The Weight of Vengeance

The Weight of Vengeance

The United States, the British Empire, and the War of 1812

TROY BICKHAM

OXFORD
UNIVERSITY PRESS

OXFORD
UNIVERSITY PRESS

Oxford University Press, Inc., publishes works that further
Oxford University's objective of excellence
in research, scholarship, and education.

Oxford   New York
Auckland   Cape Town   Dar es Salaam   Hong Kong   Karachi
Kuala Lumpur   Madrid   Melbourne   Mexico City   Nairobi
New Delhi   Shanghai   Taipei   Toronto

With offices in
Argentina   Austria   Brazil   Chile   Czech Republic   France   Greece
Guatemala   Hungary   Italy   Japan   Poland   Portugal   Singapore
South Korea   Switzerland   Thailand   Turkey   Ukraine   Vietnam

Published by Oxford University Press, Inc.
198 Madison Avenue, New York, New York 10016

www.oup.com

Oxford is a registered trademark of Oxford University Press

Library of Congress Cataloging-in-Publication Data
Bickham, Troy O.
The weight of vengeance : the United States, the British empire, and the War of 1812 / Troy Bickham.
p.   cm.
Includes bibliographical references and index.
ISBN 978-0-19-539178-7 (hardcover : alk. paper) 1. United States—History—War of 1812—Political aspects.
2. United States—History—War of 1812—Causes. 3. United States—Foreign relations—Great Britain.
4. Great Britain—Foreign relations—United States. 5. United States—Foreign relations—1801–1815.
6. Great Britain—Foreign relations—1800–1837. I. Title.
E357.B53   2012
973.5′2—dc23   2011042065

1 3 5 7 9 8 6 4 2

Printed in the United States of America
on acid-free paper

For Rachel

CONTENTS

ACKNOWLEDGMENTS

The writing of history is almost invariably a collective effort, despite the miscue of having only a single author listed on most books. *The Weight of Vengeance* is no exception. The staffs at the British Library, British National Archives, British Museum, National Library of Scotland, Bodleian Library, Library and Archives of Canada, Huntington Library, Library of Congress, Evans Library at Texas A&M University, and the Texas A&M University Library at Qatar provided immeasurable assistance in helping to identify and permit access to the sources that are the foundation of this book. Essential travel to archives and conferences, acquisition of resources, and dedicated time for writing resulted from the generosity of Texas A&M University, the Huntington Library, a Ray A. Rothrock '77 Fellowship from the College of Liberal Arts at Texas A&M, and the Qatar Foundation.

Various drafts of chapters benefited enormously from the reading and insightful comments of James Bradford, Katherine Carté Engel, April Hatfield, Daniel Walker Howe, Joanna Innes, Roger Knight, Sarah Pearsall, and David Waldstreicher. Their influence can be seen throughout the book, and, if I had taken on board more of their advice, it most likely would have been better. The comments of the anonymous readers proved equally important in shaping the direction and tone of the book. The British Group of Early American Historians' annual conference in 2010, Oxford's eighteenth-century research seminar in history, the history department colloquium at Texas A&M, and the British Studies Seminar at the University of Texas in Austin were wonderful venues for testing out some of the main arguments presented here. Oxford University Press has been the ideal publisher, and Susan Ferber the ideal editor. Her comments and encouragement from the inception of the project through to completion have been nothing less than stellar.

In 2009, Texas A&M University allowed me to take up a joint faculty appointment with its branch campus in Qatar for three years. The campus in Qatar is part of a larger higher educational endeavor being implemented by the Qatar Foundation, which includes a number of other American and European university branch campuses most commonly referred to collectively as Education City. They and the students and communities they serve have benefited greatly from the belief on the part of the leaders of Qatar that a nation's future prosperity is best secured through education, regardless of the extent of a country's natural resources. Consequently, the book that follows profited from my participating in two vibrant university communities. My colleagues on both campuses proved to be invaluable sources of wisdom, support, and timely light-heartedness, especially Quince Adams, Terry Anderson, Todd Kent, Thomas Nester, Homar Ramirez, Rebecca Schloss, Ernest Obadele-Starks, Jeff Sulik, Douglass Thornton, and David Vaught. I am also grateful to Ian Abbey for his contribution as a graduate research assistant in the later stages of the project. My teaching in the United States inspired me initially to pursue the topic of the War of 1812, and my students in Qatar, where a class of twenty-five can include representatives of a dozen nationalities, have constantly reminded me that neither American nor British history belongs solely to the peoples residing in those countries today.

None of the words that follow would have been possible without the love, support, and patience of my family: Rachel, George, Henrietta, and Beatrice.

NOTE ON TERMS

Many of the terms used here to identify cultural and national groups are admittedly sometimes anachronistic and ambiguous, but they are nevertheless useful. The term *Americans*, for example, could be used by contemporaries to refer to the whites living in the United States, the federal government of the United States, the American-born subjects of the British Empire living in Upper Canada, and even the indigenous inhabitants of North America. Similar problems surround the use of terms such as *Canada, Canadians, French, British, America*, and *American Indians*. For the sake of clarity, I have followed convention by using *Canada* and *British North America* interchangeably. *Canadians* refers to all the legal inhabitants of British North America of African, Asian, and European descent. *Americans* refers broadly to the citizens of the United States. *American Indians* refers to the indigenous peoples living throughout North America, but especially within the territorial claims of the British Empire and the United States. *Britain* and *British* refer to the United Kingdom and its inhabitants, respectively. Where necessary, I have, of course, distinguished the various ethnic and cultural groups living in all of these places. Along these lines, the capitalized *Republican* refers to the loose political party of Democrat-Republicans that dominated the federal government of the United States, and the lowercase *republican* refers broadly to the political ideology in which sovereignty ultimately rests in a nation's citizens. Following more recent convention, *tory* and *whig* are not capitalized on the grounds that they were more akin to political outlooks than parties. Virtually all of these terms were, of course, ambiguous and contested during this period, which in no small way contributed to the War of 1812 itself. Quoted material appears in its original form, despite the spellings and grammar that may appear unusual to twenty-first-century readers; alterations are signified with brackets.

The Weight of Vengeance

Introduction

In March 1815, Anthony St. John Baker was tidying up some final business related to the treaty that brought to a close the second and final war between Britain and its former American colonies. Having been negotiated in Europe in the town of Ghent, the treaty was ratified first by Britain and then carried to the United States by this veteran British diplomat. Congress quickly approved the treaty, but James Monroe, the secretary of state and future president, castigated Baker on multiple occasions for the order in which the countries' names and the signatures appeared on the treaty and related documents: Britain before the United States. Although Baker pleaded that no insult had been intended, Monroe remained unsatisfied. Before joining President James Madison and Congress for the annual spring exodus from the American capital, Monroe proceeded to give Baker a final stern lecture on the subject, knowing it would be conveyed verbatim to America's former colonial masters. Ignoring the fact that the United States had barely escaped a disastrous war with the world's foremost military power, Monroe declared that "[t]he United States have acquired a certain rank amongst nations, which is due to their population and political importance, and they do not stand in the same situation as at former periods." Baker warned his superiors in London that Monroe was insistent: in the future, the order of the countries and the signatures must be alternated.[1] The United States, Monroe made clear, would be the subordinate of no nation, whether in practice or in form.

Monroe's comments demonstrated once again that what the American government lacked in bite it more than made up for in bark. Britain had tens of thousands of troops in Canada and more massing in Britain, naval supremacy in the Atlantic, and a strangling blockade of the entire American Atlantic coastline. The British government also had earlier informed the governor of Massachusetts that, if the United States rejected the treaty, Britain would agree to his request for armed support of a New England secession. Meanwhile, the United States had defaulted on its debt payments the previous November, its navy was bottled up in port, and it had not paid its army for nearly a year. Yet Monroe was not being obtuse. He spoke with the conviction of a young nation that went to war largely because senior peers would not grant the esteem its leaders believed was deserved. The War of 1812 was, at least in part, America's grand attempt to compel Europe to take the United States seriously as a sovereign nation. By the same token, the war was Britain's concerted effort to keep America under the umbrella of British authority.

The War of 1812, or "the American war" as it was known in Britain, is often overlooked. By contemporary standards it was short and bloodless, lasting a mere two and a half years and resulting in fewer than four thousand combat deaths. By contrast, Britain's wars against Revolutionary and Napoleonic France lasted more than two decades and resulted in millions of deaths in Europe alone. Yet these statistics do not convey the full picture. Although few saw combat, as many as seven hundred thousand men and women served as soldiers, sailors, militia, auxiliary fighters, and camp followers among the American, British, and American Indian forces during the War of 1812. This figure is particularly impressive considering that the population of the United States, Canada, and the American Indian communities that participated in the war was not more than eight million.[2] The comparatively low casualty rate also meant little to those who suffered personal loss. Tiger Dunlop, a surgeon in the British army who served in Canada during the war, described a moving scene in which "a respectable elderly looking" American woman came to see her husband, a sixty-year-old farmer and militia man of "Herculean frame" who had been mortally wounded in battle and was under Dunlop's care. Seeing her husband writhing in agony, she "sat down on the ground, and taking her husband's head on her lap, continued long, moaning and sobbing while the tears flowed fast down her face." She then lashed out at those around her, exclaiming "O that the King and the President were both here this moment to see the misery their quarrels lead to they surely would never go to war without a cause that they could give as a reason to God on the last day for thus destroying the creatures that He hath made in His image." Such a scene, Dunlop angrily remarked, "would be a useful lesson to cold-blooded politicians, who calculate on a war costing so many lives and so many limbs as they could calculate on a horse costing so many pounds—or to the thoughtless at home, whom the excitement of a gazette or the glare of an illumination, more than reconciles to the expense of war to witness such a scene."[3] Dunlop's reflections serve as a stark reminder of the genuine human drama behind every statistic, no matter how small.

Often labeled a "forgotten war," the War of 1812 has traditionally received little attention in general histories of the United States and is virtually ignored by historians of Britain and its empire. Even as the War of 1812 approaches its bicentennial and historians revisit the subject or make a greater effort to incorporate it into their examination of other historical topics, they remain too willing to accept aged conclusions about the causes, consequences, and significance of the conflict.

The exception is Canada, where the War of 1812 remains a founding block of Canadian nationalism and the myths that envelop it. In the War of 1812, so the myth goes, the motley ethnic mix of British North America's inhabitants unified in a common, successful defense against their larger and more aggressive neighbors to the south, thereby securing the independence of Canada from the rule of the United States. In histories of the United States, the war sits awkwardly between the early national period and the era before the American Civil War.[4] This period was a crossroads at which the United States turned its collective gaze more decidedly westward, taking control of North America and avoiding wars with Europeans for almost another century. In consequence, the War of 1812 typically receives only a passing glance, as part of the conclusion or introduction of some larger examination of American history. In those instances when the conflict is the primary object of study, historians focus overwhelmingly on reconstructing the military narrative or the views of the American political elite.[5] Though an essential element to any conflict, such imbalance has nevertheless skewed our broader understanding of the war: we can confidently discuss the impact of American frigate design on single-ship battles, but we know comparatively little about how the American public discussed the war and virtually nothing about how the British public responded to the conflict.

More important, the military narrative alone cannot explain the timing or motivation behind declaring war. The overwhelming consensus is that militarily the war was a catalogue of American disasters and the decision to declare war on the British Empire in June 1812 bordered on criminal negligence. As Jon Latimer recently remarked in his detailed study of American wartime strategies and tactics, "defeat was practically guaranteed from the moment Madison and Congress stepped onto the warpath with risible preparations that undercooked the navy and put a half-baked army into the field."[6] And many participants recognized this. As Harmanus Bleecker of New York declared on the House floor on the eve of war, "for the Government to go to war in our present unprepared state, would be little short of an act of treason."[7] Even in an ideal situation in which Congress properly financed the war and the U.S. Army met enlistment goals (neither of which ever came close to happening), the United States had no realistic hope of defeating Britain. In fact, America's entire strategy hinged on the ridiculous notion that if the Americans took part of Canada they might negotiate its return in exchange for British concessions on trade and maritime rights—issues the New England states that dominated overseas trade ironically did not think sufficient grounds for war.[8] From this perspective, the war takes on the appearance of a horrible mistake that resulted from the negligence and incompetence of those who declared and waged it. More forgiving observers sometimes point to the slowness of transatlantic communication as the real culprit, noting that Britain conceded America's primary stated grievance—Britain's interference with America's maritime trading rights—as Congress declared war. Such observers also remark that Britain's bloodiest battle, the Battle of New Orleans, took place after the peace treaty had been signed in Europe. Thus the war takes on the hue of a tragedy.

But this war was no accident. Although the peculiarities of early-nineteenth-century communication played a role in the war, their effects on its outbreak have been exaggerated. The Republican-led government of the United States wanted war, and the British government was more than willing to oblige it. Following a saber-rattling president's message from James Madison in November 1811, Congress began preparing for war. Preparations were so public, including widely reported congressional debates on armaments and strategies, that few on either side of the Atlantic could possibly have been shocked by America's declaration of war in June 1812. Newspapers such as the North Carolina *Star* snickered as early as January at those who "are so incredulous as yet to believe there will be no war."[9] There were plenty of opportunities to avoid war or, once begun, shorten it. After all, the two issues on which the United States formally declared war—America's trade rights as a neutral in the ongoing European wars and Britain's impressment of sailors from American ships—were redundant following France's defeat in the spring of 1814. Britain's last-minute suspension of the Orders in Council, the centerpiece of Britain's limitations of neutral trade, failed to persuade the United States to halt the war, and not long afterward the British government rejected outright the offer of its ally, Russia, to mediate a settlement. When Britain finally came to the negotiating table in 1814, it purposely dragged its feet for months to allow the war to play out a little longer. This raises a pair of crucial questions: Why did the American government take the nation to war in the first place? And why did the United States and Britain continue to fight as long as they did?

This book answers these questions largely by placing the War of 1812 in a global context. The chapters that follow do not chronologically narrate the conflict in detail; nor do they offer an acute analysis of the tactics and strategies employed by the war's commanders. Instead, this book takes a broader view of the war, interpreting it not simply as a North American affair but as an Anglo-American struggle set against a global backdrop of armed conflicts. The first two chapters consider the American and British cases respectively for war, in order to determine why both sides willingly resorted to armed conflict in 1812. Together, the chapters argue that there was no single cause or explanation for the outbreak of war in June 1812. Rather, the war erupted, and continued, as a result of a perfect storm of grievances and conditions on both sides of the Atlantic. Chapter Three examines the months just prior to declaration of war by the United States, explaining not only the timing of the war but also why the United States was so unprepared to wage it. The chapter also describes the key role the British government consciously played in pushing and prodding the American government into declaring war. Next, the book offers two chapters that examine the war itself, particularly in terms of how it had an impact on the various home fronts across the Atlantic. The war caused considerable hardship in Canada, parts of the United States, Britain, the British West Indies, and among the American Indians. The war also created innumerable opportunities. Canada in particular experienced the worst and best of the war, enduring terrible hardships but emerging with considerably greater respectability within the British Empire. The chapters also highlight how different the War of 1812 was from the American Revolution for the Americans in terms of national spirit, while many Britons' attitudes toward the Americans as colonists remained remarkably steadfast. Chapters Six and Seven describe the considerable opposition to the war in both the United States and Britain, and Chapter Eight reveals how the British government dominated the peace negotiations as well as why it effectively capitulated at the end. By way of conclusion, the final chapter directly addresses the elusive question, "Who won the War of 1812?"

The world in 1812 was a violent place. During the course of its war with Britain, the United States also engaged in an undeclared quasi war with Spain over the Floridas, aided a rebellion in Texas, and fought a series of wars with American Indians, most notably against the northern confederacy led by Tecumseh and against the Red Sticks, so named for their vermilion-stained war clubs, in the Creek War. Meanwhile Britain waged a global war against France. Yet to depict these conflicts as branches of the War of 1812 is to miss the forest for the trees. North America was not the center of the world in 1812. Europe was, locked in an unparalleled struggle that had littered the world with the corpses of tens of millions of soldiers, sailors, and civilians. The wars in Europe engulfed much of the world, precipitating and facilitating innumerable local conflicts in Asia, Africa, and the Americas, including the Haitian Revolution, the Fourth Anglo-Mysore War in South Asia, and the rise of the nationalist Muhammad Ali in Egypt. In North America it was the War of 1812. Although rooted in larger Anglo-American differences, the immediate causes of the war between the United States and Britain arose from disagreements over the rights of the United States as a neutral nation to trade with the French Empire and Britain's need to man the Royal Navy. The European wars also weakened Spain's ability to control and protect its empire in North America, enabling the United States (via France) to slice off the Louisiana Territory and make inroads into the destabilized Floridas and Texas. And even though the European wars did not drive American Indian resistance, American fears that Britain was aiding dissident Indians within American territory prompted the United States to launch a preemptive strike against the followers of Tecumseh and his brother, Tenskwatawa, at their headquarters of Prophetstown in the Indiana Territory in late 1811.[1]

Yet depicting the War of 1812 as a branch of the Napoleonic Wars or the Creek War as a branch of the War of 1812 is to miss what most participants recognized: Anglo-American differences were distinct and deep-rooted. Certainly there were opportunists and people, including Andrew Jackson himself, who allowed Anglophobia to distort his vision into seeing any threat to U.S. ambitions as being orchestrated by Britain. However, most Americans, along with the majorities in Congress who consistently rejected calls for an invasion of Spanish East Florida during the War of 1812, were able to make the distinctions, just as most Britons recognized that the American war could not be dismissed as the result of a secret pact between Napoleon and Madison—despite the propaganda in the London press. Consequently, this book treats the conflict between Britain and the United States as distinct, but it also recognizes the roles that other, simultaneous conflicts had in shaping the War of 1812's origins, context, and outcome.

Despite the tendency of historians to localize the War of 1812, contemporaries were fully aware of its larger implications. American war supporters argued that giving Britain a good drubbing would send an equally effective message to any other European power thinking of interfering with the United States. As Tennessee's *Carthage Gazette* remarked, American success against Britain will "shew the infamous Napoleon, that not withstanding his success with most of the powers and potentates of Europe . . . the people of America, the great sovereigns of the nation, are firm and united; impatient under injuries, and jealous of their honor to the last punctilio."[10] In Canada, colonists constantly argued that America was the de facto ally of France, thereby linking their struggle in North America to the empire's global struggle. A number of Americans agreed. John Randolph, a Republican congressman from Virginia, declared in an open address to his constituents on the eve of the War of 1812 that the war Napoleon waged "is a war against the liberty and happiness of mankind. It is a war in which the whole human race are the victims, to gratify the pride and lust of power of a single individual." By declaring war on Britain, he warned, the United States aided Napoleon. "Are [you] willing to become the virtual allies of Bonaparte?" he asked.[11] The British connected the conflicts when it suited them. At the start of the war, they justified their alliances with Tecumseh's confederacy and other Indians living within the United States on the grounds that America had already declared a separate war on them. But at the Ghent negotiations the British attempted to attach America's war against the Indians to the peace terms, arguing that the Indians were Britain's junior partners in the North American contest, much as Portugal was in Europe.[12]

Despite these complex alliances, histories of the war are almost exclusively written as part of the national histories of either the United States or Canada.[13] The British, for whom the war is described as a "distraction," "sideshow," and "irritant," are largely ignored in histories of the war, just as the war is virtually absent from histories of Britain.[14] The wars with France dominate the historical narrative of Britain for this period to such an extent that there is room for little else. Britain's politics, culture, economy, and military are all understood largely through the lens of the wars with France, and the victory over Napoleon is portrayed as the culmination of Britain's divergence from continental Europe a century earlier. Protestantism, liberty, free trade, the Royal Navy, constitutional monarchy, industrialization, the union with Scotland, and the military-fiscal state are all vindicated through Britain's victory. And why not? After all, victory ushered in a century of global dominance. Armed with unchallenged footholds in Asia and Africa and control of the world's oceans, Britain had the building blocks necessary to create the empire on which the sun never set.[15] The war in North America does not fit neatly into this narrative, and so it is easier to treat it either as a cursory event or as being driven by America, with Britain as a mere respondent. British contemporaries were not much different after 1815: whereas the "Great War" with France shaped British national identity until a new Great War erupted a century later, the less romantic and more ambiguous war with America was quickly forgotten.

Such a portrayal, however, is problematic. The war was not militarily, strategically, or emotionally a peripheral event for Britain and its empire at the time. By the end of 1814, Britain had more subjects under arms in Canada than it ever did on the Iberian Peninsula, and with an annual price tag of about £13 million the War of 1812 cost the rough equivalent of the famous subsidies Britain doled out to its European allies to keep the pressure on Napoleon.[16] The war figured heavily in public discussions, as ordinary Britons debated the nation's policies toward the United States and the way in which the war was handled. At times it dominated the press and parliamentary debates, pushing affairs in Europe into the background. Nor was the War of 1812 a peripheral event for Britain's leaders. The prince regent, who acted as head of state during his father's illness, which lasted for the duration of the war with America, often spoke more about American affairs in his speeches than he did about France. More important, ministers refused to give commanders and agents on the ground in America much latitude, instead micromanaging affairs from London. This is because the British government was not a spectator. Rather, it had a postcolonial agenda with regard to the United States that did not include its rise as the undisputed power in North

America or as a commercial rival to Britain, and the War of 1812 was Britain's opportunity to advance that agenda. Britain's failure serves as a stark reminder of the limits of Britain to assert its will overseas, despite being successful on a global scale during this period.

The War of 1812 might be mistaken as ambiguous to the point of irrelevance. Neither Britain nor the United States set out to eradicate the other—a rare outcome in the vast majority of wars between European states during the eighteenth century. Concluding the war with a status quo ante bellum treaty meant that neither side accepted responsibility for the war, surrendered, or ceded any territory. But this was still a war of high stakes. American supporters of the war argued victory would signify that the United States had shed its colonial past once and for all, placing Americans in control of what they increasingly believed was their destiny: dominance of the North American continent.[17] War would purge the United States of the last vestiges of toryism and Anglophilia and unite the nation behind Republican leadership. The American "experiment," as republican rule came to be known across Europe, would be proven successful, and the American revolutionaries who had rejected monarchy and aristocracy would be vindicated. Moreover, European powers would be compelled to respect American sovereignty. America's ships could sail freely, its citizens would not be seized by a foreign power, and European governments would have to respect the United States in matters involving the Americas or face the consequences. In the minds of many Americans, the United States would not simply be recognized as equal to European nations but be among the elite. For these gains, James Madison and his fellow Republican leaders wagered almost everything. After all Madison knew that New England secession was always a risk, and few had any doubts that defeat would have shattered Madison's Republican party, opening the United States to a host of ruling ideologies and alternative futures.

Even though Britain had no intention of reabsorbing the United States formally into the empire, keeping the former colonies as a client was a real possibility. The fear of an American rival drove the British West Indian planters and merchants in London in the decade before the war to place enormous pressure on the British government to stifle America's rise. Along with support from the Royal Navy and similarly interested parties, they crafted the policies against American trade and sovereignty that James Madison cited as justification for going to war in 1812. If the British government had achieved by force or diplomacy the original proposal its peace negotiators presented to their American counterparts at Ghent in August 1814, any possibility of an American manifest destiny would have been crushed. The British originally demanded a sovereign American Indian state carved out of American territory and control of both shores of the Great Lakes, giving Canada an insurmountable defensive advantage and leaving the United States exposed to invasion. With the help of the Spanish, the British Empire and the Indian state could have easily hemmed in the Americans, and the Royal Navy would have continued to dictate the terms by which Americans could operate on the high seas. Furthermore, Britain was more than willing to assist American secessionists, particularly the New England Federalists, in breaking up the vast United States into more manageable units.

Thus for Britain the War of 1812 became a gamble for renewed empire in North America and the retention of British hegemony over the Atlantic world. Defeat was not a possibility in the same way it was for the United States, but American success could have cost Britain its North American empire, trade concessions with British Caribbean islands, and a great deal of credibility among its European allies and enemies at the very moment it was attempting to assert its leadership. Even worse, American success would have left Britain with an ambitious, aggressive, and confident rival in its backyard that could steadily erode Britain's commercial, industrial, and naval supremacy.

It is almost impossible to overstate the significance of the postcolonial relationship between Britain and the United States. In economic terms, ties were closer than ever following the American Revolution. Trade increased as the United States remained Britain's top overseas market. Meanwhile American grain continued to feed African slaves in the Caribbean and American lumber was used for the casks that transported the sugar-based products the slaves produced. American merchant shipping boomed during Britain's wars with France to become the world's second largest carrier, not only transporting American and French products but also making sizable inroads into routes between Britain and its colonies in Asia and the Caribbean. As poor growing seasons in Europe combined with the ravages of war, American grain also fed the armies there. In fact, Britain's forces fighting on the Iberian Peninsula relied almost exclusively on American grain even after the outbreak of the War of 1812.[18]

On the backs of trade routes follows culture—fashion, news, literature, and music—and the Anglo-American relationship was no different. A common language ensured the strength of the bonds. America was a dumping ground for Wedgwood pottery, English books packed American libraries, and American elites in New York dressed in the latest British fashions and danced the latest creations from the assemblies of London and Bath.[19] The social elite in America in particular expressed their refinement in English terms, yearning for the latest clothing, trinkets, and scientific knowledge from London. This desire, along with the snobbish refusal of Britain's social elite to accept Americans as equals, helped to create an enormous chip on the shoulder of America's elite that bled into Anglo-American foreign relations.[20] But too often overlooked is that the exchange went both ways. In Britain, the Wedgwoods' potteries produced busts of George Washington and Benjamin Franklin for British admirers, images of

American plantations in British tobacco advertisements lent authenticity to "Virginia's Best" tobacco, and cookery books featured favorite recipes for "Carolina rice pudding" and "New England pancakes."[21] Many Britons openly applauded the protesting American colonists in the 1760s and 1770s and envied them following American independence. In consequence, the British elite knew and resented, if not feared, the export of republicanism to the discontented peoples of the British Isles.

Even after two decades of independence, Americans were not easily distinguished from British subjects. Immigration further muddied the picture, with Irish subjects pouring into the United States and American-born families flowing into Upper Canada first as political refugees from the American Revolution and later as economic migrants. By 1812, Upper Canada for all intents and purposes was equally a colony of Britain and the United States—a point of concern for its British governors and a fact many in the United States hoped would facilitate easy conquest.[22] In fact, the inability to distinguish American citizens from British subjects was at the heart of the disagreement over impressment, as British naval officers who boarded American merchant ships had a difficult time telling which sailors were British deserters and which were genuine Americans. A white man might look and sound like someone from East Anglia, and American blacks, who constituted a sizeable minority of sailors on American ships, routinely found themselves being seized as British West Indian subjects.

To many participants, the cultural similarities lent a civil war quality to the War of 1812. In November 1812, the London *Times* lamented that "[n]o two nations in the world are so strongly bound together in interest; none are so identified in sound policy, as Great Britain and the North American Republic."[23] John Le Couteur, a junior British officer from the English Channel Island of Jersey who sometimes took messages and women across American lines, got along famously with the American officers he met. With regard to one of them, Le Couteur remarked, "[w]e got to be excellent friends in a Jiffy for I talked to Him as if He had been of our mess, asked Him how he liked it, how He roughed it and was so friendly that we both forgot the Ladies & walked pleasantly on." He even encountered an American artillery officer "in English shooting toggery, shooting Jacket, & gatters as well as if Buckmaster had turned them out, a beautiful double-barrelled Joe Manton and a fine setter." After exchanging a few jokes, they agreed that hunting birds was "much pleasanter Sport . . . than shooting one's own kindred and language." Le Couteur remarked that when they parted company "we three young Men were like brother officers." After further encounters with the Americans, Le Couteur reflected how "[s]trange indeed did it appear to me to find so many names, familiar household words, as enemies—the very names of Officers in our own army. How uncomfortably like a civil war it seemed when we were in good-humoured friendly converse."[24]

The Anglo-American split was, of course, not always as good-humored as Le Couteur described. American loyalists who fled to Upper Canada following American independence volunteered during the War of 1812 in disproportionate numbers, and, as Upper Canada's elected House of Assembly made clear at the start of the war, they had not forgotten their former countrymen's cruelties during the American Revolution. The Americans, assembly publicly declared, were "a people whose lands are manured with the blood of our friends and kinsmen, who drove our wives and children from their houses into the woods, or threw them into dungeons." Now was the moment for revenge.[25] Tiger Dunlop described an instance in which one such loyalist discovered after a battle that he had killed his own brother, who had split with the rest of the family decades earlier and joined the American Revolution—the last time they had seen one another. After taking possession of his brother's valuables, the man "coolly" remarked that it "served him right for fighting with the rebels, when the rest of his family fought for King George."[26]

Public opinion mattered in the Anglo-American world, and few doubted that the press both shaped and reflected it. In consequence, to recapture the broader experience of the War of 1812 and describe the forces that shaped it, this book draws largely on newspapers to relate both what people were told about the conflict and how they responded to the news. The early-nineteenth-century newspaper was the world in microcosm. Global communications networks and the absence of adequate copyright laws enabled even provincial towns to provide political news for local readers. For example, a reader of the September 2, 1814, issue of Lexington, Kentucky's *Western Monitor* would find news from Paris, New York, Nashville, London, Washington, Erie, and Charleston. In Baltimore in the summer of 1812, Americans rioted and killed each other over the reporting of political news, and when the British diplomat Baker conveyed the Treaty of Ghent to America in 1815, his instructions, if Madison rejected it, were to release the terms to the American press in order to bring public pressure to bear on the federal government.[27] The American and British governments invested heavily in the press, supporting official and unofficial organs, and high-ranking members routinely wrote articles and employed mercenary writers. Madison, just like governors, military commanders, and the prince regent, published his official messages and speeches, knowing full well his words would be reprinted at home and abroad.

Yet the press was too profitable, too independent, and too widespread for any national government to control. Only on the local level did governments manage to control the media through stationery contracts to the local printer, but this rarely occurred outside of small markets in North America and the Caribbean, as any sizable town could generate enough advertisements to support two or more papers. London had at least forty-nine. In Britain, the advertising business was so complex that the Scotch, English, and Irish Newspapers, and Advertising Office in Edinburgh offered clients access to 115 newspapers across the empire, including the *Botany Bay Gazette* and the *Madras Courier*.[28] Good communications networks and fierce competition meant that even rural people had a choice of private subscriptions, and taverns, inns, and coffee houses regularly subscribed to a host of newspapers to lure customers. A comparatively high literacy rate and a long tradition of popular interest in politics ensured that ordinary free inhabitants of the Anglo-American world avidly read newspapers, and part of the legacy of the American Revolution on both sides of the Atlantic was a popular willingness to critique the government's handling of domestic and foreign affairs—often much to their social superiors' ire. Women in the British Empire and the United States also read newspapers and contributed to them, and female printers were not unusual.[29]

Equally important, the press was relatively free, even by modern standards. Libel laws, not government censorship, resulted in fines and prison sentences for printers. In short, an Oxford printer had to be more careful about printing a story about the Duke of Wellington's mistress than about printing the exact number of troops and types of supplies being sent to reinforce his army. In consequence, though the fog of war afflicted both sides' military commanders on land and at sea, the domestic presses kept even remote readers almost as informed as government leaders. Editors helped readers size up one another's fleets by providing explicit tables detailing individual ships' location, commanding officer, tonnage, number of guns, and crew size. The *Kingston Gazette's* news briefs from April 1813 were typical in that, from its own sources and by gleaning news from other Canadian and American papers, it informed readers of the movement and strength of every British regular, volunteer, and militia regiment into Upper Canada for that season's campaigning. In fact, through a series of reports a reader could follow along as four companies of the 104th Regiment of Foot of the British Army received orders to move from Lower Canada, embarked, arrived in Upper Canada, and were deployed for service. The American press was no different. From the British papers that flowed into the United States, *Niles' Weekly Register* in Baltimore regularly offered readers elaborate tables detailing the Royal Navy's presence in North America during the summer of 1812, which other papers around the country subsequently reprinted.[30] Paralleling these reports were equally vivid details of the American navy and army, including regimental strengths and movements. When government lists were unavailable, inventive editors simply trolled through private insurance records to see which ships had been sunk or captured.

Cheap pocket maps made visualizing this information easier, enabling civilians to follow the movements of loved ones' regiments and ships or to play the era's popular pastime of armchair commander—the game Tiger Dunlop had belittled after watching an American widow mourn her husband. A reader's letter to the *Oracle* described the typical scene at an English village "newspaper reading club" after receiving news of an overseas battle:

> [Y]our paper . . . had just been received by the Club, who, long before I arrived, were hard at it, with their books of maps displayed on the table, which leaning three deep over one another, in a very hot day, and a very close room, they were consulting most eagerly and most unsuccessfully . . . the heat of the room, the tobacco, the punch, and the porter, so bewildered, muddled and perplexed the pates of several members.[31]

Even at the highest levels, the press became a key source for information, as leaders tried desperately to manage a war that stretched halfway around the globe and deep into some of the most isolated places in North America. American and British diplomatic agents alike routinely sent newspaper clippings to their governments as information and evidence of public opinion. Members of Parliament regularly cited extracts from American newspapers in debates, such as Samuel Whitbread, who in February 1812 complained that the press's discussion of Madison's inflammatory message to Congress calling for military increases was more detailed than the one transpiring in the House of Commons. Madison referred Thomas Jefferson to newspapers for the latest congressional transactions, telling the former president that "the Newspapers give you a sufficient insight into the measures of Congress." Most of Madison's British intelligence came via British newspapers, and even the American peace delegation at Ghent relied heavily on British newspapers for information about public opinion and government policies in Britain and back home.[32] Editors took the same approach, and throughout the war American newspapers reported on British public opinion by extracting editorials from British papers, just as British, Canadian, and Caribbean newspapers did with American ones. Because trade, rather than news, dictated regular communication, the direct geographical route was not always the fastest or most reliable. As a result, news from Britain typically reached Upper Canada faster when it traveled via Boston or New York. In fact, the *York Gazette* in Upper Canada changed its publication date in January 1812 to coincide with the arrival of American newspapers. The British Caribbean received most of its Canadian news via the Charleston and Savannah press, which in turn lifted stories from northern American papers, and when the British government attempted to keep the details of the peace negotiations at Ghent quiet, British editors simply reprinted accounts from better-informed American newspapers.[33]

Such access to relatively reliable information meant that for most Americans and British subjects the press was the glue that bound the otherwise disparate fighting across the Atlantic world together into a single, digestible event. Combat transpired almost entirely in the thinly populated border regions and oceans, which meant that for most Americans and British subjects, the press was how they experienced the war. Such practices helped to create "imagined communities" that connected people who would otherwise never meet.[34] Margaret Bayard Smith, a Washington socialite who had just endured the British destruction of her town, felt a melancholy camaraderie with other women across the country through her "perusal of the papers." "At Plattsburgh, N. London, and N. Haven, all was consternation and alarm," she worried, "families removing their property, and many, I suppose, as in this place wandering from their homes, without knowing where to find a shelter."[35]

The specter of the American Revolution haunted those who lived through the War of 1812. In the United States, the revolution was the defining moment in its history. Commemorated publicly every July, by 1812 it had become the national litmus test for good governance and citizenly virtue.[36] George Washington was revered almost as a god during the War of 1812, with competing factions battling over his legacy in an effort to lay claim to his blessing from the grave. As one commentator declared at a Massachusetts Fourth of July celebration in 1812, "Washington was the sun, around whom the American planets revolved, and which enlightened and cheered our political heavens."[37] Daniel Webster, then an aspiring politician, instructed his New Hampshire audience the same day that "it should be our constant aim to exhibit WASHINGTON's example as the true fruit and genuine effect of our revolution." Calling this "an infallible criterion," Webster argued that "we should point to [Washington's] principles as the true principles of our Government, and to his Administration as the best practical development and application of those principles."[38] Commentators across America relentlessly offered what-would-Washington-do analyses that inevitably reached the same conclusion: Washington would most certainly agree with the commentator. Even in Britain critics weighed in, arguing that Madison had betrayed Washington's legacy and with it the legacy of the American Revolution. In the same editorial in which London's *Times* lamented the war between the two nations, it firmly blamed the Madison administration as the nefarious instigator, remarking that "Together with the civil policy of the immortal WASHINGTON, which these poor creatures (we mean the ruling faction) affect to despise, they have lost the inheritance of his military talents."[39] American opponents of the war, like Webster, draped themselves in the language of the revolution in an effort to assert the righteousness of their cause. This laid the foundation of America's first loyal wartime opposition, in which critics asserted their love of country and disdain for its leaders in the same breath. The opposition to the war in Britain, too, resurrected old arguments in favor of conciliation and trade over coercion when dealing with the Americans. In contrast, the war's supporters in America clung to the memory of the American Revolution as an example of the power of American unanimity at a time when political dissent could be quieted by popular force. As Jefferson half-jokingly remarked to Madison at the outbreak of war, "a barrel of tar to each state South of the Potomac will keep all in order, and that will be freely contributed without troubling the government."[40]

From a global perspective, the War of 1812 was a continuation of the clash of the American and British systems that became apparent during the Seven Years' War, or the French and Indian Wars as it was known in North America, and first erupted into armed conflict in the American War of Independence. The Seven Years' War required an unprecedented expenditure of blood and treasure, as Britain battled France and its allies across the world. Often described as the first global war, it cost Britain more than any previous war and carried a price tag equivalent to the entire estimated gross national product of Britain for 1759 (the height of the war).[41] The series of victories in Africa, the Americas, Asia, and Europe drastically altered the British Empire not only demographically—the majority of people living under its control were no longer of European descent, but Asians in Bengal—but also in ways that transformed British culture at home into one that imagined the empire as intrinsic to the nation's economic prosperity and security.[42]

The Seven Years' War experience prompted British elites to reorganize governance of the empire into what has been dubbed an "empire of authority," in which control shifted decidedly to London, where the king, government ministers, and a host of bureaucrats attempted to direct it.[43] This new approach proved successful for Britain, when taken from the perspective of the empire as a whole. The exception was thirteen of its American colonies, which rejected the new system as interfering, conniving, and unjust; or, in the words of the American Declaration of Independence, "The history of the present King of Great Britain is a history of repeated injuries and usurpations, all having in direct object the establishment of an absolute Tyranny over these States." In short, from a British imperial perspective the crisis that preceded the American Revolution was less a case in which American colonists were targeted for persecution than a case in which many (but not all) Americans elected to opt out of the new centralized system being applied throughout the empire. Other colonists, particularly in the Caribbean, complained, but only thirteen colonies took up arms. What followed in America during the war and afterward, historians have long argued, was a purge of many of the remaining monarchical and hierarchical systems in America, along with many of the tens of thousands of loyalist colonists who subscribed to them.[44] In this narrative, the primary issues leading to the outbreak of war and during the war itself revolved far more around American sovereignty than re-publicanism or expansion of individual liberties.[45] In 1812 the United States again declared war on remarkably similar grounds, leading many participants and subsequently early historians of the conflict to portray the War of 1812 as a second American Revolution. As the more than five hundred citizens meeting at Woodville in the Mississippi Territory in 1812 declared in a public letter to Madison in language reminiscent of 1776, the present crisis "calls on our free and Independent Government either to proudly assert its inalienable rights, or dastardly submit to the humiliating impositions of our overbearing foe."[46]

Without doubt, the conclusion of the war in 1783 left much unresolved. Among Britain's ruling elite at least, the American success did not represent a moral victory in which the rebellion proved that either the British system of constitutional monarchy or the new empire of authority was somehow faulty. The Americans cast Washington as a demigod and wove myths about the superiority of the militia and the Spirit of '76; the British did not agree, demonize George III, and usher in parliamentary reform. In fact, they did exactly the opposite: George III soon became the most popular monarch in nearly two centuries, conservative ministries under William Pitt the younger and his successors would dominate Britain well beyond the War of 1812, and political reform would wait for more than a generation. British control over the empire was more centralized than ever in the wake of the American Revolution. British Canada was recast into colonies in which any popular voice was carefully curtailed by the government in Britain and a local British elite that was loyal to it; Britain increased its influence over the East India Company's possessions in South Asia, even dragging the governor of Bengal back to Britain to face a dramatic show trial for corruption and mismanagement; and, most notably, Parliament and the wider British public stood up to the powerful colonial West India interest and abolished the slave trade.[47] The French Revolution completed any rehabilitation by allowing British critics to unmask once and for all the true tyrannous nature of republicanism; when war broke out again, Britain was once more the protector of human liberty against French oppression. As a result, both America and Britain entered the War of 1812 espousing a sense of moral superiority.

As the War of 1812 entered its second year, the *Jamaica Magazine* comically captured the essence of why the conflict continued even after the Americans' stated reasons for declaring war had become redundant. "The people of those [United] States have long been in the habit of viewing their own political importance through a medium similar to that by which a man comprehends the magnitude of his own nose." "[T]hey have," the magazine continued, "like many eminent liars, told over their falsehoods so repeatedly, that they have at length worked themselves up to a belief of their reality." America's self-importance grated at

British sensibilities, and the war, as the magazine noted, was the opportunity to correct this.[48] A thorough military chastisement of the United States would burst the Americans' bubble and reassimilate them into the proper world order, in which Britain's name came first on treaties with client nations, and statesmen such as Monroe did not dare challenge it.

The fact was that Britain sometimes treated the United States like a colony—offering preferential trading rights but then disregarding its sovereignty and dictating the terms by which it could trade and its people could claim citizenship. Worse still, the rest of Europe continued to see the United States as part of Britain's sphere of influence, as the Americans discovered when they sought European assistance during the war. The War of 1812 was a rematch between Britain and the United States in which both sought to settle unresolved issues. The Americans fought for their definition of postcolonial independence—self-determination in trade and expansion, sovereignty over its citizens, and the right to be treated as an equal by European nations. American victory would quiet such dissension and demonstrate to the world the validity of republicanism—a system of government whose legitimacy had declined markedly as a result of the French Revolution—and that Americans' commitment to defending themselves and their freedoms had not waned with the passing of the revolutionary generation.

Though not interested in asserting direct rule over the United States, Britain pursued an informal imperialism that sought to stifle American ambition and turn it into a client state—a colony in all but name. For many Canadians and American Indians, as well as plenty of others in Britain and the Caribbean, the war offered the opportunity to erase some of their earlier losses by reestablishing British dominance in North America, albeit this time with the Indians (and possibly the Spanish) as junior partners. These were the primary reasons the War of 1812 continued long after the official stated causes of neutral wartime trading rights and impressment had become largely irrelevant, and it is on these criteria that the successes and failures of the United States and the British Empire during the war should be judged.

|| 1 ||

The American Case for War

In early June 1812, James Madison laid out his case for war in a message to Congress. The message, which appeared in newspapers throughout the Anglo-American world, was not the president's best propaganda. It rambled, lacked punch, and betrayed what might be mistaken for a lack of conviction. Portraying the United States as the victim of British imperial aggression and demanding the esteem that the United States was due, Madison's message reflected the arduous journey to the War of 1812. The fact that Madison opened with the caveat that he would restrict his description of British abuses to after "the renewal in 1803, of the war in which Great Britain is engaged [with France]" suggests how lengthy the history of animosity between Britain and its former colonies was.

There was no single cause for the War of 1812; nor was there a single catalyst that prompted the United States to declare war on Britain and its empire that June. Madison needed a dozen pages to list his reasons, and even then he covered only the previous decade and "omit[ted] unrepaired wrongs of inferior magnitude." Officially, Madison offered three primary reasons: Britain's ongoing interference with the overseas trade of the United States as a neutral nation, most specifically Britain's Orders in Council; Britain's standing policy of impressment of sailors from American merchant ships on the high seas; and, to a much lesser degree, Britain's encouragement of American Indians living within the territory of the United States to rebel against American authority. Trade received the most coverage by far, followed by impressment. By contrast, the grievance regarding Indians received little attention and appears clumsily attached to the end of the message. Although each issue was important and merits individual investigation, treating them only as a checklist misses the larger subject at stake: sovereignty of the United States in a postcolonial world. After all, during the course of the war neutral rights and impressment became redundant when Britain suspended the Orders in Council on June 18 and when Britain and its allies defeated France in the spring of 1814, removing the need for impressment. Moreover, the American government had never considered its Indian relations as grounds for war with Britain in the past, and the Indian communities to which Madison alluded had been at war with the United States at least since November of the previous year. If only these issues mattered, then the war should have ended much earlier.

To be sure, the case for war was partisan. The United States was a divided nation—sectioned off by religion, race, ethnicity, politics, social class, geography, and economic interests. No Federalist in Congress voted for war, and many Americans opposed it and worked to undermine it. In consequence, the case for war reflects a specific American demographic: generally white males living predominantly in the southern and western states, who identified with the Republican party or at least such values as expansion, minimal taxation, and limited federal government. Yet such generalizations oversimplify the lack of agreement even among those who supported the war; and the opposition to the war was equally disparate. Even Madison's fellow Republicans in Congress, who provided all the votes for the war, were fractured, barely mustering enough votes to pass a declaration despite their substantial majority in both houses. This partly explains why Madison's war message was so clunky; it had to appeal to as many constituents as possible while offending as few as possible. It does not mention expansion of the United States or its military operations in Spanish East Florida, partly because such issues were too controversial and risked alienating would-be supporters of war against Britain—including the Senate, which twice voted against authorizing action in East Florida and only barely approved the declaration of war against Britain. In consequence, Madison's war message is a document that aims for consensus—or at least enough agreement to pass a declaration of war—and so it selects those issues on which a majority of members of Congress could agree. And these issues all speak to a single theme: equality of the United States among European nations and sovereignty over its own affairs. Thus the war was not merely about British officers seizing sailors from American merchant ships or the Royal Navy intercepting American grain bound for France; rather, the war was about stopping Britain and other European nations from believing they could do such things. The government of the United States and its supporters believed that for too long Britain had directed the Anglo-American relationship, fostering deep-seated resentment for what many believed was Britain's continuing imperial attitude. Declaring war in June 1812 was an American attempt to redefine that relationship and turn the United States into a leading protagonist.

National sovereignty was the ideological heart of the American case for war. Whether from the pulpit, at the dinner table, in the editor's office, or in Congress, most justifications for war with Britain were ultimately linked to concerns about sovereignty. The hot topics of Britain's impressment of American seamen and European interference with neutral shipping were all discussed by contemporaries in terms of how they impinged on American sovereignty. Such issues, proponents of war regularly insisted, could not be measured simply in dollars and cents, especially considering that the vast majority of Americans were not directly and significantly affected by any one of these issues. It was a matter of principle. As one public orator representatively declared at a Massachusetts Fourth of July commemoration in 1810: "Should the European powers *imprison* our seamen, *burn* our ships, *bombard* our cities, and *murder* our citizens, let us not tamely submit our *freedom,* and our *rights* . . . [let us] *oppose the terror of empires, and sacrifice our lives on the altar of* PATRIOTISM, LIBERTY, AND INDEPENDENCE!"[1] In the minds of many Americans, including many of those in power, allowing Britain unilaterally to restrict American commerce and to decide on the validity of a sailor's claim to American citizenship made Americans colonists once again.

To some extent, this sensitivity to issues of national sovereignty and honor can be linked to Americans' tendency toward individualism and personal ambition. The American Revolution had promoted notions of popular sovereignty and ushered the colonists from a more deferential style of politics into a more participatory culture in which public opinion was a critical judge of public affairs. Combined with postrevolutionary America's commercial prosperity and the growth of a consumer culture, this fashioned a society in which individuals were more materially and socially ambitious. Ambition switched from being a vice to a virtue, and personal financial worth became a key indicator of success.[2] It was an age of the self-made man.

Postcolonial Americans had a large chip on their shoulder when it came to dealing with Europeans. Objects of refinement, from silk gowns to scientific instruments, were produced in Europe; even the language of refinement, whether mingling at a Charleston ball or giving a lecture on horticulture at Harvard, came from Europe. The books American children read had European (usually English) heroes and heroines, and the action took place largely in Europe. The United States appeared on only the most modern world maps. and even then it was on the edge, not the center, of the page.[3] Disenchantment with their provincialism led to what historian Gordon Wood has described as postcolonial Americans' "extraordinary emotional need to exaggerate their importance to the world."[4] The War of 1812 took place during the founding of the myth of American "bigness." In response to European snubs, both real and perceived, Americans boasted that things were larger, and thus more impressive, in the United States. They highlighted such massive engineering marvels as the Erie Canal, and even the discovery of the American mastodon, which Jefferson and others promoted in Europe as evidence of North America's invigorating climate—a response to European scientists' claims that everything, including humans, degenerated in the American climate.[5]

Many of the Americans' concerns might be dismissed as oversensitivity, but they had valid reasons to be worried about Europe's respect for the legitimacy and sovereignty of their country. After all, the United States in 1812 was a new nation, carved by force from an existing powerful empire and governed in a manner quite unlike the European monarchical system. Worse still, for all its size and wealth, the United States was a military runt. It had no ships of the line—the largest class of warships with multiple decks sometimes boasting more than a hundred cannon—at a time when Britain commanded one hundred or more, and America's effective regular army could be measured in the thousands, while the major European powers measured their forces in the hundreds of thousands. Only a small slice of America's claimed territory had been settled by its citizens, leaving the rest vulnerable to the occupying American Indians and ambitious European empires. The Louisiana Purchase in 1803, which comprised roughly half of the territory of the United States in 1812, was at best a shady deal in which Napoleon bullied and defrauded Spain out of territory that he promptly sold to the United States, despite his promise not to do so.[6] Some Americans and plenty of Britons, who by 1812 were Spain's closest allies, had avidly challenged the legality and efficacy of the purchase. Even after nine years, it remained a contested issue. As an orator at a Fourth of July public celebration in Worcester, Massachusetts, summarily declared, Louisiana was "an abounded and untitled territory, stolen from an unoffending nation, and our own government privy to the theft."[7]

Equally worrying, the European monarchies had demonstrated their willingness to use force against republican movements and weaker nations. Plenty of Europeans had attempted to assert their independence, only to be squashed by the old world order. Thomas Jefferson and John Adams had watched from their diplomatic posts in Paris and London in 1787 as Frederick William II, the King of Prussia, marched twenty thousand troops into the Netherlands under the pretext that his sister had been insulted there. This crushed the Dutch patriots' movement for republican reforms and bolstered the hereditary powers of the Netherlands' aristocracy, into which Frederick William's sister had married.[8] Poland, which reemerged as an independent nation under a new constitution in 1791, had been riddled by the same sectionalism and factionalism that plagued the United States, and, despite being far more formidable militarily, was easily partitioned and then absorbed by Austria, Prussia, and Russia.[9] The French rampage, under the revolutionary and then Napoleonic governments, through Europe—in which borders were repeatedly redrawn, countries erased, and monarchies abolished and replaced—seriously challenged the centuries-old system of the law of nations that emphasized national independence and autonomy.[10] As the Danish learned in 1807, when the British Royal Navy bombarded their capital, killing thousands and destroying much of the city in order to compel neutral Denmark to surrender its navy, neutrality offered no protection. From such widely reported incidents, Americans could take the valuable lesson that being passive in the protection of one's national sovereignty invited aggression.

Britain's interference with the maritime trade of the United States was the most commonly cited reason for the American declaration of war. The subject received the most attention by far in the American press, diplomatic correspondence, and Congress. When war erupted between Britain and France in 1793, the United States asserted its neutrality. Neither side respected America's neutrality to the extent its leaders demanded, as both Britain and France sought to limit each other's overseas commerce and supply routes. Like many neutral nations, the United States fell prey to the navies and customs officers of both countries and, like some European nations, was willing to back its perceived rights with force. This contributed first to what has been dubbed America's Quasi War with France from 1798 to 1800 and ultimately to the War of 1812 with Britain.

Ordinary consumers throughout the Anglo-American Atlantic world appreciated the importance of overseas trade to their own lives, which helps to explain why so many Americans and Britons took a keen interest in the trade restrictions Britain and France placed on neutral countries. Material things mattered to a greater number of people during this period than in any before it. In Britain and the United States in particular, the standard of living as measured by the quality and number of luxuries that average individuals possessed had risen rapidly in the eighteenth century. The remotest areas had access to such foreign luxuries as Chinese teas, Indian textiles, and West Indian sugar, and even the poorest consumers accessed these goods by purchasing smaller amounts and lower qualities.[11] This "breaking and dividing," as Adam Smith described it in his *Wealth of Nations*, was a pillar of the consumer revolution.[12]

That consumers associated these goods with the faraway places that produced them and the ships that transported them is evident in both consumers' politicization of goods and contemporary advertising. During the colonial American boycotts of the 1770s, tea became a symbol of British imperialism, and British abolitionists in the 1790s successfully linked West Indian sugar to the evils of the African slave trade and slavery in the minds of British consumers. British advertisements linked such staple overseas luxuries as tobacco, coffee, and tea with the regions that produced them and the naval power that secured their trade.[13] The engine was the contagious power of *want*. Preceding the industrial revolution's increased capacity for production by at least a century was what has become known as the "industrious revolution."[14] In this revolution ordinary people's desire for more and better goods drove them to work longer hours and more days; thus increased production through greater toil preceded the technological and organizational innovations that allowed higher production in the industrial revolution. The little luxuries people craved were often foreign luxuries—Wedgwood pottery from England, American tobacco, and a host of spices and textiles from Asia.[15] The transportation of these goods, or carrying trade, became an important business, because it was lucrative in its own right and it secured those goods ordinary Americans and Britons sought. Consequently, maritime trade was a matter of national and personal importance to ordinary Americans and Britons.

Americans' opposition to British and French restrictions stemmed from practical and ideological concerns. From a practical perspective, neutrality had made the United States rich. The nation provided agricultural products to a Europe whose young men had given up the plough for the sword. American commerce also profited by taking over the carrying trade between France and its colonies, particularly in the Caribbean, because British naval superiority prevented the French from handling this themselves. American ships took an ever-growing share of trade between the British and French empires, too, as neutrality gave American ships access to the markets of both. Neutrality also protected the ships from French privateers. This lowered insurance rates for American ships, which meant they undercut British ships even in the carrying trade of British goods. As a result, American merchants went from sending their first ship to India in 1784 to exceeding all European nations' carrying trade with India just over a decade later. By 1810 the American merchant fleet's tonnage had reached 1.25 million, making it a major rival and second only to the world's leader (Britain).[16] The official annual value of American exports peaked at $108 million in 1807, less than half of which consisted of goods originally produced in America. In fact, the value of foreign goods funneled through the United States and transported by American ships increased by a multiple of 120 between 1790 and 1807. Such figures are even more impressive when one considers that the U.S. Treasury collected a mere $13.5 million in 1810.[17]

That Britain did not immediately dismiss America's interpretation of its rights as a neutral nation speaks more to America's commercial importance to Britain than to the persuasiveness of America's interpretation. Lower costs for American-shipped goods meant cheaper prices for British consumers and gave British producers, ranging from Staffordshire pottery manufacturers to Jamaican sugar-growers, access to French-occupied Europe. Moreover, Britain supplied the United States with roughly 80 percent of the total value of its imports, to the tune of at least £8.6 million (about $38 million), most of which were goods manufactured by the tens of thousands of Britons working in the booming early industrial economy.[18] The American trade was not only central to Britain's manufacturing regions; it was also the lifeblood of port cities such as Liverpool, whose merchant community had evolved to specialize in importing American cotton, exporting British manufactures, and organizing the finances for th⁻ complicated exchanges. William Rathbone, a leading Liverpool merchant, estimated in 1808 that the American trade accounted for more than a quarter of Liverpool's commerce.[19]

Nonetheless, the British government ratcheted up its interference with American shipping, responding to changes in French policies on neutral nation trade, pressures from within the British economy, and its own rising desperation to win the war against France. At first, Britain followed the "Rule of 1756," a practice unilaterally established during the Seven Years' War by which a neutral could not engage in trade during wartime that had been prohibited to it during peacetime. In other words, American ships that transported sugar from French islands in the Caribbean to French ports—a carrying trade that was closed to American ships before the war—were acting illegally. Britain never sought the consent of the United States or any sort of a consensus of international opinion on the Rule of 1756, but with the world's most powerful navy it did not require permission.

American merchants, however, were nothing if not adaptive, and when Britain began to restrict American shipping in the 1790s, they developed the "broken voyage." Under this system American ships first brought the foreign goods to American ports, went through the charade of unloading and reloading them, and paid customs duties, which were typically nominal. The goods technically were now "American" and free to be exported to any market open to American trade. The British government accepted this laundering scheme as legal in the *Polly* case of 1800. That was during America's Quasi War with France, when the United States was a de facto ally of Britain. Five years later, Britain's High Court of the Admiralty reversed itself in the *Essex* decision, ruling that broken voyages did not protect neutral ships from the Rule of 1756. By this time, the situation had changed: the Quasi War was over, and the United States was governed by the far-less-cooperative Republicans. With the approval of the conservative tory government, the Royal Navy soon began seizing American ships trading in French goods and contraband. The next year, "the Ministry of All the Talents," a whig coalition, came to power in Britain. It was more sympathetic to the American trading interest, and so it had the *Essex* decision set aside. However, the ministry was short-lived, and the tories were back in power a year later and ready again to pounce on American ships.

The British Orders in Council marked the pinnacle of infringements on neutral America's commerce. First issued in 1807, they came to symbolize for many Americans all that was wrong with America's postcolonial relationship with Britain. A series of major French victories in 1805, capped by the epic victory at Austerlitz in December, made France the undisputed master of continental Europe, but Britain's victory at Trafalgar six weeks earlier underscored that the Royal Navy was the master of the oceans and secured Britain from invasion for the time being.[20] Napoleon responded to the stalemate with economic warfare. He first issued the Berlin decree, which excluded any neutral merchant ships that had been in British ports from entering French ports. Moreover, any British goods found on neutral vessels could be seized as prizes, even if the neutral merchant had lawfully purchased them. In essence, this was Napoleon's attempt to blockade Britain despite France's inability to challenge the Royal Navy at sea. His aim was to deprive Britain of European markets and goods, and thereby bring the British economy to its knees. Not to be outdone, Britain issued a series of executive orders the following year that became known as the Orders in Council, one of which claimed that all ports from which British goods were excluded would be considered to be under a blockade and that any neutral ship wanting to trade with those ports had to submit to a search, stop first in Britain, and pay a duty. In other words, Britain declared what became known as a "paper blockade" around Europe, just as France had done around the British Isles. If that was not enough, Napoleon then issued the Milan decree, which stated France could seize any neutral ship that complied with British regulations. In short, no American vessel could trade with French-controlled Europe without violating either French or British restrictions.

That this new round of European regulations grossly violated the traditional rights of neutrals to trade was beyond doubt. Neither side sincerely claimed that it was behaving legally; instead, each pointed the finger at the other and said it had no choice but to behave aggressively so long as the other was doing so. The American position was that both Britain and France were out of order and that who started it did not matter. As a frustrated John Russell, America's chief diplomat in London, explained to Lord Castlereagh, the British foreign secretary, for what must have seemed the thousandth time by April 1812, "The United States have never considered it their duty to inquire nor do they pretend to decide, whether England or France was guilty, in relation to the other, of the first violation of the public law of nations."[21]

Led by first Thomas Jefferson as president and then James Madison, the United States responded diplomatically and commercially. The measures included a series of disastrous embargoes and nonintercourse acts that lasted intermittently from 1807 until the outbreak of war with Britain, and they crippled the American economy. During the first year of Jefferson's embargo, Massachusetts's merchant fleets alone lost upwards of $15 million in freight revenues—more than the federal government's entire income the previous year. Nationally, the total value of exports declined by 80 percent and imports fell by 60 percent in the first year. Matters only worsened as Jefferson and his supporters attempted stricter enforcement of the acts, violating constitutional protections against illegal search-and-seizure in the process.[22] The failure of economic coercion highlighted America's inability to significantly affect the direction of European affairs.

Jefferson and his supporters assumed that withdrawing the United States commercially from Europe would make the two nations see sense. The United States was, after all, economically important to both. In fact, France, whose merchant marine had largely been destroyed, was even more dependent on American trade than Britain was.[23] Jefferson correctly estimated that the British and French economies would suffer from America's absence, but he underestimated both sides' iron resolve to defeat the other and their willingness to forgo American trade to do it.

This miscalculation, which ultimately laid ruin to America's economy and hobbled the nation's ability to wage war in 1812, highlights the inflated self-importance of the American federal government. England (Britain after 1707) and France had been engaged in an intermittent struggle since 1689—a conflict that spilled onto other continents as both nations built vast empires. In fact, when taken from a global perspective, the American War of Independence was another chapter in the Anglo-French conflict—with thirteen of Britain's colonies switching sides just like so many European, African, Asian, and American Indian nations had and would continue to do during what has been dubbed the "second hundred years' war." Precipitating a global war was, of course, a key component of the American rebels' strategy. Only when France entered the war in 1778 as an ally of the American colonies did Britain mobilize its economy and military, and even then it redeployed troops and ships away from North America to other parts of the empire, winning major victories in the Caribbean and Europe and making gains in Asia that partly offset the loss of the American colonies.[24] Britain's wars with Napoleonic France were its most expensive ever in terms of blood and treasure, with Britons experiencing higher rates of military service and taxation than ever before. By 1815 Britain was raising £80 million in tax revenues a year—roughly thirty-five times that of the United States. This does not include the massive national debt Britain amassed to fight the French, which in 1815 reached nearly £850 million—more than seventy times what it had been in 1700. These measures helped to enable Britain to assemble a force of sailors, troops, militia, and volunteers in excess of six hundred thousand men by 1805, or one in five eligible men.[25] Given the scale of the conflict and the resolve of each to beat the other, neither seriously considered acquiescing to American demands until 1812.

By 1812 Americans' frustration with the Orders in Council had reached fever pitch. As one New Yorker railed that summer in a widely reprinted pamphlet, there was little left to say: "The flagrant iniquity and unhallowed tyranny of those orders beggar all comment." Discussion was at an end, which "left the question for the American people singly between SURRENDER OF THEIR SOVEREIGNTY, or an open efficient support of their rights"—in another word, war. Failure to resist, he continued, would be nothing short of abandonment of "our national honor, our national character, and our national rights."[26] Government officials and public commentators depicted the orders as part of a secret British agenda to crush America's overseas commerce. "It was no longer a question about the colonial carrying trade—that was at an end; because Great Britain might now be considered as possessing all the West India islands," Nathaniel Macon of North Carolina explained to his fellow congressmen. "As we have now neither sugar nor coffee to carry," he continued, "she has determined to execute with rigor her unjust orders against our carrying the productions of our own soil to any market except her own, and that of her allies."[27] Jealousy, Speaker of the House of Representatives Henry Clay declared soon afterward, was the "real cause of British aggression"; Britain's true aim "was not to distress an enemy [France] but to destroy a rival [the United States]."[28] Besides, a number of Americans asked, Britain's attacks on America's maritime interests were tantamount to war, so why not declare war and get on with it? According to Augustus Foster, Britain's minister to the United States, even the president had bluntly stated in April that the orders were nothing short of an act of war, and even "he was perfectly of the opinion the United States would be amply justified in going to war with us, whatever reasons of expediency there might be to prevent it, for that Great Britain was actually waging war upon them."[29]

Americans' fury over the continued assaults on their overseas commerce is most evident in the willingness of some to consider war with both Britain *and* France in 1812. America's infatuation with the French Revolution had waned by 1812, and most Americans dismissed Napoleon as a conquering tyrant and poked fun at anyone who sought his approval. As one New England clergyman sarcastically remarked, "it is said that Bonaparte loves America. Yes, he loved Spain, Portugal, Prussia . . . and they now enjoy the fruits of his love."[30] Calls for war against France appeared with increasing regularity in the American press after France issued its decrees severely restricting neutral trade, with most critics contending that the United States should be consistent by retaliating against all European abuses of America's neutral commercial rights. After all, the French confiscated more American ships under the Berlin and Milan decrees than the Royal Navy had seized under the Orders in Council.[31] John Burnham's remarks at a New Hampshire Fourth of July celebration were typical of advocates for a triangular war. Lumping Britain and France together as a common foe for their similar offenses, he complained that "against our peaceful commerce they wage an unprovoked, a perpetual, and an unrelenting hostility. All prospects of an accommodation are seen to have vanished. We must therefore exchange the olive branch for the sword."[32]

Sincerity for declaring war against France is hard to measure in most of these statements, as many of their authors had already expressed opposition to war

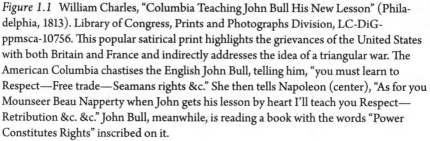

Figure 1.1 William Charles, "Columbia Teaching John Bull His New Lesson" (Philadelphia, 1813). Library of Congress, Prints and Photographs Division, LC-DiG-
ppmsca-10756. This popular satirical print highlights the grievances of the United States
with both Britain and France and indirectly addresses the idea of a triangular war. The
American Columbia chastises the English John Bull, telling him, "you must learn to
Respect—Free trade—Seamans rights &c." She then tells Napoleon (center), "As for you
Mounseer Beau Napperty when John gets his lesson by heart I'll teach you Respect—
Retribution &c. &c." John Bull, meanwhile, is reading a book with the words "Power
Constitutes Rights" inscribed on it.

with Britain and most likely advocated war with France as a bluff to highlight the
folly of war with either. Yet plenty of stalwart war supporters advocated, or at
least considered, the possibility. In late December 1811, the hawkish Kentucky
legislature passed a series of resolutions tantamount to endorsing war, the fourth
resolution of which singled out the "unjust violations of our commerce by
France" and promised to support "any measures which may be adopted by the
general government, to counteract [them]."[33] Madison discussed the possibility
with Jefferson as late as May 1812, remarking that political expediency might
demand war with both. "To go to war with England and not with France arms
the federalists with new matter, and divides the Republicans," he worried. The
downside, Madison admitted to his old mentor, was that a war with effectively all
of Europe would potentially be ruinous, but he predicted that a mere declaration
of war might compel one or the other to yield to American demands in an effort
to concentrate America's fighting power against the other.[34]

Most advocates of war with Britain, however, took a more pragmatic approach when it came to a triangular war. Jefferson, who took Madison's letter seriously, responded almost immediately with clear opposition to the idea. Jefferson dismissed the notion of declaring war on both as a way to demonstrate America's consistency and impartiality, bluntly stating "all the world will laugh."[35] He warned that war with both would prevent American privateering, and thus alienate merchants and seamen and keep them at home "idle to swell the discontents." Henry Clay agreed, remarking pragmatically, "The one we can strike, the other we cannot reach."[36]

Britain's impressment of America's sailors never matched the agitation caused by the Orders in Council. Madison's description in his war message of American citizens being "torn from their country, and from everything dear to them" and turned into the "melancholy instruments" of their "oppressors" may have tugged at Americans' heartstrings, but the topic received comparatively little attention in diplomatic, public, and government discussions.[37] However, when the British government yielded to domestic pressure and suspended the Orders in Council at the start of the war, by default impressment became the leading American justification for war.

Three major factors hampered impressment's ascendancy as the major justification for war. First, not that many Americans were pressed into service on British ships. Estimates varied enormously, but the number is unlikely to be much above a few thousand in the decade before the War of 1812.[38] With duplicated names and hearsay evidence, the Madison government struggled to produce a number above 6,500, and many of them were either deserters who had legitimately signed up for service in the Royal Navy or British subjects who had become naturalized American citizens and put their citizenship into question.[39] Second, most Americans did not care enough about common sailors to go to war to protect them. Sailors were well known for their antisocial behavior—drunkenness, associating with prostitutes, gambling, blasphemy, and other practices that were likely to alienate them from the overtly pious American middle class. In fact, evangelical Christians such as the Boston Society for the Religious and Moral Improvement of Seamen had been fighting a losing battle for the souls of sailors for years, publishing special tracts aimed at sailors and distributing bibles in places sailors frequented.[40] Even in the most egregious violation of American maritime sovereignty—the 1807 firing on the USS *Chesapeake* by the Royal Navy in order to capture deserters—the American public and government alike focused primarily on the violation of the American flag and the American sailors killed rather than the seized men.[41] Of course, it did not help that all four of the captured men were in fact deserters from British warships, although only one had been born in Britain. Third, many Americans sympathized with Britain's position as a wartime nation in need of its manpower—the American government itself estimated that some nine thousand Britons served on American merchant ships—and Britain released those men who were later proven to have been falsely impressed.[42]

Impressment as a solution to the Royal Navy's chronic manpower shortages had been a controversial part of Anglo-American maritime life since the midseventeenth century. Flexibility of size was a key component to keeping the enormous cost of the Royal Navy under control—demobilizing its sailors in peacetime to work in the merchant fleet and then rapidly mobilizing them in times of war. At the start of the American Revolution in 1775, the Royal Navy had about 16,000 sailors. By the end of the war that number had risen to 100,000. When Britain went to war against France a decade later, the peacetime navy that had returned to 16,000 rapidly grew to reach its previous size a few years later and hovered around 130,000 sailors in 1812.[43] Typically better pay and conditions aboard merchant vessels meant that more than a few sailors were reluctant to join the navy in wartime. Under a series of laws and precedents, English, and then British, governments had allowed the navy to abduct able seamen and force them to serve aboard warships. The practice was detested by most Britons. Press gangs in colonial American ports prior to independence greatly aggravated American colonists as examples of British tyranny, and in Britain in 1803 alone press gangs had prompted eighty-eight riots or violent affrays, affecting every major port.[44] Nevertheless, most Britons also recognized impressment as absolutely necessary in time of war. Impressment peaked during the wars against Revolutionary and Napoleonic France, when the desperate demand for manpower forced the government to extend the practice well beyond the traditional hunting grounds of southern English ports. In 1805 the government began imposing quotas by county.[45] By 1812 as many as 75 percent of sailors serving in the navy had been impressed.[46] The system worked. With its navy of impressed sailors, Britain managed to defeat the navies of France and its allies time and again, giving legitimacy to the popular claim that Britannia ruled the waves.

That the British targeted American vessels is hardly surprising. The problem was not merely quantitative, but qualitative. Whereas the British Army could train a soldier in a matter of months, a decent sailor required years of transoceanic experience. The British Admiralty estimated in 1812 that twenty thousand British sailors were working on American merchant ships—more than double the American government's earlier estimate—and enough to put a big dent in the Royal Navy's manpower problems.[47] Ideally, Britain would have preferred that the United States prevent British subjects from working on American ships and hand over violators. Stopping and searching merchant vessels on the high seas was ineffective. Roughly 30 percent of the men impressed from American ships were later released after providing satisfactory proof of their American citizenship. As a result, the Royal Navy's efforts to seize British subjects aboard American ships netted a paltry seven thousand sailors between 1796 and 1812.[48]

In principle, the United States did not object to the Royal Navy impressing British subjects from American merchant vessels—so long as they were either in British ports or subject to the normal searches that accompanied legal blockades. The major problem arose from conflicting views of who was a citizen of the United States. Neither side took an entirely consistent position, and no recognized global definition existed. Generally Americans held that citizenship was a choice and thus allowed naturalization, while Britain held that an individual's subjection to the sovereign of the country of his birth was indissoluble.

The citizen-versus-subject argument was at the core of the ideology of the American Revolution, with the Declaration of Independence serving as perhaps the clearest assertion that an individual had a right to choose his allegiance.[49] In the wake of the revolution, the United States created a relatively liberal process through which foreigners could become citizens and avidly defended the nation's right to do so. As the American secretary of state, James Monroe, impatiently stated to Britain's minister for the United States in June 1812, "The Government of the United States can make no distinction between native and naturalized Citizens, as has been already remarked to you."[50] Disallowing naturalization, or "expatriation" as most commentators called it, would have rocked the very foundations of America's creation myth—that the United States was founded and fought for by volunteers. As *Niles' Weekly Register* of Baltimore remarked in stirring up support for impressment as a cause for war in July 1812: "Future generations of the American people will not surely believe their ancestors, immortal in the history for their resistance of oppression and earnest devotion to independence and liberty, really submitted to such outrages from the cruel agents of that country they had so recently humbled." As for the naturalized citizens, it continued, "we are bound to protect them, for we make them our brethren."[51]

In truth, the American position was much fuzzier. The concept of citizenship was still novel in 1812, with the vast majority of people who were living in North America and Europe placing far more value on residency, race, ethnicity, and gender in determining an individual's place in society. After all, most of the leaders of the United States had been born British subjects, so there was not a great stigma attached to it. Being a white, adult male in the new state of Tennessee meant serving in the militia—something women and nonwhites could not do; whether a person had been born in New York or London mattered comparatively little. Following its declaration of war, Congress through a supplemental act in July 1812 required British aliens in the United States to register with a marshal in their state or territory. The response reveals both how awash the United States was in British subjects as well as how lax many American residents were about the formal process of citizenship. Roughly ten thousand heads of household registered themselves and their dependants in compliance with the act. This meant that if naturalization were disallowed, there would likely be more British subjects living in the United States than in Upper Canada. Many of those who registered were recent arrivals, such as Edward Henry, an English laborer who arrived in Boston in June 1812 and quickly married an American-born woman. Others had clearly been in the United States much longer but never bothered with citizenship. In the case of Mary Grace, a widow of a Boston merchant, this is not surprising, because citizenship for women afforded few benefits and her children were citizens by birth. But there were plenty of cases similar to that of Josiah Hunter, an Irish-born farmer living in Cape Girardeau, Missouri, who married an American-born woman, fathered seven children, and lived in the United States for twenty-nine years but never bothered to become a naturalized citizen.[52]

American federal law has been equally ambiguous. The refusal of the United States to recognize a state's right to secede, and its willingness to go to war to preserve the Union in 1861, is the greatest example of America's rejection of a free individual's right to choose national allegiance. In the wake of the American Revolution, Federalists especially tended to take a more traditional view of citizenship. Alexander Hamilton argued against punitive laws against New York loyalists who fled the United States, asserting they were American citizens and that declarations or actions of loyalty to Britain could not alone dissolve those bonds.[53] The U.S. Supreme Court concurred in the 1795 *Talbot v. Janson* decision. Talbot had renounced his American citizenship, declared himself a French citizen, and then seized foreign ships as a French privateer. Despite the arguments of Alexander James Dallas, Madison's future treasury secretary, the court unanimously denied Talbot's renunciation and rejected the validity of a personal declaration of a change in nationality. Although the court did not deny the right of expatriation outright, it made clear that citizenship and allegiance were not entirely the prerogative of the individual and that the state had rights as well. Three years later, during the Adams administration, Congress exercised these rights with the Naturalization Act, which changed the residency requirement for citizenship from a modest five years to fourteen. The goal was to stifle public criticism in the short run and stave off growth of the opposition Republican party, which most new citizens supported.[54] The plan backfired, and Jefferson, who considered expatriation a natural right, was selected the next president, beginning the Republicans' long dominance of the national government.

A practical problem British officers faced when impressing sailors from American ships was determining who was British. Centuries of migration and the constant flow of goods, people, and cultures across the Atlantic erased many of the distinctions among colonizers, colonized, and colonists. Most spoke English, and distinct national accents had not yet evolved. Physical differences between them were nonexistent: a white Irishman looked like his cousins living in Upper Canada and Boston, and sailors of African descent, who made up a sizeable portion of the Atlantic sailing community, looked and sounded similar whether they were born in British Jamaica or New York.[55] Moreover, sailors constituted a community apart. National language, dress, and custom were often muted among men who had spent nearly all their lives away from their place of birth. Such conditions allowed men like the Liverpool-born Henry Donaldson to avoid impressment for more than a decade, despite regularly visiting British ports as an "American" sailor, and made desertion for many sailors as easy as walking into the crowd whenever a Royal Navy vessel visited a North American port.[56]

Making matters worse were the flagrant abuses of American naturalization laws. For as little as four dollars, a British sailor could obtain a false certificate attesting to his American birthplace and citizenship. Some of the documents were outright forgeries, but plenty of others were genuine, having been obtained by American citizens and sold to foreign sailors. Lack of a centralized, uniform certification of birth in the United States was a major part of the problem. American notaries, port authorities, local governments, customs officials, American diplomats in Britain, and British agents issued certificates, which varied wildly in reliability. A British Admiralty report in January 1812 estimated that ten thousand false certificates were circulating, remarking that "it is quite obvious that the collectors of the two principal Sea Ports of America grant their certificates without any proof at all, and it is equally certain from the concurrent testimony of hundreds of seamen, that there is no difficulty whatsoever in procuring such certificates in any part of America." Many certificates were laughable, the report continued, noting that "it not unfrequently happens that a man with a fair complexion, produces a certificate describing a half-cast, and a West Indian mulatto, is not unfrequently described with blue eyes, and long sandy hair." By this time the Royal Navy as a matter of policy refused to recognize any American-issued certificates that did not come from a customs agent. Even these certificates were to be disregarded, explained the report, "If the person bearing one of these protections varies in the least in the age or description, if he is ignorant of the place in which it was granted; if he is discovered to be married in Great Britain or Ireland, if he speaks in an Irish, Scotch, or North Country accent."[57]

In other words, British officers were to employ an impossibly broad definition of "British" and err on the side of assuming the sailor met the definition of being British. Consequently, British subjecthood trumped the citizenship of Britain's former colonies; this is what made British impressment so vile in the minds of many American war supporters. As Madison explained to Congress as justification for his decision to remain at war solely on the grounds of impressment, ending the war would have acknowledged Britain's right to invoke policies that trampled America's rights, which would have meant "that on the element, which forms three fourths of the globe we inhabit, and where all independent nations have equal and common rights, the American people were not an independent people, but colonists and vassals." Failure to fight for America's self-determination would have violated the legacy of the American Revolution and, according to Madison, marked a fall "from the high rank, where the virtuous struggles of our fathers had placed us, and betrayed the magnificent legacy which we hold in trust for future generations."[58]

While Madison's grievances about Britain's interference with America's overseas trade and impressment required a new postcolonial rhetoric, his complaints about American Indians came straight out of the old colonial playbook. Throughout the eighteenth-century colonial wars with France, American colonists had demonized the French for employing Indian allies, and this was carried over into the American Revolution, when Britain was allied to the vast majority of American Indian participants. In 1812 the American line of argumentation had not changed: the European enemy enticed Indians within the United States and on its borders, in the words of Madison, to carry out "a warfare, which is known to spare neither age nor sex and to be distinguished by features peculiarly shocking to humanity."[59] Although the American anti-Indian rhetoric was simple, it was extremely effective, and American leaders knew it. As Jefferson remarked to Madison at the start of the war, "stopping the Indians barbarities" in the northwest was the best way to keep the conflict popular.[60] Yet the rhetorical simplicity of Americans' "Indian hating" masks a more complicated situation in which American Indians, the United States, and the British Empire negotiated their futures in nineteenth-century North America.

Depicting deteriorating relations between the United States and American Indians living within or on its borders as a catalyst for the War of 1812 is problematic. The United States had fought intermittently with its Indian neighbors since its foundation, and, despite plenty of accusations that Britain assisted them through Canada, this was never enough for the United States to declare war on Britain. Nor did many Americans in 1812 pretend that Britain's alleged Indian policies alone were sufficient grounds for declaring war. Madison's war message included this complaint, but it was brief, came at the end, and was likely intended primarily to illustrate the ruthlessness of Britain, not to be grounds for war. Moreover, the subject of American sovereignty did not weigh heavily into the early discussion regarding the Indians in arms. Some American commentators certainly saw a war with Britain as an opportunity to purge the United States of its disgruntled or disloyal Indians, such as *Niles' Weekly Register*, which remarked that the "advantage of a general war with Britain" was that "every *savage* in alliance with that magnanimous country may be expected to unbury the tomahawk."[61]

But only later in the war, when British promises for an independent Indian state carved out of the northwest territory of the United States became widely known, did Americans embark on a serious discussion of Indians in terms of the national sovereignty of the United States.

That war with Britain would include Indians was taken for granted by all sides. Every previous war in North America had involved Indians, and no one at the time expected 1812 to be any different. After all, the Great Lakes region, where the vast majority of the land fighting between the British Empire and the United States took place, was home to some fifty thousand Indians, roughly two-thirds the size of the colonial population of Upper Canada.[62] Moreover, the United States had been at war with the large intertribal collection of followers of Tecumseh and his brother, the Shawnee prophet Tenskwatawa, since the previous November. Declaring war in Britain in 1812 made these Indians and Britain what London's *Times* called "natural allies."[63]

The American Indians living within the territory of the United States had a better case for war than perhaps anyone else at the time. When taken from the perspective of Indian history, the War of 1812 was one episode in a half-century-long resistance movement rooted in an anti-European, pan-Indian ideology.[64] Indian country at the turn of the century was not a sanguine place. Disease, warfare, and displacement had scarred most of its Indian inhabitants, and the survivors faced the British and Spanish empires and the United States—all of which had histories of expansionism and deep hostility toward the Americas' indigenous peoples. Moreover, these Indian communities were deeply divided between those leaders who followed accommodationist policies—ceding and selling land to the imperial powers, adopting new technologies and gender roles, and encouraging intermarriage with whites—and the disgruntled Indians, who were typically younger and often lived on the margins of established Indian power structures. Indian religious prophets abounded, preaching apocalyptic messages and emphasizing a nativist ideology that embraced older Indian traditions and religions, or what has been aptly termed "sacred power." They appealed especially to the most disgruntled and marginal Indians. The most remembered of these prophets was Tenskwatawa. Often known simply as "The Prophet," he began preaching in earnest in 1805 and included in his message a call for a pan-Indian state. Squatting with his supporters on Miami land in the Indiana Territory, he responded to resistance from within existing Indian governing councils in the northwest region of the United States by accusing moderate members, particularly those who had profited personally from treaties that accommodated American demands for land, of being witches. Many of the victims were tortured and executed or, if they escaped, hunted down and murdered. The causes of Tenskwatawa and prophets like him benefited from Americans' insatiable hunger for land and established Indian leaders' willingness to accommodate the United

States. From the accommodationists' view, such dealings were seen as a means of averting wars the Indians would likely lose, but from the perspective of Tenskwatawa and his supporters, these leaders were traitors who betrayed their people out of either cowardice or greed.[65]

The last straw for many Indians in the region was the Treaty of Fort Wayne in 1809. Ohio, which achieved statehood in 1803, grew from a modest white population of forty-five thousand to nearly a quarter of a million a decade later.[66] This growth spilled into the Indiana Territory, which had a white population of sixty-three thousand by 1815.[67] To meet these migrants' needs and entice new ones, land cessions, whether by sale or force, from the region's Indian inhabitants were deemed essential. Following their defeat at the Battle of Fallen Timbers in 1794, most of the region's Indian leaders agreed to the Treaty of Grenville, which ceded large parts of modern Ohio and established an annuity system, whereby participating tribal leaders received annual payments of goods and money in exchange for cooperating and ceding lands. Although the treaty promised a permanent border, over the next fourteen years the United States government approved eight further major land cessions, typically with those tribal leaders who benefited from the annuity system. The Treaty of Fort Wayne was the most egregious in that some of the region's Indian leaders ceded three million acres of land without gaining the approval of all of its occupants. Among the excluded Indians were a number of Tenskwatawa's fellow Shawnees, and their outrage ushered in a new wave of military resistance, personified by his brother, Tecumseh. Prophetstown, established a year earlier near the junction of the Wabash and Tippecanoe rivers and little more than a day's journey from the capital of the Indiana Territory, became the headquarters of the resistance, attracting delegates from Indian communities from a 600-mile radius and sending its own deputations even further.[68] William Henry Harrison, the governor of the Indiana Territory who had negotiated the Treaty of Fort Wayne, realized his territory's vulnerability to the increasingly hostile Indians and decided to lead a preemptive strike on Prophetstown, ignoring orders from the secretary of war, William Eustis, to proceed with caution and not attack unless provoked.[69] Although technically a success—Tenskwatawa and his followers temporarily abandoned Prophetstown—Harrison's force suffered heavy casualties, endured the ignominy of retreat, and played right into the script of Tenskwatawa's prophecies of American aggression.[70]

Tecumseh was not present at the battle, because he had left to spread his militant message in the South. There he and his companions struggled to find immediate supporters among most of the Indians they visited, but he received a warm reception from the growing number of Creek Indians who had grievances similar to those of supporters in the North. A series of treaties over the previous two decades had transferred substantial Creek lands to the Americans with the aid of annuities to chiefs who brokered the deals. Tecumseh's visit coincided with the latest push by the United States: building a controversial federal road through the heart of Creek country capable of allowing thousands of wagons of goods and settlers to traverse the land. In fact, Tecumseh gave an hour-long speech calling for the Creek Indians to join him at the very meeting at Tuckabatchee, where Benjamin Hawkins, the long-time federal agent to the Creeks, had earlier informed the Creek National Council that the federal road would be built regardless of Creek approval. "The period has now arrived when the white people must have roads to market and for traveling wherever they choose to go through the United States," Hawkins bluntly announced.[71] The annuity-receiving chiefs on the national council acquiesced over strong objections, particularly from the younger generation and the Upper Creek. Tecumseh left behind a number of his companions, some of whom were prophets in their own right who claimed supernatural powers, to encourage an alliance. The nativist Red Stick movement, spawned in part by Tecumseh's visit, grew in numbers and vehemence, fueled by increasing opposition to the federal road and the apparent servility of the national council to the interests of the United States. In spring 1813, civil war broke out after the national council's warriors hunted down and killed Little Warrior, a Red Stick leader who the United States demanded be executed for his attack on a Tennessee settlement, which had been sensationalized in the press. Rather than intervene with a preemptive attack, as it did in the North, the United States initially left the Creek government to handle the problem internally, not entering until that summer as allies of the national council. Together, and with the aid of neighboring Indians, they crushed the Red Sticks over the course of the next year.[72]

Britain's involvement in the Creek War was minimal; nor was there much military cooperation between the Red Sticks and those American Indians to the north who did fight alongside the British forces. After returning Florida to Spain in 1783, Britain maintained modest trading relations with Indians in the region, but it lacked the sort of presence necessary to counter American authority. By the time Britain shifted its military ambitions to the Gulf of Mexico in 1814 and was in a position to influence the Creek War, the Red Sticks had already been soundly defeated.[73] The situation in the North was, of course, entirely different. Because Indians did not live or conduct trade solely in the neatly divided zones prescribed by Europeans, diplomatic and economic relations with most major Indian nations meant dealing with delegates on both sides of the United States–Canadian border. As a result, Britain had ongoing, substantial relations through trade and diplomacy with most of the Indian communities living in the Mississippi and Ohio river valleys and adjacent territories.

Though devoid of solid evidence, Madison's inclusion of complaints about savage Indians was a savvy move for the Americans in 1812 for the same reason it was in 1776, when the Continental Congress accused King George III in the Declaration of Independence of employing "the merciless Indian Savages whose known rule of warfare is an undistinguished destruction of all ages, sexes and conditions." Most Americans detested and feared the Indians, and accusing Britain of allying with them made the British seem all that more despicable and dangerous. Whereas the Orders in Council and impressment were divisive subjects in America, particularly with regard to whether or not this justified war with Britain, few Americans expressed objections to fighting Indians. Public declarations of sympathy for the Indians' plight were extremely rare. Critics instead deplored the lack of evidence that the British government was aiding Indians hostile to the United States. The *Alexandria Daily Gazette* insisted that "the government of Canada [has] amply executed all the offices of friendship and good neighborhood as well" and had made "earnest endeavors to prevent the late inroads of the Indians upon our frontiers." That the Indians could not always be controlled, it concluded, was hardly Britain's fault.[74] Others accused Madison and his supporters of building a false case in order to rally support for the war. As William Ellery Channing, the minister of the Federal Street Church in Boston, fumed in his widely reprinted sermon at the start of the war, "I blush to repeat, the accusation which we have brought against England without a shadow of proof, that she has stirred up the savages to murder our defenceless citizens on the frontiers."[75] Thus the stated problem for most of these critics was not waging war against the Indians but unfair association of the British with them.

Yet, as far as many Americans were concerned, Britain had been waging a war against the United States via Tecumseh in the north long before June 1812, and it needed to be punished along with the dissident Indians. As an orator declared at a Vermont Fourth of July celebration, "It [war with Britain] has long since been begun. Our brethren on the borders of the wilderness have already felt the stroke, from the savage executors of British vengeance!"[76] The federal government inflamed such perceptions. Clay bluntly informed the House of Representatives in April 1812 that "he had no doubts but that the late Indian War on the Wabash [Prophetstown] was executed by the British."[77] The congressional committee on Indian affairs' special report "relative to the Excitements, on the Part of British Subjects, of the Indians" was carefully timed to appear at the height of Congress's deliberations on declaring war against Britain. Not surprisingly, the Republican-dominated committee found the British government guilty of encouraging and supplying the Indians, citing such flimsy evidence as increased activity of deliberations with Indians, as well as private claims that some Indians had reduced their trade with Americans and abandoned their subsidies—clear evidence, according to the report, that they had found an alternative supplier in Britain. The lengthy report then went on to cite the resolutions of frontier county meetings, which loudly condemned the British and Indians alike, as evidence of

British activities. How reflective this was of the genuine views of Madison, his administration, or other Republican leaders is impossible to determine, but there are good reasons for scepticism.

Augustus Foster's vehement official denials of British involvement were reprinted throughout the United States, but his denials had little impact on public opinion because they were drowned out by accounts of Indian attacks on family farms. Little had changed in the half century since Samuel Johnson's comment on the British press coverage of the frontier violence during the Seven Years' War. "Scarce any thing awakens attention like a tale of cruelty," he declared, "the writer of news never fails, in the intermission of action, to tell how the enemies murdered children and ravished virgins; and if the scene of action be somewhat distant, scalps half the inhabitants of a province."[78] The response of many commentators was to hold entire Indian nations accountable, rather than the renegade few acting outside the official sanction of their leaders. In the case of the Red Stick Little Warrior, whose attack on a Tennessee settlement resulted in multiple deaths and abductions, his action enraged the readers against the Creek people as a whole. As the Tennessee *Carthage Gazette* railed, the raid had not been conducted by "a wild young man which the nation cannot manage, but in fact a principal chief and one of the most distinguished warriors of the Creeks." "If any evidence was wanted of the hostile disposition of the Creeks," the article concluded, "it is now furnished."[79]

Americans had good reason to fear the British Empire's relations with American Indians. The British government walked a tightrope in 1811 and early 1812 between encouraging Indian hostility to the United States and checking that it did not erupt into armed conflict prematurely. The British military leadership in Canada worried that Indian military strength would be spent too early and would be of little use to Britain should it later find itself at war with the United States. Without substantial Indian allies, the British government and military leaders expected the United States to easily overrun Upper Canada and its thinly spread collection of a few thousand defenders. Thus, although the British establishment committed to supplying the Indians in case of a general war, British agents urged patience. As an officer in the Indian department told a delegation who arrived at the Upper Canada fort at Amherstburg in 1810, "keep your eyes fixed on me; my tomahawk is not up; be you ready, but do not strike until I give the signal."[80]

The British Empire was every bit as pragmatic and self-interested as the United States when it came to Indian affairs, and in many respects it was not so much an obstacle to the western expansion of the United States as it was a rival.[81] The Canadian press sometimes shamed the United States for its treatment of Indian, such as the *Quebec Gazette's* comments after the battle at Prophetstown. "They [the United States] will not yield up the smallest portion of their interest on the ocean to England even in a case wherein she considers her existence as a nation at stake," the paper mocked, "but they expect of the Indians that they should deliver up their country and their means of subsistence, in subserviency [sic] to the interests of the United States."[82] The British Empire's record was little better.[83] British governments in London and Canada treated Indians as consumers and military allies, not as romanticized savages, and like the French, Dutch, and Spanish, the British made and broke alliances as best suited their ambitions. As with France after the Seven Years' War, Britain readily abandoned its Indian allies after the American Revolution, leaving them to make their own way with the victor. Britain would do so again in the Treaty of Ghent in 1814. Assessing the possibilities of a war with the United States, public comment in Britain gave virtually no consideration to the likely suffering of Britain's Indian allies. Instead, readers greedily anticipated the commercial benefits of a war that would expand British interests in North America. "In case of war," the *Ipswich Journal* confidently declared, "the trade with the Indians will then fall entirely into our own hands. . . . [W]e should secure the affection and co-operation of those tribes by our ability to supply their wants, and the United States would not only be deprived of an extensive branch of trade, but would meet with none, or few allies among the uncivilized and warlike nations that line their frontiers on land."[84]

Like the United States, the British Empire was in the habit of brokering dubious deals for Indian lands to allow its expansion, steadily slicing away at the territory of Indians within the imperial borders. Only at the local level would some of these practices take on a more sympathetic hue, but this was often a consequence of British agents and traders, who typically had Indian families, looking out for their relatives.[85] British–American Indian relationships in 1811 were based more on convenience than a deep mutual admiration or respect. The Iroquois, who were Britain's oldest allies and arguably suffered the most from a series of British abandonments, were slow to involve themselves in the War of 1812.[86] In fact, the vast majority of Britain's American Indian allies in the war came from within the United States, not from loyal Indians living in Canada, thus highlighting that a common disgruntlement with the United States, and not any positive feeling toward or connection with Britain, drove Indians' wartime alliances.[87] These were parallel struggles in which peoples with a common enemy became temporary allies when it suited them.

The territorial expansion of the United States, though not examined in Madison's war message, was an important part of the contemporary discussion surrounding the declaration of war in 1812. American expansion, after all, was the primary reason the United States was battling Tecumseh and his supporters, fighting a quasi war in Spanish East Florida, and fomenting a rebellion in Texas, as well as the main reason for the Creek War that would erupt soon afterward. The United States was undeniably imperialist in 1812. Within two generations it had doubled its size, dispossessing the native inhabitants of their land and stripping the declining Spanish Empire of huge swaths of its territory. Like their colonial forefathers, Americans interchangeably employed violence, diplomacy, and commerce (sometimes simultaneously) in an impressive pace of growth. Although given various ideological veneers, among them "manifest destiny" in 1845, the American impulse for expansion had colonial roots, and it seemed unquenchable. Cheap and abundant land was crucial to the Republicans, who idealized the small farmer and relied heavily on his vote. Expansion was also highly controversial, as opponents, particularly in New England, worried about the necessity, cost, legality, and consequences of expansion.[88]

This "land hunger," as it came to be known by historians, is evident in prewar discussion in the press and Congress. A number of war advocates openly embraced the idea of annexing Canada, notably Thomas Jefferson, who proudly wrote to Madison on the eve of the war that the young men of Virginia are ready to fight, and "the only enquiry they make is whether they are to go to Canada or Florida?"[89] Far more Americans, however, used the opportunity to rail against territorial expansion, accusing war advocates of rushing to war for the trivial sake of conquering new lands. As one commentator mockingly reflected before a Philadelphia audience nine months into the war, "If it is a war of conquest, there should be some promised gain,—some treasure; but, surely, every man is sensible, that the British possessions in America, will yield us nothing but, a miserable population."[90] In fact, opponents of the war brought up the subject of expansion far more often than did its supporters. Only a minority of the latter focused on the issue, and the western states that clamored most for it did not have enough votes in Congress to tip the majority one way or the other. In fact, there is little evidence that a majority of Americans wanted to retain Canada if they conquered it.[91] In consequence, and despite such quotable remarks as those from Jefferson, historians rightly have long dismissed the idea of land hunger as being the hidden force behind America's declaration of war on Britain in 1812.[92]

The cold war between the United States and the Spanish Empire in North America had little to do with the War of 1812 and is best understood as a conflict that ran parallel to the war between the United States and Britain.[93] Many Americans supported the overthrow of Spanish rule in North America—particularly those Americans living in the southern states and territories that bordered the Spanish Floridas and Texas. Jefferson and Madison challenged the legitimacy of Spain's claims over the Floridas and Texas, asserting they had been included as part of the Louisiana Purchase and Americans were involved in invasions of both. Such papers as the *Military Monitor* referred to the rebels in Texas as "our Spanish American brethren" and likened their struggle to the American Revolution's quest for personal

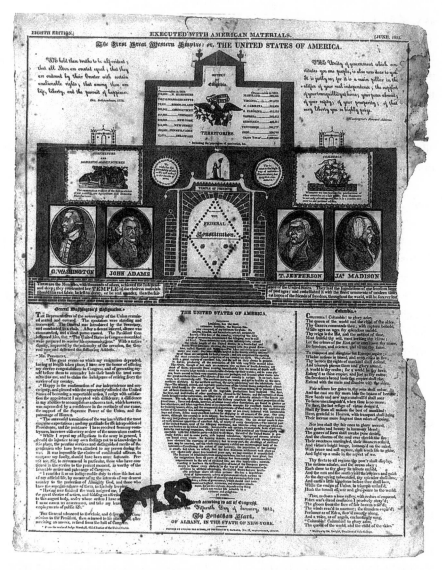

Figure 1.2 Jonathan Clark, "The First Great Western Empire: or, the United States of America" (Albany, 1812). Library of Congress, Prints and Photographs Division, LC-USZ62-40915. This patriotic broadside from Albany, New York, celebrates the United States as a new empire. Employing the shape of a temple, the artist uses the four presidents and columns, which support the domestic economy and overseas commerce. At the top of the temple is a table listing the names and populations of the states and territories, and the heart is the Federal Constitution. The foundation consists of Washington's resignation of his commission, a description of the United States, and the song "Columbia," a popular patriotic anthem. Such images as this celebrated America's size, growth, and power, and the use of such terms as first and empire underlines the perception of the United States both as being akin to a European nation and as expansionist.

and religious liberty, while at their annual Fourth of July celebration in 1812 the citizens of Carthage, Tennessee, included in the evening's toast one to the demise of Spanish America.[94] Others, particularly in the South, even attempted to link the war with Britain to ongoing hostilities with the Spanish Empire, such as the Charleston *City Gazette's* lengthy editorial in April 1812 detailing how Britain as Spain's new ally "seeks to establish a new Bengal in Mexico," but this was decidedly a minority viewpoint and more about legitimizing the undeclared Patriot War in East Florida by connecting it to the declared war on Britain.[95] Such efforts, however, were entirely in vain, and there is little evidence to suggest that more than a few Americans accepted such claims. In fact, the United States Senate twice rejected bills during the first year of the war authorizing the government to conduct military operations in East Florida. Besides, even though the British and Spanish functioned as close allies in the campaigns against Napoleon on the Iberian Peninsula, military cooperation in North America against the United States was minimal.

British Canada was a different matter. The federal government's case for attacking Canada was far more about strategic interests than it was about expansion. Britain's North American possessions made an obvious target. They were vast and thinly populated; they appeared to be poorly defended, and most important the United States did not have to contend with the might of the Royal Navy to reach them. That the Americans planned to invade Canada in the event of a war with Britain was public knowledge. It had been discussed openly in Congress, Parliament, and the press throughout the Atlantic world for years. The United States designed not only its battle plans but also its armed forces on the premise that Canada was the target. As Madison explained to Jefferson in February 1812, the aim of the military measures going through Congress was to "enable the Executive to step at once into Canada."[96] Yet only a few Americans, whether in the press or in government, initially expressed a desire to take Canada for its own intrinsic value. To the Republican national leadership, it was a way for the United States to strike at the world's greatest maritime power, whose home was an ocean away. Overestimating Canada's strategic and commercial importance to Britain, Madison and leading war advocates in Congress hoped to exchange Canada for Britain's acquiescence to American interpretations of neutral rights.[97] The United States was a David fighting a Goliath, which meant using any means at its disposal. As a young John C. Calhoun argued in Congress in December 1811, the United States had the right to defend itself against Britain's assaults on America's maritime rights by striking Britain in any way possible. In a widely adopted analogy that likened the contest between the United States and Britain to a fight between two men, he poked fun at his opponents who considered Canada off limits. "By this system, if you receive a blow on the breast, you dare not return it on the head," he mocked, "you are obliged to measure and

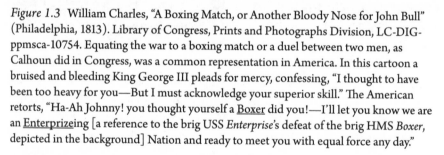

Figure 1.3 William Charles, "A Boxing Match, or Another Bloody Nose for John Bull" (Philadelphia, 1813). Library of Congress, Prints and Photographs Division, LC-DIG-ppmsca-10754. Equating the war to a boxing match or a duel between two men, as Calhoun did in Congress, was a common representation in America. In this cartoon a bruised and bleeding King George III pleads for mercy, confessing, "I thought to have been too heavy for you—But I must acknowledge your superior skill." The American retorts, "Ha-Ah Johnny! you thought yourself a Boxer did you!—I'll let you know we are an Enterprizeing [a reference to the brig USS *Enterprise*'s defeat of the brig HMS *Boxer*, depicted in the background] Nation and ready to meet you with equal force any day."

return it on the precise point on which it was received." "If you do not proceed with mathematical accuracy," he teased, "it ceases to be just self-defence."[98]

Because Upper Canada was the main conduit through which the British Empire traded with and supported Indians hostile to the United States, hobbling it had a strong strategic appeal for Americans concerned about Indian affairs. A weakened Canada meant isolating hostile American Indians, which in turn enabled the United States to continue its expansion into Indian territory, thereby pleasing the land-hungry settlers who voted for Madison and his party. Consequently, popular cries for attacks against Canada sometimes coincided with calls for vengeance against neighboring Indians. As the president of the Association of Democratic Young Men of Philadelphia declared at a meeting, "our savage neighbours on the frontiers have disturbed and will continue to disturb our peaceable inhabitants, and burn their dwellings and massacre their families, as long as we suffer their Christian ally to have a communion with them."[99] Peace, declared another commentator in the most sensationalist language possible, was unattainable so long as the British could ally with the Indians. "While our western wilds are whitening with the bones of our murdered women and children—while their blood is yet trickling down the walls of their former habitations—while the Indian war-whoop, and the British drum, are in unison saluting the ears, and British dagger and the Indians tomahawk suspended over the heads of our citizens," no American could consider peace with Britain.[100] So while territorial acquisition for the purposes of expanding the United States was not a central wartime goal, many Americans believed in the idea that the United States was contending for future control of the continent.

Ironically, the American government's insistence that it did not want war was central to its case *for* war. According to the Madison administration and its supporters, the United States was a victim, a peace-loving nation provoked into drawing the sword. Britain disregarded America's commercial rights as a neutral; Britain seized American citizens and impressed them into its navy; and Britain armed and incited Indians to attack American settlements. In short, Britain was ignoring American sovereignty, and Americans had to protect or relinquish it. By the winter of 1811–12, an increasing number of Americans argued that diplomatic efforts had been exhausted and the choice made clear. As the Pennsylvania Senate resolved in December 1811, "when submission or resistance to the unjust demands of a tyrant, is the alternative, the latter only can be chosen by the freemen of America."[101] To be fair, the federal government did not rush to war. Under the direction of Jefferson and Madison, it attempted for well over a decade to achieve its goals diplomatically or through economic coercion—much to the frustration of many of their supporters. As Vermont's governor, Jonas Galusha, reflected in his speech to the state's legislature at the outbreak of war, "I sincerely believe it to have been the unremitted endeavors of our national government, by every means in their power, to maintain the blessings of peace . . . without our resorting to the last and most dreadful remedy, of repelling aggression by force." Ultimately, he declared, the only choice was for Americans to either surrender their independence to Britain or defend themselves. "Such has been her [Britain's] conduct towards the United States," he continued, "that we had no alternative, but to submit to her arbitrary edict, and abandon our real independence, or with manly fortitude, contend for our sacred rights, at the expence and hazard of war."[102]

Britain had backed the United States into an impossible corner by June 1812. As William Parkinson proclaimed before his congregation at New York's First Baptist Church, the declaration of war was just, because Britain had "impressed our citizens, blockaded our harbours, and crimsoned our waters with American blood."[103] To their American critics, the war's supporters asked what the realistic alternative was. "Under such accumulated circumstance of insult and of injury . . . what was your government to do?" challenged one proponent of war. "Was she basely and inglorious to abandon the rights for which you and your fathers had fought and bled? Was she so early to cower to the nation who had sought to strangle us in our infancy, and who has never ceased to retard our approach to manhood?" The answer, he declared, was as simple as it was obvious: "No."[104]

2

The British Empire's Case for War

The Canadian historian William Kingsford remarked at the end of the nineteenth century that the events of the War of 1812 had not been forgotten in Britain, "for they have never been known there."[1] Unfortunately, historians have since taken this for granted, despite it being a chimera. The war against Napoleonic France has come to overshadow the War of 1812 in Britain's national memory to such an extent that referring to it even among British historians almost invariably provokes the question, "War of 1812 with *whom*?" Yet modern perceptions seldom are reliable reflections of the past. It is true that Britain's ongoing conflict with France demanded the lion's share of resources and manpower, making the war in North America a comparative military sideshow; however, this dominance was not mirrored in how the British perceived the American war. The British government and wider public cared deeply about the crisis and conflict with the United States, albeit for a variety of reasons. British policies toward the United States were neither ad hoc nor left to the management of those on the ground. Policy was crafted in London and then administered through regular instructions to relevant officials abroad. The subject often topped the agenda of cabinet meetings and parliamentary debates, and it regularly appeared in the prince regent's speeches opening Parliament. American news also made headlines, regularly squeezing out France. As the *Leeds Mercury* reflectively declared in the summer of 1812, as the nation collectively held its breath to see if war with the United States would be averted, "The question of Peace or War with America takes the precedency in public importance of all other foreign news." "The happiness and tranquility of this country," it continued, "are much more closely connected with this subject, than with the victories in Spain, or the movements of contending armies in Russia."[2]

British interest in American events reflected growing cosmopolitanism and the widespread recognition that activities abroad could have profound consequences at home. Although England had possessed an overseas empire since the sixteenth century, widespread national interest in empire and the world outside

Europe was born in the mid-eighteenth century, as the ongoing struggle between Britain and France went global.[3] Largely through the press, but also through museums and visual advertisements, Britons came to believe that the empire and wider world were vital to their prosperity and security at home. Juvenile literature and games as well as liberal admittance policies at museums, menageries, and panoramas ensured that children were indoctrinated at a young age.[4] This generally was not chauvinistic national imperialism, although evidence of it can be found. In fact, such acutely watched events as the American Revolution had taught the British to be critical both of the idea of empire and of the government's management of it, and since then the British public had declared war on the African slave trade and expressed deep concerns over the mishandling of the British East Indies.[5]

Many Britons looked upon the United States as the future, for better or for worse. Like Alexis de Tocqueville two decades later, they recognized that its sheer size would make it a global player—an awareness that stretched back well into the eighteenth century.[6] Other Britons looked upon the United States as a rival unlike any other. Like the British, the Americans were ambitious for greater commerce and territory, and also like the British, the Americans were ready to take advantage of any situation to forward their goals. Conveniently forgetting that Britain was amassing an overseas empire with the aid of less-than-scrupulous practices, critics poured scorn on the ambitious American republic. Writing to his wife in 1805, Augustus Foster, who in 1811 would become Britain's minister to the United States, declared that "from the Province of Main[e] to the borders of Florida you would not find 30 men of Truth, Honour, or Integrity. Corruption, Immorality, Irreligion, and above all, self-interest, have corroded the very pillars on which their Liberty rests."[7] The experience of the American Revolution also made clear that Americans were not willing to yield to British direction—as smaller European states often did—regardless of how much more powerful and wealthier Britain was. This last point was a thorn in Britain's side, exacerbated by renewed war with France in 1793. Thanks in no small part to the war in Europe, the neutral United States had grown rich supplying the opposing armies and assuming the carrying trade between Europe and its colonies. Amidst the chaos of wartime Europe's secret treaties, shifting alliances, and shady diplomacy, the United States also managed to double its size relatively cheaply by conveniently acknowledging France's dubious right to sell Louisiana out from under an embattled Spain.[8]

All of this served to frustrate many Britons. In the popular British imagination at home and abroad, Napoleonic France was a force of darkness bent on the subjugation and tyrannical rule of all humanity. As the *Bermuda Gazette* declared in response to news of the American declaration of war, the French regime was a "murderous despotism" led by the "demi-god of slaughter and infamy" that "laid waste" to its conquests. Britain, in sharp contrast, it continued, was the "generous and enlightened country" that "for five years past has . . . almost single handed and alone, opposed and defeated the hitherto overwhelming, and invincible armies of France." Meanwhile, the paper complained, the Americans were "meanly profiting" from the situation. While the British sacrificed their wealth and sons for the sake of all humanity, the American government whined about Britain's tactics, namely its need to restrict French commerce and secure the service of its own seamen. In short, the tedious, litigious complaints about legal precedent and practice be damned. "Engaged in a contest for liberty, a gift dearer than existence," the paper concluded, "Great Britain must have recourse, without scruple, to any measures, which can preserve her independence and retaliate a loss of honor and wealth upon our inveterate opponent."[9] Such sentiments were echoed throughout the press, public meeting places, and government houses across the British Empire. To be certain, most Britons, including those in government, would have welcomed a peaceful solution to the country's disagreements with the United States—albeit a solution in which the United States acquiesced to virtually all of Britain's demands. Failing that, the British government was willing to go to war in 1812; Britain had preemptively struck obstinate neutrals before, and plenty of people thought the United States deserved similar treatment.

Whereas jealous protection of national sovereignty was the heart of America's case for war, Britain's was *order*. A conflict from which Britain emerged triumphant would restore order, humble the boisterous Americans, quiet their incessant protests, and squash the pretense of the United States being Britain's equal among nations. The erratic nature of the American republic, with its embargos and complaints about neutral rights, upset the order of the British Atlantic. Worse still, American insolence was spreading. In March 1812 the British Caribbean press described how the British squadron based at Jamaica had earlier captured a "Haytian frigate." In response, the paper reported, "the Haytian chief, Bourgelas" had threatened to kill "all the remaining white inhabitants" in his district of the island unless the Royal Navy returned the frigate. Jamaica's *Royal Gazette*, like most papers, quickly dismissed the threat, remarking that "When threats so insolent are made by so base a foe, it would be a dereliction of all national dignity were the same passed over with impunity." Yet, according to the *Gazette*, the real problem was not the Haitian republic, but the mildness with which Britain treated the North American one. "The tameness with which we have hitherto borne the insults and the aggressions of the American republic," the paper complained, "might well have led the Haytian chief to suppose that his conduct would be equally unnoticed." The time had come for the British government to "punish by one blow the presumption of both those petty states." The paper then called for the Royal Navy to act the role of the adult and immediately seize all armed vessels of the fledgling republics in the Americas and prohibit those countries from owning them in the future.[10]

Although some Britons admired the United States and the pluckiness of the colonists who rebelled to create it, still more resented the Americans as unruly upstarts.[11] As during the American Revolution, some of the anti-American rhetoric of the early-nineteenth century manifested itself in the language of social class. Under the heading "Character of the Americans," the *Edinburgh Star* took a typical shot at Americans via a letter from a Scots clergyman who had emigrated to the United States but later returned. Americans, he insisted, were not like Europeans once one scratched the surface: "Mankind here seem to be a different race from those in Europe; they shew well at their first appearance, but there is no depending on their friendship." "Men think much less here, and more superficially than with you," he continued. "They have little knowledge, and less taste, but great vanity, and a comfortable portion of impudence and obstinacy." The problem, he and so many others in Britain concluded, was republicanism. In America "the great equality of people" made everyone fancy himself a politician and a lawyer, despite knowing precious little about those subjects, the clergyman postulated. But there was no arguing with these narrow, arrogant people, as "Truth seems to make no impression on their minds when it is opposite to their prejudices, but they are satisfied with the slightest shadow of argument when it is on their own side." Therefore, he lamented, "it is rare to see them convinced of any thing, and almost impossible to make them acknowledge that they have ever been in the wrong." Worse still, the American form of government put these sorts of people in power.[12]

The long war with Revolutionary France and fears of similar upheaval at home had clarified and entrenched British antipathy for republicanism and democracy. For many of the middling and elite Britons who dominated both the public sphere and government, "republic" was a dirty word associated with the violence of the mob rule of the French Revolution.[13] Although the American Revolution had evoked feelings of sympathy and admiration among many Britons, by the early nineteenth century most commentators stopped distinguishing between American and French republicanism. Even Lord Grenville, the leader of the ministry most sympathetic to the United States during the Napoleonic Wars, referred to the United States in 1806 as a "Mob government."[14] In fact, for Britons the United States was the better cautionary tale against republicanism because of the two nations' shared history and cultural similarities. As one critic remarked in the lengthy diatribe *Democracy Unveiled*, "the example of France has proved a warning to Britain. To make the United States, (a country whose manners and habits bear a much greater resemblance to our own, than any other) equally a beacon, is the object of these pages."[15]

Incidents such as the widely reported 1812 Baltimore riots, in which a mob besieged a Federalist newspaper printer and later attacked the jail in which he and his companions took refuge, only underscored such arguments for the British.[16] The seeming complicity of the local authorities and the mobs' torture and murder of its quarry reminded British commentators of the French *sans-culottes*, who regularly dispensed their own brutal interpretations of justice on the critics of the French Revolution. The *Caledonian Mercury* likened the American rioters to Parisian mobs, remarking that "the democratic mob had committed outrages equaled only by what took place in the French revolution." The London *Examiner* concurred, condemning the "barbarous actions" as "disgraceful." Even William Cobbett, the most prolific British apologist for the Americans, denounced the riot. The editor of the paper may have been a "corrupt tool," Cobbett argued, but this was no excuse for such a violent attack on the liberty of the press.[17]

Republican government, British critics argued, brought out the worst in men. The constant rotation of governments and elections made the American leaders short-sighted men who pandered to the masses, who more than one critic described as Europe's refuse. Most attacks on the American system began with a lengthy defense of the British model, which used hereditary privilege to temper popular impulses. In Britain, explained one commentator before launching into an invective against American republicanism, the king is "Elevated by his station, no less above the cares of private industry, than the paltry avocations of political intrigue[;] he surveys, with calm deliberation, as from another planet." In such a position, the king can act as "a check on the jarring interests and selfish designs of his subjects."[18] In contrast, contended another critic, the American system created rulers who with "an eye to elections, at short recurring periods, become influenced by motives the most secret and selfish, unchecked by that spirit of honour which gradually guides the conduct of persons of good education, and possessing pecuniary independence, not acquired by traffic with the lower classes of society." In other words, America's rulers did not come from a social class bred to rule, resulting in a nation that was as "mercenary" and "selfish" in its international dealings as a common butcher might be in running his shop. "Laws and foreign relations of the state are determined by the speculative views of the jobber, and the arithmetic of the ledger," the pamphlet sneered, "and as every man fancies that America was made for himself, so the State, in its aggregate capacity, fancies that all the rest of the world is made for America."[19]

The British Orders in Council were among the most discussed government acts in the five years following their creation in 1807. As the Dublin *Freeman's Journal* groaned in March 1812, the orders seemed to be an "inexhaustible theme" in the press.[20] The case for the orders, made both in government and general public discussions, was fairly straightforward. Napoleon's Berlin and Milan decrees essentially outlawed the British, and anyone trading with Britain, from trading with French-controlled Europe. The decrees constituted a serious threat to two of Britain's greatest assets: the commercial economy and naval supremacy. The decrees left Britain little choice but to retaliate with a series of executive orders that declared a blockade on all ports excluding British goods and requiring neutrals to stop first in Britain for inspection and to pay a duty. Such stops, of course, made the goods and ships subject to seizure in French ports by the terms of the decrees. Few in Britain bothered to defend the orders' legality in their own right. Instead, most advocates simply called them retaliatory measures, and the British government continuously reiterated to impatient Americans that it would repeal the orders as soon as France repealed its decrees.

Britain was able to compete successfully against the larger and more populous France throughout the eighteenth century in no small part because the British could more efficiently raise revenues through taxes and thus outborrow and outspend its opponents.[21] During the first decades of the eighteenth century, Britain's tax revenues shifted decidedly away from the aged and inefficient land tax to taxes on internal and overseas commerce, thus intrinsically linking maritime trade in such commodities as tea, sugar, tobacco, and cotton to the government's ability to wage war. The customs duty on coffee alone in 1774 was enough to build five ships of the line, and the annual duty on sugar in the 1760s was roughly equivalent to the cost of maintaining all the ships in the British navy.[22] The change from a taxation system in which an elite few paid the bulk of the taxes to a broad-based system in which even the poorest Britons contributed to the state's coffers had a profound effect on British society, not least of which was a rapid increase in popular interest in how the government spent the hard-earned money of its constituents. At least partly in consequence, ordinary Britons became more critical of their government and demanded more political influence.[23]

By the time of the Orders in Council, the British adamantly believed that naval supremacy was central to their nation's security and prosperity and any compromise to those rights was courting disaster. As Sir Frederick Morton Eden argued in a pamphlet published in the wake of widely reported American hostility to the Orders in Council, the British ruled the seas as a conqueror's right. "You have, now, one plain open course of policy to pursue," he declared, "to vindicate your right to the dominion of the sea, which the valour of British seamen has acquired; and to prove that what they acquired is not a barren scepter, or empty title, invented by flatterers to gratify your vanity with the swelling theme of 'Rule Britannia.'" For Eden and many others, such measures as the Orders in Council were the "only" way to combat Napoleon's "Continental Aggrandizement."[24] Eden's rhetorical use of the second person reflects the wider sense that Britain's command of the oceans was a national asset from which all Britons benefited, rather than a royal privilege or the preserve of the governing elite.[25] When it appeared that the British government might compromise those rights in 1812 by repealing the orders, many Britons expressed outrage. At the annual countywide meeting of Perthshire's freeholders that spring, the possibility of a repeal created considerable concern and prompted a petition to the prince regent. Plenty of Britons would have disagreed with the petition's support of the orders, but its language nevertheless reflects popularly held views that Britain's maritime rights collectively were "our rights" and were rooted in "our own naval superiority." "We rely on your Royal Highness's government," the Scottish petitioners asserted, "that no mistaken or destructive policy . . . shall ever suffer those principles and rights to be compromised or abandoned."[26]

No British government could have followed policies significantly different from those pursued by the succession of governments led by the Duke of Portland, Spencer Perceval, and the Earl of Liverpool and expected to survive. The primary officially stated object of the Orders in Council was to wage an economic war against France and the countries under its control, which were expected to follow the "Continental System"—as the exclusion of British and neutral trade established by the French decrees came to be known. This sort of thinking represented a new level of sophistication when it came to economic warfare, as well as the European ruling elite's recognition of the arrival of the consumer revolution. As Eden argued: "We cannot affect her [France] by attacking her armies, or by combating her finances; but the trident of the waves enables us to draw round her a magic circle . . . and render her, during war, tributary to our merchants and manufacturers, for all the foreign produce which she and her dependants may chuse to consume." Cutting off neutrals makes that dependence even greater, he continued, so that the "people of France must, then, receive our commodities, or suffer by privation," thus bringing the "pressure of war" to the people and pushing them to peace.[27]

Others viewed the Orders in Council as a means to stifle the growing maritime power of the United States and reestablish a more mercantilist system over imperial trade. The United States had benefited enormously as a neutral power. With "free trade" as their slogan, Americans gained access to an unprecedented number of ports and trade routes. British naval supremacy meant that France had limited access to its overseas colonies, and American merchants were only too happy to fill the gap, acting as transporters in the lucrative carrying trade. Britain's own merchant fleets suffered from both French privateers and the raiding of its manpower by British press gangs desperately trying to keep the Royal Navy fully manned. American merchants took advantage of this situation, too, readily carrying British goods across the Atlantic and from Asia to British markets. By 1807 Americans were transporting the bulk of West Indian sugar, were the West Indies' primary source for grain and lumber, and had negotiated greater and freer access to the East India Company's possessions than even private British merchants enjoyed.[28] Moreover, because American ships were cheaper to build and of better quality, their sailors enjoyed better pay and conditions. In fact, the American merchant fleet had grown to 60 percent of the size of Britain's fleet—up from a mere 20 percent when Britain first went to war against revolutionary France—and, as Britain's war with Napoleon showed no signs of abating, that figure was on track to grow even further. This left the British government with a choice of either accepting the United States as the eventual preeminent merchant maritime power or taking direct action to stop it.

Many in Britain and the empire viewed the Americans and other neutrals as little more than war profiteers of the worst possible kind. As a critic remarked in one of a host of pamphlets and editorials railing against the damage being caused by neutral shipping, "their utmost united efforts could never have inflicted injuries, a hundredth part so fatal to the British Empire, as their base and venal traffic of neutrality has done." Neutral shipping was destroying British commerce, he concluded, and Britain was "being swindled out of her political existence" as a result.[29] Sympathizers with this line of thinking included many of the tories who dominated the British government in the early nineteenth century. In the wake of the American Revolution they resisted surging free-trade thinking, most commonly associated with the writings of Adam Smith, and instead continued to envision the empire as a quasi-protectionist marketplace.[30] Ensuring that Britain focused on manufacturing, while the colonies focused on producing raw materials and agricultural products, had two primary benefits according to proponents. First, the trade between Britain and its colonies required a substantial merchant fleet, making the routes a "nursery for seamen," as it was so often called. The Royal Navy's ability to expand and contract rapidly relied heavily on its ability to draft in these merchant sailors.[31] Second, although less commonly argued, was the idea that focusing on manufacturing in Britain and leaving agricultural production to the colonies allowed Britain's population to swell far beyond its natural limitations. This, in turn, enabled Britain to punch above its weight class against a much larger rival, France.[32]

The remarks of Lord Sheffield, president of the board of agriculture at the time, reflected the growing resentment of the United States and increased calls for greater protections for British imperial commerce. Only "by the artifice of negotiation, or by the insolence of menace," he argued in an influential 1804 pamphlet, had this system been recently eroded. According to his detailed estimates, between 1790 and 1800 Americans not only came to dominate their own trade routes but also made their presence felt in other routes worldwide. He argued that this caused so little alarm in Britain because many Britons still saw Americans as kin and countrymen. Yet, he reminded his audience, the United States was a foreign competitor, and conciliatory measures to placate American merchants would be detrimental in the long run because they would drain Britain of its naval strength. Echoing arguments he and other opponents of American independence had made decades earlier, Sheffield pointed out that the Americans had chosen to leave the empire and thus did not deserve any special treatment with regard to trade.[33] He was aghast at those in America and Britain who "entertained the extraordinary notion that, in matters of trade, they [Americans] should not be considered by Great Britain as foreigners, though they themselves had chosen and asserted that very situation." In fact, Sheffield argued that complaints made by the United States and other neutral nations about British trade restrictions were evidence of their effectiveness, declaring "every syllable of reprobation on this point, which is heard from abroad, should be regarded by us at home as virtual applause."[34]

When it came to the rise of American shipping, among the hardest hit British sectors was the West India trade. Although the West Indies had declined in importance since the American Revolution, they had not yet been supplanted by the East Indies as the prized jewels in the British imperial crown. Many of the major West Indian planters had long been absentee owners, choosing to live in England, where their wealth and leisure time allowed them to pursue other interests. These included politics, and together with the London merchants who handled the shipping, financing, and distribution of West Indian sugar and coffee, they forged one of the most powerful political interest groups of the eighteenth century.[35] The interests' metropolitan connections, which were reinforced by such social factors as intermarriage and an elite educational experience held in common with the ruling elite, gave them a considerable advantage over Britain's provincial manufacturing interest, at which they sneered.[36]

But by 1800 the West India interest, though still powerful, was besieged by the unprecedented public movement against African slavery, which began as an assault on the slave trade. Depicting planters and their associates as murderers and their henchmen, sugar became "blood sugar" in the popular imagination of the tens of thousands of middle-class households that pledged to boycott it.[37] In March 1807 abolitionists had rallied enough political support during the short-lived whig coalition, the Ministry of the All the Talents, for Parliament to ban the slave trade. Making matters worse for the West India interest, the restrictions of European continental markets and Britain's conquest of France's sugar-producing islands produced an enormous sugar glut that forced prices rapidly downward to little more than half their recent height, reducing producers' profit margins from a high of nearly 13 percent in the 1790s to practically nothing.[38]

Anxious to counter the antislavery propaganda and demonstrate the islands' importance to the empire, the West India interest produced a steady stream of pamphlets from the turn of the century onward. They complained about heavy taxes on sugar driving down demand, bemoaned the tiny profit margins of the sugar trade, and, important to Anglo-American relations, complained incessantly that neutral shipping was flooding the British market with cheap foreign sugar. This reached fever pitch in the wake of the abolition of the slave trade, as the West India interest scrambled to adjust and reassert the West Indies' importance.[39] Under intense pressure, the House of Commons formed a select committee to investigate the "Commercial State of the West India Colonies," which published its findings in July 1807. The West Indies' political influence is evident throughout the eighty-five-page report, which painstakingly detailed how detrimental American shipping had been to the colonies and Britain's larger maritime interests. American neutrality meant access to European ports and freedom from privateers, which in turn resulted in lower insurance rates, the report complained. British merchant vessels faced higher insurance rates, and, in accordance with longstanding British navigation laws, had to travel first to a British port, where duties were paid before the cargo could be reexported to a European port. This meant shipping sugar on British ships to continental European markets cost roughly twice as much as transporting it on American ones.[40] As a result, American shipping was in high demand, with contemporaries estimating that American ships carried as much as 40 percent of British West Indian exports.[41]

The West Indian interest appealed to the "community of interest which almost every member of the empire has in the welfare of the colonies," carefully detailing how the West India trade added to Britain's wealth and ability to wage war by producing taxable goods and training for British sailors.[42] The crux of the problem, summarized one pamphlet, was a combination of factors. "The abolition of the slave trade, the present state of the continent, and the continuance of the war, while America is allowed, without interruption, to transport the produce of the enemy's colonies to Europe," the author complained, "all combine to place the British West Indies" in a terrible position.[43] Nothing could be done about the abolition of the slave trade or the continued war with France. American shipping, however, was another matter.

James Stephen's *War in Disguise; or the Frauds of Neutral Flags* became the rallying cry for greater assertion of British maritime rights against neutrals.[44] In the widely distributed and reprinted pamphlet, Stephen, a politically connected lawyer with West Indian links, railed against the government for allowing America to drain Britain of its seamen and commerce. He detested America's naturalized citizens, advocated seizing all foreigners found on American ships, and outlined the suffering of British shipping at the hands of the undercutting Americans. The answer to this "tremendous evil" was to implement laws that limited neutral commerce and created a level playing field for British shipping. Echoing the popular view that overseas commerce produced seamen for the Royal Navy and income for the government, Stephen argued that reform was "essential to our public safety."[45]

The influence of Stephen's ideas on the Orders in Council was substantial and highlights that the West India interest, though in decline, remained powerful. William Wilberforce, Stephen's brother-in-law, credited him with writing the orders, as did most contemporaries, including William Cobbett, who printed personal attacks against Stephen in the *Weekly Political Register*.[46] The cabinet memo that circulated just before the new orders were drawn up reads like bullet points from his pamphlet, and the government rewarded him the following year with a seat in the House of Commons, where he tirelessly defended the orders. He also remained a close confidant of Spencer Perceval, who as prime minister for most of the orders' existence staunchly defended them against growing criticism.[47] In fact, only with Perceval's death would they be repealed.

Britain had an even stronger case for impressment. The low pay of seamen offered little compensation for the wretched conditions aboard an early-nineteenth-century warship, but impressment largely eliminated the need for volunteerism. Although many loathed the necessity of the system, few in Britain or the United States questioned the legality of Britain to demand military service from its subjects. The trouble derived from how Britain pursued its subjects who had absconded for a better life in the American merchant navy.

The right of an individual to choose one's own nationality and the extent to which a state had the right to pursue its errant subjects were the issues at hand. As discussed in the previous chapter, the right of "expatriation," as the process of naturalized citizenship was known, was fuzzy at best and had little formal legal foundation in either Britain or the United States. A new republic that opened its arms to foreign immigration was unprecedented, and no country had formally established an internationally recognized system for how this would work, particularly when the dual nationalities of an individual were at odds. Even the American government's insistence on the legality of naturalization was more a gut feeling than a legal framework, as demonstrated in the Supreme Court's 1795 *Talbot v. Janson* decision, which rejected the legality of an American's renunciation of his citizenship.[48]

The British government had little choice in the matter. By 1800 attrition due to death, permanent injury, desertion, and illness meant that the Royal Navy needed on average an estimated ten thousand fresh men a year to maintain its wartime naval strength during this period.[49] Meanwhile, in 1808 Isaac Chauncey's investigation of seamen in New York City concluded that a mere 42 percent of sailors were American by birth. The rest were either naturalized citizens or foreign subjects—mostly British subjects from Britain and Ireland.[50] In fact, the British Admiralty estimated that some twenty thousand British subjects worked aboard American merchant ships, making them an obvious target.[51] Acquiescing to American interpretations of nationality and the sovereignty of its merchant vessels on the high seas would have been catastrophic for Britain. Such a move would have effectively turned Britain's greatest merchant shipping competitor into a legal, wartime haven for British seamen. If tens of thousands of British subjects served aboard American ships under the threat of British retribution, it is not difficult to imagine how many would have fled to the United States if the threat no longer existed. Already desperate for men, the Royal Navy would have been crippled.

Britain consolidated its legal case behind the doctrine of "indefeasible allegiance," which rejected an individual's unilateral right to dissolve his allegiance to the country of his birth. During the negotiations for the ill-fated Monroe-Pinkney Treaty in 1806, the British commissioners asked the king's advocate general, Sir John Nicholl, for his legal opinion on expatriation.[52] For all the request's pretense of seeking an unbiased judgment, it was a foregone conclusion that Nicholl, also a member of Parliament and ministry supporter, would reject the legality of expatriation, but his unambiguous opinion gave the British practice backbone. Nicholl opened by asserting a bolder variation of William Blackstone's legal opinion from decades earlier that the authority for expatriation rested in the state, not the individual: "Individuals owe an Allegiance and Duty to the State of which they are natural born Subjects," he asserted. "From this allegiance and duty," he continued, "they cannot without the consent of the state release themselves." The indissolubility of state-subject relationship established, Nicholl addressed the more practical implications of expatriation over which the Americans and British were arguing, namely whether or not Britain had the right to compel its subjects to perform military service. Calling the duty to "assist their country when engaged in war" a "most important part of this Allegiance," Nicholl described the obligation as "prior and paramount to any contract or engagement they can enter into with another state or its inhabitants." Therefore, Britain had the right to impress natural-born subjects "notwithstanding they may have been admitted Burghers or Citizens or engaged as Mariners in the service of another State." Moreover, Nicholl recognized no legal boundaries to a nation's right to obtain its subjects' services; in other words, searching foreign vessels was perfectly legal. While recognizing in recent decades that Britain had stopped short of searching neutral warships, he explained that this practice had been grounded in the understanding that no reasonable neutral nation would employ the subjects of a nation at war. "Knowingly to employ the natural born Subjects of a State engaged in War," he insisted, was a "breach of neutrality."

Having established the doctrine of indefeasible allegiance, Nicholl proceeded to provide Britain legal justification for a British declaration of war on the United States. He argued that for a state "To harbour and to encourage Deserters from the Ships of War of a Belligerent is (I think) a breach of Neutrality. Assistance is as much given to our Enemy by weakening our Force, as by adding to his. It is therefore an injury." He concluded that "If upon representation the evil is not put a stop to, nor Redress given, it then becomes an Injury for which Reparation is refused, and is a cause of War." Although quick to point out that "unlimited war" was not necessarily the best way to resolve the issue, he insisted that it was within Britain's legal rights to declare it. After all, he explained, "War is doing yourself justice by force."[53]

In practice, Britain regularly violated the legal standards Nicholl applied to the United States. An estimated 12 percent of the seamen in the Royal Navy in 1805 were foreign-born.[54] The Royal Navy and press gangs commonly held that anyone married to a Briton, living in Britain for two or more years, or working on a British ship for more than two years was a British subject.[55] To make matters worse, the Royal Navy followed a policy in the early nineteenth century that a sailor was presumed British unless proven otherwise, and the proof had to meet British standards.[56] At great effort and expense, British courts typically released impressed Americans, but the process often took years. Moreover, throughout the history of British colonial America, foreigners had been encouraged to immigrate to the colonies and were given rights as naturalized subjects. During the Seven Years' War, Parliament passed legislation explicitly granting naturalization to foreign seamen with two years of service on a British warship or merchant vessel, and Parliament had long reserved the right to naturalize someone by a special act. When war erupted with France in 1778 and again in 1793, Britain was hardly about to recognize that France had an indefeasible right to the military service of its former subjects living under British rule in Quebec. During the War of 1812, the colonial governments in Canada allowed American-born subjects residing in Canada to serve in the local militia, and even though most Royal Navy captains allowed American-born sailors the choice of continued service or imprisonment in England, complaints regularly circulated that some captains did not offer the option.

American critics pilloried Britain for its hypocrisy on the subject, regularly interpreting its behavior as high-handed scorn for its former colonies. As Asa Aikens complained in a Fourth of July oration to the inhabitants of Windsor, Vermont, the impressment of American seamen had no foundation in law; rather it was the practice of "that lawless power who has capriciously substituted naval force for maritime right, and imperiously claims the sole dominion of the ocean."[57] Americans naturally chafed at the idea of their former imperial masters awarding and denying rights to a sovereign American nation at their pleasure. Echoing declarations and denunciations in legislatures and newspapers across the United States, an enraged South Carolina commentator at a public celebration of American independence complained: "[These were] wrongs, which we might tolerate in silence, if we had never learnt the choral song of freedom, nor fight the battles of independence. . . . But submission never was nor ever can be one of the alternatives of the American nation." The United States, he proclaimed, was no "wretched vassal."[58] As in the American Revolution, Americans had no choice but to protect their freedom by force of arms. "Again our bleeding country calls us to avenge her deep wounds," an orator declared on that same day to the people assembled at Plymouth, "and to teach our enemies a lesson of respect for our national character."[59]

Had the United States created a credible and effective system for removing British subjects from American ships, Britain probably would have backed down and stopped aggressively seizing men on merchant vessels. After all, the British government was not interested in seizing genuine American citizens. A system of self-monitoring, however, was unworkable. Americans had little reason to comply, because they relied on British subjects, naturalized or otherwise, for maritime manpower, so there was every incentive for corruption. This was particularly the case in the Southern states from which Madison and war supporters in Congress derived the bulk of their support.[60] Furthermore, a valid American system would not have resolved the problem of the legality of naturalization. To comply with British demands, the United States would have to bar all of its naturalized citizens from the sea, which would have severely handicapped America's commercial interests and thrown open the validity of America's program of naturalization. Finally, the federal government lacked the centralized infrastructure to create a reliable and efficient system. After all, the United States was ruled by a Republican national government that prided itself on minimal government and seized virtually every opportunity to reduce taxes and spending, even when it meant stripping the country's defenses bare as it marched toward war. Consequently, when the American government at various points during the war offered the concession of passing national legislation to prevent British subjects from serving on American vessels, the unconvinced British government would not budge. Not surprisingly, it refused to rely on a former enemy that many in Britain believed was erratic, hostile to Britain, and a genuine threat to its global interests. For many Britons, including most of those in power, war with the United States was more appealing than compromise on such a crucial issue.

A number of America's critics did not hesitate to call for the use of force. In August 1807, Sir George Cranfield Berkeley, vice-admiral and commander of the Royal Navy's North American station, devised a plan for a preemptive strike against the United States and sent it to Lord Bathurst, president of the board of trade at the time.[61] Although more candid and aggressive than most, Berkeley best articulated the views that many in Britain held toward the United States in the years leading up to the War of 1812. He loathed the Americans, calling them the "refuse of all countries." The dangers of their ignorance, he wrote, were multiplied by their literacy, which enabled men like Jefferson to manipulate the people through the press. "[Americans] all read," he sneered, "and look upon everything as an oracle that is published in this way, and the more abusive, the more gratifying to the mind of an American." According to Berkeley, the American Revolution had emboldened the Americans above their station, a situation fueled by the peace terms that granted Americans access to the North Atlantic fisheries and handed over vast interior lands beyond the borders of the rebelling colonies. A new war, Berkeley argued, would allow Britain to scrap that "foolish treaty of peace" and begin anew.

Berkeley's plan was intimidation followed by diplomacy. "If I had a few more ships," he explained, "I certainly should be tempted to run up to New York with the squadron before the harbour is secured and wait there for the issue of the negotiations, as having that city under the terror of destruction would insure a favourable issue to any terms you might propose." Should that fail, he suggested attaching five thousand troops to a squadron in order to harass the eastern coast of the United States and distract the Americans from launching a counteroffensive against Canada—a strategy that closely foreshadowed the British coastal campaign of 1814. "Six months of this sort of warfare and the destruction of their commerce, with taxes they will be obliged to impose on the landed interest," Berkeley promised, "will raise such a clamour, as will certainly oblige them to come into terms of peace." Better to deal with the Americans on Britain's timeline than to wait for the United States to mobilize.[62] Such plans were not mere bravado. Earlier that summer he had ordered ships at his station to begin boarding American warships in search of deserters. The decision resulted in the HMS *Leopard's* firing on the USS *Chesapeake*, killing four American sailors and wounding seven, and bringing the United States and Britain to the brink of war. Moreover, while Berkeley's letter made its way to Bathurst, the Royal Navy was bombarding neutral Denmark's capital of Copenhagen, killing thousands of civilians in order to force the Danish government to surrender its navy, which at eighteen ships of the line and eleven frigates was far more formidable than the U.S. Navy. The Danes yielded after three days of bombardment and handed over their navy.

Berkeley was not alone in imagining a war with the United States. A number of government and amateur strategists contemplated publicly and privately the various ways to defeat the Americans, with the vast majority advocating a plan akin to Berkeley's: ravage the Atlantic coastline, blockade America's ports, and, if that proved insufficient to bring America to its knees, invade from Canada. As the British were in a position to go on the offensive in the War of 1812, this is exactly what they did. As with the American advocates for war, British officials and commentators articulated a variety of reasons for wanting a war with the United States. Most motives, however, stemmed from a disdain for the United

States as a dangerous and unreliable nation that threatened British interests. Britons almost never discussed a war with America in terms of conquest. With the small exception of taking a few strategic points to benefit the fur trade and better defend Canada, territorial acquisitions rarely fit into prewar discussions. The prevalent language in Britain was of management: humbling the upstart nation by force of arms and then managing the hobbled United States so as to make it comply with British directives. Virtually no Britons sought to reabsorb the United States into the British Empire formally, but plenty desired a postcolonial relationship in which the former colonies accepted British leadership, and they were prepared to apply force to obtain what they wanted.

The British shipping interest throughout the empire was perhaps the most vocal element in its expression of the benefits of a war with the United States. A war would allow the Royal Navy to annihilate America's merchant fleet and then blockade American ports, thereby shutting the Americans out of the lucrative carrying trade. Joseph Marryat, a member of Parliament and part of the West India shipping interest, best summarized this position in his influential 1807 pamphlet *Concessions to America the Bane of Britain*. He, and others like him, demanded rigorous regulations of maritime trade that would benefit the British shipping interest. Rehearsing the familiar argument of how the United States had benefited unfairly from Britain's war with France, Marryat angrily claimed that American ships transported over £14 million in French West Indian goods—mostly sugar and coffee—to European markets every year, noting that 211 American ships visited Amsterdam alone the previous year. This broke the monopoly the British had enjoyed over Europe since the 1790s, when the Royal Navy effectively cut France off from the trade of its West Indian colonies and sent commodity prices spiraling downward. Worse still, Marryat argued, the rise of the American merchant navy in this way came directly at the expense of Britain's own long-term maritime power: "That naval power, which constitutes the safety and the glory of the empire, will lose its best nursery for seamen; and the more our carrying trade decreases, and that of American increases, the greater temptation will our seamen have to engage in her service."

Marryat's solution was to create a more aggressive form of the Orders in Council aimed specifically at handicapping American shipping. There was no need to veil it with rhetoric about fighting France, according to Marryat, because Britain had the power to increase regulation as it saw fit, and the United States could do little about it. The idea that Britain would "in the plenitude of her naval power, tamely surrender to America, who has no means whatever of enforcing her lofty demands" was "absurd," he railed. Marryat fully accepted that such measures carried a serious risk of war, but this did not bother him. Force, he asserted, was the best tactic, because "Concession has ever led to new demands, as the history of all our negociations [sic] with America has abundantly demonstrated." The war he envisioned was a limited naval conflict in which a few British ships would sweep the seas of American vessels and then blockade America's ports. The risk to Britain would be minimal, he contended, and a monopoly over the West Indian trade would offset any temporary loss of American markets.[63]

Support for a limited naval war against the United States gained momentum among Britons connected to overseas trade as the years progressed. In the unambiguously entitled 1811 pamphlet *Animating Hints; for British Statesmen; British Merchants; and Britons in General: On Going to War with America*, a commentator using the pseudonym "Briton" went so far as to indulge readers with a description of the parliamentary scene upon the declaration of war on the United States: "It should be like a grand national concert, beginning with a solemn dirge, expressive of sincere regret; but closing with the highest strains of animating sounds, declaratory of our determination to make them regret the hour they forced us to become their enemies."

According to "Briton," this "wholly maritime" war would remind the Americans of who was in charge and who must obey in this transatlantic relationship. "The Yankees should be thus convinced of our decisive character and our power," he declared, "that when provoked to martial enmity, we will make our enemies duly sensible of our vengeance, and means to punish them. We have had *too much* insolence from American threats."[64] A year later, most comment within the West Indian and shipping interest circles greeted the American declaration of war exactly as "Briton" had predicted if Parliament had declared war. As the *Bahama Gazette* reflected, "as individuals," Britons might lament the outbreak of war with the United States thanks to "natural feelings" towards their cultural kin, but "in a national point of view, the event is one that promises the most advantageous usage." The paper explained that "the present American war will inevitably end in the dismemberment if not in the annihilation of what was lately a growing power of considerable promise, and [what] . . . might ere long have become a formidable rival to all Europe, and particularly to Great Britain."[65]

Worrisome for the British both in and out of the government was the favoritism that Madison and his fellow Republicans who dominated the federal government appeared to show to France. As the *Glasgow Courier* complained in response to one of the many Congressional reports that circulated in the British press on the eve of war, "Bonaparte is treated with becoming gentleness but every line of it is expressive of a jaundiced eye towards Great Britain—every line of it in which Great Britain is mentioned, is filled, if not with lies, with the most barefaced exaggerations."[66] From the British perspective, the United States enjoyed a cozy relationship with France during the tenures of Jefferson and Madison. American ships handled the carrying trade between France and its colonies, France sold the Louisiana territory to the United States for a bargain price, the United States opened harbors to French privateers and warships that were closed to the Royal Navy, and the Americans seemingly accepted all of Napoleon's restrictions on neutral trade while railing at Britain. That Jefferson and most other American admirers of the French Revolution had by 1812 long since abandoned any illusion that France was a functioning republic worthy of admiration did not seem to matter.[67]

British concerns about Franco-American relations were rooted in a polarized British worldview in which foreign nations either openly supported Britain or were in league with France. Few saw neutrality as either virtuous or sincere, and plenty had a hard time accepting that Britain's former colonies could function without European guidance. In consequence, papers such as the *Bahama Gazette* were quick to see any official American action against Britain as the work of the "Corsican usurper" manipulating his puppet, Madison.[68] When the United States refused to negotiate a quick peace after Britain suspended the Orders in Council in June 1812, commentators such as the editor of the *Edinburgh Star* claimed their suspicions had been confirmed, declaring "American was never sincere" in wanting peace. According to the *Star* the official list of reasons for war—the Orders in Council, impressment, and aid to the Indians—were just a thin veil over the real reason: a desire to assist France.[69]

The American press was by far the greatest contributor to the impression in Britain that the American government was under France's thumb. Public expressions of support for France in America had waned decidedly since the early years of the French Revolution, but Madison's opponents took every opportunity to portray members of his administration as Napoleon's pawns. "So long as the councils of America are under the influence and controul of France," complained a Vermont critic, "and so long as we can serve his interest in the war with England, he will not suffer us to make peace." Diplomatic concessions from Britain were useless: "The British government may make restitution for the attack upon the *Chesapeake*; they may repeal their Orders in Council; they may give up the right of Search and Impressment; and when all this is done, some new ghost will be conjured up by our political jugglers to stand in the way of peace."[70]

The primary purpose of these public attacks was to associate the president with a known tyrant who had destroyed a republic for his own glorification— something of which Madison's opponents regularly accused him. This criticism also highlighted that under Madison's leadership the United States was not an independent nation—an alternative attempt to play on Americans' sensitivity about national sovereignty.

Although critics intended these remarks for American audiences, the transatlantic nature of the Anglo-American press ensured they received a great deal of attention in Britain, too. With such remarks as "the war is undertaken not for our interests, but for France," John Lowell's widely extracted and reprinted pamphlet

Figure 2.1 George Cruikshank, "The Happy Effects of that Grand Systom [sic] of Shutting Ports Against the English!!" (London, 1808). Library of Congress, Prints and Photographs Division, LC-USZ62-121460. In this print a group of American merchants protest Thomas Jefferson's embargo. One complains "my family is starving," while another declares "yea friend though may as well tell us to cut of [f]our our nose to be revenged of our face." Although the embargo applied to both Britain and France, the artist asserts that Jefferson's system is meant to aid France. Jefferson encourages the merchants to endure the embargo "for about fifteen or twenty years" and to employ the idle sailors in "various works of husbandry" in support of "that great and mighty Emperor & King Napoleon!!" Meanwhile Napoleon hides behind Jefferson, promising that "You shall be King hereafter" in exchange for America's compliance.

Mr. Madison's War is a classic example of the sort of bold accusations emanating from opposition critics that made their way across the Atlantic.[71] In some cases, British publishers simply reprinted the entire American pamphlet, as with *Inquiry into the Past and Present Relations of France and the United States of America*, written by the editor of Philadelphia's *American Review*. Reflecting the tenor of the author's original remarks, the preface to the British edition refers to the Madison administration as "the Gallic confederacy at Washington" before asserting that America's trade embargos against Britain made the United States a de facto part of Napoleon's Continental System.[72]

That the Americans would seemingly take France's side was a bitter pill for Britons to swallow. Many Britons had sympathized with the "no taxation without representation" ideology of the American Revolution, and even many of those Britons who detested the rebellion nevertheless developed a begrudging admiration for the courage and conduct of some of its leaders.[73] For most Britons, regardless of who they blamed for the American Revolution, the conflict had been a tragic civil war. Reformist figures such as Edmund Burke and William Wilberforce cut their teeth as critics of the British government's colonial American policies before taking on British rule in India and the African slave trade, respectively. Partly in consequence, though Lord Sheffield was ready to label Americans as foreigners, a perception of a shared Anglo-American culture lingered among many Britons from across the political spectrum, with both the pro-ministry *Edinburgh Star* referring to the Americans as "brethren" and the opposition Dublin *Freeman's Journal* calling them "our countrymen on the other bank of the Atlantic" within weeks of each other in early 1812. Even the fiercely anti-Madison *Times* lamented the outbreak of war as a division of "the two great British families."[74]

Many of those Britons who attacked the early French Revolution as bloody, vicious, and anarchic had held out the American Revolution as a respectable example of republicanism.[75] Britons in the 1790s took heart in the Federalist-led national government's decision first to remain neutral and then to conduct the Quasi-War against France. When Thomas Paine, the one-time literary voice of the American Revolution, renounced Washington for having betrayed his French brethren, the Westminster Forum, a London debating society, came to the American's aid and "carried with universal approbation, by an audience consisting of upwards of five hundred persons, among whom . . . [were] several Noblemen, Magistrates, and Gentlemen of the first respectability of the Country" the resolution that Paine's attack "deserved the reprobation of every Friend of Liberty and Humanity."[76]

As a result, many in Britain and the empire viewed the policies of the Jefferson and Madison administrations as acts of betrayal—of both Britain and America's revolutionary legacy. In a series of published letters from a British merchant recently returned from America that the British press extracted, the author voiced the widespread indignation that surfaced across the British Empire and would remain throughout the War of 1812. "Hatred of tyranny, the admiration of valour are the shared principles of the British and American people," he argued, "and France has laid prostrate the liberties of continental Europe, and openly aims at the subjugation of the world. The downfall of America would follow that of England, as certainly as the rising of the sun is followed by the diffusion of light." Why then, he asked, did the American government and its supporters aid and abet Napoleon, "the Gallic tyrant"?[77] The answer, argued critics, was gratification of the personal ambitions of America's leaders. According to one, "Jefferson's public virtue was insufficient to contend with his private ambition," and in the French Revolution "He saw the sweets of power and emolument."[78] The *Jamaica Magazine* argued that Madison, who it styled as "his Republican majesty (the

Figure 2.2 George Cruikshank, "A Sketch for the Regents Speech on Mad-ass-son's Insanity" (London, 1812). Library of Congress, Prints and Photographs Division, LC-USZ62-1554. Typical of British critics' emphasis of Madison's coziness with Napoleon, this print highlights the folly of Madison's decision for war through word play on the president's name. The Archangel Gabriel blows "Bad news for you" through his trumpet as a distressed Madison moans to Napoleon and the devil that "'tis you two that have brought this upon me—Support me or I sink!'"

humble slave of his Corsican majesty)," was no different. He had "moulded himself into something similar to an absolute monarch" aided by "an artillery of sans-culotte manifestoes, addresses, and speeches, while not but a band of raga-muffins, the scum of the union, who have nothing to lose, either of character or property, are his only associates."[79]

The British government generally reflected the public's frustration with what it saw as the Americans' failure to recognize that Britain, not France, shared the best interests of the United States. In the decade prior to the outbreak of war, a string of British foreign secretaries and diplomats regularly tried to impress upon the Jefferson and Madison administrations that France, not Britain, was the real threat to American security and commerce. Throughout 1811 and 1812, this was a central theme of the instructions from the foreign office to Augustus Foster in Washington. In August 1810, France had offered to repeal its decrees if Britain repealed the orders or if the United States made Britain respect its neutral rights. This marked the beginning of a series of bluffs and false diplomacy in which the United States insisted that France had repealed its decrees and demanded Britain do the same, while Britain, knowing full well France continued to seize American ships and goods, refused to comply. The instructions Foster received included an array of accounts and affidavits describing the seizures in detail. In April, Castlereagh, as foreign secretary, resorted to sending French newspaper clippings for Foster to pass on to Madison and his secretary of state, James Monroe. In the accompanying forty-three-page letter, Castlereagh's frustration with the American government, and with Foster's inability to persuade it to see "reason," was evident. Castlereagh insisted that the evidence he provided "confirms if any thing were wanting to confirm, the repeated assertions of Great Britain that the Berlin and Milan decrees have never be[en] revoked." That the American government would insist the opposite and then press the British government to revoke the Orders in Council was simultaneously "suspicious" and "outrageous."[80]

Yet Castlereagh and those near him patronizingly contended that misinformation and prejudice were to blame. British officials continued to believe that all would be resolved if only the youthful Americans would listen to their British schoolmasters. They completely underestimated the complexity of the situation for the Madison administration, which was fully aware of France's duplicity but sought to use this for its own agenda.[81] On more than one occasion, Castlereagh mused on the outcomes of Foster's meetings with Madison and Monroe. In one of Castlereagh's especially fanciful imagined encounters, he arrogantly described to Foster how, on learning of France's falseness, the American government would "deeply feel the embarrassments" of its previous faith in France and recognize the trustworthiness of Britain. This evidence, he postulated, would "awaken them to a sense of the desperate policy of attempting either to force or intimidate Great Britain." He expected that following this realization, the Americans "may with more prudence than has lately marked their councils, see in this new posture of affairs, an opportunity of recoiling without disgrace from the precipice of War, to which they have been so inconsiderately approached." Castlereagh pompously concluded with the insistence that Foster represent Britain's magnanimity to the newly humbled American government, instructing him to "assist their retreat without any unnecessary sacrifice of [American] dignity."[82] Such comments not only betray the British ministers' arrogance toward the United States but also reveal their overestimation of how easily they might bully Britain's former colonies.

British North America's colonial inhabitants also made a case for war with the United States, or rather they and their supporters in Britain made a case for why Canada was an important part of the empire and worth defending, as war with the United States seemed increasingly likely. Invested merchants had long publicly advocated Canada as an alternative to the United States as a source of timber and grain, calling for economic protections and encouraging British immigration.[83] Canada also maintained a healthy trade with Britain. In 1805, before the American embargoes skewed trade estimates, Upper and Lower Canada imported some £767,000 worth of British goods, a large portion of which came from the West Indies in the form of rum and sugar. By comparison, the expense of the military establishment was a mere £150,000.[84] The real importance of Canada, however, was its potential as a major market for British goods and as a major supplier of raw materials and grain for the empire. An editorial in the *Times* in February 1812 declared, "It is a possession, therefore, which must, under all circumstances, be defended by Great Britain."[85] Throughout 1811 and 1812 British newspapers printed detailed descriptions of troop levels and defenses, along with a host of maps, while Canadian merchants met directly with ministers to discuss how the provinces might be defended. Even Sir Isaac Brock, the reluctant military governor of Upper Canada, who earlier told his brother "You, who have passed all your days in the bustle of London, can scarcely conceive the uninteresting and insipid life I am doomed to lead in this retirement," believed Upper Canada worth defending for its potential resources.[86]

Through the provincial press, the colonists made their own case for Canada's relevance to the British Empire as war approached. Although not run by the state, the press was dominated by the loyal Anglophone establishment, and through the press they articulated a vision of Canada as strategically important, inherently British, and loyal. There were other responses in Canada to the War of 1812, which were manifested outside the arena of the press. In particular, the press highlighted Anglo-American differences in readers' letters and editorials that found a transatlantic audience. None were more widely distributed than the letters of Richard Cartwright, a wealthy Upper Canadian loyalist and key architect of early Canadian nationalism, who wrote for the *Kingston Gazette* on the eve of the war.[87] Using "Falkland" as his *nom de plume*, Cartwright described Britain in one letter as "the only remaining barrier against that universal dominion to which the powerful Usurper of France hath long aspired" and declared that one cannot help but to "feel proud to be numbered among such a Nation as this." He railed against what he saw as "tame submission to France" on the part of the United States and warned his fellow subjects that life under the American republic would be a far cry from the mild, pleasant, and liberal rule of Britain: "Under the Government of the United States the widest scope is given to the violence of factions. Every family is agitated by political discord. The intrigues of a few artful demagogues pervade every State and dictate every public measure. Domestic happiness and tranquility is disturbed by party feuds; they pollute even the administration of justice." Other republics had concluded bloodily with a tyrant taking control, he declared, and the United States would end no differently.[88]

Like their counterparts in Britain, loyal critics in Canada highlighted American self-interest and greed as a product of republican government. Whereas the British system induced its government and people to serve humanity and fight against French tyranny, they contended, the selfish Americans and their government acted only to line their own pockets. This clash of worldviews, explained the *Quebec Gazette*, was at the root of Anglo-American animosity. "Let the hostility of the United States to Great Britain be attributed to its true cause," the paper declared, "an habitual hatred—that vicious love of power, engendered by their political institutions; that insatiable thirst to gain which so invariably prevails in a country where money is the only source of distinction, and that inquietude which is never contented with present enjoyments."[89] To emphasize the steady, dignified governance the British system engendered, commentators regularly contrasted what the *Montreal Herald* styled as "those tedious and violent declarations made in the American States by their President and Governors to their legislative Bodies," with the dignified statements of the empire's rulers. The February 1812 address of George Prevost, the commander-in-chief of British forces in North America and Lower Canada's appointed governor, to that province's assembly caused the paper to remark that it "cannot but be read with much satisfaction by every good subject of these provinces. . . . Here are not illiberal reflections, no unfounded complaints, nor disgraceful aspirations." The following month the paper responded to the prince regent's message to Parliament with similar praise, noting that "This message . . . exhibits a wonderful contrast between the high honorable and exalted sentiments of the most distinguished and respectable nations in Europe, and the violent, illiberal and undignified declarations of the American Republic." The American republic, like its French counterpart, had fallen prey to its own inherent weaknesses; left unchecked, such a government became a danger to its neighbors.[90]

British rule, commentators in Canada incessantly contended, was just. "We have real liberty," declared a letter signed "A Canadian" to the *Quebec Mercury*, "grounded upon the most wise and equitable laws; we have property, either transmitted to us by our ancestors, or acquired by our own industry, arising out of the happy connexion subsisting between us and the parent state." In Canada, the letter concluded, "the husbandmen [sic] cultivates his farm with the comfortable assurance, that when he sows with hope, he will reap in safety."[91] Cartwright as "Falkland" concurred, pointing out that British subjects in Canada enjoyed extensive personal liberties, low taxation, and security of their persons and property. "Those amongst us who are capable of comparing their situation here with that of the inhabitants of any other country must see and acknowledge that their own is superior," he declared, "that in every point essential to human comfort, they enjoy greater advantages, and are subject to fewer inconveniences than any other people whatever." Britain, he continued, was the savior of the "whole civilized world" and "the only remaining barrier against that universal dominion to which the powerful Usurper of France hath long aspired." One could not help but to "feel proud to be numbered among such a Nation as this."[92]

According to critics in Canada, the United States betrayed its liberal inheritance by harassing and provoking Britain in its fight for freedom against the tyrannical France. Some reacted with humor and bravado, such as in the ballad "A New Hail Columbia," printed in the *Montreal Gazette*. Intended to be sung "to the tune of 'Yankee Doodle,'" it chastised the Americans for their association with France and ingratitude:

> On parent England their good nurse.
> Who made them what they are now,
> They gratefully pour evry curse
> And strive to cramp her power.
> Instead, the Americans served as France's willing pawns:
> Bona, the tyrant, bid them fight;
> Now there's true independence,
> T'obey [sic] the Emp'ror is quite right;
> To disobey rank nonsense.
> As for American military prowess:
> The Jonathans [Americans] grown woundly brave,
> So swear they'll take Quebec town;
> But let them come, no town they'll have,
> For we will mow them right down.[93]

Britain, argued an open letter in the *Quebec Mercury* addressed to the governor of Massachusetts, was justified in using any means necessary in so noble a cause, even if it meant trampling on a few petty neutral rights. In fact, "Great Britain would be justified in interdicting the trade of the whole world with France, because such interdiction would *reduce the power* of an exterminating enemy."[94] In its war address to the province, the Upper Canadian assembly highlighted Americans' duplicity in favoring France, describing the situation as "this degrading picture, at which the Friends of Mankind and Posterity will weep."[95] John Strachan, an Anglican clergyman and a leading voice of the loyal establishment in Upper Canada, complained before that assembly that "we expected" our American cousins to join the fight against "the most formidable tyrant that ever lived" and, failing that, "if they had not the magnanimity to assist in the contest, they would at all events abstain from weakening [Britain's] means of factory and defense." The British Empire had tried to be reasonable. "We looked for peace, we persuaded ourselves that the similarity of manners, habits and opinions, the warm connexions which still subsist between the two Nations, the tender recollection that they once stood in the relation of parent and child, would have taught the States moderation," but, he lamented, instead they demand war.[96]

A war with America was an opportunity for Britain's colonists to make a contribution to the empire. While Britain spent almost two decades protecting the world from French aggression, subjects in Canada led lives of relative ease. Now they could repay that debt by fighting the North American equivalent of France: the United States. As a letter to the *Kingston Gazette* explained, "it behooves every one, who justly appreciates the blessing of living under the constitution of G. Britain, to step forward in its defence—and it is to you, Canadians, that this principle more specially applies. You, I say, who have been nurtur'd up to your present prosperity and enjoyments under its diffusive and benign influence."[97]

As one commentator remarked, Canadians had read for years about the exploits of Nelson and Wellington and "were eager for an opportunity to emulate the brilliant exploits of their fellow soldiers in Spain and Portugal."[98] Recruiters in particular highlighted the war as an opportunity for those subjects who had avoided military service by virtue of being in Canada to demonstrate their allegiance to what a recruiting advertisement in the *Quebec Gazette* called "the only remaining Free and happy country in the world."[99] Whereas recruiters used shame, Strachan employed guilt in his sermons: "Our Mother Country hath contended with very little respite upwards of twenty years with the most powerful and implacable enemy that ever threatened her existence as a Nation, while we have enjoyed peace and tranquility, and received the most solid proofs of her affection, tho[ugh] bleeding at every pore."[100] Now was the time for Canadians to assuage that guilt.

In 1812 the most alarming aspect of the American republic for the British Empire was America's ambition. A United States that had kept to itself and remained relatively small was perhaps an irritant and possible ally, as with the Dutch Republic, but the Americans were not content with independence. Land-hungry leaders set their sights on the remnants of the British and Spanish North American empires. From the British and Spanish perspectives, the Americans had already swindled the Spanish out of a huge slice of its territory through the Louisiana Purchase nine years earlier, but this whetted the Americans' appetites rather than quenched their thirsts. Meanwhile, the Napoleonic Wars drained Britain and Spain of their resources, leaving both vulnerable. Spain's situation was worse in that it was in the midst of a civil war as the British allies and French armies used the Iberian Peninsula as a battleground. Spain's ability to support, let alone protect, its colonies was minimal. Although by far the stronger of the two, Britain's situation was not much better. Its commitment to fighting France drained virtually all of its military resources, leaving protection of its North American possessions to a handful of regular troops, a largely untried colonial population, and American Indians, who had their own agendas.

At first glance, a war in 1812 would seem to favor the United States. Certainly plenty of contemporaries thought so, including a number of American leaders such as Thomas Jefferson, who notoriously declared that Britain's distraction in Europe would make conquering Canada a mere "matter of marching."[101] Yet for Britain, 1812 was a pivotal year, too. Napoleon looked nearly invincible in the summer of 1812, and virtually no one expected his rapid demise over the next two years, least of all the British government. Meanwhile, the United States threatened Britain's best assets for continuing the war: the Royal Navy and commerce. Through guile and protest, the Americans had steadily eroded Britain's maritime supremacy by constructing a rival merchant fleet, which they partly manned with British sailors, thereby also draining power from the Royal Navy. Worse still, the American government showed neither remorse nor any indication that it would change its course. In fact, the United States grew bolder in its dealings, as Congress approved plans in 1811 and 1812 to dramatically increase the size of its armed forces. That Canada would be the expanded American military's object was perhaps the worst-kept military secret in all of history. As the *York Gazette* remarked in March 1812, "Nothing but Canada, Canada, Canada, was heard from every seat in Congress—and Canada, repeated, by the speaking-trumpets throughout the Union."[102] By summer 1812, the United States had already attacked Britain's most likely Indian allies at Prophetstown and was operating an unofficial war in East Florida. Time was running out for the British Empire.

3

Declaring War

In February 1812, James Madison paid $50,000 to a spy for a packet of letters the president thought would reveal British treachery, shame the New England Federalists, and bring the nation closer to supporting a war with Britain. Three years earlier, Sir James Craig, governor-in-chief of British North America, had commissioned John Henry, a former U.S. Army captain and outspoken critic of the Republicans, to investigate New England attitudes toward the Madison administration and Britain. It would be Henry's second such mission for the British. Receiving about $900 in compensation, Henry felt cheated and spent the next two years seeking further payment, reportedly asking for either $142,000 in one lump sum or $2,200 a year for life. Rebuffed by Craig and other British officials, Henry decided to sell his correspondence with Craig to the U.S. government, promising it to be confirmation of the duplicity of the British government and enough evidence to topple the Perceval ministry in Britain. Using a French intermediary, Madison immediately bought the letters unseen for what amounted to America's entire secret service fund. Henry promptly sailed away without even being interrogated.[1]

Madison must have been disappointed when he read the letters and realized why the British had not paid Henry his asking price. Virtually all of the intelligence Henry provided could have been obtained from reading the local press—which was openly hostile to Madison, the ongoing embargoes, and the possibility of a war with Britain. In fact, Henry regularly cited the very American newspapers that Craig and officials in Britain could easily have accessed themselves. At most, Henry's reports underscored the accusations of disloyalty and sectionalism about which Republican papers such as the *Niles' Weekly Register* had been complaining for years. Craig's instructions to Henry were an embarrassment, particularly the lines that authorized Henry to insinuate that Britain would assist New England separatists; but the information was three years old by the time Madison purchased it, and Craig, who suffered from poor relations with the French majority in Lower Canada, had returned to Britain the previous year. Perhaps hoping people would read the headlines rather than the actual letters,

Madison had them printed with the sensationalist title *Message from the President of the U. States, Transmitting Copies of Certain Documents Obtained from a Secret Agent of the British Government, Employed in Fomenting Disaffection to the Constituted Authorities, and British about Resistance to the Laws; and Eventually, in Concert with A British Force, to Destroy the Union of the United States.* The letters, either in part or in whole, appeared in virtually every newspaper in the United States and most of those in Britain, the West Indies, and Canada.

The reaction did not meet Madison's hope for a popular surge to war. Federalists dismissed the charges, with the *New England Palladium* calling it an election ploy by the Republicans to win the Massachusetts gubernatorial election. They then accused Madison of squandering public money.[2] The Republicans in Congress, although condemning the British and declaring the letters authentic, admitted they could not take the matter further, because Henry had cleverly concealed the identities of any Americans who had furnished him with intelligence. In Britain, the Perceval ministry denied any knowledge of Craig's actions before Parliament, with Lord Castlereagh, as secretary of state for foreign affairs, "disclaim[ing] most peremptorily on the part of the British Government, any attempts to dismember the Unites States."[3] The ministry's supporters in the press, such as the *Aberdeen Journal*, declared the government's innocence. The *Journal* assured readers that "we believe we may state with confidence, that there is not the least foundation for the charge brought against the British Government"; it then chastised Madison for not "taking any steps with our Minister in America, or our Government at home, to ascertain the accuracy or inaccuracy of Henry's correspondence."[4] Critics readily took the opportunity to attack the ministry, but even their efforts were largely half-hearted, especially given the content of Henry's reports, Craig's already having left Canada, and the events having taken place years earlier. Few commentators, however, doubted Madison's warlike intentions, including the sometimes-sympathetic *Carlisle Journal*, which remarked, "that this communicating from Mr. Madison to Congress, is likely to lead to open war, is, we fear, pretty evident."[5]

The Henry affair highlights the desperation of the Madison administration to build a convincing case for war in the spring of 1812. Faced with a divided nation, factional party, and lukewarm Congress, Madison blindly invested a great deal of public money—roughly the equivalent of 0.5 percent of the entire federal budget from the previous year—in a risky scheme. Yet the affair also reveals the duplicity of the British government and its strategy to portray Madison and the pro-war members of Congress as the aggressors while simultaneously considering its own war plans. The British government lied about the Henry affair. Craig had recommended Henry to Castlereagh, who in 1808 was secretary of state for war and the colonies, as a useful gatherer of intelligence, sending along reports from Henry's first mission. Castlereagh responded favorably to Craig, calling Henry "a person of good information and discretion," and authorized his future use, stating "his exertions deserve your Encouragement." Yet when the affair become public in 1812, Castlereagh instructed Augustus Foster, Britain's minister to the United States, to deny "on the part of this government, any knowledge of the nature of the Mission upon which Mr. Henry was sent by Sir James Craig until several months after the whole was terminated." Then in a clever diplomatic trick that had become the hallmark of the ministry's policy toward America, Foster was directed to shift the blame onto the United States by attacking the Madison administration for releasing the letters of a self-avowed spy and traitor before allowing the British to respond through normal diplomatic channels. Such "extraordinary" actions, Foster was to imply, was nothing short of warmongering, and Britain was its victim.[6]

Perhaps most surprising about the outbreak of war between the United States and Britain in 1812 was that it did not happen earlier. Disagreements over trade, impressment, American Indians, and expansion were decades old by 1812, with the crisis over maritime issues having peaked five years earlier when Britain attacked the *Chesapeake* and introduced the Orders in Council. Threats of war and last-ditch diplomatic efforts to avert it had become something of a normal state of affairs for Britain and its former colonies. In fact, when the United States declared war in June, many on both sides of the Atlantic doubted the crisis would amount to much more than another round of threats, gestures, and inconclusive negotiations.

Whereas the timing of the outbreak of war might be described as arbitrary or coincidental, the major factors that led to it cannot be. There is no single explanation for the outbreak of war in June 1812. Americans' grievances were combined with such domestic political factors as Madison's upcoming bid for reelection and changes in Congress; these American factors then confronted British concerns about America's growing merchant fleet and territorial expansion, as well as Britain's own domestic politics, to create a perfect storm in 1812. This war was no accident. The word "inevitable" is too cavalier, but the case for the likelihood of a second war between the United States and Britain is strong, and the emphasis is best placed more on *when* than *if*. Although subtle changes in diplomacy or timing of events might have avoided an American declaration of war in June, equally slight alterations could have provoked an American (or British, for that matter) declaration of war in the months and years surrounding June 1812. The failure of Britain's suspension in June of the Orders in Council—by far the leading grievance of the United States as presented in public discussions and diplomatic exchanges—to halt the war underlines the determination of America's national leaders to let the war play out.

The Liverpool ministry's refusal even to consider using suspension of the Orders in Council as a foundation for further discussion of Americans' other grievances highlights the British government's willingness to go to war, too. It is a mistake to view the United States as the sole protagonist in this pageant. Britain did not enter this war in the same way it stumbled into the American Revolution.[7] The case for war in Britain was substantial and deep-rooted, and as the following chapter reveals, Britain's leaders were wholly aware of the severity of the situation throughout the spring of 1812. They knew their actions, or inaction, risked open war with the United States. Weary of ongoing diplomatic dramas with the Americans, British leaders and public commentators alike accused Madison and the Republicans of bluffing, knowing full well that calling the bluff risked war. The British government had plenty of opportunities before and after June 1812 to avert war, if that was their primary goal. Ultimately, the Perceval and Liverpool ministries both chose courses of action that allowed the war to play out, as did their parliamentary supporters, the British electorate, the king, and the prince regent, when the king became indisposed due to mental illness. All of these contributions ultimately enabled the government's course of action.

Among the most important factors that led to the declaration of war by the United States in June 1812 was the changing political scene in Washington. Sectionalism and fragmentation within the Republican party, rather than lack of conviction on the part of America's leaders or genuine grievances, prevented the war from erupting earlier.[8] When the Twelfth Congress first met in 1811, one-third of its members were new—representing the largest turnover since the founding of the federal government.[9] At the helm of the House of Representatives was the newly elected Henry Clay from Kentucky. Although the son of a Baptist minister, Clay preferred late-night gambling to early-morning church services; still, his childhood in Virginia had taught him how to captivate, rouse, and control a room. After a spell as a senator, Clay moved to the House of Representatives, where he was elected speaker by an unprecedented margin of two to one on the first day. Among his first orders of business was to assert control over his party and the House. He ignored precedent and seniority in selecting committee chairs, instead favoring like-minded supporters, and he reined in and isolated the likes of John Randolph, a powerful Virginia Republican who was critical of Madison and had an intimidating habit of bringing his large dog into the chamber and talking loudly about his love of dueling pistols.[10] Few congressmen in 1811 brought their family with them to the capital, lodging instead in taverns and widows' spare rooms. Such living arrangements became the basis of lasting friendships and political alliances, and so it was with Clay and six of his colleagues, who all lived above the same tavern, which came to be known as the "War Mess."[11] These fellow lodgers— Langdon Cheves, Felix Grundy, George Bib, William Lowndes, and John C. Calhoun—became the nucleus of what was known as the war hawks, who with Clay plotted how Congress might push the country into war with Britain.

Entirely Republican and predominantly Southern (three of the core group were from South Carolina), the war hawks argued incessantly that America's national honor was at stake. The concept of manhood among the generation of elite Southerners being raised in the early republic placed a premium on personal honor and self-determination. Not surprisingly, the Twelfth Congress, which saw an influx of these young Southerners, styled foreign relations, and Anglo-American affairs specifically, in terms that emphasized rights, honor, and independence far more than any previous Congress.[12] On the international stage, this translated into a group of unbridled, patriotic congressmen hailing from the South who likened national sovereignty to self-determination and saw violations of American sovereignty as an insult to the nation's honor. The hierarchy of nations meant relatively little to these men, who tended to reject the authority of institutions and their indulgent parents. They were natural risk takers, and they believed history rewarded such men. When describing the celebrated late William Pitt the elder, Britain's leader in the Seven Years' War and defender of American colonists' rights in the 1760s and early 1770s, Calhoun highlighted to Congress those qualities he found worthy of imitation in history's great leaders: "It is his ardent patriotism; the heroic courage of his mind that could not brook the least insult of injury offered to his country, but thought that her interest and honor ought to be vindicated at every hazard and expense."[13] In consequence, British and American critics' arguments about the imbalance of power, the vulnerability of the United States, and the deference America owed to Britain only stirred these men.[14] Calhoun chastised Randolph for making such arguments before Congress, remarking, "Supposing a speaker of that day [when the Continental Congress met on the eve of the American Revolution] had risen and urged all the arguments which we have heard on this subject. . . . With what sentiment, think you would have [sic] such doctrines have been received?" "Happy for us," Calhoun declared, "they had no force at that period of our country's glory."[15]

Arguments of this sort played out well nationally. Virginia's House of Delegates declared its support for war against Britain in December 1811 by pledging "our lives, our fortunes, and our sacred honor"—a phrase taken from the Declaration of Independence and serving the dual purpose of legitimizing the present contest and reminding everyone that honor trumped all.[16] In the North, the Connecticut *American Mercury* endorsed the Kentucky legislature's warning that "should we tamely submit, the world ought to despise us—we should despise ourselves—Great Britain, herself would despise us."[17] The citizens of the First Congressional District of Pennsylvania issued a nationally circulated public statement in late May expressing their firm support of war with Britain, explaining that the "legitimate and inevitable cause of war" was not financial gain but "our imprescriptible rights of sovereignty, the liberty of our citizens."[18] Moreover, such arguments became the bulwark of continuous justification of the war when the stated reasons of maritime rights lost relevance after the British suspended the Orders in Council and France's defeat in the spring of 1814 ended the need for impressment. The regular invasions of Canada and attacks on American Indians were also justified in Congress and in the press in the language of national honor and sovereignty. In fact, when the war concluded, Madison and the war hawks were able to claim victory on the grounds that the protection of America's honor and sovereignty had always been the root causes of the war; such issues as the Orders in Council, they argued, were mere examples of the matter of Britain's disrespect for America.

In the year before the declaration of war, Clay and his associates persuaded— and at times pushed, shamed, and bullied—the House, delivering the necessary support for a declaration of war to Madison in March 1812. When Madison appeared hesitant, in April Clay led a delegation to the president. They demanded war, promised the House's support, and made a thinly veiled threat that if Madison was not up to the task they could find a new president in the upcoming elections.[19] The details of the meeting are sketchy at best, but the agreed outcome was clear. War would follow a brief embargo allowing American ships to return to port. The only question was how long the embargo would last. The embargo, Clay assured a concerned supporter, was not another commercial measure: "[it] is not designed as the substitute of War, but as a component part of that system which government is deliberately forming."[20] When war finally came, Clay reacted with unbridled joy: "We shall have war. Every patriot bosom must throb with anxious solicitude for the result. Every patriot arm will assist in making that result conducive to the glory of our beloved country."[21]

Yet Clay and his war hawks did not control the country's fate. He did not have the powers of a dictator, Madison was not his client, and the war hawks were a vague faction, not a majority in either Congress or the Republican party.[22] In fact, Jefferson seriously doubted Congress's ability even to prepare for war without the president's leadership. "That a body containing 100 lawyers in it, should direct the measures of a war, is, I fear, impossible," he wrote to Madison in February 1812.[23] The Republicans controlled the federal government, but they were notoriously divided. The Republicans suffered from their success, as ambitious Americans filled their ranks in hopes of joining the ruling party. To consider the Republicans as a single party by 1812 is debatable. Sectionalism along with differences on states' rights, federal authority, foreign policy, taxation, and virtually every other issue, divided the party, and Madison was hardly the party's unanimous choice in the presidential succession. George Clinton, Thomas Jefferson's vice-president, and James Monroe had garnered significant support in the 1808 election, and plenty of prominent Republicans, including members of Madison's cabinet, joined the oppositional ranks during his first term. Many British observers, as well as American ones, doubted Madison would be reelected.[24] In short, a declaration of war required cooperation, and cooperation required negotiation and compromise.

The bungling of the war preparations highlights both Republican divisions and the limitations of their leadership. Despite clamoring for war, the Republican-dominated Twelfth Congress balked at the idea of preparing properly for it. To some extent overconfidence hampered American preparation. Britain was, after all, tied down in Europe, leaving Canada seemingly undefended. As Clay brazenly remarked, "the militia of Kentucky are alone competent to place Montreal and Upper Canada at our feet."[25] But such statements are more a reflection of contemporary bravado than an explanation of Republican leaders' failure to prepare adequately for war. Congress refused to recharter the national bank in 1811, despite its necessity in financing the looming war and the pleas of Albert Gallatin, secretary of the treasury and Madison's favorite in the cabinet.[26] The commercial war on Britain and France had shattered the American economy by 1811, leaving the federal government with a revenue of $11 million, decreasing by a projected further $2 million the following year. Faced with a war preparations bill of an estimated $22 million, Gallatin recommended sharp increases in taxes and loans. Congress stalled before reluctantly accepting a doubling of tariffs and a loan for half the amount, just four months before the outbreak of war—hardly adequate, and a worrying omen of things to come.[27]

The sluggishness with which Congress acted is particularly egregious considering that, for all intents and purposes, the United States was starting from scratch. Whereas Britain measured its warships in the hundreds and its fighting men in the hundreds of thousands, the United States struggled to maintain a poorly equipped and badly officered national army of a few thousand men and a seaworthy navy of seventeen ships. Yet the Americans dragged their feet. Congress began enacting a serious war program a mere six months before the war, increasing provision for the number of regulars in the army to 35,000 men and offering enticing bounties to new recruits. Arguments broke out over recruitment, the authority of the president to call out the state militias, appointment of officers, and provisioning of the army. The U.S. Army never reached this target— let alone the higher ones set in subsequent years—during the course of the entire war, peaking in September 1814 at 29,107 officers in men. In fact with 6,744 men at the start of the war, the U.S. Army was comparable in size to the force of British regulars defending Canada, yet weaker in experienced officers, equipment, organization, and training.[28]

The American navy fared much worse. With only seven frigates, the United States was entirely at the mercy of the Royal Navy, so Madison and others simply abandoned the idea that the navy would be a factor.[29] Oceanic navies were fabulously expensive to build and maintain, and the penny-pinching Republicans under Jefferson and then Madison had allowed even the small force built during the Federalists' administrations to rot, choosing instead to focus on cheaper and smaller short-ranged gunboats to defend the coast. Little had changed by 1811, except that even most of the gunboats were in disuse. As the *National Intelligencer*, the recognized organ of the Republican national leadership, remarked in August, "Let the watchwords of the current wisdom, virtue and patriotism of the day of trial be—no increase of the national debt—no navy."[30] The navy had major supporters among the war hawks. Langdon Cheves, Clay's fellow lodger at the "War Mess," was the chairman of the House Naval Affairs Committee. His task was to ready the navy for war, and so in the autumn of 1811 he asked fellow South Carolinian Paul Hamilton to produce a report that outlined targets for naval growth. Hamilton responded with an ambitious plan that called for construction of twenty new frigates and a dozen ships of the line. A force of this size would make the United States a formidable naval power in the Americas, enabling it to engage the British openly in line battles at sea. Britain, which kept only a modest force in the West Indies and Canada by this point, would either have to deploy a much greater force to its American stations or accept the naval supremacy of the United States in North American waters.[31]

At first glance, it seems that Cheves should have had little difficulty implementing this plan. He was a core member of the war hawks, the Federalist opposition had long bemoaned the lack of American naval power, and America's primary stated grievances were maritime. Even the *National Intelligencer* changed its tune and offered initial support by temporarily reversing opposition to a larger navy, printing a lengthy letter in December 1811 in favor of an immediate building plan.[32] Moreover, the planned navy was modest by European standards, and downright tiny given the size and importance of America's merchant marine. Yet the Republican Congress rejected the plan outright, largely on matters of cost. When Cheves later proposed watered-down versions, he faced further rejections. His only consolation came in March via a bill authorizing refurbishment of three mothballed frigates and stockpiling of lumber to build three more. Neither Clay nor Madison publicly spoke in support of Cheves or directed Republicans to do anything other than vote against his proposals.

Cheves's failure highlights the limitation of both the war hawks and the Republican leadership and underlines how much the declaration of war was a compromise. Madison has long been denigrated as a weak, overwhelmed president who could not manage his own party.[33] Yet he deserves more credit for his political survival skills. By the autumn of 1811, it was evident that the Republican party was in serious danger of collapsing under the weight of its success. The Republicans of the Twelfth Congress controlled 75 percent of the seats in the House and 82 percent in the senate. This meant the real threat to any bill was not the marginalized Federalists but dissent among Republicans. Although only

Republicans ultimately voted to declare war in 1812, there were no guarantees that the measure would pass.[34] As was the case with Cheves's plans for the navy, Republicans regularly voted against their own. Trying to force unpopular bills risked alienating supporters who could choose other candidates within the party for president and speaker. Augustus Foster best described to his superiors in London the web of American domestic politics in which Anglo-American relations were trapped. They could

> depend upon this as being the fact—that whatever measure is resorted to at this time, it is with a view to the approaching election of a President, which takes place in November. Whatever will secure the re-election of Mr. Madison be it embargo, non-intercourse, war, repeal of the non-importation act (which is not improbable) or reconciliation, it will be recommended by the Government, and many members who would otherwise be against any one of these measures will for the sake of the party vote in its favour. In this view it is not unlikely that the session may terminate favourably to our interests after all.[35]

Madison responded to the factionalism and rising pro-war sentiments in the autumn of 1811 by abandoning more than a decade of moderate Republican foreign policy in favor of an aggressive, explicitly warlike stance. Cleverly construed, Madison's foreign policy would unite Clay and other war hawks, who were critical of his timidity, with moderates who would have no option but to support the new majority or defect.[36] When Congress convened in November, Madison made his new stance clear. In his formal address, he put foreign affairs first on the agenda, blasting Britain and calling on Congress to approve substantial increases in America's military and measures to finance them. "With this evidence of hostile inflexibility, in trampling on rights which no independent nation can relinquish," Madison declared, "Congress will feel the duty of putting the United States into an armour, and an attitude demanded by the crisis and corresponding with the national spirit and expectations."[37] America was to go on a war footing.

Over the following six months, the Republicans in Washington were more united than ever.[38] Yet this unity masks continued deep divisions within the party over such key issues as taxation and federal power. Had the Republican leadership vigorously pursued adequate war preparations, they would have shattered the illusion of party unity. Making the United States even moderately competitive on the British model was impossible, as it would have required abandoning key republican principles. Per capita, Britain's government outspent the Americans by a ratio of 25 to 1 in 1811, and Britain's military-fiscal state had been efficiently collecting revenues to wage war against France for the better part of a century.[39] Britain was able to tax subjects' property, internal and external commerce, activities, and (from 1798 for the first time in modern history) personal income. The British state employed tens of thousands of men and women either directly or largely through private contracts to equip and supply its forces. This meant legions of tax collectors, civil servants, lawyers, contractors, and suppliers. In fact, management of the Royal Navy was so organized that by 1812 seamen had the option of splitting their wages, allowing their dependents to collect a portion each month in offices around the country without interruption as the men sailed around the world, transferred ship, or became ill.[40] In comparison, the United States had effectively relinquished its ability to tax anything other than overseas commerce years earlier, possessed practically no system of contractors, and rarely paid its troops and seamen on time.[41]

In sharp contrast to Britain's military-fiscal state, the United States at its core in 1812 was a coalition of peoples whose pursuit of their individual and sectional interests naturally slowed and diluted bold national policies. Even Federalists likely would have rejected many of the ambitious war preparations for fear of the powers they would give the Republicans. Americans granted power to the federal government with the greatest reluctance, inherently fearing large standing armies, navies, and the financial tools a federal government needed to maintain them.[42] In consequence, the American government approved trifling military budgets of only $4.75 million in 1808 and $7.75 million in 1811, a drop in the ocean compared to what European nations were willing to spend.[43] Republicans in Washington avoided properly financing the war throughout its duration, refused to recharter the bank, rejected significant naval expansion, and were abysmal in implementing even approved war measures. As a result, the United States staggered into a war with scarcely a navy and the skeleton of an army. As historian Jon Latimer recently summarized, such poor preparations and planning meant that "defeat was practically guaranteed from the moment Madison and Congress stepped onto the warpath."[44] Yet, realistically these were the only terms on which an American declaration of war and Madison's political survival were possible.

According to the party line, Jefferson and then Madison had tried everything short of war—disastrous commercial restrictions and negotiations ad nauseam—but pacific measures had accomplished nothing. The lack of alternatives to war was a central tenet of the case made by Madison and the war hawks in Congress, and supporters across the country took every opportunity to drive this point home. As South Carolina's governor explained in a widely reprinted address to the state legislature in November 1811, "We have long witnessed the United States pursuing a course of policy entirely pacific, impartial and conciliatory, and displaying, in all their transactions with foreign powers, a degree of mildness and forbearance almost without example in the history of nations." Britain has taken advantage of American mildness with abuse and aggression, he continued, and if the United States must "suffer nearly all the privations of war," then it was time for America to declare one.[45]

Worse still, America's moderation was beginning to look like prostration. As Hezekiah Niles explained with his usual literary flare in his Baltimore *Weekly Register*:

> [I]n the valley of humiliation, at the foot of the throne of her ideot [sic] monarch, at the threshold of the palaces of knaves who administer the government in his name, we sought justice and begged for peace; not because we feared war, but from that moderation which distinguishes the people, as well as the government of the United States.[46]

In short, the United States had no choice. As the popular pamphlet *Free Trade and Sailor's Rights!* argued, America was the victim acting in self-defense against a well-known, relentless foreign aggressor: "After years of forbearance, in despite of concessions without number, and we had almost said without limitation, that cruel and unrelenting spirit of oppression and injustice, which for centuries characterized the spirit of the British cabinet, overwhelmed nation after nation, and caused humanity to shed tears of blood, has involved us in a war."[47]

As in the arguments about national sovereignty and honor, depiction of America as the victim remained part of the pro-war rhetoric for the duration of the war—much to the ire of its opponents. Clay reminded Congress the following year during the debate on increasing the size of the army that "the war in fact was announced, on our part, to meet the war which she [Britain] was waging on her part."[48]

In spring 1812 this was a legitimate argument. The diplomatic toolbox of the federal government was empty, and Britain showed no signs of yielding. Castlereagh explicitly repeated his standing instructions to Foster in April: no matter how hard the Americans push "you will not express yourself in such a manner as to encourage the most distant hope of our being induced to make such a sacrifice."[49] The prince regent publicly reinforced these sentiments a few days later in a declaration that made clear Britain's long-standing position that it would not repeal the Orders in Council until France proved beyond a doubt that it had repealed its own system of commercial restrictions. To demand otherwise, as the United States had done, was a summons for Britain "to submit, to the abandonment of its most ancient, essential, and undoubted maritime Rights."[50] Moreover, Britain showed no signs of accepting American claims that France had rescinded its decrees limiting neutral trade.

Madison was resigned to war by this point, remarking to Jefferson in April, "They prefer war with us, to a repeal of their Orders in Council." As a result, "We have nothing left therefore, but to make ready for it."[51] Monroe's mood was also one of resignation. After meeting privately with him, Foster used the words "despondency" and "melancholy" to describe the secretary of state's mood as he told Foster that the United States could not change its course without Britain yielding: "Mr. Monroe confidentially spoke of the impossibility there was for this Government now to recede without a change of any kind, whatever on the part of England." "He even said that he should feel like a man disgraced and ashamed to shew his face," Foster relayed, "if after the steps which were taken they were now to submit . . . and that he for his part would rather quit the United States at once and go somewhere else where there was a Government that could make itself respected."[52]

Supporters of war throughout the country therefore argued that the War of 1812 was a defensive war for the United States, regardless of who declared it or how the United States prosecuted it. The Republican minority in the Massachusetts legislature, having earlier been outvoted in a series of resolutions condemning the declaration of war, petitioned Washington as a show of support, describing it as a "war to resist depredations the most wanton and edicts the most barbarous, savage and tyrannical" and as a "war to save our commerce from destruction, and our citizens from slavery."[53] Niles and a host of other editors fought against accusations that Madison had plunged America into an offensive war, declaring "It is the *law of the land* that we defend ourselves from British aggressions; it is the legal authority of the country that we shall retaliate our wrongs as the only means to end them." To explain his argument, Niles employed a parable that would be reprinted across the country. In the story, a well-known thief and murderer set upon a peaceful farmer, stealing his grain and sometimes snatching one of his children to be "transported to *Turkey* and sold as a slave." "Suppose," Niles continued, "that not content with these, the marauder should sometimes approach the threshold of the good man's house and discharge his pistols at the family, killing some and wounding others." "Would the husbandman, that took up his rifle and went to seek this wretch, be considered as acting offensively?" Niles raged. "This metaphor is strictly applicable to our present controversy," he concluded. "We have suffered all these things in their most extensive latitude."[54]

By extrapolation, the war's supporters insisted that invasion of Canada was a justified measure and part of a defensive strategy. As Monroe explained on the eve of war, Canada should be understood "not as an object of the war but as a means to bring it to a satisfactory conclusion."[55] Though critics argued that starting a land war to assert maritime rights was nonsensical, Madison and his supporters insisted they had no other choice if America was to wage war on Britain. Deprived of funds for so long and slighted during military preparations in 1812, the American navy was incapable of defending the American coast, let alone conducting offensive operations in other parts of the Atlantic. Like Napoleon's armies, America's forces were landlocked, and so Madison orchestrated his entire war strategy around an invasion of Canada.

The Republican leadership defended themselves against accusations of aggrandizement by insisting that their aim was not permanent conquest of Canada. Territorial expansion appealed to some Americans, particularly those in the land-hungry West, when it meant forever depriving the American Indians in the vicinity of allies and supplies. As Felix Grundy, a lodger at Clay's "War Mess," exclaimed, "We shall drive the British from our Continent—they will no longer have an opportunity of intriguing with our Indian neighbors, and setting on the ruthless savage to tomahawk our women and children."[56] But western states such as Grundy's Tennessee were sparsely populated, and so lacked the necessary votes in Congress to direct national policy. In fact, the myth that the United States declared war on Britain primarily to gain Canada developed more from the propaganda of the British and Americans opposed to the war than from Americans who supported the war. Even Clay privately reflected in 1812 that "When the War was commenced Canada was not the end but the means; the object of the War being the redress of injuries, and Canada being the instrument by which that redress was to be obtained." If Canada could be captured and retained at the negotiating table, then fine, but it was not essential.[57] Of course, this did not prevent an overly optimistic Congress from briefly debating during the summer of 1812 how a conquered Canada would be ruled, but even then there was no consensus in either house that Canada should be retained over exchanging it for British maritime concessions.[58]

Proponents of the invasion were optimistic about the strategy, and to be fair, at first glance their confidence seems justified. Britain's naval presence on the Great Lakes was minimal, and only a few thousand troops defended a border with the United States that stretched for hundreds of miles. Furthermore, these defenders suffered from appalling morale and a high rate of desertion to the United States, where a common laborer earned as much as four times the wage of a private soldier.[59] Committed to defeating Napoleon in Europe, Britain would not send significant reinforcements; even if it did, they would be unlikely to reach Canada for a year. The American regular army was not much larger than the small force defending Canada, but the population on which it could draw was enormous—some 8.5 million Americans (including slaves) versus about half a million subjects in all of British North America.[60] Moreover, Upper Canada in particular was packed with tens of thousands of American-born colonists of dubious loyalty. These "late loyalists," as they came to be known, had for the better part of two decades poured into Upper Canada, where land was cheap and taxes were low.[61] America's war advocates believed that at worst the late loyalists would stay home, and at best they would, as John Harper declared in Congress in January 1812, "sigh for an affiliation with the great American family" and join the cause of the United States.[62]

More important, war supporters in the United States believed Britain did not have the stomach for a land war with the United States. As the *National Intelligencer* outlined in a lengthy, widely reprinted editorial in April, the United States had little to fear from Britain. "Where are her troops?" it mocked. "The war in the [Iberian] peninsula, which lingers, requires strong armies to support it. She maintains an army in Sicily; another in India; a strong force in Ireland, and along her own coast and in the West Indies." "Can any one believe," the editorial wondered, "that, under such circumstances, the British government could be so infatuated, or rather mad, as to send troops here for the purpose of invasion?" As for the colonists in Canada, "Seven or eight millions of people have nothing to dread from 300,000."[63] Moreover, Americans held fast to the prerevolutionary belief that the British government was vulnerable to popular opinion—despite the string of American failures dating back to the 1760s to co-opt it through economic coercion. James Lloyd explained to the Senate in February, "the Government of Great Britain is in some degree a popular one. . . . Touch the popular sentiment effectually, and you control the Commons, the Commons, by withholding supplies and the civil list, control the King and obtain a change of Ministry and a change of measures."[64] And the British public, insisted the American war supporters, did not desire a war in North America.

The close, and often selective, coverage in the American press of Britain's domestic opposition to the Orders in Council led many in the United States to believe that the pressure of a looming war would lead to repeal. The economic depression in the manufacturing districts brought on in part by closure of American markets created a firestorm of public opposition and protest. American readers in even the most remote corners of the republic could count on their regional paper to reprint selective parliamentary debates, provincial meetings, popular petitions, and parliamentary committee testimony relevant to the Orders in Council. William Cobbett's inflammatory diatribes against war with America addressed to the prince regent made for particularly popular reading, appearing in full form and extracts in papers from Maine to Tennessee. Reading some American newspapers, one can easily understand why many Americans believed Britain was extremely vulnerable to American pressure, if not on the brink of a government collapse. In this context, Jefferson's infamous remark that the conquest of Canada would be a "matter of marching" was perhaps not so brazen after all.[65]

The declaration of war by the United States would have surprised few people in the British Empire with access to the tens of millions of newspapers that circulated annually. The increasingly aggressive tone of Madison's addresses, Congress's war preparations, state governments' resolutions encouraging war, and the militant hostility in the Republican press were all closely monitored across the empire. As the *Bahama Gazette* remarked in February 1812, it is "evident that the negotiations are rapidly drawing to a determination, which we always predicted, namely, an open breach and declaration of war."[66] "They [Americans] have been going to war with us as fast as they can," declared the *Times* the following week, "and if they at all halt, it must be for want of breath, rather than want of will."[67] The week after that the *Montreal Herald* agreed, stating that "It is now evident that war can no longer be avoided."[68] Through its North American agents and the British press, the British government, too, was well informed of the war intentions of the United States. In fact, Americans counted on this flow of information to put public pressure on the British government to meet American demands. To a great extent, Britain's failure to yield has been dismissed by historians as a combination of British ignorance and arrogance, but such explanations seriously underestimate the depth of British interests in the conflict.

Britain had little reason to yield to American demands in 1812. France and its allies were largely cut off from overseas neutral trade; the merchant fleets of the United States had been dealt a serious blow by the Orders in Council, albeit in no small part due to America's own disastrous retaliatory measures; and the Royal Navy was able to man its ships. Yielding to American demands would have jeopardized all of this. As described in greater detail in Chapter Seven, the Liverpool ministry suspended the Orders in Council only as a means to ease domestic political pressure on the fragile new ministry. The demise of the orders reflected the growing political clout of British provincial manufacturers and was timed to avert a political crisis in the wake of the assassination of Spencer Perceval in the lobby of the House of Commons on 11 May. The only prime minister ever to have been assassinated, Perceval was killed by John Bellingham, a mentally unbalanced merchant who acted alone and blamed Perceval for his economic and personal misfortunes. In the government crisis that followed, the new ministry, led by the Earl of Liverpool—which was a slightly revised version of the one that ended with Perceval's death—attempted to gather support by softening its position on a number of issues, including the Orders in Council. Madison made a poor assessment of the situation, first underestimating the significance of the prime minister's assassination and later claiming the Orders in Council were repealed because of popular pressure in Britain galvanized by the fear of war with America.[69] This partly led him and other Americans to believe wrongly that suspension of the orders was a clear indication of the British government's crumbling resolve on all of America's grievances—a false hope that lulled Madison into the disastrous assessment that his opponents were not as sincere about pursuing the war as he was.

In fact, for many Britons war was preferable to the status quo, because a wartime setting would allow Britain to thwart more aggressively the rise of the United States. In a war, the Royal Navy could seize American merchant vessels and sailors without all the peacetime legalities, Americans could be excluded from all British trade to the benefit of the West Indian interest and Canada, American expansion could be curtailed, and perhaps greatest of all, the United States would at last be put in its proper place. Against these advantages, Britain's only risk seemed to be continued disruptions to its trade with America, and perhaps Canada.

British proponents of war identified other potential benefits, too. Powerful elements of the West Indian interest, merchants involved in the Canadian trade, and advocates for more protectionist trade policies continued to argue that the British Empire would be better off economically without a large American presence. Supporters admitted that war might initially hurt the West Indies, which relied heavily on Americans for supplies, but this would be offset by higher prices for coffee and sugar caused by elimination of the Americans from the carrying trade. Moreover, they argued, such a situation would force the West Indies to become more self-sufficient and reliant on other suppliers, such as Canada.[70]

Elements of the powerful landed interest also welcomed reduction of commercial intercourse with the United States. The Americans had undercut British grain producers and fueled the rise of provincial manufacturing, which competed with agriculture for cheap labor and was run by *nouveau riche* industrialists whom the more established landed elite detested.[71] As one commentator remarked, "I can see no good that can arise to England from being the workshop for America, while we do not raise corn enough to feed ourselves."[72] The series of American embargoes taught the British that the United States was a volatile nation, which could not be depended on to act in harmony with British economic interests. As a reader of the *Leeds Mercury* remarked, paying the Americans £7 million a year to provide cheap grain so that British laborers could focus on manufacturing rather than agriculture was proving dangerous. "We have upon this island several millions of acres of land uncultivated, and our produce is very much short of our consumption," the reader stated. "Could not some plan be devised to employ many of our starving Manufacturers in improving our waste lands, and thereby produce at home a sufficiency of grain for our own consumption, without subjecting us to the necessity of importing?" Such sentiments were not in vain. Although unable to act during the wars with France, the British government shortly afterward passed the Corn Laws, a protective, and controversial, system that effectively subsidized British grain producers and severely curtailed foreign imports.

A war would also offer Britain the opportunity to check American expansion. Spain was Britain's ally, and the collapse of its empire both threatened the war effort in Europe and hurt the British West Indies, which traded extensively with the Spanish colonies. As the governor of the Bahamas, who was concerned about American advances on the Spanish Empire, reminded Liverpool in July

1812, "Your Lordship knows that the principal support of the Islands is the trade carried on with the Spanish Colonies."[73] Although Spanish Florida itself was not that important to Britain either economically or strategically, the American incursions into East Florida in the spring of 1812 set off alarm bells in the British West Indies. Foster received immediate instructions from the Foreign Office to make clear in "firm language" Britain's "protest against any attempt to seize that Province from our Ally."[74]

Short of declaring war on the United States, however, there was little Britain could do. The alarmed *Royal Gazette* in Nassau explained to its readers, "it seems that both West and East Florida, are condemned to be annexed to the territory of the United States, and we fear there is no way to avert their fate—Great Britain has already too much to do, and Spain of herself is too weak, to prevent it." The United States, the editorial railed, was an expansionist nation in the class of France: "This proceeding well accords with the general tenor of the conduct of the American Government, which, like its Prototype, of France, readily throws aside the principles of Honour and Justice, to effect its objects of ambition and aggrandisement."[75] Following continuation of American exploits and official denials over East Florida, the *Bahama Gazette* called the Americans out. "Their conduct in this instance is of a piece with the other acts perpetrated by a Government held together by the basest of intrigues," the paper proclaimed, "and is equaled only by the supineness with which the country permits an atrocious aggression on the rights of a friendly power, at a time they are so clamourous about their own."[76] When the British government discovered American involvement in the 1812–13 rebellion in Spanish Texas, more alarm bells rang. The worry was that Texas would become another Florida, enabling the United States "to extend the boundaries of Louisiana as far as the Rio Grande, to which River the American Government assert that their claims extend," according to a British agent's report.[77] A regular theme in the West Indian press was that if the Americans ran out of space in North America they would be next. After all, remarked the *Jamaica Magazine*, "Most [American] politicians are agreed that these little islands must one day become the colonies of their natural lords of that continent to which they append."[78]

Yet despite the economic drawbacks and the risk to Canada, 1812 was as good a year as any for the British Empire to go to war with the United States. British naval success had secured Britain from French assault for the time being, and Napoleon was focused on a massive invasion of Russia. The British, who would play only a minimal role in Russia's defense, were largely reduced to spectators of the major actions for at least the next year.[79] As the *Times* explained in the midst of its coverage of Napoleon's invasion preparations, "We who are in England view the motions of the Gallic ruler through the mystery in which he involves them; as people at a great distance observe horses on a Race-course, at the point of the starting plate."[80] Meanwhile, proceedings in the Iberian Peninsula (Britain's greatest military commitment) were going well, and Napoleon's eastern focus gave every reason to hope for success.

Moreover, Britain was already equipped to wage a war against America, having been in a global struggle with France for nearly two decades. Britain had evolved into a massive, efficient military machine that could outspend its enemies and enlist its men into service at a rate three times that of France. At the height of the Napoleonic Wars, Britain had nearly a thousand warships in service and well over six hundred thousand men in arms.[81] Everything the British did or owned was taxed to the extent that the average Briton paid twice the percentage of his income as he did a century earlier and more than 50 percent higher than during the American Revolution.[82] This in turn meant government revenues of roughly forty times what the American treasury secretary projected the United States would raise in 1812.[83] A war with America in 1812 would change none of this. Britain's war machine would neither increase nor grind to a halt in the event of a war with America. Because the war could be conducted largely as a matter of redeployment rather than increased mobilization, virtually all of the costs could be absorbed, or at least masked, by the existing establishment.[84] As a result, any apprehensions the British nation or its leaders might have had in peacetime about the hardships of war were largely muted by the fact that the nation had already been enduring them to an unprecedented degree for so long. Furthermore, Britain had become adept at fighting imperial wars overseas since the American Revolution, having recently added a great deal of South Asia, parts of Africa, and France's West Indian colonies to the British Empire.[85]

From a strategic perspective, the only obvious vulnerability besides Canada was the British Army's dependence on American grain. By 1812 the Americans were the major supplier of flour to British forces fighting in Spain and Portugal. With the aid of thousands of British-issued trading licenses, which safeguarded American ships from the Royal Navy, and the dummy Portuguese merchant house of Henrique Teixeira de Sampaio, which officially imported the flour so as to get around any American embargoes or nonintercourse acts, the Americans shipped a whopping 830,000 barrels in 1811 alone. This trade accounted for 70 percent of total American grain exports, and American ships transported practically all of it, as well as a substantial portion of the supplies coming from the British Isles. Yet the British remained calm. The Duke of Wellington, who commanded the British forces in Spain and Portugal—countries that struggled to feed themselves, let alone tens of thousands of British troops—supported the continuation of the Orders in Council, even though he knew it threatened his supply of grain. The British need not have worried. They found alternative suppliers in South America and North Africa, and American grain kept flowing, thanks to a system of British licenses and the limitations under which the Madison administration was forced to conduct the war. For the same reason Congress was reluctant to implement new taxes, Congress did not want to interfere with the lucrative grain trade.[86] As Jefferson wrote to Madison, the American people were far more likely to support the war if they could "dispose of their produce," even if it meant supplying the enemy. Besides, Jefferson explained on another occasion, "if we could by starving the British armies, oblige Them to withdraw from the peninsular [sic], it would be to send them here; and I think we had better feed them there for pay than feed and fight them here for nothing."[87] In 1813 American grain exports to the British Army in Portugal and Spain increased more than 15 percent. Britain, not the United States, ultimately stopped the flow of American grain to Europe, when Napoleon's retreat from Russia gave Britain renewed access to Northern European suppliers.[88]

The United States was vulnerable in the spring of 1812, or so many Britons believed. In a letter to his superiors in April, Foster described America's defenses and ability to prosecute a war as poor. He dismissed the militia outright, explaining that "they are however not at all counted upon as an efficient force for any other purpose of defense," and described Henry Dearborn, the senior general in the American army, as "a heavy unwieldy looking man" whose "military reputation does not rank very high."[89] British agents rarely bothered to comment on America's navy, and when they did it was merely to dismiss its handful of ships as no match for "the leviathan of the ocean."[90]

Even better for Britain, Madison appeared to be ruling over a fractured party and nation. The British press routinely reprinted stories from the American newspapers that thoroughly abused the president. In fact, apart from *Niles' Weekly Register* and the *National Intelligencer* (most British editors treated the latter as the official government newspaper), pro-Madison administration newspapers received comparatively little attention in Britain. Stories from New England newspapers that railed against Madison's sycophantic subservience to Napoleon or complained about the possibility of war with Britain were far more abundant. Anyone reading a British newspaper in early 1812 could be forgiven for concluding that the United States was on the verge of breaking up, or at the very least that the vast majority of Americans opposed the war. The reasons for the lopsided coverage were not nefarious but a consequence of the structure of trade networks on which information and news always piggybacked. Northern states, along with *Niles' Weekly Register's* home of Baltimore, dominated America's trade with the British Empire, and so their voices were the loudest.

Based almost exclusively in the major port cities, the British government's commercial and diplomatic agents came to similar conclusions. Foster regularly reported on the sectionalism and party strife that defined the national government, often relying on conversations with American officials and private friends

Figure 3.1 W. Holland, "John Bull, the leviathan of the ocean; or, the French fleet sailing into the mouth of the Nile!" (London, 1798). Library of Congress, Prints and Photographs Division, LC-USZC2-1857. Celebrating Britain's decisive victory over France at the Battle of the Nile, this print encapsulates popular British attitudes toward the Royal Navy as dominant. The artist reflects the popular notion of the Royal Navy as the embodiment of the British people by employing John Bull, the personification of the British people in satirical prints during this period, rather than symbols of the nation or military power, such as Britannia, a lion, or George III. The British government and people were supremely confident in the Royal Navy in 1812 and did not perceive the U.S. Navy as any sort of threat.

for insights. One such person who had Foster's confidence was Rosalie Stier Calvert, a wealthy refugee of the European wars who joined the American elite by marrying one of the descendants of the proprietors of colonial Maryland. Calvert closely followed American politics, because she invested her money and the money of her extended family residing abroad in American bond markets. She had a low opinion of the Republicans. In a letter to her brother, she described Madison as being "in reality an honest man," but alas "one of those wavering, weak characters . . . he will do as much harm as his predecessors." To her sister she described how sectionalism and party strife might result in civil war if war with Britain erupted. "Do not think these idle crotchets," she cautioned, "the best informed and most weighty people are of my opinion, and it is that of the most prominent Senators and members of Congress."[91]

Foster's reports may have been detailed and mostly accurate, but his power of prediction was poor. In the six months prior to America's declaration of war, he consistently downplayed the likelihood, portraying the Madison administration and the war hawks as too weak to lead the nation into war. In response to the war preparations approved by Congress, Foster assured ministers that they were mere bluff and bluster. The January bill for increasing the army, he explained, "has in the opinion of the well informed persons now become more an electioneering than a war measure."[92] As more measures were passed, Foster did not budge from his position. In March he stated resolutely that although a war bill might pass the House, it would never win approval from the Senate.[93] The following month he declared, "I should not be at all surprised if the war spirit that has prevailed so long and all the preparations attendant upon it were entirely to disappear before the present month."[94] A few weeks later he wrote that impressment alone was not sufficient for America to declare war.[95] In June he estimated that "Four fifths of the people of the United States" opposed going to war, and that America and its relationship with Britain was being held hostage by a radical minority. "I have every reason to be convinced that the President has been forced into [going to war]," he asserted, "by a faction composed principally of Southern and Western Members, whose leaders are said to have threaten'd to abandon him if he flinched."[96]

Even though some of Foster's assessments of the situation might be ridiculed in hindsight, at the time they reflected the fractured and often contradictory messages of the American government. To be fair, Jonathan Russell, America's chief diplomat in London, similarly misjudged the domestic political situation in Britain, sending messages to the British government that contradicted Monroe's meetings with Foster in Washington.[97] In particular, Russell relentlessly hammered on about the evils of the Orders in Council, while impressment received hardly any attention. In fact, on learning of suspension of the orders in June, Russell immediately sent Castlereagh a magnanimous letter about how this event heralded the bright and peaceful future of Anglo-American relations. The word "impressment" does not even appear in the letter.[98]

The Federalists were especially vexing. In Congress a number of them supported war preparations out of the hope that Madison was indeed bluffing and that by giving him enough rope he might hang himself through either declaring an unpopular war or being forced to suffer the humiliation of backing down.[99] Some Federalists, however, did not stop there. On several occasions they met secretly with Foster and urged Britain to force the United States into a war. Writing in code, Foster reported an early February 1812 meeting with two Federalist leaders in which they advised "We should neither revoke our Orders in Council nor modify them in any manner. They said, this Government would, if We conceded, look upon our Concessions as being the Effect of their own Measures and plume themselves thereon." What transpired next was treason. Their request, relayed Foster, was to push Madison and the Republicans "to the Edge of the Precipice, by an unbending attitude, that then, they must be lost, either by the Disgrace of having nearly ruined the Trade of the United States, and yet failed to reduce Great Britain, by their system of Commercial Restrictions, or else, by their Incapacity to conduct the Government during war."[100] A month later, Foster described how a number of prominent Federalists continued to push their duplicitous agenda, complaining to him whenever it appeared that Britain might concede and that peace might prevail. Some even accused Foster of making secret deals with Monroe.[101]

The language the Federalist leaders used in their discussions with Foster is especially revealing in terms of how they perceived the postcolonial relationship between Britain and the United States. Britain, they argued, was in the driver's seat, not the United States. In fact, they concluded in their first meeting that "Great Britain could by management bring the United States into any connexion with her that she please." Variants of the word *manage* appear regularly in Foster's descriptions of these encounters, underlining Britain's continued role as the senior state. A letter to Foster from "a Federalist of influence" that he included in one of his dispatches revealed this most obviously: "you clearly discern that you have in your hand the fate of the party now in power. You can out [remove] them if you will it." The letter then proceeded to outline in detail how British resolve would split New England Republicans from the rest of the party, cause the "extinction" of Madison's faction, and usher in a new age for the Federalists. Once war erupted and Foster departed the United States (as was customary when two countries went to war), these men complained to the remaining British diplomatic agents that Britain was ruining the Federalists' chances to defeat Madison in the autumn elections by being too lenient in its prosecution of the war. One agent reported to Castlereagh, "it is not to be concealed that a considerable number of the federal party do not view the lenient and conciliatory measures which have been adopted by His Majesty's Government since the war with feelings of satisfaction, and that should Mr. Madison be re-elected his success will be attributed by them to that cause."[102]

Interestingly, Foster thought little of the Federalists, whom he depicted as the greater threat to Britain. He believed the Federalists would ultimately create large navies and an industrial base that would compete with Britain, whereas the Republicans were "contented with the humble pursuits of peace and agriculture."[103] He spoke warmly of Madison and his most trusted members of his cabinet, Gallatin and Monroe, calling Monroe "a very mild moderate man, and with whom I am happy to say it has been my good fortune to be on the best of terms."[104] Such poor impressions of the Federalists and positive personal views of members of the Madison administration likely contributed to Foster's continued hope for peace as well as his underestimation of the Madison administration's resolve to declare war.

The British government consciously worked to "manage" the Americans, but not quite in the way the Federalist who contacted Foster wanted. The government's policy in 1812 was to force the United States to make the decision for war or peace. Whereas an open war with the United States had its advantages, the British government was not in a position to make the declaration itself. The Perceval ministry and the Liverpool ministry that followed were vulnerable at home. Neither had come to power following an election and so had a weak mandate, limited popular support, and declining support in Parliament.[105] The prince regent supported both ministries, but he was still a generally unpopular, temporary substitute for his ailing father. Moreover, the British nation was tired of war, and broadening Britain's war efforts to include a separate war with the United States risked a backlash strong enough to tip the balance against the already precariously placed ministry.

An American declaration, however, would shield the British government from much of the negative fallout of an American war. Ministers could assert that Britain was not the aggressor, they had not asked for the war, and they had no choice but to defend existing British territory and maritime rights against the aggressor Americans. They concluded that Madison and his government would have to decide on war or peace. Either way Britain stood to gain from its passive-aggressive handling of America: if America yielded, the Orders in Council and impressment policies stood firm, and if America declared war, Britain would have license to pound the Americans into submission, with wartime restrictions of America's commerce far harsher than the Orders in Council.

Consequently, Castlereagh repeated explicitly to Foster in April that Britain would not yield its maritime rights, leaving the Americans with a clear choice: "Every minor question has been conceded, and nothing remains but fundamental Rights, which can admit of no compromise. The decision therefore rests with America." Although Foster was to "conduct [himself] with the utmost Conciliation towards America," he was to make Britain's position crystal clear. "Should the councils of America reject every pacifick suggestion," Castlereagh explained, "it will be your object to regulate the discussion in such a manner as to throw distinctly upon the United States the option of War." In so doing, explained Castlereagh, the intention was to cast publicly America's declaration of war as "a war undertaken to compel Great Britain to submit to France Her inveterate enemy, her maritime Rights and Power."[106] British ministers meanwhile instructed agents in North America not to give the United States an obvious pretense to declare war. Writing in May to Prevost, Lord Liverpool (who would soon become the new prime minister) made clear that he expected war with the United States shortly but that neither Britain nor its colonies were to provoke it. "I cannot however avoid repeating to you," Liverpool concluded, "their [His Majesty's government's] earnest desire that you should cautiously avoid any act which can have the effect of irritating the Government or the People of the United States, or can tend in any way whatever to accelerate the resort to actual hostility against this Country."[107] America was intentionally being forced into a corner, leaving its government no choice but to yield or to fight its way out. Either way, ministers held, Britain stood to gain from a resolution.

Meanwhile, the Perceval ministry and its supporters publicly maintained the position that Britain did not want war, but neither would it budge. Speaking before the Commons to resounding shouts of "hear, hear!" Perceval "acknowledged, that the question of war with America was one of great importance, and that a breach with that Power would deeply affect our interests . . . our endeavours at conciliating America had been sincere; at the same time Ministers were aware, it was their duty not to give up those rights which Britain had always maintained." Shouting over cheers from his own party, he declared that he did not doubt that the Orders in Council had caused suffering in Britain; "but for these Orders, the distress would have been ten-fold." Britain, he declared, would fight. "He thought war with America, if possible, should be avoided," reported the *Edinburgh Star*, "but though war would be attended with loss to this country, he did not apprehend ruin from it; nor must peace be purchased at too great a sacrifice."[108]

Both the British and the American governments underestimated each other's resolve to go to war. The British government believed that the weak hold Madison had over his party and the federal government, along with the half-measures to prepare for war in 1811 and 1812, most likely signaled a bluff. Foster might be blamed partly for such a false impression, but his assessments were accurate in that the decision of the United States to go to war in June 1812 was strategically illogical given that the nation was so divided and grossly unprepared to wage it. What Foster and his superiors in London misjudged was the willingness on the part of Madison and his supporters to go to war even under such conditions. Therefore, many Britons in and out of government were caught slightly off guard when the United States rejected suspension of the Orders in Council as grounds for an armistice. Some commentators and officials believed that Madison and Congress were, to an extent, bluffing, and that the suspension would sufficiently satisfy the American government to call off the war without losing credibility at home. But the United States went to war for a range of reasons, and maritime rights were merely manifestations of larger issues about national sovereignty, expansion, and the continued reign of Madison and the Republican party.

The greater error of judgment, however, belonged to the Madison administration, its agents, and its supporters in Congress, who earnestly believed they could bluff and bully the possessor of the world's largest overseas empire and navy out of what it perceived as maritime rights. Failing that, many saw war against a vastly superior, albeit distracted, opponent as a viable alternative. Perhaps it was, but only if the Americans could swiftly take possession of a lightly defended Canada and then hold it before Britain mobilized its military strength—assuming the British government would negotiate favorably for the return of Canada. This, in fact, was the plan in the summer of 1812. But unfortunately, the United States was not capable of effectively carrying it out. Even two years later, the U.S. Army had not met its prewar recruitment goals, and by then British forces were pouring into Canada and assaulting America's coastline.

The grave underestimation of the Liverpool ministry's willingness to go to war is best seen in Russell's correspondence with Castlereagh in London over the summer and early autumn of 1812. After learning of the suspension of the Orders in Council, Russell conveyed his assumption that war had been averted in a congratulatory note to Castlereagh. Wrongly assuming the repeal was a British capitulation and a victory for America's saber-rattling diplomacy, Russell went back to Castlereagh in late August after learning the United States would continue the war despite the suspension of the orders. Russell, taking his cue from Monroe, was less than conciliatory. Believing he had the advantage, he proceeded to dictate to Castlereagh harsh terms for an armistice: repeal of the orders, compensation for all ships and cargoes seized under the orders, cessation of impressment of any persons from American vessels, and release of all American citizens being held by Britain. In exchange, the United States would agree to an armistice and pass a federal law forbidding British subjects from serving on American merchant vessels. Russell's tone was haughty throughout, and he concluded with a warning that even these terms were temporary and that the British government would need to act immediately to take advantage of them, threatening "passions exasperated by injuries—alliances or conquests on terms which forced their abandonment—will inevitably hereafter embitter and protract a context which might now be so easily and happily terminated."[109] Russell expected an immediate response that would open negotiations.

Castlereagh's reply highlights both his veteran diplomatic skills and the Liverpool ministry's willingness to pursue the war. First, he waited five days to reply. He then pretended to take Russell's claim that the conditions of the armistice were unconditional (Russell stated they were, but Castlereagh knew such a claim was a matter of form), telling Russell that if he was not in a position to negotiate the terms, then there was no reason to engage with him any further. "Under the circumstances of your having no Powers to negotiate I must decline entering into a detailed discussion of the propositions which you have direct to bring forward," Castlereagh replied. "As you inform me that you are not at liberty to depart from the conditions set forth in your letter," Castlereagh continued, "it only remains for me to acquaint you, that the Prince Regent feels himself under the necessity of declining to accede to the proposition therein contained, as being on various Grounds absolutely inadmissible."[110] Russell replied a few days later, feigning his plans for an immediate departure; Castlereagh wrote back to wish him a safe journey.

A newly humbled Russell, still in London, then wrote to Castlereagh the following week in an attempt to start discussions of the armistice that Castlereagh had rejected. The haughty tone was noticeably absent, and the terms were severely reduced, requesting only repeal of the Orders in Council, return of the American citizens, and the vague need for an "understanding" regarding impressment.[111] Again, Castlereagh ignored him, despite Russell calling on him in person. Then Castlereagh demeaned Russell by having a secretary reply that Castlereagh was too busy to address the letter personally.[112] When Castlereagh finally responded, it was only to reject Russell's proposal and admonish him for sending it. After first describing the proposal as having "the same purpose in a more covert and therefore in a more objectionable manner," Castlereagh eviscerated Russell, concluding that "this course of proceeding as having on the face of it, a character of disguise, is not only felt to be in principle inadmissible, but as unlikely to lead in practice to any advantageous result."[113] Castlereagh did not write to Russell directly again, despite his repeated pleas to start negotiations, and he eventually left Britain in October. The United States and Britain finally had their war.

|| 4 ||

America on the Offensive

The United States began the War of 1812 on the offensive. Because it declared the war, its forces were in a position to take advantage of the difficulty of communications in North America and the Atlantic world. The declaration can hardly be called shocking, but even so the United States decided exactly where, when, and how hard it would attack, leaving the British to react. For the first half of the war, the conflict was America's to win. Britain's distance and its commitment to defeating France meant that the empire was not able to go on the offensive. As a result, the United States set the early agenda and pace.

What transpired highlighted the inability of the United States to wage war. Most observers expected the Americans to make serious inroads into Canada, and the British commanders in Canada had assumed this in developing a defensive strategy. Yet the land campaigns of the United States were so poorly conceived and executed that historians' neatly structured books on the military aspects of the war unintentionally create the illusion that it was well organized.[1] In fact, the Americans failed miserably on the battlefield from the moment the war started with the invasion of Upper Canada—an invasion that resulted in loss of the Michigan Territory when the British-led forces counterattacked. Few American officers had commanded more than a thousand men, and the organizational structure that supplied and paid them was practically nonexistent. Attempts to rally popular support through creation of a Spirit of 1812, reminiscent of the early days of the American Revolution, also failed. Moreover, Britain's ability to defend Canada with the assistance of American Indian allies alarmed Americans who had thought British North America too weak to pose a significant threat to the much larger United States. Only the American Indians who fought against the United States—both as British allies and, especially in the South, independently—fared worse. American success at sea was nothing short of shocking; however, minor victories over the Royal Navy could not have an impact on the war's outcome, because the disparity in the size and strength of the two navies was too great. At best, the Americans could hope for a boost in morale and enough British prizes to help offset some of the economic losses associated with the massive disruption to overseas trade caused by the war. Yet throughout the conflict, Congress balked at providing the resources and organization necessary to create an efficient military machine, and in less than two short years the United States government was bankrupt, the nation's economy lay in ruins, its troops were deserting in droves, and Britain was ready to take control of the war.

The primary aim of America's campaigns in 1812 was to deal a decisive blow to Canada before the British Empire could mobilize its resources for a defense. Press reports from Canada and Britain made clear that British North America was vulnerable in 1812, with only a few thousand reliable defenders, a population of questionable loyalty, and a modest presence on the part of the Royal Navy. The original plan was for a rapid, three-pronged assault into Canada, targeting Amherstburg near Detroit, the Niagara region, and Montreal. Victories, the government's strategists believed, would deal a severe blow to Britain's Indian allies, leave the United States poised to capture the rest of Canada the following year, boost public confidence in the Madison administration, and force Britain to either negotiate on America's terms or face losing its North American empire. Though the plan was overly ambitious, it is seen to be ridiculous only with the benefit of hindsight. While descriptions of Quebec in *Niles' Weekly Register* read like a real-estate brochure with images of happy people and fertile lands ripe for the taking, reeking of ill-fated overconfidence, many Americans and Britons following the war expected at least Upper Canada to fall— including Britain's commanders charged with defending it.[2] Yet 1812 proved militarily disastrous for the United States.

Formal campaigning began with William Hull's invasion of Upper Canada in July. Anticipating a declaration of war, the Madison administration had sent him and supporting troops and supplies to Ohio months earlier in order to take advantage of the slowness of communications and hopefully catch Canada's defenders off guard. His plan was to capture the British fort at Amherstburg, a move that would give the United States a toehold in Upper Canada and severely disrupt British-Indian relations by demonstrating British weakness and stripping it of a key fort deep in Indian-occupied territory. Unfortunately for Hull, his plans were intercepted earlier by the British, who were preparing their own defense, and his progress was anything but rapid. Hull's army was a motley crew of regulars and militia hailing from several states, which meant rivalries, conflicting orders, and a mingling of command structures that ruffled the feathers of many officers, making his force more a coalition than a proper army.

After an apprehensive crossing into Upper Canada, hampered by the refusal of two hundred Ohio militiamen to serve outside the United States, and paranoia about imminent Indian attacks, Hull vacillated between bravado and timidity.

He issued a proclamation to the local inhabitants declaring that he had come to liberate them from British rule and warning them to stay at their homes. "Separated by an immense ocean and extensive wilderness from Great Britain, you have no participation in her councils, no interest in her conduct—you have felt her tyranny, you have seen her injustice," Hull declared. Ever mindful of Indians, he also threatened to execute anyone caught fighting alongside Britain's Indian allies, vowing that "No white man found fighting by the side of an Indian will be taken prisoner." When faced with news of British forces moving against him, however, he abandoned his attack plans and, to the disgust of many of his officers, quickly retreated his numerically superior force to Detroit. Well-supplied and secure in a fort that had become famous for withstanding a lengthy Indian siege fifty years earlier, Hull nevertheless panicked again and quickly surrendered his army, the fort, along with enough arms and supplies for an entire campaign season, the Michigan Territory, and sixteen hundred Ohio militia who were not even at the fort, to a much smaller counterattacking British force. Meanwhile the Americans lost or abandoned the key Great Lakes forts of Mackinac and Dearborn. Within a matter of weeks the entire Northwest frontier of the United States collapsed.

Although the other two prongs of the invasion did not match Hull's debacle, they were utter failures as well. Commanded by the often confused and complacent Henry Dearborn, the forces were mired in the same sort of conflicts of command between regulars and the state militias. In October, American forces attacked Queenston Heights across the Niagara River, but their early success, which included killing the British commander and victor at Detroit, Isaac Brock, was offset by the refusal of the New York militia to cross into Canada. This forced the invading troops to surrender once British reinforcements arrived. Dearborn's own force of eight thousand men did not even bother to carry out its planned invasion of Lower Canada, which was supposed to be the main attack. Instead, Dearborn readily accepted a British ceasefire—established under the auspices of giving the American government time to end the war in response to Britain's suspension of the Orders in Council. An exasperated Madison administration rejected the offer on the grounds that it would just buy time for the British to ready their defenses, and Dearborn meandered his way northward in late autumn, scrapping his attack plan when some of his militia refused to cross into Canada and the weather turned cold.[3]

All of this was dissected and rehashed in newspapers and government houses throughout the Anglo-American Atlantic world. No one denied that the planned invasion of Canada had been an unmitigated disaster for the United States. The American responses to Hull's surrender were full of disbelief followed by outrage. The war's critics not surprisingly railed against Hull's hubris as reflective of the Madison administration and the folly of the war. The war's proponents searched for someone to blame, and Hull was the primary target. *Niles' Weekly Register* was typical of pro-war papers in that at first it refused to believe early reports of the surrender and then assumed traitors in Hull's army had sabotaged it, before finally accepting the original accounts and lashing out against Hull. The *Missouri Gazette*, like other Western papers, headlined the account with the word *treason* in large type.[4] James Monroe called the fiasco "this most mortifying and humiliating event." Hull and his force, stated Monroe, had panicked.[5] Thomas Jefferson was even less sympathetic. After excusing Madison for making a poor choice in appointing Hull, Jefferson argued, "We can tell by his plumage whether a cock is dunghill or game. But with us cowardice and courage wear the same plume." He expected that "Hull will of course be shot for cowardice and treachery."[6] Though a court martial later found Hull guilty and sentenced him to be executed, Madison proved more merciful than Jefferson and gave Hull a reprieve.

A number of war supporters also took aim at the federal government. In his speech to the state legislature at the end of 1812, Ohio's governor tactfully affirmed his resolute support for the declaration of war but blamed poor preparation on the part of the federal government for the disastrous campaigns: "It is to be regretted that the congress of the United States has not provided a more efficacious system of militia organization, discipline and duty," leaving Ohio citizens little choice but to take defensive matters into their own hands.[7] Henry Clay was more blunt, blasting Madison in a private letter in December 1812, and declaring "[i]t is in vain to conceal the fact . . . Madison is wholly unfit for the storms of war."[8] Madison publicly blamed the state militias for failing to support the invasions. In his November message to Congress, he singled out New York's militia for the defeat at Queenston Heights, saying they did not provide "the expected support" for the nation's troops who had executed the initial attack "with distinguished gallantry, and were for a time victorious."[9]

The most finessed apology came from the Republican leadership's bugle, the *National Intelligencer*. In an editorial that was widely reprinted and plagiarized in newspapers throughout the nation, the paper argued that by their very nature republics were doomed to struggle in the first years of war. Claiming that because of popular peacetime aversions to standing armies, taxes, and strong national governments "it was impossible to make those provisions antecedent to a declaration of war, which are indispensable to its successful prosecution." "Ours is a government, whose operations must be slow and limited," the editorial explained, and although "we rejoice that it is so" in peacetime, war exposes its limitations.[10] Thus the disasters of 1812 were, according to the official line, at least in part the fault of every American who desired civil liberties, low taxes, and a limited government.

To counter the disasters in the field, the war's supporters worked tirelessly to create the idea of unified national support for the war. As in the American Revolution, they contended that the once-divided American people would be united in a trial by fire. Madison, Jefferson, Clay, and a host of other Republican leaders and public supporters asserted that war would unite Americans and call out its internal enemies.[11] Even John Adams declared that a victory would "generate a national self-respect, a Spirit of Independence and a national Pride which has never before been felt in America."[12] From this seed the popular notion that the War of 1812 was a second war of independence was born. As an orator proclaimed at a Massachusetts Fourth of July celebration, the present conflict was about securing Americans' revolutionary legacy: "At the moment we are celebrating the triumph of the fathers in the acquisition of independence, their sons are challenged to vindicate their title to this fairly purchased inheritance." In a fashion that was typical of the war's public supporters that summer, he continued by styling the War of 1812 as a test for the next generation, asserting "the period has arrived when the basis of our independence and the stability of a republican government are to be proved by adversity."[13]

Faced with a divided nation, supportive editors packed their newspapers and magazines with accounts of patriotism, unity, and valor in an attempt to create something akin to the Spirit of '76—the mythological moment in which Americans set aside their differences and united to expel the British from America. The Fourth of July celebrations in 1812 signaled the launch for this ideal. As the Charleston's *City Gazette* reflected, "there has not been a return of the Anniversary [of independence] calculated to excite such sentiments and feelings as the one so recently passed." "Sentiments that have been smothered beneath the ashes of oblivion, after a lapse of near thirty years appear," the paper continued, "again in all their original splendor, and the 4th of July 1812 will be looked upon, by the future American patriot, as the day when political animosities were merged in the love of country, and one undivided sentiment of patriotic ardour animated every American bosom."[14] Newspapers across the country printed accounts of celebrations far and near, with the *National Intelligencer* acting as chief compiler. By mid-August, the editor feigned a protest under the headline of "Public Feeling," stating that "[w]e found these evidences of patriotic sentiment . . . so numerous as to make the narrow limits of our paper."[15] Poems such as "Incentives to Valor," first published by the *Albany Register*, even rewrote the story of 1812 so that it more closely paralleled the American Revolution. Calling on the "Sons of valor," the poem commanded them to "Rise, avenge our injured fame" and to "repel their bold invasions"—despite the only invaders in 1812 being from the United States.[16]

The idealized Spirit of 1812 was gendered. Men were expected to express their patriotism through military service. Service in the militia as proof of manliness

Figure 4.1 John Lewis Krimmel, Fourth of July in Centre Square (1812). Courtesy of the Pennsylvania Academy of the Fine Arts, Philadelphia. Born in Germany but a resident of Philadelphia, Krimmel depicted the festive scene at the city's Fourth of July celebration following America's declaration of war. The scene highlights the social diversity that could be found at the celebrations that took place throughout the country: Quakers, affluent women, children, members of the lower ranks, and blacks—albeit often clustered. The celebrations often included parades, balls, dinners, and plenty of alcohol. They also featured public orations, many of which found a national audience as pamphlets and through extraction in newspapers.

was a long-established tradition in America, which continued to hold sway particularly in the South and the West, where a white male could assert his status by participating in something from which blacks and women were excluded.[17] Recruiting advertisements and calls to arms consistently emphasized that Britain had insulted the United States (often depicted as the female Columbia), and it was the job of America's men to protect her and her children. As the popular poem "Incentives to Valor" proclaimed, America was where "liberty her throne's erected," and defeating the British invaders would save her and result in "unborn millions shout[ing] your praises." The symbolic passing of this responsibility from father to son was emphasized in such widely reprinted accounts as the petition made by fifty-eight retired Tennessee war veterans, who volunteered to serve in garrisons in order to allow the young men to fight outside the region. "In doing this," the veterans declared, "we feel a pride in offering ourselves a second time on the Altar of Liberty. Although with the fatigues of the war, and the wear of many years since, our bodily powers are much impaired, yet our zeal for our country's good is not abated." Although first printed in Tennessee's *Carthage Gazette* a few months before the war, the account became a staple in the autumn of 1812. "He must deserve to be a slave," proclaimed the *Gazette*, "whose pulse does not beat in union with these grey headed volunteers, called by the Genius of Liberty, once more from their peaceful dwellings to the tented field, to protect that Independence they fought to purchase."[18]

Even James Monroe, the fifty-four-year-old secretary of state and Revolutionary War veteran, felt some pressure to defend his manliness. Writing to the much younger Henry Clay in late August, Monroe claimed that he wanted to participate in a campaign to reclaim Detroit. "I most sincerely wish that the President could dispose of me, and at this juncture, in the military line," wrote Monroe. "If circumstances would permit, and it should be thought that I could render any service, I wo[ul]d. In a few days, join our forces assembling beyond the Ohio, & indeavor to recover the ground which we have lost." Just in case Clay had not been sufficiently impressed, Monroe wrote a few weeks later reporting that he had asked the president's permission to go west. According to Monroe's account, Madison originally consented, but "on mature reflection," insisted that Monroe stay in Washington. A likely relieved Monroe offered the improbable claim to Clay that "I had no opinion on the subject but was prepar'd, to act in any situation in which it might be thought I might be most useful."[19]

The war's supporters also called upon women to make specific contributions as part of the push for a Spirit of 1812. Although thousands of poor women endured considerable hardships as camp women attached to both armies, theirs was not a role that the nation celebrated, or even significantly discussed.[20] Instead, pro-war commentators took a classist approach, addressing middling women and calling upon them to encourage the military endeavors of their men folk and remember their deeds. "Incentives to Valor" charged women in its concluding lines:

> Daughters of immortal story,
> Ye who boast Columbia's name,
> Oh! Inspire the love of glory,
> And record your heroes' fame!

Women's diaries and private correspondence of the era indicate awareness of political events and willingness to comment privately on them. Rosalie Stier Calvert regularly used her analysis of politics to assess the stability of the American bond market for the investments of her relatives and herself, and many

American women undoubtedly had similar concerns, albeit on a more modest fiscal scale.[21] "Incentives to Valor" was signed "Emma," and similar non-partisan essays and poems generically imploring Americans to do their duty appeared regularly under female pennames. Yet premeditated public statements by women that sharply criticized the government or supported a particular political action or military strategy were almost entirely absent from the public record. The *Alexandria Daily Gazette* was rare in engaging a female reader's critique of the federal budget in May 1814, and the editor clearly felt uncomfortable doing so. While declaring he did not subscribe to the popular adage "a woman in politics, is like a Monkey in a China Shop—She can do no good, & may do a great deal of harm," the editor still insisted that "the *political* favors of our female friends are less acceptable, than any other they could confer upon us."[22]

The prescriptions for women and their actions were not unique to either 1812 or the United States. To a great extent what became known as "female patriotism" in the War of 1812 was defined by memories of women's activities in the American Revolution, which provided a narrow, yet still public, scope for women's participation in national events.[23] Thus, just as their mothers had supported the troops via an extension of their domestic duties by making homespun shirts and organizing charity drives, their daughters were expected to do the same in 1812. As one commentator remarked in September, "In the revolutionary war our females acquitted themselves well and so will their daughters of the present day."[24] Americans could also take as their example the heavily publicized conduct of middling and elite British women, who had been implored during the wars against France to extend their domestic sphere so as to offer public endorsements of the war effort. They responded by churning out tens of thousands of socks, waistcoats, and shirts for their fighting men; they raised funds for the care of those who were wounded; and they organized parades to send them off in style and hosted balls to celebrate their return.[25] In fact, between 1798 and 1800 alone, more than ninety women in Britain were known to have presented flags to volunteer regiments, typically in public spaces with the full regiment assembled and almost always covered by the press.[26] Having a son in military service was celebrated in the press as a badge of feminine honor, as when the dowager Viscountess Charlotte Howe attended court in 1776 to mark the occasion of the elevation of her son, Sir William Howe, the commander of Britain's armies in America, to the Order of the Bath. The *General Evening Post* offered its congratulations to her, noting "this worthy Lady had had the singular happiness of seeing three of her sons head the British armaments against the common enemy" and likening her to a "Roman matron, in the virtuous times of the republic."[27]

In an effort to rekindle female patriotism, the pro-war American press abounded with stories in the summer and autumn celebrating women's contributions that fit this model of extended domesticity. As in the American Revolution, women made clothing and raised funds for soldiers, such as the Ladies Stocking Society of New York, which knitted "Socks, Mockasins, Mittens, and Cloth Hoods" for American soldiers and raised six hundred dollars, and the "ladies" of Frankfort, Kentucky, who established a subscription to collect funds for soldiers.[28] During the embargoes that preceded the war, women had been called on to make material sacrifices too, just as they had during the boycotts of British goods during the 1760s and 1770s. This expectation continued once the war began.[29] One commentator reminded South Carolinians that in times of war "the women of Sparta carried their jewels into the public treasury, and became 'when unadorned, adorned the most.'" North Carolina's *Federal Republican* took particular pleasure in relaying a supposed British account damning English women's excesses in times of war while celebrating the corresponding austerity of American women. In America, the account argued, "each mother emulates the Roman matron Cornelia, and tells her daughters they are more precious objects in her sight, as they appear before her without jewels; since those ornaments cannot be had without strengthening the hands of the English, who hold up a sword to slay their fathers and brothers!"[30]

Women's symbolic support of military action could be shown through presentation of a flag made by their own hands or a sword purchased for the commanding officer. Such ceremonies were purposely public, with the receiving regiment parading through town in anticipation of the gift and recruiters standing ready to enlist any young men moved by the occasion. Such events were common in America's large towns and cities, but even small communities emulated these public acts of female patriotism. St. Louis's *Missouri Gazette* recounted for its readers how the "patriotic ladies" of Chillicothe, Ohio, raised money to purchase a sword to present to the commander of the local fort. "This tribute to valor," declared the paper, "is honorable to the character of the fair patriots . . . and will undoubtedly stimulate [the officer], as well as his competitors in the field of honor, to redouble their efforts in the service of their country in order to merit the future approbation of their country women."[31]

According to this ideal of republican motherhood, the greatest contribution a woman could make was to donate her sons for service in the state's armies. The pro-war press in the summer and autumn of 1812 overflowed with accounts imploring mothers to encourage their sons to enlist, and celebrating those that did. "Mothers, exercise over your children, the influence of the Spartan women, and bid them court glory in the face of death!" commanded William Crafts at Charleston's St. Michael's Church during his oration celebrating American independence. "Remind them of the valor of their ancestors, teach them the lessons of patriotism, and implant the spirit which is to protect your daughters."[32] The case of Mrs. Mary Pruitt is a typical example of the many (largely embellished) cases that the press celebrated. The wife of an independent Georgia farmer and mother to fourteen sons and two daughters, Pruitt enjoyed the pride of having eight sons on the militia's muster rolls, one of whom commanded a company. The widely reprinted account carefully noted that the Pruitts were not poor. They lived without debt, owned their farm, and had "the goodwill and esteem" of their neighbors. During a recruiting drive two sons were so "warmed by the sacred love of country, and glowing with patriotic zeal" that they enlisted in the regular army. The father, a veteran of the revolution, hesitated to give his consent out of "paternal affection" and called upon their mother to persuade them out of enlisting. Mary Pruitt, however, responded with "the heroic firmness and public virtue of the Spartan females" and encouraged her sons, addressing them "My children I will not say one word nor shed a tear to oppose your wishes—go and serve your country like men." And as they departed, she told them "My sons, do not shed a tear, and I will not shed one—go, in God's name—if you fall in your country's cause I will not regret it—be virtuous, faithful, and honest, and my fears are at an end." The editor of New York's *Military Monitor*, which like most papers that supported the war reprinted the story in some form or another, used the account to remind readers that women too must play their defined roles in this conflict—as supporting mothers, wives, and daughters. "Let those who think lightly of female virtue and patriotism," the *Monitor* extolled, "read this and blush for shame."[33]

Yet for all its supporters' efforts, the War of 1812 failed to produce a public patriotic outpouring comparable to the one in 1776, let alone their idealized version of the Spirit of '76. Female patriotism was ultimately partisan, with few women in districts opposed to the war producing clothing for troops or raising funds in the support of the war.[34] The tales of mothers enlisting their sons originated in the southern or western states, not New England, and alcohol was a far more common tool in recruitment than a mother's shaming.[35] The actual recruitment figures temper claims of the effectiveness of such tales. By 1813 only 9,823 of the pre-war authorized regular army of 35,000 had been recruited.[36] The war's critics also latched onto the public memory of the American Revolution and argued that the War of 1812 was a dishonor to its legacy. In this vein, Phinehas Cooke proclaimed at a New Hampshire celebration of American independence in 1813 that the people's rejection of regular military service shows how empty the claims of patriotic fervor were. "Was it a real, or bastard patriotism, which inspired the armies of our revolution, when our ranks were filled with men, who had something near or dear to protect?" he challenged. "Cast your eyes on our *present army* and see what composes it," he continued. "Are they the owners of the soil? Have they domestic altars, and fire-sides to defend? I believe this can hardly be said, even of all their officers."[37]

Madison won reelection in 1812, but it was not a wave of populism that kept him in office. His victory was the closest margin in twelve years and owed almost entirely to the will of the South, and even in several of these states the Republicans lost ground to the Federalists. Such stark regional divisions in a presidential election would not be witnessed again until the election of Abraham Lincoln.[38] Madison also failed to tie patriotic duty to congressional willingness to raise taxes and citizens' readiness to pay them. Despite a plea in his May 1813 message to Congress that "in recommending to the national legislature this resort to additional taxes, I feel great satisfaction in the assurance, that our constituents . . . will cheerfully give any other proof of their patriotism which [their country] calls for," neither Congress nor its constituents ever enthusiastically, or even properly, funded the war.[39]

The United States did not fare well in subsequent offensive campaigns. Despite mounting a series of invasions into Canada, the Americans came up largely empty handed as the combination of British regulars, Canadian militia, and American Indians consistently pushed them back into the United States. Problems of supply, recruitment, communication, inexperience, and an uncooperative militia beset the American forces' every attempt.[40] In his December 1813 message to Congress, Madison insisted that these setbacks were making the United States stronger. He argued that "the war, with all its vicissitudes, is illustrating the capacity and destiny of the United States to be a great, a flourishing, and a powerful nation."[41] Few Americans, however, shared Madison's public confidence, including the president himself in private. Public optimism waned rapidly in 1813, as the wealthy began to evacuate coastal towns for fear of British attacks, and the Royal Navy's blockade of America's ports was expanded and strengthened. Desertion mounted in the army and militia, and harsh attempts to stop the flow instilled only bitterness in an American public already suspicious of government power and armies. In a pitiful scene that became increasingly familiar, an emotionally moved camp guard at Plattsburgh, New York, described how a woman had rushed to see her husband, a Vermont man caught deserting the militia, and plead for his life. Exhausted from the hasty journey, she entered the jail, "and without speaking a world she fell at his feet, and for some time they both seemed to have lost the power of speech. She choked, sobbed and cried; and her cries and sorrows seemed more than a young and delicate female out [sic] to bear." She begged for his life with the commanding officer, but her husband was executed soon afterward.[42] Such scenes contrast sharply with the confidence and bravado at the start of the war.

Yet there were some bright spots for the Americans. York, the capital of Upper Canada, fell to American forces in April 1813. Led by Zebulon Pike, the sixteen hundred American raiders burned and looted (with the help of locals) much of the small town of six hundred inhabitants, escaping with about £2,500 worth of booty and the governor's mace, which the United States kept until 1934.[43] The raid cost a number of American lives, including Pike's, and gave further cause for later British retaliation against the United States. Although far short of the conquering expectations from the previous year, some Americans, such as the editor of South Carolina's *Pendleton Messenger*, celebrated the victory as "a presage of glorious events" to come that "will have a great effect on the British allies."[44] Most commentators, however, did not make much of the raid, instead simply printing the particulars. Papers in Britain and the West Indies followed suit, merely reprinting a few extracts of the official reports without commentary. Madison gave York less than half a sentence of his May address to Congress.[45]

Far more significant was Oliver Hazard Perry's victory in September over British naval forces on Lake Erie, which gave the United States control of the lake and cut off western Upper Canada. This forced the British to withdraw from Detroit and enabled American forces under William Henry Harrison to cross Lake Erie and achieve a major victory over the retreating British and Indian forces at the Battle of the Thames. Total casualties in the battle were light, fewer than a hundred dead for both sides, but the American victory included the death of Tecumseh, capture of the bulk of the British regulars in the district, and the return of the territory Hull had lost at the start of the war. Yet this dramatic victory fell far short of the nation's initial expectations for the war. Even Tecumseh's death, which devastated the morale of his followers, had a limited impact on the outcome of the Anglo-American war, because the Americans could not follow up the advantage and returned to American territory shortly after the battle.

Following the disastrous summer of 1812, Indians became a central part of public discussion surrounding the war. Complaints about trading rights declined rapidly after Britain suspended the Orders in Council, and American seamen were more imperiled by naval battles than by impressment once the war started. In fact, the subject of maritime rights appeared with less frequency in the press, all but disappearing by 1813. The exception was the opposition press, which occasionally raised the subject to mock the Madison administration for dragging the nation into a fruitless war for a forgotten cause. As the *Boston Spectator* summarily remarked, under a story with the headline "Free Trade and Sailors' Rights," "This ridiculous imposition has now lost its charm, even among the most perverse and ignorant."[46] Even *Niles' Weekly Register* admitted at the end of the war that the issue has been "partially forgotten."[47] All that remained of Madison's June 1812 war message to Congress were his brief complaints about Britain stirring up Indians living within the borders of the United States.

The events of 1812 demonstrated that the United States had good reason to fear British-Indian cooperation. Britain's alliances with Tecumseh's confederacy and other communities in the Ohio River Valley and Great Lakes region had proven crucial to the defense of Upper Canada, with nearly half of Brock's force that counterattacked Hull consisting of Indians.[48] Worse still, popular American fears of Indian warfare proved well founded, as a number of surrendering garrisons, retreating columns, and frontier families soon discovered. At the present-day site of Chicago, the American column of soldiers and civilians that had evacuated Fort Dearborn were slaughtered by several hundred Potawatomi allied to Britain, "without distinctions of age or conditions," according to one witness.[49] At the River Raisin in the Michigan Territory in January 1813, Indians allied to Britain turned back an American attempt to retake Detroit, massacred wounded American soldiers, and pillaged the surrounding area.[50] News of these attacks underlined the general American public's hostility to Indians—an enmity on which politicians played to drum up support for the war. Madison railed against Britain's Indian allies in almost every one of his addresses to Congress, continuously linking their attacks to the British government. In his November 1812 message, he complained that the "benevolent policy of the United States" was being undone by the British, who sought only to take advantage of Indian savagery as a tool for their own ends. In employing Indians, he continued, the British commanders had committed an "outrage against the laws of honorable war, and against the feelings sacred to humanity." Moreover, he concluded, British commanders and their governments cannot feign ignorance, "since the savages are employed with a knowledge, and even with menaces, that their fury could not be controlled."[51]

An Indian war was something virtually all Americans could understand and few would oppose publicly. The pro-war press chastised newspapers that failed to print a sufficient number of stories covering the Indian attacks, or even worse, stories that sympathized with the Indians. Public sympathy for the Indians hostile to the United States, such as the Massachusetts governor's remark that "the late unfriendly dispositions of the Indians may be accounted for, by the march of a hostile army into their country and the battle which ensued, many months before the war *was declared against England*," were rare; however, the pro-war press unfailingly reprinted them in an effort to show readers how shameful opponents of the war were.[52] The *National Intelligencer* led the charge against the opposition press, complaining that "these degraded journals, at the moment the British and their savage allies are ransacking our shores, and butchering helpless women and children on the frontiers, can occupy their columns . . . with falsehoods so base, as to be unequalled by any thing we have ever seen."[53]

As a result, real and imagined attacks by Indians under real or imagined British direction became a key rallying cry to arms. As a poem in William Charles's popular print, "A Scene on the Frontiers as Practiced by the Humane British and their Worthy Allies!" which played on popular fears, proclaimed:

> Arise Columbia's sons and forward press,
> Your Country's wrongs call loudly for redress;

The Savage Indian with his Scalping knife,
Or Tomahawk may seek to take your life,
By bravery aw'd they'll in a dreadful Frights,
Shrink back for Refuge to the woods in Flight;
Their British leaders then will quickly shake,
And for those wrongs shall restitution make.

Throughout late 1812 and 1813, war advocates packed the press with accounts describing Indian attacks. No detail was too gruesome or far-fetched to be omitted. That the British and Indians often played on these fears did not help. Brock threatened Hull with an Indian massacre when demanding the American surrender of Detroit, writing to the American general that "It is far from my intention to join in a war of extermination, but you must be aware, that the

Figure 4.2 William Charles, "A Scene on the Frontiers as Practiced by the Humane British and their Worthy Allies!" (Philadelphia, 1812). Library of Congress, Prints and Photographs Division, LC-DIG-ppmsca-10752. The image visually underlines the view that the Indians were brutal mercenaries rather than worthy allies who were defending their homes. The print shows Britain's American Indian allies scalping American soldiers and handing the trophies to a British officer, whose pockets are filled with money to distribute as a reward. One Indian's weapons have markings to indicate their British manufacture; he also has a medal with the royal seal, and his rifle has a price tag that reads "Reward for Sixteen Scalps." In the background British officers and Indian women dance around a bonfire.

numerous body of Indians who have attached themselves to my troops, will be beyond controul the moment the contest commences."[54] Meanwhile, Tecumseh underlined Brock's threat by parading his warriors in full view of the fort—circling them around to give the appearance of an almost infinite Indian coalition.[55] A terrified woman witnessing the display of painted warriors from inside the fort described the scene as akin to "standing at the entrance to hell, with the gates thrown open to let the damned out for an hour's recreation on earth."[56]

War supporters in the United States argued that Britain's alliances with the Indians made the British culpable for any violence or treacherous act the Indians committed. As Madison remarked in his March 1813 inaugural address:

> [The British] have not, it is true, taken into their own hands the hatchet and the knife, devoted to indiscriminate massacres; but they have let loose the savages armed with these cruel instruments; have allured them into their services, and carried them to battle by their sides, eager to glut their savage thirst with the blood of the vanquished, and to finish the world of torture and death on maimed and defenceless captives.

Other commentators went further, such as Richard Bache, who at a Pennsylvania Fourth of July celebration in 1813 declared that "allied with the savages in arms, and almost assimilated with them in nature the troops of Canada are ferocious ... [and] like the savages themselves, they seek not an enemy, but a victim." Operating with "the sanction of an organized government," he continued, these allies are "Excited only by a thirst of blood, they are equally gratified by the stream, whether it flows from the head of the old or of the young;—from the heart of a woman, or a man!" Panning Britain as "the self-created asserter of the civil liberties of mankind," he bemoaned "the blended trophies of the tomahawk and the scalp, the mace and the mitre."[57]

According to a number of war advocates, the choices were simple: either suffer an eternity of these attacks or remove the British from North America, and with them the Indians' ability to resist the will of the United States. As a result, the public call for taking Canada shifted away from the strategy of forcing Britain to negotiate on maritime issues advocated by Madison in the summer of 1812 and toward an unabashed demand for conquest. So long as Britain armed and supported the Indians, railed Jonathan Smith to the Philadelphia Association of Democratic Young Men, "our savage neighbours on the frontiers ... will continue to disturb our peaceable inhabitants, and burn their dwellings and massacre their families." The only solution, therefore, was the seizure of that "poison tree in our neighbourhood," Canada. "God forbid that I should defend a war merely of conquest," Smith assured his audience. "But to a politician or a soldier, Canada is no barren rock; it is a fort ... from which troops may pour at a moment's notice and deluge our people in their own blood." Canada, he argued, was not a colony, but a "foot hold" of British imperialism akin to "Gibraltar, Malta, Calais and Calcutta," designed by the British government to drain the blood and resources of the United States. In consequence, Smith, like a host of others in similar letters, addresses, and speeches proclaimed, "this is a war of preservation: a war in defence of our own constitution, our own laws, and our people and our own security."[58] Although Madison did not directly subscribe to these views, plenty of other politicians did, including the governor of the Indiana Territory, who, in a December 1813 message to the legislature that the *National Intelligencer* enthusiastically endorsed, declared, "It is essentially necessary that the United States should hold possession of Upper Canada at least, and true policy would dictate to our government to get possession and keep it, of both Upper and Lower Canada."[59]

During 1813, the American mood became vengeful. As the *Baltimore Whig* declared in May, "Hang *four or five* Indians for every American massacred, and if it does not bring them to their *senses* it will at least go some way towards their *extermination*."[60] Although the war with the Creek Red Sticks was seen by most Americans in and out of government as a conflict largely separate from the war with Britain and its Indian allies in the North, American animosity toward the Indians was evident in the Creek War. Under the command of Andrew Jackson, the American forces and their Indian allies annihilated the Red Sticks in a series of decisive battles that culminated in the summer of 1814 in the harsh terms of the Treaty of Fort Jackson, by which the United States demanded more than 22 million acres of Indian land, some of which did not even belong to the Red Sticks.[61] Although the Madison administration was privately upset with the harshness of the terms, the president had earlier driven the bandwagon of national animosity that led to the terms. Singling Jackson out for praise in his December 1813 message to Congress, Madison announced that he wanted to "not only chastise the savages into present peace, but make a lasting impression on their fears."[62]

The British knew full well that by courting the Indians they were playing a dangerous game that stretched the rules of so-called civilized war. Lord Bathurst, as secretary for war and the colonies, expressed concern about the negative publicity the alliances would bring, but he willingly took the risk. Writing to Sir George Prevost, Canada's governor general, in August 1812, Bathurst had little illusion that the commander's plans to use Indians as a key component in his defense strategy would not result in a number of atrocities. Yet, Bathurst argued, the warlike nature of the Indians gave Britain little choice: "I fear, there can be little doubt that if not retained as our Friends, they will act against us, as Enemies, and that if We decline to employ them, we ensure to ourselves all those

Evils from which we are desirous of exempting our Enemies."[63] Comment in the British press generally agreed, with such papers as the *Carlisle Journal* excusing the British alliances on the grounds that when the United States declared war, "many of the Indian nations were engaged in active warfare with the United States."[64] Moreover, added the *Aberdeen Journal*, the Americans knew they were playing with fire when the "American force invaded the territory of the Indian nations, with whose mode of warfare (established for ages before Europeans had a settlement in the country) they are well acquainted."[65]

The British had little love or even genuine concern for American Indians. The press during the Seven Years' War had demonized them as the basest and most savage of human societies past and present. Parents, judges, and social commentators used the "known cruelty" of Indians to reprimand impolite children, chastise criminals, and shame the London rabble. In fact, British disdain for Indians was so deep that during the American Revolution a public outcry followed news that the government had employed Indians to attack the rebelling colonists. After the American Revolution, the image of Indians had been somewhat rehabilitated by the Romantics as heroic victims of European imperialism.[66] Yet the entrenched image of the Indian as a remorseless brute had not been entirely shaken. Travel accounts continued to treat Indians with disgust, as when Hugh Gray in 1809 remarked to readers that, "[y]ou probably expect that I should give you some account of the Indians. Doubtless I have seen hundreds of them; but those were such miserable-looking disgusting creatures, that I do not undertake the task of describing them with any degree of pleasure." In keeping with British assessments for the past half-century, Gray poked fun at the French Enlightenment figures who depict Indians as noble savages, telling readers hoping for "a very pretty story about the dignity of the Indian, you have only to consult *Raynal*, who says a great deal more for them than dame nature warrants."[67]

The lack of popular outrage in Britain to Indian alliances ultimately spoke more to Britons' changing perceptions of Americans as members of the wider British family than to a massive shift in attitude toward Indians. Although Bathurst worried about negative publicity from Indian alliances, most of the public had moved on. During the French and Indian Wars, scarcely a tear was shed in Britain for the French colonists killed by Britain's Indian allies. During the War of 1812, Americans received similar disregard, thus representing the continuing shift toward viewing the Americans as foreigners. On the eve of the war, the *Times* openly called for Britain to establish alliances with Indians, noting their connections of commercial interest and a shared animosity toward the United States, while other commentators salivated at the possibility that a British victory would push the United States out of the Indian trade permanently.[68] Besides, others argued, it was naïve to assume Britain would not use every means available to defend its possessions from invaders. As a widely reprinted piece in the *Quebec Mercury* argued in December, "Can the Americans suppose that the British commanders, in these Provinces would suffer the Canadas to be wrested from the crown of Great Britain, if that evil could be averted by calling in the aid of auxiliaries who have a common cause with them?" "Is it the fault of the British if they cannot wholly induce [the Indians] to change their system of warfare?" it continued. The Indians fought as savages, and the Americans should have considered that before making "enemies of them by unfair usage, and now impute it to Britons, as a crime, that they make common cause with them, in the defence of British and Indian territory."[69]

Despite a common cause, the British and Indians had little trust and much apprehension between them. Brock was in awe of Tecumseh and reported to Lord Liverpool that "a more sagacious or more gallant Warrior does not I believe exist. He was the admiration of every one who conversed with him."[70] But this admiration did not transfer to other Indians the British general encountered; nor did it alleviate his general distrust of his Indian allies. He fully believed in August 1812 that these allies might turn on his troops at the first opportunity and slaughter them.[71] A few weeks later he wrote to Liverpool and complained bitterly about the decision of the Iroquois initially to remain neutral. Although a traditional ally of the British, the Iroquois had suffered heavily from the relationship—both in the wake of the American Revolution, when the victorious Americans seized much of their land in New York, and afterward as the British in Canada steadily chipped away at the remaining Iroquois homeland on the Canadian side of the border.[72] Brock's advice to his superiors on how to handle the situation reflected his belief that the Indians were neither sovereign nor equal to the British. "I shall think it my bounded duty at some future day to call your Lordships attention to the absolute necessity of removing this infatuated people from their present situation," he scoffed. "The loud voice of self preservation, every consideration of Policy recommends the measure,—although they have changed their tone with the late success yet the necessity of guarding against the evil they may still commit, is not less imperious."[73]

British regulars and the Canadian militia and volunteers shared Brock's fears, if not his disdain. Reports from the British commander of the recently taken Fort Michilimackinac pleaded for supplies on the grounds that without them "I fear there will be great murdering."[74] Officers used Indians to hunt down deserters, playing on popular fears, and the Canadian militia refused to turn out in some districts for fear that the Indians would attack their homes in their absence. John Le Couteur, a young British lieutenant who served in Canada for the duration of the war, complained in his journal about Indians scalping wounded Americans and stealing from British supplies. In a particularly moving account, he describes encountering an American prisoner of some allied

Indians, who begged the British for help. While "it was very lamentable to Him and excited our sympathy," Le Couteur wrote that "rescue Him we dared not, it would have lost us an alliance of seven hundred Indians, most invaluable allies they were." Such experiences so moved him and his fellow soldiers that when they went into battle, they gave the prayer "that no worse than a wound might befall me—nor fall into the hands of the Savages—death we thought preferable."[75]

Brock and other officers' complaints about Indian duplicity and unreliability are best interpreted as Indian independence. The nativist ideology that drove Tecumseh, whose warriors formed the core of Britain's native allies, applied almost as much to the British Empire as it did to the United States. The British had been less egregious in their abuses in recent years, but then there were fewer British colonists than Americans to cause offense.[76] To counter Indians' suspicions, the British government made an array of attractive promises. Liverpool wrote directly to Brock after studying the general's reports from the summer of 1812, instructing him not only to supply the Indians but also "to give them every assurance that in any negotiation for peace which may be hereafter entered into with the American Government their interests will not be forgotten."[77] Though perhaps sincerely given at the time, such pledges, like so many others made by Europeans over the centuries, proved disingenuous when Britain signed a peace treaty with the United States two years later. Indians, therefore, had every reason to be suspicious and pursue those policies that benefited their own interests.

In sharp contrast to the failures of the American forces on land, the success of the tiny American navy sent shockwaves throughout the Atlantic, starting with the American frigate *Constitution's* victory over the British frigate *Guerrière* in a single-ship action in July. Over the next year the United States chalked up a series of victories over British warships, including the defeat of two more frigates, the *Macedonian* in October and the *Java* in December, in single-ship actions. Strategically, the American triumphs meant little, as the loss of a few warships barely counted as a scratch on the power of the Royal Navy. Besides, the *Macedonian* was the only British frigate that the Americans managed to bring into a home port—the rest being too damaged or other British ships being too near to permit salvage. Moreover, America's success was short-lived, with the naval war effectively ending once Britain more than doubled its naval force in North America in 1813 and bottled up the American navy in ports for the remainder of the war. The Royal Navy did not lose a single frigate after the *Java*.[78] Most important, the American navy was unable to prevent Britain from blockading America's coast or from conducting coast raids at will. Yet from a morale standpoint, the American victories were critical. In the more than two decades of the ongoing war against France, the Royal Navy had lost only one frigate in a single-ship action.[79] The Americans defeated three in six months. As a popular orator boldly declared at a Philadelphia celebration of American independence in 1813, the "Spell of British power is broken!"[80]

Americans looked on the Royal Navy with a mixture of hatred and awe before 1812. As the enforcer of both the Orders in Council and impressment, the Royal Navy was a source of loathing. Yet the spectacular victories of the most powerful navy the world had ever seen were well known in America and begrudgingly admired. Against this goliath the United States had no ships of the line, a mere eight frigates to Britain's 124, and twelve sloops; and of these twenty American ships only seventeen were fit for service.[81] News in early 1812 that Congress might boost its naval strength prompted some chuckles in Britain. As the *Ipswich Journal* remarked, "with all due deference to the sagacity of the American Legislature, it seems rather an inversion of the natural order of proceeding, first to recommend a Maritime War with Great Britain, and then to set about building a Navy."[82] Such remarks would not have seemed out of place in Washington, where under Republican leadership the navy had been neglected for more than a decade. Last-minute efforts to boost its strength in late 1811 met with derision and failure, and Madison's original wartime strategy did not include the navy on the grounds that it was so small.[83] A minister's remarks to his Salem congregation on the national fast day in August 1812 epitomized the prevailing sense of impending maritime doom: "Where are the fleets and navies of those nations of Europe? In their fate we may read an instructive lesson."[84]

Americans reacted to the victories with euphoria and more than a little exaggeration. *Niles' Weekly Register* called the *Constitution's* victory over the *Guerrière* "one of the most splendid naval achievements in maritime history," and at the end of the year the paper likened America's success at sea to Britain's victory at Trafalgar—the greatest naval battle of the age of sail, which defined the popular image of the Royal Navy and its most celebrated commander, Horatio Nelson, in which the clash of some seventy warships resulted in more combat casualties than for the whole of the War of 1812.[85] Scarcely a negative word was printed about the American navy even by commentators hostile to the war. In his melancholy oration on the state of the country given before the Washington Association of Philadelphia, Charles J. Cox included praise for the navy, admitting that "amid the gloom and misery which surrounds us, let us still rejoice, at the valorous achievements of our little navy."[86] Even in St. Louis, the town took notice of naval victories. When news of Perry's decisive victory at Lake Erie reached the town, "the citizens with gladful countenance congratulated one another on the happy event, at night their joy brought forth the firing of cannon musketry, bonfires and a general illumination."[87]

Figure 4.3 Benjamin Tanner, "Capture of H.B.M. Frigate Macedonian, Capt. J.S. Carden by the U.S. frigate United States, Stephen Decature, Esqr., Commander," after the painting by Thomas Burch (1813). Library of Congress. Engraved and sold in celebration of the American naval victory, the triumphal print depicts the American frigate *United States* firing on the British frigate *Macedonian*, whose masts and sails are destroyed.

The American navy became what Jefferson described to Madison as the "balm" for the wounds the defeats on land inflicted on America's pride.[88] Biographies of American naval heroes past and present circulated throughout the country, with no detail too small to deserve mention. Recognizing that many Americans would be unfamiliar with naval warfare matters, a number of editors produced informative basic guides, such as a question-and-answer session in the *Niles' Weekly Register* with Charles Stewart, captain of the *Constellation*, who answered questions about ship classes, types of cannon, rules of engagement, and tactics.[89] Artists produced commemorative prints of the victorious moments, and the Boston Federal Street Theatre, deep in the heart of opposition territory, reenacted the scenes for eager audiences, even hosting the *Constitution's* crew on a special occasion.[90] Dinners for the commanding officers became national events, such as the one hosted in New York for Isaac Hull, captain of the *Constitution*, that fawning newspaper editors throughout the country meticulously described down to the menu.[91]

Bravado was never in short supply as Americans pretended that a handful of single-ship victories marked the decline of the Royal Navy. The *Philadelphia Aurora* printed a popular song called "Yankee Frolics" that began

> No more of your blathering nonsense,
> 'Bout the Nelsons old Johnny Bull!
> I'll sing you a song, 'pon my conscience,
> 'Bout Jones, and Decatur, and Hull.
> Dad Neptune has long with vexation,
> Beheld with what insolent pride,
> The turbulent, billow-wash'd nation,
> Has aimed to control his salt tide.[92]

Hardly a public dinner or celebration passed without a toast to the American navy. At the Fourth of July celebrations in the Navy Yard in Washington, the toast that received the greatest number of cheers (nine) was to the "American Navy, youngest son of Neptune, but heir apparent to glory."[93] Even after the American warships were bottled up in ports, Americans continued to celebrate their early naval victories. Following the usual Fourth of July festivities of a parade and oration, the people of Waterville, Maine, in 1814 held a dance at which toasts were given. Like other communities throughout the country, they raised their glasses to the American navy, in celebration of "Our Navy—The gallant exploits of which, cover its commanders with glory, and reflect a luster on the nation."[94]

The only significant partisan debate about the navy was who should take credit for its success. Federalists claimed vindication in their attempts to build the navy during the Washington and Adams administrations and defense of it as the Republicans dismantled it under Jefferson and Madison. As the war erupted, staunch Federalists such as Daniel Webster railed against the Republicans for America's weak naval state. "Without loss by accident, or by enemies," he argued, "the second Commercial Nation in the world is reduced to the humiliation of being unable to assert the sovereignty of its own seas, or to protect its navigation in sight of its own shores." "What war and the waves have some done for others," he lamented, "we have done for ourselves."[95] When news arrived of American victories, Federalists wondered at how great the victories would have been if their plans to build the navy had been carried out, and they were furious at Republicans who took credit for the navy's success. As North Carolina's *Federal Republican* remarked in mock magnanimity, "We are very well pleased to find that those who are in power, do now favor a Navy, and of course, that they have renounced their former opinions upon this subject."[96] Consensus, however, could be found in agreeing on the need to continue to develop the navy even after the war. As New York's *Military Monitor* remarked as early as December 1812, with devoted resources America "will, in a few years, be in possession of a fleet sufficiently powerful to cope with the utmost maritime force which Britain can send into the American seas."[97] A previously reluctant Congress authorized construction of new ships, and Madison, who had not given much attention to the navy before the war, endorsed naval expansion. Although the Federalists had lost the national elections, they won the fight over the navy. As a Philadelphia Federalist declared in 1814, "We now behold men exalting to the highest pinnacle of glory the navy which but the other day they affected to despise."[98]

The British reacted to the early defeats with horror. In 1812 the Royal Navy held pride of place among the armed services in the hearts and minds of the nation. The strength of the navy was how ordinary Britons measured the nation's health, for the navy protected the empire and the trade routes that made Britain strong, and so whereas army bills met with groans in the House of Commons, calls for increased naval spending typically aroused nods of agreement.[99] In fact, the navy was so foremost in the public imagination that the news of the loss of the single frigate *Guerrière* overshadowed the nearly simultaneous arrival of accounts of Brock's far more strategically important victory over Hull and the capture of Detroit. As Henry Goulburn, Bathurst's undersecretary for war and the colonies and the man on whose shoulders the daily burden of running the war fell, reflected, the "public . . . scarcely appreciated this [Brock's] success as the ship which brought [it] home brought also the intelligence of the capture of the British frigate *Guerrière*. . . . The feeling in the British Public in favor of the Navy rendered in their eyes the military triumph no compensation for the Naval disaster."[100] The *Times* called the loss of the *Guerrière* a "disaster" with which "England is but little familiar." Admitting the "loss of a single frigate by us, when we consider how all the other navies of the world have been dealt by, is, it is true, a small one . . . it is almost nothing," the *Times* confessed that "we know not any calamity of twenty times its amount."[101] Even the prince regent expressed his frustration when opening Parliament in November, noting that although "We rejoice that the attempts of the United States to invade Upper Canada have added laurels to the many victories of our soldiers" it was shocking that "the only maritime trophy, on either side, [was] the enemy's."[102]

As the Royal Navy suffered a string of defeats, the embarrassment and frustration only increased. Writing in response to the loss of the frigate *Java*, the *Times* printed a lengthy editorial summarizing the outrage of a nation that was expressed from Plymouth to Aberdeen. "Any one who had predicted such a result of an American war, this time last year, would have been treated as a madman or a traitor," the *Times* raged. "He would have been told, if his opponents had condescended to argue with him, that long ere seven months had

elapsed, the American flag would have been swept from the seas, the contemptible navy of the United States annihilated, and their maritime arsenals rendered
a heap of ruins." The truth, exclaimed the paper, was worse than could have been
imagined: "not a single American frigate has struck her flag. They insult and
laugh at our want of enterprize and vigour." In a fit of exaggeration worthy of its
American counterparts, the *Times* proclaimed that the consequence of such an
embarrassment would be ruinous: "It will waste away the strength of the country, and what is worse, it will break down the national spirit, so that gallant enterprise and far-sighted undertakings will become foreign to our very nature, and
the English character will dwindle into effeminacy and decrepitude."[103]

Excuses and finger pointing began soon after news of the *Guerrière* arrived.
Commentators quickly pointed out that the *Constitution* was significantly larger
in tonnage, guns, and crew, and that in many ways the new American frigates
were closer to ships of the line than British frigates. The proliferation of tables,
detailed eyewitness accounts, and in-depth analyses throughout the British
press verified all of this. Even in Oxford (one of the furthest points from the sea
in Britain), the local paper printed a slew of articles that offered statistics by way
of apology for the defeat.[104] Not surrendering, argued the *Caledonian Mercury*,
would have resulted in needless further bloodshed and would have made the
British captains executioners of their own men.[105] Naval historians have since
agreed on all these points, and at the time so did the British Admiralty, which in
July 1813 ordered its frigate captains not to engage in single-ship actions with the
American frigates.[106]

Papers from across the political spectrum took the opportunity to blame the
Liverpool ministry for its role in the fiasco. "The war with America ought to
have been foreseen" years before, complained the *Morning Chronicle*, "yet such
was the total want of foresight, or of ignorance" that Britain's merchant shipping was being ravaged and its flag insulted.[107] For the *Times*, writing in response
to the capture of the frigate *Macedonian*, the problem boiled down to a simple
question. "The American frigates are said to be equal to line-of-battle ships,"
the paper stated. "The reply to this is very obvious," it continued, "Why, then,
had not we line-of-battle ships to fight them?"[108] In response, John Wilson
Croker, secretary to the Admiralty, in 1813 wrote ten letters to the sympathetic
London Courier under the penname "Nereus." Croker defended the actions of
the Admiralty and Liverpool ministry, insisting that adequate ships were in
American waters and that Britain's defeats were a case of ships meeting in
chance encounters.[109]

Nevertheless, few Britons took comfort in the statistics and official assur-
ances. Setting aside arguments about deployment, cannon size, and seamanship,
the *Naval Chronicle*, a much respected magazine established for the use of
navy men and amateur enthusiasts, printed a reader's letter that best summarized

Figure 4.4 George Cruikshank, "British Valour and Yankee Boasting or, Shannon versus Chesapeake" (London, 1813). Library of Congress, Prints and Photographs Division, LC-USZC4-5918. The print celebrates the victory of the HMS *Shannon* over the *Chesapeake* by depicting a British boarding party easily subduing the cowardly American crew. One British sailor calls out, "Stand and clear messmate whilst I heave a few of these lubberly Yankee Doodles overboard." In the background, a group of American men and women gaze disappointedly at the empty table at which they had planned a celebratory dinner for the *Chesapeake*'s officers. The host ominously tells waiting guests, "Friends, I think you had better come & sit down for if we wait till the Chesapeake comes back I am afraid the Dinner will get Cold."

the national mood. Defeat "has produced no slight sensation in the mind of every man, interested in the honour of his country, and that of the British navy," it stated. The American frigates were superior in weight, metal, and size of crew, and the British seaman had fought well, it continued, but such excuses did not counter the "stain on our naval arms." In a call to arms, the *Chronicle* declared that only vengeance and punishment would remove it. "Let us not, however, trifle with them longer," it asserted, "or allow their temerity, in pretending to dispute the command of the ocean with us, to remain longer unpunished."[110]

E. BOASTING or, Shannon *versus* Chesapeake

A modicum of redemption came the following summer, when the British frigate *Shannon* defeated and captured the *Chesapeake* in June. It had been an unusually long wait for the British for good naval news, and never before in the history of Britain had a single frigate prompted so much rejoicing. The ship's captain, Philip Broke, became a national hero whom the prince regent singled out for praise and made a baronet.[111] Most formerly critical papers held out the victory as a vindication of the Royal Navy, including the *Liverpool Mercury*, which declared that "we do not recollect any naval occurrences which has excited so much expression of general congratulation, as the recent capture of one of the American ships of war" that marks "a glorious retrieval of our naval reputation."[112] "American Vanity," smiled the *Edinburgh Star*, "raised to the most inordinate height of their former successes in three very unequal contests, has been mortified in the extreme . . . by this unequivocal proof of their inferiority to us in fair and equal combat."[113] Only the *Times* refused to participate in the celebration, stating to its readers that "we do not think it proper to express an extraordinary degree of exultation on the present occasion." The *Shannon* and its crew had merely done what the nation had expected from all its ships. In the meantime, the paper mocked, "We look forward with confidence to a period, when it will excite no more surprise, to see an English ship conquer an antagonist of equal force, than the same circumstance used to occasion in the days of NELSON."[114]

Privateering—the age-old system by which governments authorized private ships to attack the enemy—proved more of a mixed bag for the United States. Hailed by war supporters who were too cheap to fund a professional navy as the "militia of the seas," privateers offered the federal government an inexpensive way to strike at British shipping, while simultaneously boosting the suffering American maritime economy with employment for sailors and seized goods for domestic markets. The venture could be lucrative. The *Rossie*, which operated out of Baltimore, was the most successful, seizing eighteen ships worth in excess of $1.5 million. The *Yankee*, operating out of Rhode Island, hit the jackpot when it captured the *San Jose Indiano*, which was laden with silks and other cargo from Asia that sold for half a million dollars. Even a cabin boy's share was $1,122— more than a year's wages for an ordinary seaman on an American ship or fifteen years' wages for an ordinary seaman on a British warship.[115] Such success attracted hoards of adventurous and desperate men to try their luck, thanks in no small part to the American press, which closely followed their exploits. In September 1812, *Niles' Weekly Register* began printing a list of the names and locations of all British merchant vessels taken by the American navy and privateers. By November, it had reach 253, and it finished the year at 305. Each number included by way of celebration the name of the capturing ship, its port, and a brief description of its cruise. Soon the list appeared in part or in full in virtually every town in the United States. Even the Ohio *Western American* regularly selected some of the exploits for reprinting, and in September 1814 it thanked the *Register* for its service, remarking proudly that with the list at over one thousand "this is certainly doing the enemy some damage."[116]

Privateering was something of a lottery. Crewmen typically received pay only by way of shares of the value of the captured ships and their cargoes, thus rewarding risk-taking behavior, and like most high-stakes gambling the house (in this case the Royal Navy) almost always eventually won. The Royal Navy captured 150 privateers in the first eight months of the war—roughly half the American privateers sailing in that period—and British prisons in North America, the Caribbean, Africa, and Britain teemed with nearly nine thousand American seamen taken from privateers by war's end—partly because so many had been caught but also because the British were reluctant to exchange them.[117] The life of a privateer was, therefore, a dangerous one, and the risk attracted a variety of men—even some who had no seafaring background at all.[118] In consequence, although the average haul for the roughly five hundred ships that sailed as American privateers during the course of the war was 2.6 prizes each, three-fifths of all voyages yielded nothing. Worse still, the British captured at least 228 privateers by war's end, meaning that far more often than not privateers returned to their home ports empty handed or not at all.[119]

The impact of American privateers on British shipping is hard to estimate. At their height of activity, they pushed West Indian insurance rates upward by 30 percent, and estimates for a loss to British shipping range from 6.3 to 25.8 percent of total merchant tonnage, although the actual figure is likely closer to the lower estimate. Authorized privateers captured prizes worth an estimated $45.5 million, nearly four times the prewar annual income of the federal government.[120] The reaction in Britain was apprehension followed by fury. News of the outbreak of war coincided with reports that privateers were swarming through the Atlantic. The stretched Royal Navy did its best under the circumstances, but soon American privateers were striking in British waters. The widely distributed *Morning Chronicle* expressed the rage of the merchant community in October when it lashed out against the government in a lengthy editorial. "We have in commission above 1,000 ships of war, the Americans have but five or six that deserve the name, and yet they have been allowed to commit the most extensive depredations on our commerce!" the paper raged. "Surely," it seethed, "if our Ministers by their obstinate perverseness precipitated their country into this war, they ought at least to have taken measures to protect our trade from the only molestation of which the Americans were capable."[121]

The British took an equally heavy toll on American shipping. British privateers operating from Britain, Canada, and the West Indies poured into the Atlantic and with the Royal Navy chalked up comparable successes. Three dozen privateers operated out of Halifax and, along with the Royal Navy, brought hundreds of prizes into its port. West Indian newspapers brimmed with advertisements of auctions for seized American prizes and goods.[122] So great was the flow of American prizes into West Indian ports that the American newspapers found on board became a steady stream of information for the local press, which routinely thanked British naval officers for donating them. The British press also kept score, with most papers printing the list compiled by Lloyd's insurers either in full or in part and gleaning whatever they could from the American press. By November 1812 the score appeared to be tied, with the Americans and British taking 187 and 185 merchants vessels respectively.[123] As with the American press, the most successful captures became the stuff of legend, such as the capture of the *Montesquieu* off the coast of Delaware on its way to Philadelphia from Asia laden with a reported $800,000 worth of goods.[124] At the end of the war, the British government estimated that British forces had seized 20,961 American seamen along with 1,407 merchant ships—more than the number of British merchant ships taken by the Americans, according to Lloyd's list.[125]

Figure 4.5 A typical advertisement for one of hundreds of prize auctions of American merchant ships that appeared throughout the British Atlantic. This one is for the *Lydia* and the *Columbia* that appeared in the February 2, 1813, issue of the *Bermuda Gazette and Weekly Advertiser*.

Yet the British public was not mollified by this news, expecting far more from its navy. The *Morning Chronicle* unabashedly printed readers' letters complaining about the "unfavourable" naval situation in the same issue as numerous advertisements for auctions of American prizes.[126] This frustration continued unabated throughout the war as outraged merchant communities attacked the government for what they perceived to be its failure to protect British commerce. Even as the Royal Navy asserted its authority over the Atlantic and bottled up the American navy, American privateers continued to cruise successfully. This stemmed partly from the Royal Navy's strategy of focusing on the American navy and blockade, but mostly this was a case of the Atlantic being an enormous place and the privateers being too quick and too many.[127] As the *Liverpool Mercury* railed in August 1814 following another summer's listing of British vessels captured in the English Channel and the Irish Sea, "We have naval strength far greater than our enemy; but we must now confess, that we have neither his vigilance or his activity." That privateers operated with seeming impunity along Britain's coastline was especially galling. What was the point of paying for the world's largest navy, the paper asked, if it could not protect its charges? "It is impossible to witness our present situation—insulted and injured, within sight of our own shores, without the conviction that there must be negligence somewhere," the *Mercury* asserted. "We pay for the protection to our trade, and we do not obtain that protection."[128]

Late that summer anger reached fever pitch, as merchant communities throughout the country organized highly publicized meetings to petition the government to express their lack of confidence in the Admiralty and demand greater protection.[129] In Glasgow, 554 merchants meeting in the town hall sent a petition to the prince regent complaining that privateers had "infested" Britain's waters and "proved injurious to our commerce, humbling to our pride, and discreditable to the directors of the naval power of the British nation."[130] A Bristol meeting of ship owners, traders, and merchants drew similar conclusions, resulting in yet another petition to the prince regent—this one with the lord mayor's signature. The higher insurance rates were worse than when fighting the French, ruining Bristol's merchant community, they complained. The navy was proving "incapable of preserving our own shores from the ravages of this infant state," and what was worse was the "flippant manner in which official answers have been lately conveyed" in response to merchants' concerns.[131]

Early American victories and complaints of British merchants aside, Britain had won the Atlantic naval war by the end of 1813. The U.S. Navy was bottled up in American ports, and by the following summer the Royal Navy had blockaded the entire American Atlantic coast. The British blockade was porous—at first to allow a limited trade to continue and later because of limited resources and bad weather—but official American exports fell from a peak of $108 million in 1807 to $7 million in 1814, while declared imports plummeted from $138 million to $13 million over the same period. This in turn deprived the federal government of its primary source of income of import duties, and so revenues fell from $13 million in 1811 to $6 million in 1814. Considering that annual federal spending during the war averaged in excess of $20 million, this was disastrous and forced the government to rely ever more on creditors who had waning confidence in the government's ability to repay its debts.[132]

Blockade runners, privateers, overland smugglers from Canada, and American merchants with British licenses and other prearranged agreements lessened the impact on the consumer economy.[133] James Ingraham's grocery store in the Maine village of Hallowell in July 1814 advertised a host of foreign luxuries, including an array of European wines, Chinese teas, Asian spices, and West Indian sugars and coffee, and Samuel Gilbreath was able to open a new country store in Ohio in the autumn of 1814 that sold plenty of overseas luxuries, including Asian and British textiles, West Indian sugar, and Asian teas and spices.[134] Perhaps the hardest-hit of the major ports was Baltimore, which endured an ever-tightening blockade for most of the war, but even its markets still traded in overseas goods—albeit usually at higher prices. Caribbean products from sugar to cigars, typically either produced in the Spanish colonies or funneled through them, remained on offer with minimal price fluctuations until the last months of the war. Even then, sugar in October 1814 was trading at only 52 percent higher than before the war. Asian teas and spices, such as cinnamon and nutmeg, were traded throughout the war. Even Jamaican rum continued to be sold on the Baltimore market until 1814.[135] But much of the continued trade in small luxuries came through less-than-legal channels, and such trade did not render much revenue to the federal government. Considering that the Madison administration estimated it needed $50 million in 1815 to continue the war on an offensive footing, the Royal Navy's superiority ultimately proved crushing for the government of the United States.

By the autumn of 1814, the American war machine had ground to a halt. The U.S. Army regulars showed promise in the Niagara campaign that year when they faced British regulars, but the tactical successes proved too small to make a lasting impact and, more important, the fruitless campaign drained the little that was left in the American treasury.[136] The treasury secretary, Albert Gallatin, had been a true magician, conjuring financing in the first two years of the war that largely did not exist, but by the autumn of 1814 he was negotiating for peace at Ghent, and his successors were less capable and working in more difficult circumstances. The federal government's finances, although precarious from the start, were in ruins.[137] Troops were not being paid, leading to mass desertion, and commanding officers were routinely forced to feed and supply them privately. Yet Congress feared its constituents more than the British, and it would not approve the necessary tax increases. As Madison admitted to Jefferson in May, "procuring money without heavy taxes" was essential for fear that the administration's internal enemies would use tax increases against it.[138] Creditors refused to lend the federal government money or buy its paper currency, and Europe's nations, broke from their own wars and deliberating their own futures, would not assist. Secretary of Treasury George W. Campbell determined in autumn 1814 that the United States needed $50 million to continue the war, and with no way to raise it he resigned in October. The following month the United States defaulted on repayments of the national debt. With no money for bounties, supplies, and wages, recruitment effectively ground to a halt, and when the Madison administration sought to solve its manpower problems with national conscription, Federalists and Republicans in Congress joined hands and bluntly refused.[139] The national outcry was intense, with only a handful of newspapers offering support. Boston Federalists called it unconstitutional, while Kentucky Republicans equated it with naval impressment.[140]

Yet the Madison administration's greatest tactical blunder in the war was its misinterpretation of Britain's early limitations in conducting the war against the

United States as a lack of resolve. As Madison remarked in his public message to Congress when it convened in May 1813, "That no adequate motives exist [for Britain] to prefer a continuance of war with the United States . . . is certain."[141] The American people would pay a heavy price for such misconceptions during the last year of the war, because in 1814 the British military was finally in a position to commit to the North American war. By the end of summer, Britain had a regular army in North America that outnumbered the active regular U.S. Army, and it was ready to pursue the longtime objective of hobbling the United States once and for all.[142]

5

The Empire at War

In the frozen depths of the Canadian winter in January 1814, Sir George Prevost, the governor-in-chief and commander of British forces in North America, planned his military campaign for the next season. Canada had been ravaged by a series of American invasions, and although he and his forces thwarted each one, the attacks were taking a heavy toll on Canada's inhabitants—particularly those living in Upper Canada, where most of the fighting took place. The American invaders were increasingly aggressive, destroying bridges, seizing stores, and most recently burning entire villages. Committed primarily to the war with France, the British government offered limited assistance at first, but by late 1813 the situation in Europe had changed and Prevost finally began to acquire enough resources to go on the offensive. Writing to Lord Bathurst, the secretary for war and the colonies, Prevost tellingly declared that the enemy's aggressions "set an example" that would "produce calamitous consequences to himself since the Theatre of war has been transferred into his own territory. Painful is such a retribution to those who execute it."[1]

The first eighteen months of the War of 1812 brought great hardships to the British Empire, as Canada suffered invasion, the West Indies struggled for resources, and American privateers ravaged British maritime commerce. Yet as the United States steadily spent its capacity to wage war, the British Empire was mobilizing its resources for an American war, and by 1814 Britain was setting the pace and direction of the war. By that time, Britain could have ended the war without any strategic loss. The war with Napoleon was almost over, and the maritime issues of impressment, neutral trade, and blockades over which the United States and Britain had quarreled were irrelevant in peacetime. The Royal Navy redeemed itself against initial embarrassments by bottling up the American navy, strangling American commerce, and attacking America's coast. Moreover, the Americans were afraid. Margaret Bayard Smith, a Washington socialite, felt the calamities of war for the first time in July 1813 as the British raided the American coast. "Until the late alarm I have never been able to realize our being in a state of war," she confessed privately, "but now when such active preparations are made, when so many of our citizens and particular acquaintance have marched to meet the enemy, I not only believe but feel the unhappy state of our country."[2] But this was not enough to satisfy the British desire for vengeance, and in 1814 British forces launched a series of offensives, wreaking havoc across the North American continent and exposing the vulnerability of the empire's enemies. Consistent with its initial aims before the war erupted, Britain pursued an aggressive strategy that aimed to humble the United States into accepting British superiority and to curtail its expansionism. Nevertheless, like the United States in the first half of the war, the British Empire failed to achieve its goals.

Yet the experience of the War of 1812 cannot be dismissed merely as a strategic defeat for Britain and its empire, because the war was a series of opportunities, struggles, and failures, for subjects from Kingston in Upper Canada to Kingston in Jamaica to Kingston-upon-Thames in England. Canadians won widespread support and admiration for their very public endurance of the hardships of war, which in turn more tightly bound Canada to the British Empire. West Indian planters and merchants paid dearly for their prewar push for a coercive American policy, but adaptive individuals benefited from privateering and increased trade with the Spanish Empire. In Britain, the government and public alike clamored for the punishment of the United States in tones that reflected the harshness of the cries for vengeance against Napoleonic France, but they ultimately learned the limits of British power overseas and relinquished the goal of a submissive United States and, for some, the dream of a resurgent British Empire in North America.

For inhabitants of British North America, the War of 1812 was a high-stakes affair that carried great risks but also potential rewards. Few Britons before 1812 had given much thought to Canada. Travel accounts were available, but they rarely went through multiple editions and were almost never extracted in newspapers before the war. Books on Canada rarely show up in the surviving records of circulating libraries and book clubs, even though travel accounts and histories were two of the most popular genres. On the eve of the war, William Cobbett even welcomed the loss of Canada, declaring "the *loss* of Canada I should deem a gain" for the nuisance and expense it caused.[3] The allegiances and interests of Canada's inhabitants proved ambiguous at best—despite early historians' attempt to treat the War of 1812 as the birth of Canadian nationalism in which the loyal inhabitants rose up and defeated the would-be conquerors. Canadian historians have since shattered that myth, but the importance of the War of 1812 to the rise of Canada's stock as a loyal, worthy component of the British Empire should not be underestimated.

In 1812 the British government did not expect Canada to withstand an American invasion. British animosity toward the United States was so great by

1812 that the government was prepared to go to war even though it would jeopardize Canada. Years of prioritizing Europe, the Caribbean, and Asia had left little for Canada's defense, so much so that its generals' military strategy was to fall back on the fortified city of Quebec and hope for the best—a strategy with which the British government agreed.[4] The British government made clear to Prevost that he should not expect significant reinforcements in case of an invasion. As Lord Liverpool reminded Prevost in April, Canada was not a priority. "It must be needless for me to point out to you that the Exigencies of Public Service in Europe, render it desirable that every Reduction of the British Force should be made in our distant possessions," he explained, so "that His Royal Highness The Prince Regent may be enabled to prosecute the contest with additional vigour in that quarter of the World, in which the Interests of the Country are, at the present moment, more immediately committed." In fact, Liverpool expected Prevost to return some of his troops, barring an immediate American invasion. "Under any other circumstances than those above mentioned [American invasion], I feel confident that you will see the Expediency of enabling His Majesty's Government to avail themselves of the services of these Regiments in Europe."[5] When war erupted, Bathurst, as the new secretary for war and the colonies, sent the prince regent's good wishes rather than troops, "on account of the warfare in which he is engaged, & the vital importance of the object for which he is contending."[6] This did not prevent Prevost from pleading for reinforcements. An exasperated Bathurst responded in November 1812, "I have already had occasion frequently to express the difficulty which exists of providing reinforcements of troops to the different quarters in which they are demanded, and I fear that I must still refrain from giving rise to any expectation on your part of considerable additions to the force now under your Command."[7]

In consequence the British defenders' initial successes over the American invaders in the summer of 1812 prompted shock and congratulations throughout the empire. The *Oxford Journal*, like most papers throughout the empire, was elated with the surrender of the American army led by William Hull, and it took the opportunity to mock the American general for his hubris. "There are not many instances on record of a General being so soon compelled to *eat his words*, as has been afforded in the case of General Hull," the *Journal* declared. "When he entered Canada, he published a proclamation to the inhabitants, in which he said, 'The Army under my command has invaded your country; the standard of the Union now waves over your territories.'" "Where, we ask, is the standard of the Union now?" the paper chided. "It has been sent to England."[8] The West Indian press chimed in with similar remarks, such as a sneering comment in the *Jamaica Magazine* that "This was the army which was to conquer all our northern provinces in the course of a few weeks!"[9] The news of Queenston Heights, at which the British again thwarted an invasion from the United States, reached

Britain in late November, resulting in further excitement. The *Times* featured the story in a lengthy editorial belittling the United States, praising Britain's troops, and likening the fallen general Isaac Brock to the Spartan king Leonidas, anticipating that "national gratitude will doubtless raise" monuments in Brock's honor.[10] Yet on reflection, most agreed that the long-term outlook for Canada remained bleak. Britain's diplomatic agents in the United States informed the government that the Americans would likely overrun Upper Canada in 1813, and few in either public or private doubted this. As the *Leeds Mercury* reflected after the first year of war, "This news taken collectively, and divested of all false colouring, will, we think, appear to our readers to afford little cause for exultation." It continued, "That our troops have fought most gallantly, will be universally allowed; but that there is too much reason to suppose that they will ultimately be obliged to give way before superior numbers is much to be dreaded."[11]

Most inhabitants of Canada were equally pessimistic and far more apathetic when it came to defending the British Empire. But then Canada was hardly "British" in 1812. In Lower Canada, the descendants of French colonists were in the majority, and in the sparsely populated Upper Canada, three-fifths of the inhabitants were "late loyalists"—Americans who had arrived in the 1790s or later in search of cheap land. Neither was especially loyal to the British government, but neither had an established opposition either.[12]

In Lower Canada, French-language newspapers that criticized the government had been squashed, and leaders of the Catholic Church, which was part of the establishment and enjoyed privileges equal to that of the Church of England, needed only look at Ireland or France to realize how much they depended on the favor of the British government. Despite the Concordat of 1801, in which the Catholic Church was nominally restored as the majority religion in France, many French-speaking Catholics during this period detested Napoleon for France's annexation of the Papal States and imprisonment of Pius VII, regarding Napoleon as determined to destroy the Church.[13] The British government also had the good sense in 1811 to replace Sir James Henry Craig, the conservative military governor-general of Canada who deeply mistrusted the French-speaking inhabitants, with the far more compromising and ingratiating Prevost, an American-born son of a Francophone Swiss colonel in the British army.[14] Although Prevost proved to be a poor commander, he deftly handled the diverse population of Lower Canada. In consequence, such incidents as the riot at Lachine in the summer of 1812, in which a number of French Canadians refused to join their militia regiment and rioted with locals, did not lead to a full-scale revolt.[15] The French Canadian judge in the trial that followed chastised them for being ingrates: "Canadians live so happily under the British government, without taxes or imposts, protected in their religion that they may exercize freely.... For 52 years you have lived under the present government. What complaints would you dare to make against it?"[16] Compared to other parts of the empire where non-Britons made up the majority of inhabitants, such as Ireland or the West Indies, Lower Canada required little maintenance. In fact, it proved less troublesome during the War of 1812 than the manufacturing districts in Yorkshire, where the British government sent thousands of troops to keep the peace against bread rioters and machine breakers.

The situation in Upper Canada was far worse. It was contested territory in that it was as much a colony of the United States as it was of Britain. Few of the colonists had come directly from Britain, and the local elites, who were tied commercially to the United States, shared an ideology that was more akin to the Federalists than to any party in Britain.[17] Brock, the military governor, took the provincial assembly's hesitation to adopt his war preparations as a sign of disloyalty. Sounding like Madison and his cabinet, Brock complained to his commanding officer, Prevost, in early 1812 that "I had every reason to expect the almost unanimous support of the two houses of the legislature to every measure the government thought it necessary to recommend, but after a short trial, I found myself egregiously mistaken in my calculations." The problem, as Brock perceived it, was "the greatest influence which the numerous settlers from the United States possess over the decisions of the [elected] lower house." Writing directly to Lord Liverpool that spring, Brock openly worried about the "Aliens, emigrants from the United States, who have acquired property, and consequently vote for Members to the House of Assembly" and complained that he was "surrounded by a population a great part of which profess strong American feelings, and attachments."[18] The long-term solution was to "remove the evil" and then find "real subjects to settle this province." With a war looming, however, the short-term solution was more problematic.

Even when the war began, the assembly blocked Brock's attempts to grant officers more powers to punish militia deserters and again rejected his attempts to suspend *habeas corpus*—a move that would have allowed him to more easily arrest suspected traitors. Martial law was not an option, he informed Prevost, because in such an event "I am told the whole armed [militia] force will disperse."[19] By late July Brock was nearly despondent, convinced that the population had already given up the fight. "My situation is most critical, not from any thing the enemy can do, but from the disposition of the people," he wrote to one of his officers, "the population, believe me is essentially bad—a full belief possesses them all that this Province must inevitably succumb—this pre possession is fatal to every exertion—Legislators, Magistrates, Militia Officers, all, have imbibed in the idea." "Most people," he concluded, "have lost all confidence."[20] Much of the militia was refusing to embody, and many of those men who did report refused to march. "What in the name of heaven can be done with such a vile population?" moaned Brock.[21]

Following Brock's successful defense of Upper Canada and the conquest of the Michigan Territory, the assembly slowly offered more support for his measures, but popular support for the war never manifested. Brock and many of his fellow officers and superiors in London interpreted the lack of support as disloyalty, but apathy might be a better term. After all, many advocates for war in the United States had been equally disappointed in their expectations that the American-born inhabitants of Upper Canada would embrace and aid the invasion. Assumptions that the late loyalists remained American in outlook proved entirely true, but what both sides failed to grasp was that being an ordinary American typically meant not wanting to risk one's life or property in a war. Mostly poor farmers hailing from the mid-Atlantic, the late loyalists were in many ways quintessential Americans; like their brothers and sisters to the south, they avoided military service, regularly absconded from militia duties whenever conditions became difficult or a harvest beckoned, traded with the enemy when a profit could be had, and remonstrated against the hardships of war. To be fair, British regulars were not keen on service in Canada either. Brock and his fellow officers complained about being relegated so far away from the main action in Europe, and the desertion rate of private soldiers was high. Tiger Dunlop, a surgeon in the British army sent to Canada in 1813, described with disgust how soldiers in Britain awaiting disembarkation for Canada would feign illness and injury through the summer and then miraculously recover in September, knowing that the transports had left and "there was no chance of a call on their services until the month of April following."[22]

Colonists' participation in military service in Upper Canada was extremely limited. Brock was able to persuade the militia in August 1812 to march against the invading Americans and on to Detroit only by lying to them about their mission, and even then he released half of the militia with him for fear they would all desert.[23] After the British victory at Queenston Heights in October, the British commanders summoned the region's militia. Yet less than a fifth reported, and almost all of those deserted within a month.[24] Militia reform the following year attempted to use higher pay, better training, and uniforms to lure men into the quasi-regular Incorporated Militia, but the effort failed miserably with a mere three hundred recruits volunteering for three thousand spots in 1813. Following more reform in 1814 and a failed attempt at conscription, the volunteer regiment still attracted barely four hundred men. In fact, the greatest Upper Canada militia turnout of the war followed the Americans' capture of York. More than three thousand men flocked to York after the battle to surrender and thereby receive American paroles. A parole was a standard alternative to imprisonment that armies issued to surrendered militia and troops whereby the individual promised that if freed he would not fight again in the war. Therefore, a documented American parole meant being excused from military service for the duration of the war.

The figure is even more impressive considering the total number of eligible men in the entire province was not much more than six thousand.[25] Not surprisingly, British commanders for much of the war regularly complained about the militia, rarely crediting them and almost always questioning their loyalty to Britain.[26]

Some British subjects in Upper Canada openly sided with the Americans, creating a civil war atmosphere on the border. Like the American and British leaders, many of Upper Canada's residents expected the United States to conquer the province with relative ease, and so a number of them, including members of the province's assembly, decided to join what they believed would be the winning side. Some were outcasts who believed they had suffered under British rule and some were opportunists, but most were people who had business and family connections on both sides of the border and so made a choice. The numbers of British subjects from Canada who fought for the United States was small; however, at 164 men, Joseph Willcock's "Canadian Volunteers" who fought against Britain were equal to more than half the number of Upper Canadians who volunteered for the Incorporated Militia in 1813.[27] Even the so-called United Empire Loyalists, the men and women who had opposed American independence during the American Revolution and afterward sought refuge in Upper Canada, were not universally reliable. After all, men and women became loyalists during the American Revolution for a myriad reasons, most of which had little to do with affection for the British Crown or were not guaranteed to be passed down to the next generation. In consequence, though these groups fought in the defense of Canada at a greater rate than other groups and even formed their own regiments, there were still some who sided with the United States.[28]

While the Liverpool ministry encouraged harsh punishments for such traitors, the British commanders and governments treaded lightly, having a better appreciation for the murky distinctions between American citizens and British subjects. The fine for a deserter in Upper Canada was a mere £20, less than a fifth of the annual income from a small farm of thirty or forty acres, and even this was not strictly enforced.[29] Courts martial were rare and those convicted typically received light sentences.[30] When Bathurst wanted to severely punish British subjects captured fighting in the American forces in 1813, Prevost advocated temperance. He argued against transporting such prisoners to Britain for trial and suggested that the matter should be dropped altogether, explaining that "it might not be advisable to bring them to trial, and [instead] to allow them to be acquitted for the want of Proof and afterwards restored to the ordinary condition of Prisoners of War."[31] After all, executing them for treason could alienate virtually all of the Upper Canadian militia, many of whom had been born in the United States and might face reciprocal executions if captured by American forces.

The inhabitants of Upper Canada may not have turned out in great numbers to fight during the war, but many suffered horribly during it. Shortages became so acute that poorer families teetered on the brink of starvation. Advertisements for groceries and luxury goods all but disappeared from the newspapers in late 1813 and 1814, and for periodic spells even the printing presses stopped for want of paper. The records of the Loyal and Patriotic Society of Upper Canada, a charity established in the province to aid the families of the militia and volunteers during the war, reveals how the war affected individual families. Petitions typically were for £25 or less, often requests for money to pay the inflated prices of food, such as the petition for the family of John Puller of Estobicoke, which received ten shillings a week. Other common claims were for aid following the death of a father or son, such as the petition of Mrs. Murray, whose husband was one of the few who died in defense of York in April 1813. She, like most widows, received the standard benefit of £25, roughly the equivalent of a year's wages of a common laborer. Some cases were particularly tragic, as with the young children of Donald McClean, another defender of York who lost his life. Their mother could not be found, and no relatives were known, so £25 was given to a neighbor until a relative could be located. As the Americans stepped up their raids on Canadians' property in the summer and autumn of 1813, claim amounts increased considerably. The worst incident was at Newark, when in December 1813 the American forces burned the town as they retreated from Fort George, leaving the inhabitants to fend for themselves in the depths of the Canadian winter. This infamous act alone resulted in the destruction of ninety-eight houses valued at £36,570, according to the charitable society. At war's end, civilians in Upper Canada would claim property losses of nearly fifty times the province's average prewar annual revenue.[32]

In 1817 the *St. Catherine's Spectator* printed a humorous dialogue in which the devil is welcoming various souls into hell. He acknowledges the most notorious by name and honors them with a seat near him, but when George McClure, the American general in command of the forces that burned Newark, arrives, the devil gives the general his own seat, declaring "I'll be no longer the Devil" and runs away in terror.[33] Although the American invaders set out with professed good intentions not to inconvenience civilians, such promises of goodwill and protection as found in Hull's 1812 proclamation were replaced by plunder as the war effort stagnated and American forces ran low on supplies. A loyalist serving in a volunteer regiment remarked in the summer of 1814, "the Conduct of the American Army was infamous in the Extreme. Ever since their late Invasion, they plundered women of every thing they had."[34] The Canadian press relentlessly portrayed American troops as marauders. In an attempt to rally the listless inhabitants of Upper Canada to the defense of the province, a *Kingston Gazette* editorial signed "A Loyalist's son" railed at his fellow subjects' passivity in

November 1812. He insisted they were wrong to believe the American forces meant them no harm. The Americans' object was conquest, and the men attracted to such a cause were not "the farmer, the mechanic or any man who has sufficiency at home," but instead "idle vagabonds, who are induced by the promise of our possessions, to undertake the conquest of this country."[35]

Yet demonizing the American soldiers is too simplistic. Although the Americans destroyed or stole a greater amount of Upper Canada's wealth, the British and Canadian soldiers and their American Indian allies did so more often.[36] Sometimes this was strategic, such as when retreating British forces destroyed the stores at Fairfield following the Battle of the Thames for fear they would fall into the hands of the pursuing Americans. Or when a camp of British troops and allied Indians destroyed Hanna Frey's frontier farm, trampling her crops and requisitioning the "Brick, Board and Lime . . . for the use of the camp." Frey, who suffered trials during the war that would have rivaled those of Job, lost her husband in battle, and the American forces later burned her house.[37] At other times, plunder was the work of organized criminal gangs, such as the one that managed to embezzle naval stores from Kingston in early 1814.[38] Britain's Indian allies were notorious for plundering civilians and soldiers alike. John Le Couteur, a junior officer in the British army, faced off with Indians on several occasions over thefts, including one instance in which an Indian drew a tomahawk and threatened him.[39] Although Le Couteur's confrontations typically ended peacefully, many of Upper Canada's residents shared the Americans' animosity toward Indians, and more than one farmer shot at Indians he claimed were thieves, creating tensions and compelling locals to form armed bands for protection against reprisals.[40]

Underfed British-led forces regularly raided farms in search of food. Shortages were particularly acute in Upper Canada from 1813 because the province could not meet the growing military demand, and the irregularity of supplies purchased from profiteering farmers in the United States and elsewhere forced individual soldiers to take matters into their own hands.[41] Le Couteur, who was not above dealing in stolen food, relished any opportunity to take official messages to the better-supplied American forces, whose junior officers welcomed him and shared their sumptuous meals of "Capital beef steaks, Potatoes, and a bottle of excellent brandy."[42] To deal with the acute shortage of grain, Francis de Rottenburgh, the military governor of Upper Canada, prohibited distillation of grain and then declared martial law in parts of Upper Canada in November 1813 specifically so the military could requisition grain from the province's inhabitants. Although not officially plunder, the locals saw it as such, including the elected lower assembly, which called it "arbitrary and unconstitutional and contrary to, and subversive of, the established laws of the land."[43] A number of farmers and their families attacked the soldiers and refused to hand over their grain at the reduced price—sometimes motivated by a desire to make a greater profit but other times facing their own shortages.[44] As one British army officer observed, "Loyalists and malcontents, for once, were unanimous in damning the government; rebellion appeared inevitable, threats to this effect were publicly and boldly thrown out."[45]

Despite the deprivations suffered by some of the inhabitants of British North America, the War of 1812 also brought opportunities to Canada and those connected to it. Merchants, farmers, and army officers all sought ways to profit from war from the start. After all, the arrival of British troops meant contracts for supplies and soldiers ready to spend their pay, and naval warfare meant prizes to be bought and sold. Even in Upper Canada, most inhabitants initially benefited from supplying the British-led forces, as the commissariat nearly tripled its annual expenditure during the war and the price of a barrel of flour rose 130 percent. The mercantile elite did particularly well, enjoying paroles that exempted them from service and gouging desperate civilians and the military alike, creating hard feelings that lingered after the war.[46] Still others took a longer view, looking for ways to turn Canadians into stakeholders in the British Empire and to turn Canada into a jewel in the imperial crown.

Nova Scotia and New Brunswick boomed. Merchants dominated the colony's legislative council, and the lieutenant governor, Sir John Coape Sherbrooke, was no fool. He issued a proclamation at the start of the war condemning predatory warfare on its borders with New England and took no steps to interfere with cross-border trade. He readily issued licenses to American and neutral ships to continue trading for a long list of provisions and other specified items, and when the Madison administration put a stop to the licensing system in 1813, he and the council encouraged continuation of trade by prearranging with American merchants to have their ships "captured," brought to port to sell their goods, and then released. The port town of Halifax thrived, funneling men and supplies from Britain to other parts of British America. When Britain shifted toward predatory war on the high seas and strengthened its blockade in the second half of the war, the Royal Navy and British privateers brought roughly three-quarters of all their prizes from the war to Halifax.[47] In consequence, the war tripled revenue receipts for Halifax and made fortunes for many of its merchants, such as the owners of the *Liverpool Packet*—the most successful privateer on either side of the war, raking in more than £250,000 prize money—and the now-famous Cunards, who established their shipping business during the war and made their first transatlantic passenger voyage in 1813.[48]

The social scene prospered, too, with brothels and taverns mushrooming near the dockyards, and balls and dinners filling the calendar of young British officers. Le Couteur, who was stationed initially at Fredericton, recorded in his journal at the end of 1812 that "some idea may be entertained of the Society at Fredericton when I relate that I was at Thirty five dinners, evening parties, or balls since I came up here on the 4th of September."[49] Local newspapers teemed with shop advertisements for luxury goods. A single issue of the *New Brunswick Courier* in August 1814 included seven ads for goods arriving from around the world, such as sewing silks, various sugars, spices, coffees, and teas. A typical weekly advertisement for James Codner of Halifax that autumn included muslins, printed calicos, Irish linens, "fine bombazetts [silk]," hosiery, shoes, boots, cotton pantaloons; a range of teas, coffee, spices, perfumery, soaps; window glass, paints, cutlery, stationery, crockery, and much more.[50] Thus even though Upper Canadians starved for lack of flour, the prosperous inhabitants of Nova Scotia could enjoy the finest "souchong" tea in porcelain teacups.

Although no town in British North America prospered quite like Halifax, Montreal's merchants took full advantage of the opportunities presented by the war. The city acted as a depot for supplies, arms, and men, as British and neutral ships sailed down the St. Lawrence and neutral vessels sailed up Lake Champlain from the United States. One issue of the *Canadian Courant* noted seventy vessels involved in dropping off British manufactured goods to be resold to American Indian, Canadian, and American customers.[51] As in Nova Scotia, officers danced the winter nights away, charming the wives and daughters of the local elite, including Prevost's own daughter, Anne, who celebrated British victories in elaborate balls hosted by the garrison.[52]

A number of the British Empire's subjects also recognized the war as an opportunity to promote Canada and more firmly affix it to British ideas of the empire. Canada received scant attention from either the British government or the press before the war, and many in Britain (and Canada for that matter) were willing to write off Canada as a lost cause. The elites in Canada responded by asserting its economic and strategic importance as well as the loyalty of the inhabitants, in order to demonstrate that Canada was worth an investment of blood and treasure to defend and cultivate it. Although the American loyalists who fled the United States after independence were a minority in Upper Canada, their story became central to the elites' case. Framing the War of 1812 as a rematch of the American Revolution, this line of argument emphasized the abusiveness of the American republic and the unreasonableness of its people. As the *New Brunswick Courier* remarked, "The present War was declared by the Americans upon the same selfish and insidious principles as the former, equally conspiring against the Vitals of Britain, as they are against all the anciently established Governments which had stood the test of experience for Centuries."[53] In Lower Canada, too, the War of 1812 was described as a rematch of 1776, when the American rebels invaded to find a population that rejected them and remained loyal to Britain. As the *Montreal Herald* exclaimed at the start of the war, this round would be no different: "The spirit of the whole country is awakened, every man burns in ardour for a musket, supposing he already sees again the discomfited ragamuffins of 76 attacking his dwelling."[54]

Others in the Canadian press went further, insisting that the present war was an opportunity to go on the offensive for a change and redress the wrongs of the American Revolution. Calls for expanding British North America's borders and the chastisement of the United States were common. Such commentators chafed at any mention of leniency or mercy. When British forces went on the offensive, the *New Brunswick Courier*, like almost all papers in British North America, demanded that the British Empire "Strike [and] Chastise the savages; for such they are, in a much truer sense than the followers of Tecumseh or the Prophet." "Let us not be so foolishly confiding," the paper warned, "as to trust again to the honor of veracity of the Madisons, the Jeffersons, or any of a tribe, to whom we are well aware that those principles are altogether unknown."[55] In a comment piece that gained an empirewide audience, the *Quebec Gazette* argued that the Americas needed to accept full accountability for their nation's actions. Letting the United States off lightly, the editorial insisted, would be a terrible error akin to the one in 1783, when the British government offered generous peace terms. "Let the hostility of the United States to Great Britain be attributed to its true cause, an habitual hatred—that vicious love of power, engendered by their political institutions." No neighbor, it continued, could have a mutual understanding with a people who are driven by "that insatiable thirst to gain which so invariably prevails in a country where money is the only source of distinction, and that vicious inquietude which is never contented with present enjoyments."[56]

The committees of trade at Montreal and Quebec were perhaps the most ambitious, formally petitioning Prevost at the start of the war to press hard for American territory. The 1783 Treaty of Paris, they argued, was a mistake in that it sliced off a portion of what was once Quebec (essentially everything east of the Mississippi River and north of the Ohio River) and handed it over to the newly formed United States.[57] Renewed war was an opportunity to correct the "ignorance, negligence, or something worse, of the then minister of Great Britain" by seeking "reparation of a most gross and extraordinary error in the negotiation and treaty" and by demanding the return of a portion or all that had been ceded. Insisting on the importance of securing the future of Canada, the petition also called for a new boundary line that would have stripped the United States of about a quarter of its territory, including the modern states of Illinois, Michigan, and Indiana.[58]

Under the Canadian elites' cultivation, the War of 1812 became a story of redemption. Although marred by early accounts of traitors and deserters, Canadians' reputation in Britain grew as loyal defenders of the empire, thanks in no small part to a combination of savvy propaganda and Britons' readiness to believe it.

The case of Edward McSwiney personified this shift. A convicted murderer, McSwiney was awaiting his sentence in Brockville's jail when in September 1813 American forces arrived and liberated the prisoners. While everyone else made their escape, McSwiney remained, refusing the Americans' offer of freedom for military service. The local elite found in McSwiney a cause to champion, and so they petitioned Gordon Drummond, the commanding general in Upper Canada and military governor, who in turn was moved to support the cause of the man redeemed by his nationalist spirit. "[S]o strong was his attachment to his Country," Drummond wrote in a plea to Bathurst for a royal pardon, that "even under those circumstances, that rather than purchase that freedom at the expense of his Loyalty, he chose to remain in confinement, and await his fate."[59]

Generally ignoring the statistical evidence of low turnout for the militia and commanders' constant complaints, newspapers, petitions, and assembly addresses heavily emphasized Canadians' loyalty and contributions to the war effort. Disregarding the fact that Brock detested the militia and openly questioned the loyalty of the inhabitants of Upper Canada, he quickly became a Canadian hero. His death at the Battle of Queenston Heights prompted widespread public mourning, and the provincial assembly with which he had struggled helped to provide an elaborate public funeral that included men from the same militia that had balked at marching with him a few months earlier. For anyone unable to attend, the *Kingston Gazette*, in a rare move, created an illustrated diagram of the procession to accompany its detailed description of the event, so that mourners could participate in spirit if not in person.[60]

Drummond's exchange with Upper Canada's legislative assembly in February 1814 was typical. Though he credited successful defense of the province to "Divine Providence" and a "small band of British soldiers," the assembly responded by explicitly praising the militia that Drummond had ignored, declaring that "We individually have witnessed the brave, zealous and meritorious exertions of a very large proportion of His Majesty's subjects, and the privations and sufferings they have undergone in defence of this Province."[61]

Commentators in British North America also worked hard to tie their conflict to the wider global struggle between Britain and France. Tying Canada's struggles to the empire's war against France was a way to lend greater legitimacy, broader importance, and imperial relevance to the North American conflict. The wars against France had dominated the press throughout the British Empire, and the colonial inhabitants of British North America celebrated major victories publicly and lamented defeats. In 1814, the *New Brunswick Courier*, like most newspapers, dropped all other news when peace was announced, informing readers that "[t]he publication of the Definitive Treaty of Peace, *at full length*, renders all other intelligence matter of secondary consideration."[62] The Canadian press, like elements of the British, West Indian, and American press, repeatedly asserted that the United States was under the influence of France both before and during the War of 1812. Thus by extension, in going to war with the United States the Canadians joined the global struggle against France. In response to the victory at Queenston, the *York Gazette* praised the militia, rejoicing that "[t]he brief Address of the immortal Nelson to his Gallant Sailors, seems acted upon in this Province, and everyman (as was confidently expected) does his DUTY."[63] Bracing for an American invasion the next spring, papers such as the *Quebec Mercury* and *Kingston Gazette* reprinted anti-invasion rallying cries the British had produced years earlier during the French invasion scares. Even Drummond did his part by likening his British troops in Upper Canada to "their comrades in the [Iberian] Peninsula."[64] In imitation of their sisters in Britain, a number of middling and elite women of Canada publicly endorsed the war with the United States by ceremoniously presenting local regiments with handmade flags and specially purchased swords. On a frozen March day in 1813 the "Patriotic young Ladies of York" presented the assembled third regiment of the York Militia with handmade colors in a public ceremony. It was a scene that echoed hundreds like it in Britain but, according to one observer, was "novel in this country," where British patriotism was in its infancy. Local editors, whose descriptions would be reprinted across the British Atlantic, recognized the event's symbolism for what it was. As the neighboring *Kingston Gazette* remarked, "may the gratitude of the . . . militia, for the confidence reposed in them by their fair country women, truly *shew itself in deeds*."[65]

For commentators asserting the connection between Britain and Upper Canada, the Napoleonic Wars marked the final divergence between the inhabitants of that province and the United States. John Strachan insisted in his sermon at York to celebrate the defeat of France that whereas he and his fellow subjects had remained loyal to the British system, the Americans had betrayed their liberal British inheritance. "That a nation far beyond the tyrant's [Napoleon's] reach," he raged, "and enjoying peace and tranquility by the generous labour of the people she fought to destroy, would have too eagerly claimed the execrable preeminence, of being the only nation that volunteered its aid to the oppressor of the world" was abominable. Britain's victory over France and the unexpected success over its henchman, the United States, Strachan insisted, was proof of the dangers of radical republicanism, validation of the British system under which Canada had flourished, and vindication of the American loyalists who chose to live under it. The "two experiments made in *America* and *France* . . . both have completely failed," he declared. "It is by peaceable and gradual steps, and not by revolutions, that the most solid improvement in the Science of government can be obtained."[66] In consequence, newspapers across Canada latched on to the poet laureate Robert Southey's poem for 1814 not as a news piece of what was transpiring in Europe but as immediately relevant to their own struggle in

Canada as a branch of that greater struggle against the forces that threatened the British system of governance:

> Wake lute and harp! My soul take up the strain,
> Glory to God! Deliverance for mankind!
> Joy, for all nations, joy! But most for thee
> Who has so noble fill'd thy part assign'd,
> O England! O my glorious native land!
> For thou in evil days didst stand
> Against leagu'd Europe all in arms array'd,
> Signe and undismay'd,
> Thy hope in Heaven and in thine own right-hand.
> Now are thy virtuous efforts overpaid,
> Thy generous counsels now thy guerdon find,—
> Glory to God! Deliverance for mankind![67]

Even the French Catholics, long treated with suspicion by many Britons, ultimately gleamed in discussions as examples of loyalty. Despite the bad publicity of the Lachine incident at the start of the war, the French inhabitants served as effectively and loyally in the militia as any other subjects in Canada. As a widely reprinted reader's letter to *Quebec Mercury* proudly declared in reference to the province's Francophone inhabitants, "there can be no doubt whatever but the Canadian population will cheerfully come forward, and maintain the warlike character of their ancestors."[68] The timely endorsement of the war by the Bishop of Quebec in October 1812 won favor, too. His statement referred to his flock as "an entire people brimming with desire to rise in a body in order to prove their fidelity and courage" and reminded them of "how very liberal Divine Providence has been towards you" by granting them a government that protects their persons, fortunes, and freedom and "which alone in the midst of the ruins of all others has manifested its honour and glory." The statement furthermore instructed all parish priests to publish the statement, include a prayer for the success of British arms at the next mass, and at the end of mass "shall be sung a solemn Te Deum, accompanied by the ringing of bells, in thanksgiving to Heaven, for the victory" of the British-led forces over France at the Battle of Salamanca the previous July.[69]

The statement scored points with the British government, with Bathurst greatly praising it and describing it as an "example which [the bishop] has given his flock of loyalty and attachment to His Majesty."[70] British proponents of Catholic emancipation in the British Isles, such as the *Liverpool Mercury*, hailed this cooperation in Lower Canada as a lesson in how religious freedom promoted loyalty.[71] George Canning, who had split with fellow tories, including Lord

Liverpool, over granting Catholics in Britain and Ireland equal political rights, declared in the House of Commons in response to news of success in North America, "most cordially do I concur in that sentiment of approbation . . . in favour of his Majesty's Roman Catholic subjects." "[L]et me remind the House," he shamed his opponents, "that these provinces of Canada, so assailed, and so attempted to be seduced, and so inaccessible to seduction, constitute the single specimen in the British empire, in which the Catholic is allowed to sit side by side with the Protestant in the legislature, as well as to fight side by side with him in the field!!"[72]

In Britain the Canadian interest traded on Canada's potential as a loyal producer of raw materials, in hopes of arousing support for defense and acceptance as a jewel in the British imperial crown. The total value of exported goods and materials produced in British North America was just over £250,000 in 1811, making it relatively inconsequential economically in its own right. By comparison, in that same year Canada reexported six times that amount in British goods to the United States, but this position of entrepôt existed only so long as Britain's trade disagreements with the United States continued and with them the need for smugglers, neutral ships, and trading ports in close proximity to the United States.[73] In consequence, pamphlets and newspaper articles relentlessly emphasized the theme that Canada, though relatively worthless in economic terms at present, was vital to the British Empire's long-term future, because whereas Canada and the United States had similar resources and growth potential, only Canada's population was loyal. If properly developed, they insisted, Canada could easily replace the United States as a grain and lumber provider for Britain and the West Indies, while acting as a conduit for the flow of British manufactured goods into the United States. One commentator went so far as to argue that the myth of Canada's inconsequence was a conspiracy of "the geographers and historians of the United States, [who] in their details of the extent, divisions, resources, and population, scarcely condescended to notice the remaining British settlements in that portion of the globe, as if they were anxious to hide from the inhabitants of Europe, the attractions which those settlements held out to the emigrant and cultivator of the soil."[74]

One of the more zealous proponents of the British Empire's potential via Canada was David Anderson, a merchant and one-time resident of Canada who produced a lengthy pamphlet outlining how Canada could become the launching pad of Britain's reasserted imperial dominance of North America. The United States was a formidable enemy that should be feared, he argued. "In the short space of 20 years she has doubled her population . . . increased her exports from about 16,000,000 to 118,000,000 dollars; her shipping from 939,000 to 1,911,250 tons;—and," he reminded readers, "before she had either raised an army or fitted out a navy, has actually, by her threatenings and artful negotiations, nearly doubled her territorial extent, and trebled her maritime resources!" Action needed to be taken immediately to curb the power of the United States. The American Revolution, he and others like him declared, need not be the final say on who would be master of the continent.[75]

Among the most effective tools in grafting Upper Canada to the wider public consciousness was the empirewide charity drive for the aid of the province's suffering civilian inhabitants. Organized by the Loyal and Patriotic Society of Upper Canada in late December 1812, the drive brought in well over £10,000 in the first year alone—a figure that exceeded the previous totals for any charitable drives in the empire for a North American–related cause—and aided nearly a thousand families in the province. Although originally rooted in the shirt-making efforts of the "young ladies" of York, the province's male loyalist elite dominated the Society from the start, choosing a name, designing a strategy, crafting its publicity, distributing the proceeds, and excluding women from any major organizational roles. The directors were so entrenched in the establishment that they had to take a vote to admit non-Anglican clergy, and even this extension only included Catholic priests and Presbyterian ministers. [76]

Publicity for the charity invariably emphasized two points: first, that the inhabitants of Upper Canada were loyal and true subjects, and second, that they were suffering for it at the hands of the United States. A donation to the charity therefore represented an act of both kindness and patriotism. As one of the London advertisements in the *Times* noted, the relief would aid "the Inhabitants of the British North American Colonies, whose gallant exertions in defence of their country when invaded by the enemy, have subjected themselves and their families to severe sacrifices and distress."[77]

Donors from across the social and political spectrum contributed. In York, the garrison militia volunteered one day's pay. In Lower Canada, the people of Montreal and Quebec mounted effective nonsectarian campaigns that included endorsements from both the Catholic and Church of England bishops, who became members of the society. The merchant communities of both contributed generously and pushed the total to £4,641, which exceeded the annual prewar revenue of Upper Canada's provincial government. In Jamaica, planters and merchants donated cash as well as coffee, sugar, and rum to be sold in Lower Canada for the benefit of the charity. When the goods arrived, the brokers, printers, "and even the bell-men who announced the day of the sale throughout the city and its environs, spurned at remuneration." In London, Prince Edward, Duke of Kent, chaired the subscription drive, hosting the meeting in July 1813 at the City of London Tavern, one of the most famous eateries in the City and host to a legion of dinners celebrating domestic causes and imperial victories. The duke topped the list of individual donors at £105, but merchant firms dominated the list, and the Bank of England outdid every individual and firm throughout the empire by pledging £1,000. The famous Lloyd's coffeehouse, whose patrons invested heavily in maritime insurance and other overseas commercial ventures, volunteered to assist in collecting donations. The flow of cash satisfied one goal of the charity; the unanimously adopted resolutions at the meeting confirmed the success of the other. Praising the "unshaken loyalty, fidelity and attachment" of the inhabitants of Upper Canada, those in attendance also gave credence to Canada's militia myth by declaring the enemy "have been repelled by the valour of the Volunteers and Militia, in aid of small numbers of His Majesty's forces" at the cost of "leaving their farms, upon the produce of which their support depend, uncultivated and neglected." By donating to the subscription, Britons could demonstrate their recognition of and appreciation for their fellow subjects.[78]

The wider British public and government increasingly responded favorably to arguments asserting Canada's importance. Although reluctant to send reinforcements at the start of the war, the Liverpool ministry poured in reinforcements as soon as it could in 1814, and, as discussed later, at Ghent the government pushed hard for concessions that would have severely curbed the power of the United States to the direct benefit of British North America. British commanders in Canada who once railed against the vileness of the local population began to sing their praises—perhaps due to a change in impression, but also likely out of a desire to secure more resources from Britain. Even Drummond praised Upper Canada's militia by war's end, and at the conclusion he publicly gave credit for successful defense of the province to the regulars and militia, declaring to the provincial assembly that "the brave exertions of our Regular and Militia Forces have preserved this portion of His Majesty's Dominions; and it now only remains to us, this Province, to improve to the utmost, the happy consequences of that invaluable Blessing."[79]

In Britain, Castlereagh, the most reluctant of the major players in the Liverpool ministry when it came to favoring the overseas empire over European affairs, came around to the idea of Canada's value by the end of the war. Writing to Bathurst on his way to the Congress at Vienna, where the leaders of Europe were gathering to decide the fate of the continent and with it much of the world Europe controlled, Castlereagh described how he had been studying "our system towards America for years past, as well as the growing value of Canada." Castlereagh explained that from his reading "I have certainly acquired by those researches a very increased notion of the value of our North American possessions to us."[80] The public discussion in the press concurred, with such papers as the *Morning Post* declaring in a piece reaching readers as far away as Upper Canada that it believed British North America was an "invaluable resource on which can alone be founded the independence of the West Indian possessions—the independence of our navy against defective supplies of timber from the Baltic—and as the certain means, if duly cherished, of increasing our commercial wealth and maritime power."[81] The West Indian press concurred and found in Canada a new ally for pressing the importance of colonial affairs. By the end of 1813, editors were flooding their pages with reports about the transactions in Canada from British and American sources and arguing for its fellow colonies' importance. As the *Royal Gazette and Bahama Advertiser* explained to readers after reprinting petitions from Canadian merchants calling for increased protection, "We wish to press upon the minds of the colonial public, as far as in us lies, of what importance it is, that we should be prompt and united in our efforts to claim our rights."[82] Canada had finally gained acceptance both at the heart of the empire and by its fellow colonies as an integral part of the British Empire.

The West Indian interest in Britain and the Caribbean constituted one of the loudest advocates of a coercive policy toward the United States, and it paid dearly. The West Indies depended on oceanic trade for their survival and prosperity: ships brought in staples such as flour and beef and transported the colonies' cash crops of sugar-based products and coffee to Britain and other countries. This system had been the foundation of the West Indian slave economy for nearly a century, making the islands lucrative but also vulnerable in times of war to foreign navies and slave revolts when supplies ran low. To protect this commerce in 1812, the Royal Navy initially stationed a mere five frigates and nine other ships at Jamaica and the Bahamas.[83] The French navy had been driven from the Caribbean years before, and the admiralty did not take American naval forces seriously—despite fervent warnings from the West Indies about American privateers. In June 1812, those privateers and warships were poised to pounce, waiting for a formal declaration of war—just like Hull's army on the Canadian border. As *Jamaica Magazine* observed, as soon as the United States declared war, "Shoals of privateers were at sea before the end of a week, and at this time the West Indies we believe have more vessels of this description hovering about her islands, than she has British vessels in her ports."[84] Unlike America's land forces, the navy and privateers proved extremely effective, raking in British merchant vessels and ravaging West Indian shipping, which was one of the most lucrative trades in the world.

The American ships attacked anything they could reach, disrupting both trade and communications. The island governors even regularly complained to their superiors in London that postal ships had been taken, forcing them to request fresh orders and new newspapers. Privateers took two British packets bound for Barbados within months of each other, the second case "in sight of this Island," according to the apoplectic governor.[85] Complaints continued unabated for the entire war. As the *Jamaica Magazine* tellingly remarked in February 1813 in an article reviewing the state of the war, there was "nothing new" to report: "American privateers still cover the ocean, to the almost total annihilation of commerce; while the heroes of the land have failed in the wise designs against Canada."[86] Even as the Royal Navy sent more ships, complaints continued. The *Royal Gazette and Bahama Advertiser* was typical in printing its appreciation for the additional protection but in late 1814 still complained privateers were continuing to devastate West Indian commerce. "The system of privateering, is a warfare in which the Americans excel," the paper conceded, "their enterprize cannot be doubted, and their vessels are avowedly the best adapted for it."[87]

The impact of privateering on the islands was severe. Six months into the war, a special committee of the Jamaica Assembly estimated that insurance rates had already risen 10 percent—an increase that would ultimately triple for some transatlantic routes. Moreover, the committee warned, British ships with a capacity of 120,000 tons were about to set sail with the colony's produce worth an estimated £6 million—a prime target for the Americans.[88] Worse still, because the islands had converted much of the usable land to sugar and coffee production, they relied on external sources for almost everything they needed to run the plantations—from flour to feed the slaves to the lumber for the barrels in which the slaves packaged the sugar products they produced for export. The United States had been integral to this trade, both as market and supplier, since its days as colonies in the British Empire, and just as the islands suffered during the American Revolution so they would in the War of 1812.[89]

The planters and merchants pushed hard to secure their livelihood from the war, relentlessly petitioning the colonial governments and Parliament. Jamaican planters immediately requested that neutral vessels be allowed to carry coffee, rum, and sugar (the colonies' main exports) to the United States, while the island's assembly requested that American lumber be allowed into the colony. Canada and Spanish Florida, the assembly explained early in the war, lacked the infrastructure to provide decent, cheap staves (the lumber planks in the barrels used to transport goods), a problem that had driven the price upward by 50 percent. The assembly complained that the rum trade was being ruined for "want of packages" at a potential annual cost of £1.2 million.[90] In some cases governors acted unilaterally to open up wartime trade with the United States, granting special licenses just as British agents in the United States were doing to ensure the flow of grain to the British army fighting in Spain and Portugal. The governor of Barbados essentially opened up trade completely, producing an enormous list of American goods that could enter the country on neutral or licensed American vessels.[91] Thanks to Britain's agents in the United States, and the American government's reluctance to close off the grain trade at the start of the war, these licenses were readily available.

As more colonies followed suit, the British government ultimately relented and in effect retroactively endorsed these practices; yet the situation remained difficult.[92] The Royal Navy proved unable to eliminate American privateers, and

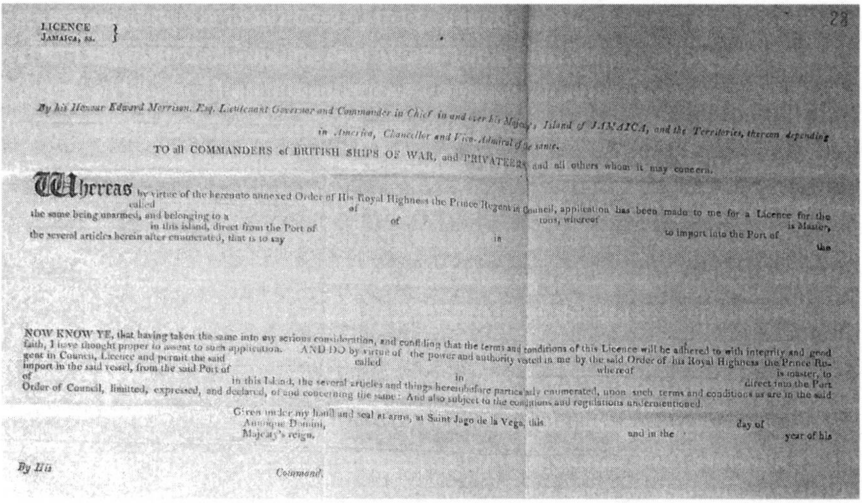

LICENCE
JAMAICA, ss.

28

By his Honour Edward Morrison, Esq. Lieutenant Governor and Commander in Chief in and over his Majesty's Island of JAMAICA, and the Territories thereon depending in America, Chancellor and Vice-Admiral of the same.

TO all COMMANDERS of BRITISH SHIPS OF WAR, and PRIVATEERS and all others whom it may concern.

Whereas by virtue of the hereunto annexed Order of His Royal Highness the Prince Regent in Council, application has been made to me for a Licence for the called of tons, whereof is Master, the same being unarmed, and belonging to a of in this island, direct from the Port of to import into the Port of in the several articles herein after enumerated, that is to say

NOW KNOW YE, that having taken the same into my serious consideration, and confiding that the terms and conditions of this Licence will be adhered to with integrity and good faith, I have thought proper to assent to such application. AND DO by virtue of the power and authority vested in me by the said Order of his Royal Highness the Prince Regent in Council, Licence and permit the said called whereof is master, to import in the said vessel, from the said Port of in direct into the Port of in this Island, the several articles and things hereinbefore particularly enumerated, upon such terms and conditions as are in the said Order of Council, limited, expressed, and declared, of and concerning the same: And also subject to the conditions and regulations undermentioned.

Given under my hand and seal at arms, at Saint Jago de la Vega, this day of Annoque Domini, and in the year of his Majesty's reign.

By His Command.

Figure 5.1 A trading license issued by Jamaica's governor. The National Archives, Kew, CO 137/136. Such licenses were printed in bulk and left to British agents in the United States to complete the details of the ship, voyage, and cargo. It instructs the Royal Navy and British privateers not to interfere with the ship.

a series of hurricanes destroyed many local attempts to convert sugar fields to grain production. The hurricane that struck a number of islands in July 1813 was the worst in living memory. As the *Bahama Gazette* remarked, "it falls to our lot to record the most dreadful calamity by which these Islands have been ever afflicted in the memory of man." "Years must elapse before the losses and injuries sustained can be repaired," it continued. "Hundreds of families, heretofore comfortable, have been reduced to beggary and want." An estimated one-third of houses were leveled, along with virtually all of the ships in the harbors.[93]

Provisions were such a problem in the first year of the war that the British officers at Bermuda petitioned the government in October to reinstate rations for their wives and children. The problem, they explained, was not pay but food on the open market, "for the pay of an officer can be of little use when (as is known to your Excellency) a single article of food (bread excepted) cannot be bought at any rate for many days together."[94] Unfortunately, the army in Bermuda could barely manage to feed its own men, let alone their dependents.[95] The situation was so dire in Jamaica during the first six months of war that, according to its assembly, only the American grain ships that the Royal Navy captured and brought to port saved the population from starvation.[96] A monthly snapshot of key commodity prices in Jamaica recorded by the governor supports the anecdotal evidence. By autumn, flour, rice, and white oak staves cost 150, 175, and 125 percent, respectively, more than prewar prices.[97]

The following year proved less volatile for West Indian markets, especially as demand for sugar and coffee rose and flour prices stabilized in response to the reopening of Baltic and Northern European grain-producing regions and markets in the wake of Napoleon's disastrous retreat from Russia. Nevertheless, prices for a number of staples, including flour and staves, remained nearly double what they were before the war. In the Bahamas, American flour continued to be available throughout the year, thanks largely to continuation of the British licensing system. Meat was another matter entirely. Although officially reported as "British North American" pork and beef, the meat most assuredly originated in the United States rather than Canada, as the Canadian sources struggled to meet the demands of their own inhabitants and resident British troops in 1813, forcing them to rely heavily on black market supplies from the United States. For most of the year, American meat was not available in the Bahamas, forcing inhabitants either to do without or to rely on Irish alternatives, which cost as much as 40 percent more. Lumber was available in most months, although expensive, while luxury goods such as Madeira wine all but disappeared.[98] Jamaica's experience was similar to that of the Bahamas in 1813, and 1814 proved stable but still expensive, with flour prices dropping to an average of 75 percent above prewar prices. In late 1814 the combination of extension of the Royal Navy's blockade to cover the entire American Atlantic coastline, deployment of more warships to enforce the blockade, and an American government embargo and attacks on the British licensing system worked against the West Indies. By early 1815, flour again cost twice the prewar price, and the essential white oak staves were nearly four times their prewar cost.[99]

The tangled web of commercial restrictions and relaxations emanating from the British colonies, Britain, and the United States, along with the slow lines of communications that relayed them, ensured that even well-intentioned officials had a hard time supplying their islands. Such was the case of the *Hiram*, an American merchant ship operating out of New Haven, Connecticut, that ran afoul of legal entanglements and miscommunications. In the autumn of 1812 Sir George Beckwith, the governor of Barbados, granted the master of the *Hiram*, John Howe, a special license for the ship to deliver a large cargo of flour and beef to the British forces stationed in the colony. During its journey the *Hiram* was captured by the British sloop *Eliza* and taken to Antigua, where the *Hiram* and its cargo were condemned by a British admiralty court and its crew imprisoned. A furious Beckwith mounted a series of challenges, questioning the court's right to overturn his license and the *Eliza's* status as a bona fide privateer. Beckwith even went so far as to make a thinly veiled accusation of corruption in a letter to the governor of Antigua, suggesting the court had taken advantage of Howe's situation—for if he contested the court's decision he faced retribution from the American government for trading with the enemy. Eventually Beckwith sent an appeal to Bathurst that included Howe's statement describing his financial losses, summaries of the court's decisions, and a racial jab at the British privateers operating nearby, who Beckwith described as being "manned principally, I believe, by Blacks [who] will not be found conducive to the honor of the British Character in the prosecution of this war."[100] The case remained unresolved for the duration of the war.

For others the war represented new opportunities. As in the United States and Canada, plenty of unemployed sailors and struggling merchants entered the fight as privateers, and although most came up empty-handed, plenty of others prospered, bringing hundreds of American ships and their cargo into West Indian ports. Some commentators argued that war with the United States would force the West Indies to become self-reliant, or at least shift their dependence to other parts of the British Empire. In Jamaica, the colonial assembly used the war as a pretext to renew calls for increasing internal land clearances—so as to produce grain and other staples for home consumption. A petition to Britain's Board of Trade signed by seventy-three merchants and planters in the Bahamas at the start of the war insisted that now was the opportunity for greater self-sufficiency, claiming it was their "decided opinion" that "with the exception of the single article of Flour these Islands possess abundantly within themselves, the means of raising provisions and Live-stock, for the consumption not only of the Inhabitants and their slaves, but of His Majesty's Troops doing duty here." Moreover, the petitioners argued, they "would long since have done so, had not our Farmers and Garrisons been discouraged by the Indulgences which have too long been extended to the vessels belonging to Citizens of the United States of America." War, they insisted, was a chance to break these old habits.[101] Merchants also argued that, with some development, Canada could meet the lumber and grain needs of the West Indies and that a war with the United States would force the transition.

Cooperation with the Spanish Empire represented another opportunity. From a political perspective, the struggling Spanish Empire was a potential ally against the United States. Although formal discussions between the two empires did not take place, Britain was sensitive to American aggrandizement in Spanish Florida and Mexico and complained about it to the United States. During the War of 1812, there was little point in formally recruiting into the fight the Spanish, whose home was a war zone and whose empire was crumbling. Doing so would have exposed Spain even further to American aggression and saddled Britain with the additional obligation to protect yet more vulnerable colonies in North America. However, the British government was thinking beyond the immediate war to a future in which a defeated United States could be hemmed in by an Anglo-Spanish–American Indian alliance. In consequence, cultivating that relationship was crucial, and the British government regularly issued orders to the colonial governors to keep its charges out of Spanish affairs, particularly sporadic colonial rebellions, and to cooperate with Spanish officials. From a trading standpoint, Spanish America could serve as both an alternative supplier and an entrepôt for laundering American goods. For colonies such as the Bahamas, which were favorably located at a nexus between the British and Spanish empires, inter-imperial trade was vital. The governor reminded Lord Liverpool in July 1812 that "the principal support of the Islands is the trade carried on with the Spanish Colonies."[102] The Spanish knew how to take advantage of the situation, too. Cuba, which quickly became the leading neutral entrepôt for American flour, taxed British buyers at a rate of seven Spanish dollars a barrel (roughly 20 percent of its market value in Jamaica), which was returned if the flour was exported on a Spanish ship.[103] Soon this "Spanish" flour became a staple in the British West Indies. Other neutral powers participated, and by the end of 1813 Swedish registered vessels were routinely carrying American lumber from the United States to Cuba, where British and Spanish vessels collected it for use as staves on British West Indian plantations.[104]

The war also gave the West Indies a chance to reassert their loyalty to Britain and the empire. As in Canada, the island legislatures sent loyalty petitions to their governors, who forwarded them to the prince regent via Bathurst, who in turn ensured that they appeared in British newspapers for the nation to see. Governors too took every opportunity to express their loyalty, echoing many of the arguments asserted across the Atlantic. When Edward Morrison, the Jamaican lieutenant-governor, addressed the island assembly in the autumn of 1812, he remarked, "that a kindred nation should become the ally of our most inveterate enemy must be a matter of great regret" and proceeded to depict Britain's war effort as a campaign to save the fledgling America from wicked and well-practiced Napoleon—a war so "that America may be preserved from the destructive influence of the present ruler in France."[105] In response to news of the American declaration of war, the *Bermuda Gazette* printed a lengthy column under the headline of "Fellow Citizens, and Native of Bermuda." Damning Napoleonic France's "murderous despotism," the *Gazette* lavishly praised "our parent country" for pursuing the "honourable struggle." While noting that Bermuda was unlikely to suffer invasion in a war with the United States, the paper declared that its inhabitants nevertheless owed it to the rest of the empire to make a gesture of goodwill. Calling for the organization of a "respectable Colonial Militia," the *Gazette* remarked that even though the need for a militia was slight the symbolism of the gesture was great: "In this way, fellow citizens, we may at least show our gratitude to that country, which has so long protected us in peace and prosperity; and borne the whole and enormous expenses of the momentous war in which she is at present engaged; without once burthening, us or any of her colonies, with taxes, imposts, or contributions."[106] Similar calls for greater self-sufficiency in defense appeared in other islands. Such fidelity proved crucial to British operations in North America, because confidence in the stability of the West Indies enabled Britain to redeploy a considerable number of troops from the islands to Canada after 1812 and triple the size of the regular force there by the summer of 1813 to more than twenty thousand troops.[107] Without this shift, Canada's chances of surviving continued invasions would have been slim.

The War of 1812 could have gone much worse for the British West Indies. After all, two decades earlier in neighboring French Saint-Domingue, African slaves took advantage of a distracted France to rebel and create the Haitian Republic, and throughout the Spanish Empire local populations were attempting to free themselves from imperial rule. As slave-holding societies, they sat on a powder keg, which remained defused only through armed force, a steady supply of American flour and lumber, and profitable overseas trade. The War of 1812 directly threatened two of the three. But while American privateers raided West Indian maritime trade, the Americans continued to trade with the West Indies directly, or later on indirectly. This trade, far more than the Royal Navy, kept the islands relatively stable for the first half of the war. During this dark period of the British Empire, there was no realistic alternative to American supplies. Upper Canada struggled to feed itself and the British forces stationed there, the British forces in Europe relied on American grain, and the Spanish colonies lacked the infrastructure and organization to supply all of the islands' needs. Alternative sources, such as converting land usage on the islands, would take years to develop. Fortunately for the British Empire, the American federal government proved at first unwilling and ultimately unable to halt commerce with the West Indies. In consequence, by the time the Royal Navy asserted its dominance in the Caribbean, British governors worried more about where to put all the captured American sailors than about how to regain control over the islands. Yet the War of 1812 proved difficult, even with continuation of the American trade, because it sufficiently disrupted trade to cause considerable inflation and anxiety and highlighted the colonies' ongoing dependence on the United States, further driving home the strategic importance of either subjugating the United States or cultivating Canada.

As the war in Europe wound down, the Liverpool ministry implemented the offensive strategy it and previous governments had considered for years: blockade America's ports, assault its coasts with a diversionary force, and invade from Lower Canada. The British government had grown more adept at conducting overseas wars since the American Revolution, and so explicit instructions to army and navy commanders in America, ranging from minute deployments to campaign strategies, flowed across the Atlantic. Prevost was not given the latitude the Howe brothers or Lord Cornwallis were afforded the last time Britain went to war in North America. For intelligence, British ministers relied heavily on newspaper reports from Canada and the United States, which almost always reached London before commanders' dispatches. As a typical remark from Bathurst to Prevost in July 1813 regarding the American capture of Fort George in Upper Canada reveals, "I cannot but be most anxious to learn how far this unfortunate occurrence may influence your naval superiority on Lake Ontario: But as far as I can judge from the American newspapers, which are as yet our only source of intelligence the impact has been modest." Ironically, Bathurst occasionally admitted the unreasonableness of trying to run the war from London, but such remarks were almost invariably followed by more instructions, as in late 1813 when Bathurst described his role to Prevost as offering only "general advice" but then followed that remark with ten pages of detailed orders. The ministry also routinely overruled Prevost's requests on such mundane local matters as recruiting bounties for Canadian volunteers.[108]

The American war was not a sideshow or distant nuisance for the British government. This was Britain's war, not a peripheral conflict of little consequence, and it was carefully planned and extremely aggressive. The Liverpool ministry did not want a compromise peace, and by the end of 1813 it was prepared to devote considerable resources to prosecuting the war to the best of its ability. First by shifting regular troops from the Caribbean and later by sending them directly from Europe, Britain raised regular troop levels in North America to twenty thousand by the summer of 1813 and well over thirty thousand the following year—putting the British Army's commitment to North America on the scale of the major campaigns in the Napoleonic Wars.[109] When Bathurst received third-party reports in the summer of 1814 that Prevost was considering an armistice in light of agreed peace talks between Britain and the United States, the British minister was apoplectic. Writing immediately to Prevost, Bathurst chastised the general for taking such an initiative, explaining in no uncertain terms that "It is the wisdom of H M's Government to press the War with all possible vigour up to the moment when Peace shall be finally concluded." If an armistice had been made, Prevost was ordered to end it immediately.[110] The United States was down, and the British government intended to strike hard to end the war on its terms.

Although the British government ordered its forces in North America to take a defensive posture at the start of the war—partly in hopes of delaying it until the empire was better prepared—the government went on the offensive as soon as it was able. Once it became apparent that Napoleon's retreat from Russia might release the Royal Navy from some of its commitments in the Baltic and the rest of Europe, Bathurst and his undersecretaries went to work implementing the plan to assault America's coastline. In a secret dispatch, Bathurst outlined the plan to Sir Thomas Beckwith, the British colonel who would implement it. With more than two thousand men under his command, Beckwith was to raid American coastal towns and villages at will in order to hurt American morale and distract attention from Canada. He was not to take or hold any territory. "As the object of the Expedition is to harass the Enemy by different attacks," Bathurst explained, "you will avoid the Risk of a General action unless it should become necessary to secure your retreat." Any naval or military stores, which included flour, would be destroyed. When it came to private property, Beckwith could either destroy it or negotiate tribute from the American civilians. "If you shall be enabled to take such a Position as to threaten the Inhabitants with the Destruction of their Property," Bathurst instructed, "you are hereby authorized to levy upon them Contributions in return for your forbearance." The only restrictions Bathurst placed on the forces regarded slaves. Beckwith was not to stir slave revolts; nor was he to take slaves as booty. If they desired to leave their masters, however, Beckwith was to assist them as "free persons" and enlist any suitable men.[111]

The coastal and border raids that Beckwith and other British officers orchestrated were often brutal. At Hampton, Virginia, in June 1813 the British stayed for ten days, after dispatching the local militia. Among the British forces were the notorious companies of French chasseurs formed from the royalist armies that had fought against the French Revolution who raped, murdered, and plundered the inhabitants—crimes for which "not a man was punished," an outraged British officer later complained.[112] The American press complained as well, and violently. Connecticut's *American Mercury*, like most newspapers, attacked Sir George Cockburn (the British admiral in charge of the coastal raiding operations) personally, claiming French deserters from the British force confessed that "Cockburn, in order to insure their fidelity to him" promised them extra pay and the right to pillage. The papers called him "the monster, Cockburn, who is a disgrace not only to his nation, but to the whole human race."[113] Some British officers expressed discomfort with the situation, but most proved indifferent if not brazen. As one British officer unsympathetically reflected afterward, when American women complained to him as his troops destroyed buildings and carried off supplies, "Our reply used to be, 'You must ask your President, Jim Madison: he invited us.'"[114] As for Cockburn, he reportedly ordered the destruction of one American newspaper's offices and type, instructing his men to "be sure that all the c's are destroyed so the rascals can't abuse my name anymore."[115]

Commanders in Canada were full of vengeance once Britain could go on the offensive in 1814. Prevost proceeded to burn towns across the border, including Buffalo, and he ordered raids on American towns and villages to gather supplies and intimidate civilians. Unlike the American commanders and editors who attempted to excuse or distance themselves from similar atrocities, Prevost made clear that the actions were deliberate acts of revenge. In a public proclamation addressed to the inhabitants of British North America, he explained that although he "sincerely deprecates this mode of warfare," the Americans left him no choice after they burned Newark the previous December—"an event the inhabitants of Upper Canada can never forget and the recollection of which cannot but nerve their arms when opposed to their vindictive foe."[116] As with their counterparts attacking the Atlantic coastline, British officers in Canada were largely indifferent to the suffering of American civilians. When the women of Hopkinton, New York, complained about the destruction of their flour, a British officer told them that his men would roll the barrels down a hill, and he would allow the women to have any flour that remained in the barrels, remarking, "Ain't I a generous man?"[117] The press was even more vociferous, with such newspapers as the *New Brunswick Courier* declaring that "we trust [the American enemy] will be followed and over taken, no matter at what distance, chastised for his wanton cruelties, and his country laid wastes.—The necessity is painful, but retaliation is the only way in which a stop can be put to this war of extermination."[118] In contrast to instructions sent to Canada at the start of the war, the British government in 1814 wholeheartedly endorsed such actions, writing to Prevost in March that "His Royal Highness entirely approves of your having retaliated on the Inhabitants of the United States the harsh measures which the American Government had adopted with respect to the population of that part of the Canadas . . . you will not fail to inflict a similar retaliation whenever the conduct of the Enemy shall render it necessary."[119]

The public mood in Britain shifted decidedly, too, by 1814. That summer, the American war supplanted European affairs to become the leading topic of conversation in the press with newspapers clamoring to provide every possible detail to readers. Puffed up by Britain's victory over France, commentators implored the government to turn its military might fully against the United States. As the *Aberdeen Journal* remarked in response to more troops being sent to North America, "The Americans are now likely to feel the full might of British vengeance; and now every preparation is made for inflicting with severity proportionate to the delay, the vengeance which has so long been suspended over them."[120] The *Times*, which in 1813 was lukewarm to the war as it threatened Britain's focus on fighting France, led the charge in favor of an expanded war against the United States, supporting naval bombardments of its cities and placing "a large army in a commanding position within its territory."[121]

Victory over France did more than inflate the British national ego. Public discussions created an expectation of total victory in which a nation was not merely defeated with minimal penalty to fight again another day; it was crushed and the ruling regime changed. Throughout 1813 and 1814 papers such as the *Times* campaigned hard for the removal of Napoleon as the only path to lasting peace in Europe. Although in violation of the law of nations, which held that monarchs were not to be removed from power following defeat, commentators and politicians argued that Napoleon was an aggrandizing tyrant. So long as he had an army, no neighbor was safe. Such assertions received widespread support throughout Britain and its empire. As a West Indian paper remarked, "no lasting peace can *ever* be made with a Power that has risen to greatness by similar crimes." To detractors balking at such a notion under the pretense of the law of nations and the "liberties of Europe," the paper asserted they "must hold in remembrance the lessons they have been so recently taught, and banish from their Counsels even the thought of Peace with Bonaparte."[122]

British supporters of the war constructed a similar case against Madison and his administration. The American invasion of Canada as well as its treatment of the Spanish Empire in North America and the American Indians was clear proof that the United States, like France, was led by "aggrandizers" who sought to expand the borders of the United States. When the Liverpool ministry laid out its case for war to the public in the form of the prince regent's "Manifesto Against America" in January 1813, it accused Madison of inflating "trivial" grievances to justify his aggressions and for good measure accused his administration of a "partiality towards France," which, the manifesto claimed, was "the real cause of the present war." Such a move, declared the prince regent, was nothing short of an act of betrayal:

> While contending against France, in defence not only of the liberties of Great-Britain, but of the world, His Royal Highness was entitled to look for a far difference result. . . . From their common origin—from their common interests—from their professed principles of freedom and independence, the United States were the last power, in which Great-Britain could have expected to find a willing instrument, and abettor of French tyranny.[123]

Britain as the victim of a mentally unbalanced Madison administration became the Liverpool ministry's mantra throughout 1813. As Bathurst rhetorically asked the House of Lords in February, "with a Government of this description, which claimed the right of absolving our subjects from their allegiance to their native country, at a time which it was involved in a war for the general interests of mankind, what hope of conciliation could be entertained?"[124] The *Edinburgh Star* agreed and concluded that "if the President will not be reasoned, he must be beat into it."[125]

Reports from the American press only reinforced this interpretation. From the war's inception, the British press and government alike generally held that both Madison and the war were unpopular with a large number of Americans. If a particularly violent antiwar column appeared in a Boston paper in April, it

Figure 5.2 William Heath, "Boney and Maddy—Gone to Pot" (London, 1814). British Museum Catalogue, 12281. © Copyright the Trustees of the British Museum. Using toilet humor, the artist plays on the popular motif of Madison's connection with Napoleon and that, like Napoleon, Madison risked forcible removal from office. The title is a play on words that refers both to the literal use of the toilet and that of insanity. Napoleon holds a paper inscribed "Orders for an Imeadiet march to Elba," the island to which he was sent following his abdication. A worried Madison holds a paper inscribed "March to the Tomahawks" and declares "see what a fine kettle of fish we have made of it, this comes of my believing you and takeing your Bribes."

would be circulating throughout Britain by summer. As the *Carlisle Journal* remarked after reprinting a slew of anti-Madison commentary from America, "the war is extremely unpopular in the United States. . . . The eastern States have already manifested a strong disposition to resist the general Government, by refusing to place their Militia at its disposal; nor will they grant the territory demanded by the general Government for military purposes."[126] Accusations of American links to France continued, with editors finding plenty of supporting material in the American newspapers. Such venomous attacks as the letters from "an old farmer" in the *Boston Gazette* (which accused Madison of an elaborate conspiracy that included an alliance with France and likened America's attack on Canada to France's invasion of Russia) found a transatlantic audience.

The public attacks against Madison in the British press worsened considerably in the wake of Napoleon's abdication. Liverpool privately confided to Castlereagh during the peace negotiations at Ghent that he thought they had a better chance of success if Madison remained in office—believing the American government weak, and therefore vulnerable to British demands—but public discussion took a radical turn.[127] The *Times*, the most widely read newspaper in Britain, led the charge, accusing Madison in September 1814 of being a "traitor" both to his own people and to the Anglo-American transatlantic relationship for having gone to war in favor of Napoleon. A few weeks later the paper called him an "ass" who should be executed by his own people and blamed him personally for the "barbarous warfare in Canada."[128] In October, the paper laid out its case for complete removal of the Republican leadership, calling it an "evil" second only to Napoleon that represented a direct threat to Britain: "the present American Government must be displaced, or it will sooner or later plant its poisoned dagger in the heart of the parent state." Moreover, the *Times* continued, the change should come by force of arms: "It [the federal government] must be displaced by the powerful effect of great military successes to our arms, continued and connected until they enable us to dictate the terms of an honourable Peace." Therefore, only with replacement of the American government and the humbling of that nation militarily could Britain have a lasting peace.[129]

Echoing the posture the Liverpool ministry would take initially at the peace talks at Ghent, British public proponents of the war demanded harsh terms for peace. A number of Britons in and out of government advocated a more conciliatory stance, but they were drowned out in the spring through the early autumn by the legions who demanded more. By 1814, few in Britain publicly advocated a negotiated compromise on America's original complaints. As one commentator remarked, "to suffer these even to be discussed would be a dereliction of duty."[130] Even the *Exeter Flying-Post*, which initially wavered on supporting the government over the war, declared in March that "peace with America, desirable as it is, is not worth purchasing with the concession of one of those rights for the preservation of which we have fought with such constancy and with such success."[131]

Many insisted on major concessions from the United States in return for peace. "Vigorous war with America, till America turn back in the spirit of peace to sue for reconciliation with her outraged parent state, is, we believe, the universal voice of the country," cried the *Edinburgh Star*. "When we consider the meanness, the cowardice of Maddison's [sic] policy, who only dared to strike us when he thought we were down," the paper continued, "nothing short of the following conditions . . . will, or ought now to satisfy the country." These included territorial concessions to Canada, an independent state for the Indians carved from the territory of the United States, exclusion of Americans from trading with the West Indies and Britain's possessions in Asia, revisiting the legality of the Louisiana Purchase, exclusion of Americans from Florida, and the cession of New Orleans to Britain.[132] In essence, the *Edinburgh Star*, along with a supporting chorus throughout the British Isles, wanted to strip the United States of everything it had gained since independence and then reduce it to a client state. As the *Times* bluntly stated on the eve of negotiations, "Our demands may be couched in a single word, *Submission*."[133] Others questioned whether Britain should be considering peace at all. After negotiations began in August, the *New Monthly Magazine* remarked, "The negotiations at Ghent are continued; but we still remain of the opinion that we must look to the sword, and not the pen, for the adjustment of our differences with the United States."[134]

The burning of Washington in August 1814 was the most infamous punitive British attack of the war. With a population of a mere 8,308 (at least 2,000 of whom were slaves), the American capital at the time was small and strategically unimportant, and so it had minimal defenses. The British landed 4,500 troops in Maryland and proceeded to march on the capital. At Bladensburg the British easily defeated a larger, but poorly trained and equipped, American force consisting mostly of militia as Madison and other members of the federal government watched. The routed soldiers and politicians fled through the streets of Washington, which the British entered that evening. According to one British officer, when they entered the White House they found a prepared dinner still warm but hastily abandoned. After dining and pillaging the president's residence for souvenirs, they burned it. The British then burned the navy yard along with the considerable amount of stores it held and two unfinished ships, the Capitol building, and the treasury along with most of the other government buildings. Further demonstrating his disdain for the American press that had regularly abused him, Cockburn also ordered the office of the *National Intelligencer* burned. Fearing a large American force might be on its way, they quickly left Washington to board their ships a few days later, leaving their wounded behind. Meanwhile another British forced moved on the wealthy merchant community of Alexandria, Virginia, which surrendered for fear of suffering a fate similar to that of Washington. The plunder was far greater, and the British sailed off with twenty-one captured ships and flour, tobacco, cotton and other goods worth in excess of £200,000.[135]

The fallout for the Madison administration was mixed. Madison's opponents and critics of the war railed against the government for the humiliating loss. As the *Western Monitor* remarked on learning the news, the disaster demonstrated how the government had misled the people: "that which is most humbling of all, and which must produce the most unpleasant feelings is, that such was the want of preparation, and such the defenseless situation of the place, that but a very feeble resistance was or could be made to their approach." "Our misfortune," it concluded, "seems to have arisen from a misapprehension of the real state of things—Exaggerated ideas of strength and preparations, together with an underrated estimate of danger, necessarily expose to surprise and disaster."[136] Madison and his supporters responded by insisting that the destruction of Washington was of minimal strategic importance, and by accusing the British of another atrocity.

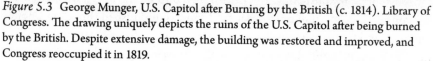

Figure 5.3 George Munger, U.S. Capitol after Burning by the British (c. 1814). Library of Congress. The drawing uniquely depicts the ruins of the U.S. Capitol after being burned by the British. Despite extensive damage, the building was restored and improved, and Congress reoccupied it in 1819.

According to eyewitness accounts, the British forces behaved impeccably in Washington, taking pains to avoid harm to civilians or private property, but this truth was quickly ignored in the public discussion. Madison set the tone in his widely circulated message to Congress following the capital's destruction by insisting that the enemy "will find in his transient success, which interrupted for a moment only the ordinary public business at the seat of government, no compensation for the loss of character with the world, by his violations of private property, and by his destruction of public edifices, protected, as monuments of the arts, by the laws of civilized warfare."[137] In a widely printed letter addressed to Admiral Cochrane, but intended for the American public, Monroe chastised the British admiral for ordering the burning of Washington, claiming (wrongly) that "In the wars of modern Europe, no examples of the kind, even among nations the most hostile to each, can be traced. . . . We must go back to distant and barbarous ages, to find a parallel for the acts of which I complain."[138] In response to British claims that Washington had been burned in response to American forces' destruction of towns in Upper Canada, Monroe defended the American government's record in Canada, insisting that Newark was adjoined to Ft. George and so destroyed out of military necessity and that similar attacks either had been disavowed or were under investigation.[139]

The attack on Washington breathed some new life into grassroots involvement in the war effort. As *Niles' Weekly Register* explained, the event showed Britain's true colors. "The hate with which we have always said Great Britain regarded us," the paper declared, "is now exhibiting by a Goth-like war. . . . The barriers with which civilized nations have circumscribed their military operations, are cast down by the foe; and the contest, began for unalienable rights on the sea, is becoming a struggle for liberty and property on the land."[140] All along the coastline, militia and volunteers shored up local defenses. In Charleston some "200 ladies" presented the local militia with a flag in a public ceremony and then in an unusual move "went to work on the fortifications and labored *manfully*."[141] In Philadelphia, the Federalist young men who had been publicly critical of the administration and of the war formed volunteer companies to aid in the city's defenses.[142] In short, the war was no longer simply one of aggression on the part of the federal government; it was a defensive war, enabling former critics to participate, albeit limitedly and usually with the caveat that they had not changed their minds on the origins of the war. Yet the administration proved unable to spin the situation to its advantage that autumn, failing to secure from Congress either a conscription bill or adequate financing to continue an offensive war into 1815.

The response in Britain to the attack on Washington bordered on euphoric, with such papers as the *Exeter Flying-Post* calling it "glorious" and the *Edinburgh Star* poking fun at Madison's retreat by asserting that, "like his master, Napoleon, he wisely consulted his personal safety by an early retreat from the field."[143] The *Glasgow Courier* typified the satisfaction that cascaded over much of the reading public calling for a severe chastisement of America:

> We never undertook a task with more alacrity and heart-felt satisfaction, than that of laying the particulars before our readers. It is not the enterprise itself, splendid as it is, and much as it enhances the lustre of our military character, that communicates this keen pleasure; but it is the *punishment*, which has fallen at last upon a *wanton* and *unprincipled* enemy, which justifies, and in a manner ennobles, our exultation.[144]

In an unusual move, even the *New Monthly Magazine*, a predominantly literary review that rarely commented on the war or politics, praised "our gallant little army," gleefully estimating that the burning of Washington "must have filled the people and government of the United States with consternation" and describing Madison's public message reprimanding Britain as "sniveling" and "impudent."[145]

Despite assumptions today that the British understood the burning of Washington as payback specifically for the looting of York in 1813, contemporary evidence suggests hardly anyone in Canada or Britain saw it as a simple tit-for-tat affair. Instead, most understood it as an expression of British power and a general

Figure 5.4 Charles Williams, "The Fall of Washington—or Maddy in Full Flight" (London, 1814). Library of Congress, Prints and Photographs Division, LC-USZC4-3115. A celebration of the British destruction of Washington, the print touches on the major pro-war themes circulating in the public discussion in Britain: the Madison administration's connection to Napoleon and the need to remove him from office. Madison, third from the left, flees with another cabinet minister with bundles of papers, one of which is marked "Boneys [Napoleon's common nickname in Britain] Instruction to Maddison" and another labeled "Project for the conquest of Canada." Two British sailors (far right) congratulate each other, as Washington burns in the background. The American onlookers discuss Madison and the war. One declares Madison will soon be with "his bosom Friend" at Elba, the island to which Napoleon was exiled. Another complains that the defeat "will throw such a light on affairs that we shall find it necessary to change both Mean and measures"—an allusion to the removal of Madison and suing for peace.

chastisement of the United States—with readers, editors, and commanders highlighting America's audacity in starting the war and more generally the Americans' behavior in Canada. Responding to an account of events from the Republican *Savannah Advertiser*, the *Bermuda Gazette* called the burning of Washington "glorious and honourable to our Forces, who, in so short a time after their victorious career in Europe, are exhibiting to the astonished Americans the power and spirit of Britons."[146] Madison's complaints about British barbarism stank of hypocrisy to many British readers. The *Morning Chronicle*, which had been highly critical of the government's prosecution of the war, had little sympathy when it came to the burning of Washington. Admitting that destruction of public buildings "must be lamented by every man of liberal feeling," nevertheless

a lengthy editorial stated that "in this case it is undoubtedly only a mitigated retaliation for the wanton cruelty exercised some time since by the Americans." In
consequence, the paper continued, "they therefore have no right to complain;
and the blow having been struck in the very centre of their power, and the seat of
their Government, it must make so much the greater impression upon the
people."[147] The prince regent gave his public assent to such views in his address
to Parliament in November by calling the operation "most brilliant" and declaring that it "has produced on the inhabitants [of the United States] a deep and
sensible impression of the calamities of a war in which they have been so wan-
tonly involved."[148] The Americans, insisted an observer, were now "paying the
price of their folly."[149]

The attack on Washington had always been intended as a diversion for the main
event: invasion of the United States from Canada. But in September Prevost's
long-awaited invasion ended before it really began at the Battle of Plattsburgh. At
the head of an army of ten thousand men that included hardened veterans from
the Peninsular wars, Prevost lost his nerve when the Americans defeated the
British naval force on Lake Champlain. Fearing he would be cut off from supplies in Canada, Prevost ordered a retreat. Although casualties were light on
either side (about a hundred each), the battle effectively signaled the end of the
war for Britain. The British peace delegation at Ghent was stalling in order to
give the summer campaigns a chance, pressure in Britain to reduce wartime
taxes was intense, and the other European powers wanted an end to the conflict.
Prevost's invasion had been the linchpin of Britain's entire North American
strategy in 1814, with all of the events on the Atlantic coastline, including the
attack on Washington, primarily being diversions. Writing to Prevost in August,
Bathurst could not have been clearer in his expectations for victory. Noting that
Prevost finally had substantial resources "both in amount and quality," Bathurst
explained that "I am bound in fairness to apprize you that if you shall allow the
present campaign to close without having undertaken offensive measures against
the enemy, you will very seriously disappoint the expectations of the Prince
Regent and the Country."[150] The *Times* attempted to gloss over the significance
of Britain's defeat and called for escalation. "Partial and insulated exploits; however brilliant,—such, for instance, as the late capture of Washington" were not
enough to win the war, the paper declared.[151] Most other commentators, however, were ready to throw in the towel, unwilling to continue the war another
year or more to gain concessions from the United States.

   Although historians have been divided on the extent to which Prevost should
be blamed, most participants and observers recognized the defeat for the fiasco
that it was and held its commander largely responsible.[152] Tiger Dunlop, a
British army surgeon in Canada, remarked in frustration that "a more incompetent

Viceroy could hardly have been selected for such trying times. Timid at all times, despairing of his resources, he was afraid to venture anything."[153] In Lower Canada, Prevost became a scapegoat for those who were unsatisfied with the war's outcome. The *Royal Gazette and New Brunswick Advertiser* described inhabitants up in arms over the defeat, remarking that "the public Mind is in so complete a state of ulceration since the receipt of the fatal news, that no other subject seems to have engaged attention" and that the public largely blamed Prevost for the disgraceful retreat of "troops habituated to Conquer the best Legion of France."[154] After the war, local fury did not abate, and in a series of letters for the *Montreal Herald* that spring "Veritas" echoed popular frustration in his painstaking review of the conflict in which he pilloried Prevost.[155]

Prevost sent a letter after the battle to Bathurst pleading for his job—an act Prevost must have known was futile. Noting that he read Bathurst's August letter "with deep concern," he provided nearly eight pages of excuses that ranged from the beginning of his command to the date of the letter.[156] Ministers in London, who were already irritated with Prevost's slowness to attack, were furious, with the prime minister declaring that Prevost had "managed the campaign in that quarter as ill as possible" and that in retrospect the troops should have been given to the force commanded by Cochrane in order to take large portions of the Southern states. Alas, the prime ministers lamented, "We thought, however, we were acting for the best, and so we were if we had had a competent officer in the command in Canada."[157] The Liverpool ministry sent immediate instructions for its negotiators at Ghent to move forward on the peace treaty and removed Prevost from command. Britain had played the game on offense, but time was called well short of victory.

6

Wartime Opposition in the United States

On July 23, 1812, less than five weeks after the United States formally declared war on Britain, William Ellery Channing took to his pulpit in the Federal Street Church in Boston to address his congregation on the subject of the war. The grandson of a signer of the Declaration of Independence, a graduate of Harvard, and later celebrated as America's foremost Unitarian preacher, Channing had impeccable American credentials. The occasion for the sermon was the day of public fasting set aside by the governments of Massachusetts, Connecticut, and Rhode Island in response to the war.

Channing did not mince his words, declaring that "this is a day, set apart for national sorrow and humiliation." This was not a time to pray for the success of American arms; rather it was an opportunity "when forsaking our common pursuits, and especially forsaking our pleasures, we are to penetrate our hearts with our national danger and sins, and to offer, in the temple of the Almighty, penitential acknowledgments and earnest prayers, that he will spare and protect our country." War, Channing and a host of New England clergymen would declare that day, was God's judgment. His favor would be shown with victories and his admonishment with defeats. In just wars, the family and friends of the fallen might take comfort, Channing explained, "for we know that they have fallen in a just and honourable cause." The present war, however, was not just. "I cannot address you in the language of encouragement," he told his congregation. "I can offer you no reflections to sustain you in your calamities—no bright prospects to animate hope and to lighten the pressure of immediate suffering." "We are precipitated into a war, which," he concluded, "cannot be justified—and a war, which promises not a benefit, that I can discover, to this country or to the world." In a sermon that must have lasted well over an hour, Channing proceeded to dissect and dismiss Madison's case for war and condemn any association with France, "the acknowledged enemy of mankind." The war could not be won, he argued, because it violated the values established by America's founding fathers, undermined Americans' moral character, and wasted the lives of New England's sons. In short, "It is a war fraught with ruin to our property, our morals, our religion, our independence, our dearest rights—whilst its influence on other nations, on the common cause of humanity, is most unhappy."[1]

Opposition to the war was widespread, and it manifested itself in a variety of ways. Militia declined to cross state and international borders, state governments refused to relinquish their militia to federal authorities, and bankers refused to acquire federal debt or back federal paper currency. Many Americans continued to trade with the Canadians and even supplied the British army, a handful of Americans fought with the British, and a few American leaders actively explored the possibility of secession. The most common expression of opposition, however, came from the combination of the pen, the pulpit, and the printing press.

The United States had inherited the tradition of public fast days during wartime from the British, who, like the Americans, included public prayers and church attendance as part of the day's events. Issued by the government, such days were intended to shore up public support for a war, or in the language of British declarations throughout this period, "the success of His Majesty's arms." During the War of 1812, fast days in the United States became contested events, as a large number of clergymen took to their pulpits and railed to their flocks about the evils of war and the Republicans in the federal government. As the *Boston Gazette* protested, that the president would even call a national fast day was outrageous: the president "is not content with forcing upon the nation a war that must destroy it, but he asks you to supplicate your God for its success ... for success in battle against your liberties and your God."

The power of the traditional religious establishment in the United States was waning, with religion in the nineteenth century becoming more "democratized" as once-small sects, such as Baptists and Methodists, flourished in era of rapid expansion, individualism, and debates about separation of the old denominations from government support.[2] Nevertheless, clergymen of all faiths still maintained a considerable hold on the minds and actions of their followers. Sally Ripley, a young merchant's wife in Boston, would not dare cross her minister, who condemned "everyone who contributed the smallest degree of their influence to aid the unjust and unrighteousness cause [of the war]."[3] In the summer of 1812, many Americans experienced three fast days, as federal and state governments declared their own fast days, which peppered American calendars along with Fourth of July services as key opportunities for America's clergy to weigh into the debate about the war. Like Channing, many clergymen published their sermons or had them extracted in local papers.[4] This set the tone for public days throughout the war; such occasions as fast days, George Washington's birthday, and the Fourth of July created opportunities for hostile opposition just as much as they did for nationalistic fervor.

Public opponents to the war first and foremost asserted their loyalty to the United States, insisting that the Constitution protected them and that proper loyalty in a republic was to the nation, not to the men who ran it. From this standpoint, critics leveled a host of criticisms at Madison and the Republicans in the federal government, declaring the war a tactical blunder, immoral, and a vehicle for Madison and his cronies to pervert the Constitution and seize permanent power. Critics of the war also celebrated Britain's triumph over Napoleon, while highlighting Madison's connections with France (real or otherwise). In short, the war became a lightning rod for all of the general complaints Americans had about a decade of Republican rule and exacerbated the existing fractures in American politics and society. Critics were not let off lightly by the war's supporters, who both physically assaulted critics (as in Baltimore in 1812) and unleashed a torrent of abuse in the press. For war supporters, such critics were traitors. Such accusations generally were unfounded, but some Americans seriously considered, and even pursued, various schemes to subvert the federal government and rebel against it.

American opposition to the war is impossible to measure precisely, not least because opposition is so difficult to define. Condemnation of the war and calls for secession can easily be categorized as opposition, but reluctance to buy government debt or serve in the army might not have anything to do with a person's political views. Unlike during the American Revolution, Americans did not take up arms against one another in any significant number. Nor did the British occupy America's major towns and cities, compelling local populations to serve the British interest as a matter of survival. Only in parts of Maine did the British occupy populated areas for any length of time, and people there generally complied, with a number of them taking oaths of allegiance to the king. The War of 1812 was also short, affording little time for dramatic shifts in public opinion. Both the war's supporters and its opponents were anxious to claim large swaths of America as their own, but sectionalism was often as much a rhetorical tool as it was an identifiable division in expressing public opinions. Although Federalists continued to play a leading role in New England politics, plenty had abandoned the disintegrating party in favor the opportunities the ruling Republicans offered. Even John Adams and his son, John Quincy, aligned themselves with Madison and his supporters, and Madison's vice-president for most of the war, Elbridge Gerry, was the recent Republican governor of Massachusetts. In consequence, claims such as David Osgood's in a sermon to his Medford, Massachusetts, congregation that in "New England, the war declared cannot be approved by any but here and there a furious party leader, a few ignorant, deluded fanatics, and a handful of desperadoes" do not ring true.[5]

Nor is it particularly useful to think of opposition to the war in strictly partisan or sectional terms. The greatest threat to Madison's reelection in 1812 came from within his own party via the New York lieutenant governor, DeWitt

Clinton, who drew support from both disenchanted Republicans and Federalists. Western and southern Republican strongholds harbored substantial antiwar sentiment. John Randolph, arguably the most articulate opponent of the declaration of war in Congress, was a Virginia Republican. Federalists also maintained significant minorities in the state legislatures of Virginia and the Carolinas throughout the war, and they retook the Maryland lower chamber during the war. The most outlandish antiwar newspaper was published in Baltimore, and well over a dozen opposition newspapers operated throughout the South during the early nineteenth century.[6] Plenty of public critics of the war also ultimately took up arms against Britain, including the Federalist youths of Philadelphia who organized volunteer companies in anticipation of British coastal attacks in 1814.[7] Even the militantly anti-Madison and antiwar Virginia *Alexandria Daily Gazette* showed its limits of opposition, when in May 1813 it apologized to readers for the disruption in service, explaining that one of the editors had abandoned the paper when he was called up for militia service.[8]

The western states were not a unanimous block of support for Madison's war either.[9] Many welcomed the support for a war on neighboring Americans Indians and accepted the attack on Canada, while others expressed a disconnect between Madison's stated maritime objectives and the needs of the Western states. The self-proclaimed Republican *Western Monitor* of Lexington, Kentucky, was typical in that it had little love for Madison as a war leader, the American Indians, or the British. At the end of the war, the editors reflected on their coverage of it, remarking that "We differed in opinion with many *honorable men* on the necessity & expediency of the war." "We were opposed to it, not because we did not believe Great Britain had injured us in various ways," they explained, "but because . . . it would cost the United States much more in the end than they would gain by it. We could not see that the end proposed would be gained by the means employed."[10] Such remarks were a world away from the unwavering condemnation found in Channing's sermons.

Although some referred collectively to the voice of the war opposition as the "peace party," this label is misleading. There was no single opposition movement, and the various factions never pretended to speak with one voice. Even southern Federalists rarely cooperated with their northern associates and typically defined their politics according to local or state issues, voting accordingly.[11] As with Americans who supported the war, opponents justified their choice on a wide range of moral and practical reasons. Furthermore, opposition to the war often had little to do with Britain or the case for war against it. Many Americans spoke out against the war for fear that it would further empower Madison and his cohort of Southern Republicans, depicting the war as a ruse to strip citizens of their rights, squash dissent, and forever subordinate New England. What the opposition lacked was national leadership to unite these disparate groups. Much has been made historically of the Hartford Convention, when a number of prominent New England leaders congregated in December 1814 to discuss their opposition to the war and the possibility of secession. However, it was ultimately a regional affair and lacked an agenda with which opponents of Madison and the war outside of New England could identify. Moreover, most opposition simply was not that radical, including many delegates at the convention. The vast majority ultimately was loyal to the United States, and they crafted their language to emphasize that Madison and his Washington supporters were the problem, not the Federal Constitution or the United States.

The overwhelming majority of the war's public critics insisted on their loyalty to the United States. At a June 1812 meeting in Montgomery County, Virginia, those in attendance produced a series of resolutions that both condemned the declaration of war and celebrated their right to do so, declaring that "the right of free deliberation ... has been secured to the people of the United States, not only by the long undisturbed usage of their ancestors, but also by express provision in all their constitutions."[12] The language of Connecticut's general assembly in a public declaration two months later that justified its refusal to release the state's militia to federal authority was remarkably similar. "The people of this state view the war as unnecessary," it insisted. Nevertheless, "the general assembly, ever regardful of their duty to the general government, will perform all their obligations."[13] These constitutional obligations, the assembly insisted, did not include handing over the militia for federal use in anything but defense.

The idea of a loyal opposition was not new to the Anglo-American world. It had been a fixture in British politics throughout much of the eighteenth century and was most seriously tested during the American Revolutionary era. Throughout the 1760s and 1770s, members of Parliament and public commentators railed against the British government's coercive policies toward the American colonies, all the while insisting they did so not to undermine the country but to protect the nation's best interests, which they believed were ill served by an American war. When the unsympathetic Samuel Johnson defined patriotism as "the last refuge of the scoundrel," he had in mind John Wilkes, the outspoken pro-American former Lord Mayor of London and member of Parliament.[14]

In the United States, the idea of a loyal opposition was in its infancy. Opponents to the American Revolution had been treated mercilessly as criminals and enemy combatants. They faced imprisonment, impoverishment, and even death for expressing their beliefs. During the Quasi War, John Adams and the Federalist-dominated national government had dealt heavy-handedly with critics, granting the executive powers to jail critical newspaper editors and deport disruptive foreign nationals. The War of 1812 was substantially different in that there was no serious legal action taken by the Republican majority to punish Americans for merely expressing their opposition to the war. Private action in terms of mob violence continued, but Madison did not order the arrest of opposition newspaper editors or governors who condemned his policies. In fact, many pro-war Republicans went out of their way to condemn violence against public opponents of the war. In consequence, even though one might argue that use of loyal rhetoric merely shielded the nefarious designs of the war's opponents, or that Madison tolerated public opposition only because he had no real prospect of stopping it, the War of 1812 marks an important episode in the history of individual liberties. In no other American conflict would the press and state politicians so freely and absolutely condemn the wartime policies of a president.

Caleb Strong, the outspoken governor of Massachusetts, best framed the idea of a loyal opposition in his widely reprinted speech to the state legislature in the spring of 1813. "We are bound to obey the laws made in conformity with our constitutions," he explained, "but those constitutions ensure to us our freedom of speech; and at this momentous period, it is our right and duty to enquire into the grounds and origins of the present war."[15] Critics were not traitors, they argued, but good Americans exercising their liberties as won in the revolution and guaranteed by the Constitution. As Condy Raguet, then a young merchant and aspiring politician, declared in a speech before Philadelphia's Washington Benevolent Society, "One of the most distinguished blessings which is conferred by our constitution upon the citizens of this republic is the liberty we enjoy of a free expression of opinions, relative to the measures and conduct of the government."[16] Americans had no obligation to the men in government, explained Channing in another sermon, because the nature of America's governing system did not require it. "Government is instituted for one and a single end,—the benefit of the governed; the protection, peace, and welfare of society; and when it is perverted to other objects," he continued, "we are authorized and even bound to make such opposition."[17]

Resistance, critics insisted, must be passive—not for fear of reprisal but out of faith in the wisdom of the Constitution. As Daniel Webster, the future secretary of state but then an aspiring politician who would shortly be elected to Congress, remarked at an 1812 Fourth of July celebration in New Hampshire, Federalists were "neither tyrants *in* power, nor rebels *out*." "If we are taxed, to carry on this War . . . we shall pay. If our personal services are required, we shall yield them to the precise extent of our Constitutional liability." Yet, "at the same time, the world may be assured that we know our Rights, and shall exercise them. We shall express our opinions on this, as on every measure of government, I trust without passion—I am certain without *fear*."[18] Exultations of the value of a free press were not surprisingly common. As Channing remarked, "At the present time, it is particularly your duty to guard with jealousy, the right of expressing with freedom your honest convictions respecting the measures of your rulers." "Freedom of opinion, of speech, and of the press," he insisted, "is our most valuable privilege—the very soul of our republican institutions—the safeguard of all other rights." Partly in consequence, war supporters often went out of their way to insist that the war's proponents had a right to express themselves. Such was the case when Bostonians abused William Widgery, a Massachusetts congressman who voted for the war, in the street. A number of antiwar papers dutifully carried apologies, including the *Salem Gazette*, which defended him by noting that "he doubtless voted according to his conscience."[19] As fine American citizens who respected the Constitution, they could publicly do no less.

Opponents criticized the war from a variety of angles. They argued it was pointless, and the United States could not possibly compel the British government to concede what were held to be its maritime rights. Antagonists highlighted the horrors of war in general and the absurdity of fighting a nation that was second only to the United States in dedication to liberty. They argued the war was immoral and the United States would suffer the wrath of God for prosecuting it. Above all, they argued it would ultimately destroy the character, if not the polity, of the United States.

That the United States was ill prepared to go to war in June 1812 seemed obvious to everyone but those who most wanted to prosecute it. As the citizens of Newbury, Massachusetts, resolved at a June 1812 town meeting, "It is a War entered into without any measure of preparation, against an enemy completely prepared to avail itself of every advantage arising from our defenceless state."[20] The Massachusetts House of Representatives concurred in a memorial sent to Congress on the eve of the war, which included the resolution passed by an overwhelming majority that "an offensive war against Great Britain, under the present circumstances of this country, would be in the highest degree, impolitic, unnecessary, and ruinous."[21] The widely reprinted August declaration of the General Assembly of Connecticut, supporting the governor's refusal to release the state militia for federal service, further highlighted the folly of going to war when the nation was so unprepared:

> War, always calamitous, in this case portentous of great evils, acted against a nation powerful in her armies, and without rival on the oceans, cannot be viewed by us but with the deepest regret. A nation without fleets, without armies, with an impoverished treasury, with a frontier by sea and land extending many hundreds of miles, feebly defended, waging a war, hath not *first counted the cost*.

As a result, the assembly explained, "the people of this state view the war as unnecessary"; the state would retain the militia to protect itself rather than waste it on supporting the ill-planned schemes of invading Canada.[22]

As the United States suffered a string of defeats over the next six months, the tone of criticism did not change; critics railed against the poor military planning and leadership at the national level. During the autumn presidential election, Madison's critics focused on his poor wartime leadership. "If suspicion could be harboured in the generous hearts of republicans," declared Madison's chief rival for the presidency, DeWitt Clinton, in a supposedly anonymous pamphlet, "we should almost be disposed to say, that all this looks like a connivance with the enemy, and that every other thing was intended, rather than a serious attack upon her." "Certainly if [Britain] had directed, or influenced our councils," he concluded, "she would not have made them more favourable to herself."[23] Speaking to Philadelphia's Washington Association on the anniversary of Washington's birth, Charles Cox summarized the rampant frustration being expressed throughout America. "We have ventured on the pennon of destructions," he declared, "without the weapons or preparation; against a nation whose natural state is war: one armed in impregnable brass;—and the strife must end like the spasms of a convulsion leaving us still more injured and debilitated." In the face of such folly, he concluded, "Every thinking man, must exclaim against this war, it is pregnant with misery, expense and dishonour."[24] The *Boston Spectator* focused on the military commanders, remarking "what a figure the biography of our contemporary generals will make, in the history of our country! What a disgrace to the annals of the United States!"

Criticism became less of a partisan or sectional issue, as the British chalked up more victories in Canada. Even such stalwart Madison-supporting papers as the Charleston *Investigator* readily printed attacks on the war's management. "The art of war is not learned in a day," a critic in the *Investigator* admitted, "But without a disposition to be querulous, and making all due allowances for the military inexperience of the United States, can we satisfy ourselves that there is no reason for complaint?—that some of these calamities might not have been prevented?"[25] By the summer, papers such as North Carolina's *Carolina Federal-Republican* were ready to admit defeat. "Without funds, without taxes, without an army, navy, or adequate fortifications, with one hundred and fifty millions of our property in the hands of the declared enemy, without any of his in our power, and with a vast commerce afloat, our rulers have promulged [sic] a war, against the clear and decided sentiments of a vast majority of the nation."[26]

The series of failed invasions of Canada was a magnet for criticism—both for their strategic folly and for the immorality of an offensive war. "If it is a war of conquest," complained Cox, "there should be some promised gain,—some treasure; but, surely every man is sensible, that the British possessions in America, will yield us nothing but, a miserable population."[27] Like Napoleon's army in Russia in 1812, America's army would waste away in the vast frozen nothingness of Canada, complained a letter to the *Boston Patriot*.[28] During the 1812 presidential election, Clinton argued that Britain would have sold Canada for less than would be required for America to seize it by force of arms. He calculated, "as to Canada, suppose we get it at the expense of ten thousand men, and we have already lost three thousand five hundred without gaining an inch of ground, and with the further loss of twenty millions of dollars; how stands the account?" "While Britain has lost what she did not want, we shall have gained what we *cannot keep*, and what we do not desire, and what Britain would have sold us for half the money," he concluded.[29]

For the war's opponents, this was a dirty, bloody business filled with human suffering—a sharp contrast to the supporters' attempts to create a nationalist spirit of 1812. As a poem in the *New Bedford Mercury* titled "War" described the scene:

> Oh! Must Columbia's sons forsake their home,
> To crimson over Canada with blood,
> Or hostile, o'er the murm'ring billows roam,
> To stain, with human gore, the ocean flood?[30]

Such men were the pawns of the good and the great, complained an article in the *Trenton Federalist*. After all, Madison and Congress were "comfortable in their seats" and were not even "dreaming of sharing the hardships and dangers of the context." Instead, the author complained bitterly, "they may vote, but others must fight." "The burden and heat of the day will fall upon the poor mechanics, the farmers and their sons, and the day-labourers," he continued. "These are the men that will ultimately be called forth to suffer the hardships of war—to be maimed and slain the day of battle. It will be their families that will be beggared—their wives and children that will be reduced to widows and orphans." Yet, bemoaned the author along with a host of critics throughout the country, such people did not want war: "A cry has gone forth that the *people* are calling for this war of conquest. It is untrue. The people do not wish—do not dream of such things. They are not such idiots as to wage war against England."[31]

Antiwar sermons in particular focused on the enormous personal suffering caused by armed conflict. David Osgood vividly described the anxieties of his Medford, Massachusetts, congregation in a sermon responding to Madison's war declaration:

> At this moment, your minds are harassed and your bosoms tortured with the idea of your sons, husbands, your brothers reluctantly torn from all the scenes and occupations of peace, from all their domestic connexion, enjoyments, pursuits, to be exposed in the tented field, subjected to the rigors of a military life, liable to the numerous and fatal

diseases of a camp, and occasionally, to stand as to many marks for the sharp shooters in the hostile army.[32]

Of course, the civilians-turned-soldiers were not the only ones who suffered.

In sharp contrast to the idea of republican motherhood espoused during the Spirit of 1812 period, in which mothers and wives encouraged the men in their families into military service and bore their deaths with pride, the war's opponents highlighted the suffering caused by the loss of a father, husband, brother, or son. The loss of any man is to be lamented, Channing argued in one of his fast sermons, but New England felt the loss of its sons more acutely than European nations, because New England had no surplus population to waste: "[The war] will cost us blood, and not the blood of men whose lives are of little worth—of men burdensome to society, such as often compose the armies of Europe." "In this part of our country," he argued, "we have no mobs, no overflowing population, from which we wish to be relieved by war. We must send our sons, our brothers to the field—men who have property, homes, affectionate friends, and the prospect of useful and happy lives."[33] On a later fast day, Francis Brown, a minister in neighboring North Yarmouth, harped on the familiar theme of civilian suffering, describing to his congregation how "in computing the destruction of life occasioned by war, the numbers actually slain in battle will not give the proper total. Famine, pestilence, and conflagrations often follow up the picture of desolation." In consequence, he estimated that the genuine total of casualties was much higher than any battle estimate, concluding, "Oh, what a dreadful aggregate of slaughter and wretchedness!"[34]

Women's diaries and private letters convey these concerns far more than they reflect the public calls for "female patriotism" at the start of the war. Elizabeth Ann Seton, at the time the head of Catholic religious society in Maryland, worried incessantly about her son, William, whom she described as "rather inclined to follow the drum. Young Brent, one of his fellow students, and some other of his companions, left the Seminary for a commission." Rather than endorsing his martial interests, she discouraged him, noting that "if it was not for the boundless love for mother, Rebecca and Kitty [his sisters] he would probably be off."[35] Rebecca Gratz, living in Philadelphia, worried equally about her brother, who had volunteered for military service. In one letter to him she confessed that local women were not being stoic supporters of the war. They wanted peace so their men would return, describing how "we sit and bewail you much more like women than patriots and turn pale at the thought of a battle."[36]

War, insisted many of the opponents in pulpits, meetings, and print, was a vile affliction. It turned honest men into immoral scoundrels whose wickedness stoked the fires of hell. Echoing innumerable commentators, Nathan Beman declared to his Congregationalist Church in Portland that "Camps and the field of slaughter are the head quarters of satan," who in wartime spreads the "depravity of morals" across the lands as good Christians ignore their duties.[37] Like many New England seaport towns, Newbury watched its unemployed men, who could no longer find work on merchant and fishing vessels, try their hand at privateering—a dangerous business dangling high rewards in exchange for great personal risk.[38] "It is a War," complained Newbury's citizens, "in which we must exchange the fair and honorable trade by which our country has been heretofore, under the wise and good Rulers, greatly enriched, of the miserable, ruinous, demoralizing practice of privateering."[39] Lust, not justice, railed Francis Brown, drove men to war—"lust of *power*, the lust of *wealth*, the lust of *praise*, and the lust of *revenge*, have kept the world in arms from age to age." In consequence, "In time of war the wicked become bold and impudent to sin." "When men are accustomed to rapine and blood," he continued, "and are constantly in the midst of all the profaneness, blasphemy, debauchery, and every contagious evil, which abound in an army, they lose every spark of kindness and mercy, and become ferocious beasts, fitted for the work of cruelty and death." Such injuries to the public body, he concluded, take "many generations" to heal, and "perhaps it is never repaired." This immoral, blasphemous episode in American history will stain America's character and propel it towards a disastrous path, he insisted: "our sons and daughters will grow up with those feelings and habits, which will prepare them to cast off the fear of God and man, and to rush headlong in the broad road to destruction."[40]

For many Americans, defense of personal or national honor—a favorite justification among the war's advocates—was not sufficient reason to risk such suffering. By opposing the war, explained Randolph to his Virginia constituents, an American did not surrender his manhood.[41] "There are not wanting men so weak, as to suppose that their approbation of warlike measures is a proof of national gallantry, and that opposition to them indicates a want of that spirit which becomes a friend to his country," he complained. Yet real manliness and patriotism was to reject the "acclamation of the day" and to exercise the "courage and patriotism . . . to oppose one's self to the mad infatuation" clamoring for war.[42] True national honor, insisted Francis Brown to his Portland flock, was founded in good governance. "It is frequently alleged, that the honor of the nation demands an appeal to arms," he admitted; however, the "real honor of a nation consists in the equitable and wholesome laws impartially administered; in the maintenance of justice, trust, and good faith, both at home and abroad." Nations were not duelists. "If it be that morbid sensibility, which is all alive to an imaginary insult, but feels not real disgrace," he concluded, this is a view that "if not nearly allied to crime, is at least consistent with it."[43]

Worse still, an offensive war was a violation of God's commandments and thus risked catastrophe for the nation. In keeping with their Puritan theological roots, many Americans, particularly in New England, held that God's wrath was both immediate and harsh. As Governor Strong warned with regard to America's aggressive war, God "would break in pieces the power of the oppressor, and scatter the people that delight in war."[44] The problem was America's rulers had turned away from God's teachings, a Salem minister worried, because the "governors of nations too generally conduct their affairs as if they believe there were no being above them." The role of war, he explained, was God's way of putting such men in their proper places.[45] In one of many sermons that questioned the Christian rigor of America's rulers, James Blyth, principal of Kentucky's Transylvania University, remarked that "the religion of the American rulers, if indeed they recognise God at all, resembles infinitely more the religion of heathens than of Christians, forms one of those numerous items which ought to fill up our cup of mourning and sorrow today."[46] And it was not just the rulers who suffer for their lack of devotion and vanity and greed. As James Abercrombie warned the congregation at St. James's Church in Philadelphia, "Innumerable are the examples, both in sacred and civil history, of the destruction of cities and countries, in consequence of the wickedness of their inhabitants."[47] Such universal application of God's wrath, explained David Osgood, was all the greater when dealing with a republic such as the United States. After all, a republic's rulers were selected by the people and could be replaced by them. "If through their [the people's] own weakness and wickedness they fail of doing this, they forfeit all their privileges, offend against God . . . and expose themselves to his heaviest judgments, not only to the calamities of the present life as a community, but individually, to the danger of everlasting punishment hereafter."[48]

The European wars, which had constituted part of Americans' daily diet of news for nearly two decades, served as the prime extended example to early critics of the War of 1812. Europe revealed the folly of war, the human suffering it caused, the rise of rapacious rulers that war fostered, and, of course, how severely God could punish the wicked for their sins. "It is sufficient that every consideration arising from good policy," pleaded the Massachusetts House of Representatives in a June 1812 address to the federal government, "and from the duty of a nation to itself, forbids us to plunge into a war which desolates the European world, and from which it seems to have been the design of Almighty Providence to exempt us . . . by placing us remote from the theatre of their contentions."[49] To disregard this blessing of distance from Europe by involving the United States in a war with either Britain or France, however justified, was folly. As an address by prominent New York Republicans in opposition to Madison explained to their constituents, "An immense ocean separates us from the old world, and it ought to be a fundamental maxim of our policy to keep aloof from the intrigues, the conflicts and the wars of Europe. . . . By entering into the labyrinths of European policy we identify our destinies with blood, prodigality and misery."[50]

Randolph offered a similar warning to his Virginia constituents. Responding to war supporters' public pronouncements that "the finger of heaven points to war," Randolph argued that "It does point to war, as it points to the mansions of eternal misery and torture; as a flaming beacon warning us of that vortex which may not approach but with certain destruction." That beacon, he cautioned, was "desolated Europe," and it "announces the wrath to come upon those, who, ungrateful for the bounty of Providence, not satisfied with the peace, liberty, and security and plenty at home, fly, as it were, into the face of the most high, and tempt his forbearance."[51] The United States, he warned, was on the brink of that same catastrophe.

A regular theme in public opposition to the war was that the greatest threat to the United States was domestic, not foreign.[52] As James Sloan remarked on the eve of the war, "the conduct of the said Democratic Republicans hath been, for five years past, more injurious to the interest, peace, and happiness of these United States" than anything yet faced by the United States.[53] Much of the blame fell squarely on Madison's shoulders. The attacks were personal and uninhibited. During the 1812 election, Clinton publicly compared his opponent for the presidency to a disease affecting the United States—a nation that "at this truly awful moment, [is] reduced, by the driveling policy and imbecile judgment of a man." Not finished, Clinton then attacked Madison's wife, Dolley. She was, after all, the daughter of a loyalist from the American Revolution, and "such is the effect of female influence on men of weak minds" that she "annihilated in his mind" any "real bias toward the republican interests."[54] So even though the clergy harped on about the immorality of the war, secular criticism depicted the war as evidence of Madison's corruption and a Republican plot to subjugate the United States.

Many critics challenged Madison and his supporters' sincerity over impressment. Why, Kentucky's *Western Monitor* continued to ask in early 1815, did Madison push the country to go to war for the sake of sailors about whom few cared, and for grievances largely focused on New England over which New Englanders themselves did not want to go to war?[55] Critics pointed out that the issue of impressment had barely been touched on in Madison's speeches or in the diplomatic correspondence appearing in newspapers throughout the country. In his influential *Perpetual War, the Policy of Mr. Madison*, John Lowell argued that "this subject of impressment is a mere instrument wielded by men who are utterly indifferent about the sufferings of the sailors or the merchants."[56] Governor Strong went even further in his widely reprinted message to the Massachusetts legislature after a year of war, publicly defending Britain's position of indefeasible allegiance and chastising Americans for knowingly employing British sailors. "All the European nations agree in founding allegiance upon the circumstance of nativity . . . [and] every government has a just claim to the service of its subjects in time of war," he declared. For Americans to deny this is hypocrisy, he continued, because "it was on this principle that our laws for the confiscation of absentees [loyalist who left the United States after the American Revolution] estates were passed." "A nation ought first to do justice to others before it demands justice of them," he proclaimed, before admonishing Americans who used these sailors "as means of acquiring wealth," whereas Britain needed them "for her defence."[57]

Some critics pointed to a conspiracy with the French. "So long as the councils of American are under the influence and controul of the emperor of France, and so long as we can serve his interest in the war with England, he will not suffer us to make peace," argued a Vermont detractor.[58] Although such comments played well among British and Canadian proponents of the war, most critics in America recognized their ridiculousness and pursued a more nuanced approach. Instead of asserting a direct connection between Madison and Napoleon, most critics asserted that Madison was acting unitarily to impress his French idol. In some ways this was even worse; it depicted Madison as a sycophantic dupe. One speaker reflected at an 1814 New Jersey "convention of the friends of peace" that the government was "under the fatal delusion that it was necessary that the super-eminent Napoleon, the mighty conqueror, the subjugation of Europe to whom was considered by our cabinet as certain, was to be appeased by whatever means."[59] And for this, critics claimed, the world mocked the United States. As the *Carolina Federal-Republican* raged, "America is now held out to the World, not as a Nation gallantly fighting for the maintenance of her own rights, but as a people duped into a War for the support of principles which they disclaim, and for the advancement fatal to their best interests, and to the dearest of humanity."[60]

Another common accusation was the more serious concern that Madison and his associates sought to use the war to circumvent the constitution and seize more permanent power for themselves. Although slavery would not be a major factor in the conflict, northern war critics were quick to draw on their disdain for chattel slavery to question Madison and his southern supporters' commitment to republicanism and accuse the president of secret plans to enslave all Americans.[61] Such public accusations and the corresponding defensive rhetoric would become all too familiar in decades that followed. Madison and his cronies, claimed Sloan in his popular pamphlet, "secretly with closed doors, surrounded by slaves and slave holders, and a set of war hawks, and other idle drones ... are perpetually striving to produce war, or any other evil change, that may increase offices, and thereby enable them to live in pride and luxury, upon the product of the labour, of honest, industrious, and virtuous citizens."[62] The idea of a Virginian plot held sway among many northern critics, who felt the last twelve years had been too beneficial for America's largest, most populous, and wealthiest state. Virginians were not like northerners. "They live in plenty and repose in ease," complained a Philadelphia critic, "the labour of their slaves supplying the necessity of corporal exertion, they are accustomed to find all their wanted relief by the issuing of a command." In short, the "spirit of enterprise" so commonly found in New York, Pennsylvania, and New England did not "correspond with their slothful and sedentary habits." Anyone who supported such a regime was "forging fetters for themselves and their countrymen."[63] Josiah Quincy declared in an inflammatory speech before the House of Representatives that appeared throughout the Anglophone world that he would resist such slavery. "If . . . my children are destined to be slaves, and to yoke in with the negroes, chained to the car of a Southern master," he railed, "they, at least, shall have the sweet consciousness as the consolation of their condition—they shall be able to say, 'OUR FATHER WAS GUILTLESS OF THESE CHAINS.'"[64] Northern Republicans also expressed this grievance, with prominent New Yorkers complaining that their party in Washington was dominated "by two or three individuals" and that their law "has not only controuled the conduct of its members; but has become the law of the land."[65]

War, opponents maintained, was the enemy of a republic and would ultimately be disastrous for the United States regardless of the outcome on the battlefield. As Samuel Clesson Allen declared in a July 1812 oration in Greenfield, Massachusetts, "a state of war is hostile to the *genius* of a republic. It cannot fail to endanger the liberties of the people; and a war of conquest is, in the spirit of it, repugnant to the principles, which are the support of a free state."[66] The federal government's attempts to impose new taxes, increase national debt, raise a national army, and draft the militia into federal service all met with hostility from the war's critics, who ceaselessly represented any executive measure as a plot to undermine Americans' personal liberties and states' rights. Madison's long record of defending states' rights haunted him throughout the war, as critics openly mocked the president for his hypocrisy. In its response to the attempt to press the Massachusetts militia into federal service, the *Salem Gazette* ridiculed Madison by reprinting his No. 46 from the *Federalist Papers*, which defended states' rights against a national government, under the headline of "State Sovereignty, or Mr. Madison's Mode of Oppugnation to the General Government."[67]

Public commentators worried especially about restrictions on the press, fearing that Madison and his cohort would strike at their critics. Over half of the Montgomery County, Virginia, resolutions against the war dealt with issues of the necessity of free debate and the right to public criticism.[68] "The mouths of the opposition abroad must next be gagged, their hands tied, and their feet made to move at the will of the war-party," fretted one.[69] Opponents of the war, especially newspapers editors, had good reason to worry. In June 1812, a mob in Baltimore attacked and destroyed the press of the *Federal Republican*, when its editor, Alexander Contee Hanson, responded to the declaration of war with a

I Josiah the first do by this my Royal Proclamation announce myself King of New England, Nova Scotia and Passamaquoddy, Grand Master of the noble order of the Two Cod fishes.

JOSIAH the FIRST

Figure 6.1 William Charles, "Josiah the First" (Philadelphia, c.1813). Library of Congress, Prints and Photographs Division, LC-DIG-ppmsc-05876. In this print, Charles criticizes Josiah Quincy, the wealthy descendant of Massachusetts revolutionaries and future Boston mayor and president of Harvard University, who sat in the U.S. House of Representatives during the War of 1812. Quincy was among the most outspoken critics of Madison, the Republican majority, and the war, and he was a known New England secessionist. In the satirical print, Charles attacks both Quincy, who is depicted as the "King of New England, Nova Scotia and Passamaquoddy, Grand Master of the Noble order of the Two Cod fishes" and New England, whose importance to the United States is panned through the suggestion that it offers only cod—inferred by placing Quincy on a barren rocky coastline with only a few cod swimming in the background.

scathing editorial against it and the Republican leadership. Nothing Hanson had written was new, and similar arguments and language abounded in the newspapers and sermons in states further north. But Baltimore during the summer of 1812 was a restless city in which men assaulted the property and bodies of anyone who appeared to oppose the war. City officials did little to halt the violence and called out the militia only when a church was threatened. To some extent, this sort of crowd violence was part of the Anglo-American repertoire of protest. As in the Stamp Act riots and the Boston Tea Party in America, and countless riots against rising bread prices and toll roads in England, the crowds of Baltimore exercised a degree of restraint. City and state officials were often at the scene, either participating to give the mob action legitimacy or negotiating.[70]

This model was shattered when Hanson returned to Baltimore in July, establishing himself and his paper in a solid brick building with the help of his supporters, which included Henry "Light-Horse Harry" Lee—Revolutionary War hero, former governor of Virginia, former congressman, and father to the future Confederate army general, Robert E. Lee. Hanson's first issue on his return was a challenge to his opponents. He viciously attacked the mob that had driven him out in June, Madison, and the war, and then he followed up with the announcement that he and two dozen armed supporters were ready to defend the paper's offices. When an angry mob arrived on cue that evening, Hanson's group fired on it, killing one and wounding others. The mob left only to acquire firearms of their own. They soon returned with an armament that included an artillery piece manned by the editor of the Baltimore *Sun*. By the next morning the crowd neared two thousand. Outgunned and outnumbered, Hanson's group ultimately surrendered to local authorities on the understanding they would be protected in the local jail. A mob broke in the next evening and repeatedly and brutally assaulted the men before a cheering crowd. By the end, one man was dead and eleven were physically broken, including Hanson and Lee, neither of whom recovered from their injuries and died prematurely a few years later. No one was punished for participating in the riots, and Baltimore endured the name "mobtown" for decades.[71]

Although Baltimore witnessed the most brutal attack on the press, it was not alone. The editor of the opposition *American Patriot* in Savannah was pulled from his office and assaulted by a mob that June and the editor of the *Virginia Patriot* received regular death threats.[72] The violence received condemnation throughout the country and from across the political spectrum. Conjuring images of the French Revolution with its mob-ruled cities and bloodstained streets was not difficult. The *Greensburgh & Indiana Register* headlined its reprinted account of the first riot with "Mobocracy!—or, The Reign of Terror!"[73] The *Newport Mercury* labeled Baltimore the "Paris of America."[74] The *Salem Gazette* headlined its account with "The Mob Government of Baltimore" and included

an editorial about how freedom prospered in New York under the wise leadership of DeWitt Clinton, the paper's favored candidate for the upcoming presidential election.[75] Most pro-war papers were tactfully quiet on the subject, with
such papers as *Niles' Weekly Register* printing the most inflammatory extracts
from the *Federal Republican* alongside official affidavits describing events rather
than an editorial condoning or condemning the riots.

The funeral of James Lingan, the Revolutionary War veteran and former
senior officer of the Maryland State Militia whom the Baltimore rioters had
tortured and killed, was as close to a national event as the opposition media
could make it. Vivid descriptions of the funeral were widely printed, along
with a diagram of the procession, so that citizens across the country could participate virtually in the event. The funeral procession was elaborate and included family, friends, an honor guard, and a host of worthies from the region.
Support of the cause in which Lingam died was made clear in the procession
including Hanson and "other survivors of the band who defended liberty and
the press." Surrounding them were war veterans, who physically aided the
weakened men and played the music. George Washington Parke Custis, the
adopted son of George Washington, set the tone of shame in the funeral oration. "Hide, hide my country, thy diminished head," he proclaimed. "*Thou*, an
empire of laws, and yet this monstrous outrage, within thy bosom!—Thou, an
empire of laws, and yet the asylum of justice, with innocent blood profaned!"
Most unsettling for Custis and much of the American elite was not the violence of the rioters, but their victims having been so distinguished. "Who were
these Prisoners?—Were they the rankings of kennels; were their shoes yet
new, since they landed on our shores?" he asked. "Or were they the sons of the
sires, who had fought the battles, and labored in the councils of their country's
glory; generous scions, sprang from the oak which had borne the hardest blasts
of liberty's storm?"[76]

The war's critics made the most of the situation, seizing every opportunity to
mention their opponents and the violence in Baltimore in the same breath. A
town meeting in Boston that August was typical in its attempt to link the riots
with Madison's presidency, calling them a "prelude to the dissolution of all free
government" in which government-supported mobs and the governors themselves would be interchangeable. The solution, they resolved, was "a change of
our present rulers."[77] Festus Foster of Vermont, a state whose government was
divided between Federalists and Republicans, called the pro-Madison press "the
mercenary scribblers in every prostitute Gazette" who justified the "Presidential
mob" that "most inhumanly mangled and massacred some of our best and wor-
thiest citizens."[78] Such arguments helped the Federalists in elections in New
England and New York and enabled them to win control of the House of Delegates in Maryland.[79]

In terms of their attitudes toward Britain itself, critics ranged from ambivalent to warmly supportive. None, despite the accusations of pro-war pundits, openly embraced the idea of reunion with Britain or appear to have been in the pay of the British government. Although plenty of Americans lamented that Britain and the United States—countries of a common ancestry and shared love of liberty—should be at war, no one publicly bemoaned the revolution or waxed fondly on the merits of the old colonial relationship. Many commentators, however, emphasized the need for Americans to break free of old prejudices and the dangers of hate being passed down through the generations without cause. In Charleston's St. Michael's Church on the Fourth of July 1810, a prominent local veteran of the American Revolution declared that the time had come for Americans to forgive Britain and move past any lingering resentment. Speaking at the invitation of the American Revolution Society and the South Carolina State Society of Cincinnati in one of the city's most prominent churches, Henry McCall argued in his opening, "now that the tree of liberty has become strong, let us forget the storms that beat upon its youthful branches, and almost shook it from its base. The brave have no memory for injuries."[80] Speaking in Dedham, Massachusetts, two years later, Jabez Chickering echoed these sentiments. "The revolutionary war has given rise to partialities and prejudices," he observed, "not less disgraceful in themselves, than dangerous in their tendency. They endeavor to excite perpetual hatred and animosity toward any nation, can originate only in corrupt hearts and darkened understandings." "Remember Carthage," he warned. "The father of Hannibal, the Carthegenian General, took his son to the altar of his country and compelled him to swear perpetual hatred to the republic of Rome. From this hatred originated those wars which laid Carthage in ruins."[81]

Many Americans celebrated Britain as the last line of defense against French tyranny. Toeing the line so often expressed in the British press, war critics in America argued that the French Revolution, though it was embarked on with such promise, had descended into brutality and darkness. From it a new tyranny was born that threatened human civilization and civil liberty throughout Europe and the world. The war between Britain and France was unlike any other, explained Randolph; it was "a war in which the whole human race are the victims, to gratify the pride and lust of power of a single individual." Only Britain could stop Napoleon. As the headline of an editorial in the *Missouri Gazette* from October 1813 declared, "the World's Last Hope—or Britain in the Bulwark of Humanity and Civilization and Civil Liberty."[82] Intended or not, explained a Philadelphia critic, a war against Britain made the United States the de facto ally of France. "Whether there is at present, or any future prospect of an alliance with France, I know not," he explained, "but this is a self-evident fact, that by declaring war against England, it is as effectually aids and assists France, to destroy that power, as if our situation was such, that our American army and that of France, were united together in one field of battle."[83]

The sudden turn of events following Napoleon's disastrous Russian campaign in the winter of 1812 and France's defeat in 1814 met with euphoria in some parts of the United States. The *Boston Spectator* went further than even most Britons in its demand to see Napoleon and France punished, declaring, "We should be sorry to see Paris in flames in revenge for the fate of Smolensk and Moscow; but the repose of the world requires that France should feel for centuries the folly and wickedness of the schemes of her unprincipled tyrant." The French deserved to suffer, the editorial continued. After all, "If Frenchmen had not rejoiced, and insolently triumphed at the injustice and foreign conquests of Bonaparte; if they had not contributed cheerfully to promote his views; if they had not boasted of their trophies, plundered from other nations . . . one might feel some compassion for them."[84] Large and small towns alike in New England, New York, New Jersey, Pennsylvania, and Maryland celebrated peace in Europe during the summer of 1814.[85] These celebrations raised the ire of local war supporters, such as Connecticut's *American Mercury*, which equated celebrations of French defeats as thinly veiled support for Britain—calls to rejoice in the "victory of the British, a victory of our deadly enemy . . . in a word, a victory over our government."[86]

Such complaints had little effect. At a Wallingford, Connecticut, celebration the featured orator openly praised Britain's senior general, the Duke of Wellington, declaring "When we behold the humble peasant rising against his oppressor; the long exiled monarch restored to the throne of his ancestors and the affections of his people; and whole nations, with one simultaneous effort, breaking the chain of despotism; who does not call to mind the name of Wellington?" Britain, he argued, deserved praise for delivering humanity from the tyrant, Napoleon. "Let not the prejudices of any, be offended by this tribute to British valour," he warned. "Virtue, even in an enemy, deserves our respect. The love of Liberty, and the spirit of resistance against oppression, have ever distinguished the national character of Britons."[87]

While Canada boasted cannon volleys and assemblies for officers and local ladies, the greatest celebration in all North America took place in Boston, where a committee of the good and great of the city planned citywide festivities for June 15.[88] The official celebrations culminated in a packed church service attended by the governor, his council, and most members of the legislature. "The musical performances, vocal and instrumental," announced one review, "were executed by a very full choir and band, in a style of enthusiasm, taste and excellence, seldom equaled in this metropolis." It included hymns by Handel and an ode by L. M. Sargent written for the occasion and sung to the tune of "Ye Mariners of England." The concluding hymn, bellowed out in unison by the choir, band, organ, and congregation, rejoiced over the fall of France:

> Of France the eagle spoils no more!
> Her lilies cease to blush with gore!
> Broken the spell, that bound the world in awe;
> And Europe wakes to freedom, peace, and law.

Although somewhat careful not to include too extensive praise of Britain, the hymn nevertheless concluded with a lament of the war in America:

> O Thou, whose mercy never sleeps,
> Though Carnage raves, and Pity weeps;
> Pardon and save our guilty, suffering land,
> Which feels thy judgements still and owns thy hand!

Channing delivered the sermon, which chronicled Napoleon's tyranny and bemoaned his negative influence on the United States. Channing then rebuked the federal government and lamented that "*As a nation* indeed, we have no right to participate in the general joy. As a nation, we cannot gather round the ruins of the fallen despotism, and say, We shared in the peril and glory of its destruction." That evening included further festivities, among them fireworks and an illumination of the state buildings—a gesture almost exclusively reserved for American victories—for the benefit "of the vast multitudes united in the celebration."

Through opposition to Madison and the War of 1812, critics argued, Americans could find some redemption. Channing argued at the victory celebrations that New Englanders

> in heart if not in act, with our prayers if not our arms . . . have partaken [in] the struggles of Europe. In this day of our country's disgrace, we can say, and the world should know it, that *we* never sung the praises of the tyrant, never joined the throng which offered him incense and bent before him the servile knee.[89]

The following month at the Northampton Fourth of July annual celebratory dinner, the toasts included one to the "Commonwealth of Massachusetts—Tho' she will long feel the burthens of the present war, thank Heaven, she participated not in its guilt."[90] Daniel Webster was among the brazen. Standing before the House of Representatives in December 1814 in opposition to the government's attempt to introduce conscription into the federal army, he waxed eloquent on various constitutional issues before declaring the war an unmitigated disaster, accusing the Madison administration and the Republicans of conniving to turn Congress into a "dictator" by introducing conscription. "May God, in his compassion, shield me from any participation in the enormity of this guilt," Webster proclaimed.[91]

The war's supporters were outraged at the flagrant public opposition to the war and criticism of the nation's leaders. Connecticut's war-supporting *American Mercury* was so frustrated with the New England war opposition by the end of summer 1812 that it declared "It is impossible to read the federal papers at the present crisis, we mean the most of them, and particularly some in New-England, without astonishment at the falsehood, the malice and the folly which their polluted columns are daily disgorging."[92] Such antiwar messages could not be ignored, because they undermined the war effort. "At a time like this," complained the *National Intelligencer* in August 1812, "when the exertions of every individual should be directed to an efficient prosecution of the war . . . such misrepresentations cannot but have the most baneful influence as well on the present as on the future prospects of our country."[93]

Many accused the war opposition of duplicity, arguing that their opposition stemmed from political, rather than patriotic, motives. In response to dissident New York Republicans' published appeal to the electorate, Madison's supporters created their own address in which they described their opponents as "a faction in the bosom of our land, whose perseverance and industry is exceeded only by their inveteracy; who seek, through every avenue, to mislead your judgment, and to inflame your passions." "While our enemies are waging against us a cruel and bloody war," the address raged, "they cry 'peace.'"[94] After all, Richard Bache pointed out in his 1813 Fourth of July oration to the Republicans of Philadelphia, these so-called friends of peace were hardly that. These were men "who were solicitous for a war with England in 1793; who waged a war against France in 1798; who demanded an act of war against Spain in 1802; who clamored, once more, for a war with England in 1806; and who, at this moment, pant for a war against imperial France." Yet they "adopt, with all the complacency of an accommodating forgetfulness, the title of THE FRIENDS OF PEACE!"[95]

To the war's stoutest defenders, opposition was treason. Leading the assault was *Niles' Weekly Register*, which in June 1812 responded to opponents' defense of impressment by declaring that "It is traitorous, and shews a mean and pitiful spirit, to palliate or *in any manner* excuse, or justify, the impressment of our seamen by the *British*." "It springs from a heart so base and sordid," the paper continued, "that he who is guilty of it may well be suspected of a disposition to sell his father, mother, wife and children to the *Turks* for a handful of sequins."[96] Asa Aikens of Vermont likened the opposition to the loyalists of the American Revolution, who, as then, must be identified and rooted out. "At this eventful moment," he declared, "when our government are calling upon us to strike and avenge the wrongs of an insulted and abused nation, it becomes our duty to point to the dangers which lurk within, as well as those which threaten from without."[97] New York's *Military Monitor* prayed vengefully in September: "may the united plagues of Egypt come upon the house and person of the wretch who refuses to raise his arm and open his purse to secure gallant American sailors from cruel, ignominious bondage, and American property from Anglo Algerine depredations."[98] Such threats were not idle, as the Baltimore mob had demonstrated.

Although the violence of the Baltimore riots was never repeated, the assault in the press upon the opposition was relentless. Throughout the war, its supporters rejected the legitimacy of a loyal opposition, insisting that opposition to the elected government was inherently disloyal to the nation. As *Niles' Weekly Register* representatively explained at the outbreak of war, disagreement in a republic was expected, but once the vote is made the minority must yield. "It is not to be supposed that every man will approve a general measure; but the minority must submit to the majority," the *Register* declared. "It is the first principle of our solemn compact with each other."[99] Madison agreed, informing the nation in his war address that all Americans had a duty to support the elected government, stating that "Whatever opinions men of different sentiments may have imbibed with regard to the prevailing policy of government, a sacred obligation is now imposed, magnanimously to drown all party contentions and political bickerings."[100] This became the mantra of the war's supporters throughout the conflict: the opposition were being poor sports; they had lost the elections fairly and now needed to accept the will of the majority.

Not surprisingly, the war's public supporters singled out the New England clergy for vilification. Critics in the press chastised them for interfering with politics on the one hand and then criticized them for not following in the footsteps of their predecessors in the American Revolution, who took to their pulpits to support the war against Britain. Critics called the opposition clergy closet loyalists, traitors, Anglophiles, and any other printable insult. As the *Boston Patriot*, a Republican newspaper that supported the war, asked in response to the "shocking" sermons heard in the city during the most recent fast day, "are we Christians? or are we Heathens? Are we Americans? or are we British?"[101] These criticisms do not appear to have affected the New England clergy who opposed the war. Some responded directly, defending their constitutional right to speak freely and calling their critics tyrants, but most simply carried on. Regardless, at every fast day and Fourth of July for the duration of the conflict, they raged relentlessly against the government's folly for taking the country into an unjust war.[102]

The New England Congregationalists and Presbyterians were especially vocal, and well organized in terms of influencing their states' policies and disseminating their message through published sermons and newspapers, but their interpretations of Christian doctrine were hardly representative of all Americans. Baptist and Methodist communities generally supported the war, and although Francis Asbury, the Methodists' unofficial head, did not embrace the War of 1812, he shamed the clergy who defied the federal government, remarking that anyone who refused to pray for his country in wartime did not deserve to be called a Christian.[103] The Catholic Church's leadership in America remained cautiously neutral. Boston's Cathedral was illuminated in celebration of Napoleon's defeat—the bishop was a refugee of the French Revolution who looked forward to reestablishment of the Catholic Church in France—but bishops also ordered priests in their diocese to participate in favor of the national fast days.[104] Even in New England a number of clergy endorsed the war from the pulpit, and some congregations took issue with ministers who opposed it, as in Walpole, New Hampshire, where the parishioners compelled their minister to write a public retraction of his fast day sermon condemning the war.[105]

Unfortunately, few Baptist or Methodist sermons dealing with politics found their way into print and survived. An exception is William Parkinson's national fast day sermon to the First Baptist Church in New York City in August 1812. Parkinson unequivocally supported both the Madison administration and justification of the war. Focusing on passages from the Christian Old Testament that describe how the Israelites' god granted them victory over a numerically superior foe in a righteous war, Parkinson informed his flock that the War of 1812 would be similar. He proceeded to espouse the standard arguments of the Republican national leadership: that Britain had violated the sovereignty of the United States, that the federal government had tried to find a peaceful solution, and that the war was therefore "self-defense." He then made a call to arms, pleaded for a renewal of the "noble spirit of '76," and railed against those who refused to support the federal government as "no longer worthy [of] the honourable distinction of an American citizen."[106] In essence, Parkinson's sermon differed from secular defenses of the war only in that he tied his arguments loosely to Biblical passages.

The argument in favor of a Christian's loyalty to the government stemmed from the Biblical passage in Romans 13:1–7, which in the favored King James version of the day instructed that "every soul be subject unto the higher powers. For there is no power but of God: the powers that be are ordained of God. Whosoever therefore resisteth the power, resisteth the ordinance of God: and they that resist shall receive to themselves damnation." Or, as a Hingham, Massachusetts, minister explained to his congregation in an 1812 Fourth of July sermon, "the constituted authorities of the Union have the highest claims to our obedience and cordial support."[107] The *National Intelligencer* was relentless, regularly reprinting and paraphrasing favored sermons and declaring that the "real Christian loves his country, and is therefore the best of patriots." As for those who opposed the war, the newspaper of the Madison administration declared "he who countenances strife and sedition, can no more be a true and benevolent Christian, than a real patriot and citizen." Moreover, he continued, while one "can find examples of pardon for the most atrocious private sins in the Bible ... [there is not] one instance of God's mercy extended to the public crime of rebellion."[108]

Concerned with the fragility of republics and factionalism within America, Republicans especially fretted over the nation's future.[109] After all, republicanism was still a fresh experiment in America, and one that had failed miserably and bloodily in Europe. Madison's June 1812 war message to Congress identified internal division as one of the greatest threats to the United States, remarking that "The evils, which have the most powerful tendency to subvert our constitution and government, are faction, party-spirit and jacobinism."[110] Such divisions, declared pundits, would be America's undoing. Employing the same passage from the Gospel of Mathew that Abraham Lincoln would use two generations later, Parkinson declared to his Baptist congregation that "A house," a family—a nation "divided against itself cannot stand."[111]

For many of the public supporters, the war provided an opportunity to secure the unity they desired. As the *National Intelligencer* proclaimed, "Unanimity is the watchword that leads to victory—divisions will lead to defeat to humiliation."[112] Declaring that "disunion is the grave of republicanism," one supporter asserted at a New Hampshire Fourth of July celebration that a war with Britain would prevent civil war at home. "Our seaports may once more be laid in ashes by the fleets of England," he explained, "but all these things, though truly dreadful in themselves, dwindle to insignificancy compared with the horrors of a civil war, which may arise from disunion amongst ourselves."[113] Some held the false hope for a unifying spirit akin to the Spirit of '76 to take hold of the nation—thus erasing the divisions that had stifled America's war preparations. Felix Grundy, one of the war's architects in Congress, optimistically argued in a speech lamenting the failure of yet another war finance bill in May 1812 that, "I venture to predict, that if war is once begun, the difficulties which now present themselves will vanish. The distinction of Federalists and Republicans will cease; and united energies of the people will be brought into action."[114] In one of his lighter moments, Hezekiah Niles likened America's domestic disputes over the war to a quarrel between a husband and wife. "A person interfered with a view to injure the man. The *pair* left their *private* quarrel to repel the general grievance—they mauled the *foreigner*, and then resumed the management of their own affairs in their own way." "So let it be with US," he concluded.[115] In contrast, Elbridge Gerry, the former Republican governor of Massachusetts and Madison's soon-to-be vice president, imagined a unity forged by purging dissent, describing a scenario to Madison in which "by war we should be purified, as by fire."[116] Writing to Madison two years later, John Adams echoed Gerry's sentiments, remarking that "It is the decree of Providence, as I believe, that this nation must be purified in the furnace of affliction."[117] Yet despite the hopes and threats of the war's supporters, the War of 1812 would create a sense of national unity only when it was over. Until then, the war drove the wedge between the Madison administration and its opponents deeper.

The fear of secession haunted the War of 1812. Threats or attempts at secession were part of the political life of the early republic. After all, just a few years earlier, the former vice president, Aaron Burr, was arrested and tried for treason over a plot to create a new nation in the North American interior out of lands claimed by Spain and the United States. Among his co-conspirators was James Wilkinson, the governor of the Louisiana Territory at the time and a major general during the War of 1812. The United States was still fragile and factious. Partly in consequence, supporters remained dubious of any opposition throughout the war, despite its members' continued protests of fidelity. Such suspicions, though exaggerated, were well founded, with Federalist leaders meeting secretly with the British before and during the war.

The British government certainly took the possibility seriously. In his 1807 plan for a preemptive strike on the United States, Admiral Berkeley estimated that the strike would result in Massachusetts and other New England states suing for a separate peace. He mused that this would permanently divide the northern states from Madison's stronghold in the South, "whose reciprocal hatred exceeds that of any two separate nations."[118] When war erupted, the Liverpool ministry immediately authorized its commanders in America to offer separate peace agreements. The island of Nantucket, whose maritime economy was at the mercy of the Royal Navy, ultimately accepted the standing offer. Petitioning the senior Royal Naval officer in North America in July 1814, the people of Nantucket pleaded that they would starve without a peace accord. After some amicable negotiations and a discussion at a town meeting, the island's inhabitants agreed to withdraw from the war and cease paying any taxes to the national government in exchange for peace and the release of Nantucket's sailors from British prisons.[119] Henry Lee, still suffering from the injuries he received during the Baltimore riots, met privately with the governor of Barbados during 1813 and 1814 to discuss the possibility of an agreement. Secession did not make the official agenda, but Lee freely contradicted Madison's positions on impressment, neutral trading rights, and expatriation. Because the United States had agreed to direct negotiations, in his role as secretary for war and the colonies, Lord Bathurst responded that Lee's services were not necessary. Yet Bathurst sent detailed comments to the governor of Barbados in which he delighted in highlighting his and Lee's agreement. Moreover, Bathurst interpreted Lee's efforts as a positive sign for the British position at the forthcoming negotiations at Ghent. "I flatter myself," wrote Bathurst, "[Lee] speaks also the language, if not of the President, at least of the American people" and that Britain will not have trouble over the issue of impressment—"a question, which has until lately been considered as indisputable."[120]

Though virtually all of Madison's critics outwardly maintained at least an appearance of loyalty to the Union, a few opponents went public. One such attack came in the form of an anonymous open letter addressed to Madison and published late in the war in New York. The attacks were vicious, personal, and relentless, accusing Madison of corruption, subservience to France, tyranny, and incompetence and dubbing him "the oppressor of the Eastern States." Impressment, the author declared, was a mere pretense for Madison to fill the north with spies and strip it of commerce. These states would not yield to tyranny. "The Eastern States are not yet prepared for an insidious Despot," the author warned, "they are not yet ripe for the chains of servitude; they will not calmly, and without struggle, renounce their birth-right, and surrender their liberties." If Madison did not fix the problem immediately, the letter warned, a "separation of the States will be an inevitable result," and, likening the seceding states to the independent Greek states and Madison's block as the Persia of Xerxes, the author had little doubt as to who would win.[121] Far more common than such bravado, however, were the subtler hints that secession was a possible recourse for Madison's opponents. Going to print at the same time, the *Boston Spectator* pitched its position in the guise of a plea to Madison to prevent secession. Invoking the spirit of the American Revolution and citing the Declaration of Independence, the paper insisted that the timetable of reform was set by the people, not the government. After all, "It is clear rulers will *never* admit that the time has come. The people, therefore, the aggrieved people, *must* be the judges." And the people had decided: "Give us a new administration, give us peace, and reform may prevent the revolution."[122]

The Hartford convention has come to embody New England's courtship with secession during the War of 1812, but the December 1814 meeting amounted to a flirtation. From first appearance, the convention had the makings of something serious. The twenty-six delegates from five states met in the chamber of the Connecticut senate and included U.S. senators, congressmen, and judges in their number. They represented states whose governments had publicly condemned the war, ridiculed the Madison administration, refused to allow their militias to serve the federal interest, and raised their own military forces. These states' governments had allowed their printers free reign to circulate the most vicious attacks on the federal government during wartime; they had enforced trade regulations only with the greatest reluctance; and they had openly celebrated Britain's victory over France.

Nevertheless, the resulting resolutions of the convention were surprisingly tame in that they fell well short of calls for secession. At their core, they demanded a rebalancing of power both between state and federal governments and between New England and the rest of the country. This included calls for a two-thirds majority in Congress being required for admission of new states, interference with international commerce, or declaration of war as well as eliminating the three-fifths rule in the federal constitution by which a slave counted as three-fifths of a free citizen for purposes of apportioning members of the federal House of Representatives and votes in the Electoral College. The three-fifths compromise of 1787, or the "federal ratio" as many called it, had been a source of discontentment in free states for some time. It, like slavery itself, was increasingly portrayed as anathema to a free republic. As one critic remarked, if the Mississippi Territory became two states, then *"one slave in* Mississippi" would have *"nearly as much power* in Congress, *as five free men in the State of* New-York."[123]

Acceding to these demands would have meant a considerable power shift in national politics in favor of New England. Had these measures been in place in 1800, the history of the United States would have been dramatically different. Neither Jefferson nor Madison would have been elected, no government could have implemented anything akin to the embargoes first implemented by Jefferson that ravaged the New England economy, territorial expansion would have been severely curtailed, and Congress never would have approved a declaration of war on Britain. New England would have either been the dominant region or at least sufficiently significant to make ignoring it (as the Republican majority had done for more than a decade) impossible. Ironically, the Federalist and Republican leaders had come full circle in 1814, with Federalists demanding limitations on federal power and protection of states' rights and Republicans calling for increased military spending, more power to the executive, and a national bank.

Yet the Hartford delegates' proposals were hardly new or radical ideas. Any tendencies toward extreme measures were checked by more moderate delegates, such as Harrison Gray Otis of Massachusetts, and by the fact that the delegates represented a broad Federalist base that was not ready to follow its leaders into secession.[124] Most of the points made by the resolution had been part of the public discussion for years—some dating back to debates over drafting and ratifying the federal Constitution. Even such Republicans as DeWitt Clinton and the self-avowed Kentucky Republican *Western Monitor* called for curtailing Virginia's apparent monopoly on the presidency by rotating the office among states (a resolution of the convention).[125] Anyone hoping for a firm stance in favor of secession would have been severely disappointed. When the resolutions appeared in print throughout the country in January, the *Western Monitor* described them as surprisingly mild, remarking that "We discover more temper & moderation in the report than had been anticipated by some." Those who expected "a different course of measures from the convention," the *Monitor* concluded, must be "painfully disappointed."[126] The most that the convention offered by way of more extreme measures was a promise to reconvene if its resolutions were not addressed.

Nevertheless, the war's supporters took every opportunity to paint the Hartford convention in the worst light possible. The Republican leadership had long been willing to tar any opponents, and particularly New Englanders, with the brush of treason. As the *National Intelligencer* remarked in January 1813 with regard to press criticism of the war, "the Eastern federal prints teem with publication which can have no other object" than "separation from the union."[127] *Niles' Weekly Register* covered the convention under the headline "Progress of the enemy," calling its supporters "the British Jacobins at Boston" and the event something "that every reflecting *American*, whether he be a 'republican' or a 'federalist' must reprobate and despise." The spy John Henry, declared the *Register*, had been right about New England's disloyalty all along: "That a revolution is *designed* is beyond all doubt."[128] John Randolph's widely printed December letter against New England secession highlighted the disunity within the war opposition. Randolph sympathized with the sufferings that drove New England to the Hartford convention, but he unequivocally denounced secession, pleading "Pause, I beseech you pause! You tread on the brink of destruction."[129]

When the convention's resolutions appeared in January, America was far more confident, thanks to the recent news of its complete victory at New Orleans. Once-alarmed papers such as *Niles' Weekly Register* summarily dismissed the threat of New England's secession.[130] Ohio's *Western American* was less forgiving, declaring that "their conduct has been reprehensible in the highest degree and deserves the punishment that ought to be inflicted on a rebellious people."[131] After reprinting the convention's proceedings in detail, the Kentucky *Union* took stock of the situation. Like many critics throughout the country, the paper raged in particular against those who emphasized the mildness of the convention's resolutions, arguing that the actions of the convention gave comfort to Britain, encouraging it to continue the war and negotiate for harsher peace terms. "The enemies of our beloved country, the enemies of our peace, happiness and prosperity," it explained, "count largely on the measures of these men, in assisting and promoting their views in humbling the pride of this Nation, and in securing a peace dishonorable and disadvantageous to America, and honorable and advantageous to themselves."[132] From this perspective, the actual resolutions did not matter.

The Hartford convention was the final nail in the coffin for the Federalist party, despite the mildness of its resolutions. America's stellar victory at New Orleans and the arrival of news of peace shortly thereafter turned the nation's gloom into euphoria and allowed Madison and his supporters to claim an honorable victory

Figure 6.2 William Charles, "The Hartford Convention or Leap No Leap" (Philadelphia, c. 1814). Library of Congress, Prints and Photographs Division, LC-DIG-ppmsca-10755. A satire on the Hartford Convention, the print depicts the delegates contemplating secession, which Charles equates to a return to the fold of the British Empire—represented as the open-armed King George III. In the center is Timothy Pickering, the former secretary of state and an outspoken Federalist in Congress, who is praying fervently (an attack on the New England clergy who opposed the war) for secession and for the personal rewards of wealth and aristocratic title it would bring him.

in the war. Because most newspapers covered these events within the span of a few issues, the sectionalist tone of the resolutions grated against the nationalist pride that was sweeping the nation. Timing was crucial, and the New England Federalists did not master it.

Yet an entirely different outcome is easy to envisage had the convention met even a little earlier, and this highlights the precariousness of the United States during the war. Opposition to Madison's prosecution of the war was widespread for the duration of the conflict, reaching deep into even his Southern strongholds. The threat of a New England secession might very well have compelled divided states, notably New York and Pennsylvania, and those with substantial opposition minorities, such as Maryland and North Carolina, to negotiate. This, of course, was what the delegates in Hartford had desired. After all, few anticipated the victory at New Orleans or the suddenness with which the negotiations at Ghent concluded. That December, even the most optimistic of Madison's supporters would not have dared hope for the events that unfolded over the next three months.

The Madison administration certainly took the possibility of secession seriously, withdrawing troops from the Canadian border, moving regular regiments recruited from New England home, and ordering the seizure of New England arsenals at the first sign of trouble.[133] The convention's greatest intended threat was its final resolution: that it would reconvene if its demands were not taken seriously. As was the case with the Continental Congress on the eve of the American Revolution, a second Hartford convention might have seen moderates pushed to the margins by radical leaders such as Josiah Quincy and John Lowell, Jr., who had become outspoken in the secessionist sympathies. Massachusetts and Connecticut were both poised to secede, or at the very least negotiate a separate peace with Britain, by 1814. They had created armies independent of the federal command and possessed the financial resources to maintain a rigorous defense against the rest of the United States. As one critic concluded in an open letter to Madison, New England had little to fear from "men whose united efforts, are not sufficient to keep in order their own enslaved population, and defend their own frontiers! By warriors whose repeated attempts at invasion of a neighbouring province, have been disgracefully foiled by a handful of disciplined troops!"[134]

The episode that best highlights the very real possibility of alternative outcomes to the war is the attempt of Caleb Strong, Massachusetts's popular governor, to negotiate an alliance with Britain. Anticipating a more radical outcome from the Hartford convention, Strong sent an agent a month earlier to meet with Nova Scotia's lieutenant governor, Sir John Coape Sherbrooke. Described by Sherbrooke as a man personally known to him and a member of the Massachusetts House of Representatives, the agent outlined Strong's plan.[135] He expected the states represented at the Harford convention to end payment of taxes to the federal government under the guise of needing the revenues for "their own immediate and joint defence." "It will require no great degree of prescience, to forsee that this measure . . . will necessarily lead to collision between that Government and these States." In such an event, these states would want an end to the war with Britain and an alliance. New England would be willing to assist in the defense of Canada in exchange for a "competent Military force" to aid the secessionist leadership in crushing any local resistance and attacks by forces loyal to the federal government. Sherbrooke forwarded the proposal to the Liverpool ministry for consideration. A covering letter outlined the governor's concerns, particularly the likelihood that the secessionists would face considerable opposition within their own states and, therefore, the likelihood that Britain would be called on for direct military assistance.

Bathurst responded immediately.[136] He remarked first that Strong's overtures justified the Liverpool ministry's policies toward the United States, as they were "undeniable proof that [Britain's] Conduct towards the United States has been duly appreciated by the most enlightened Members of the Confederacy."

Bathurst explained that because the negotiations at Ghent were nearing a favorable conclusion there was no need for action unless the American government refused to sign the treaty—something he thought a real possibility. Should that happen, Sherbrooke had the authority to sign an armistice with Massachusetts and any other state mentioned in his letter. Should any of the states that sign an armistice be attacked by the United States, Sherbrooke was to "furnish arms, accoutrements, ammunition, Clothing and naval Cooperation, on receiving application to that Effect." British assistance would not include troops. However, explained Bathurst, this limitation stemmed "solely from an apprehension that the Employment of such a force" would only agitate opposing Americans and "therefore materially counteract the advantage which would otherwise be derived by the State to whose assistance the force was sent." Meanwhile, the British would provide diversion by attacking the coasts of the other states. Moreover, should this transpire, Britain was committed not to make peace with the United States without providing for the protection of New England and any other state that signed an independent armistice with Britain. Had this come to pass, the Americans would have faced the disunity of a civil war, which all factions had professed to fear most. Only the unexpectedly rapid conclusion to the War of 1812, described in Chapter 8, would save the United States from this fate.

7

British Opposition to the War

In the wake of the British frigate *Leopard's* unprecedented attack on the USS *Chesapeake* to retrieve deserters in 1807, war between Britain and the United States seemed more likely than ever. London's *Morning Chronicle* responded to the crisis by featuring a series of letters that criticized the British government for setting a collision course with the United States and pleaded for a more conciliatory approach. Perhaps the most important political newspaper in Britain, the *Morning Chronicle* gained fame decades earlier under the leadership of William "Memory" Woodfall for an independent and reliable source of parliamentary debates at a time when reporters faced enormous obstacles in reporting parliamentary news.[1] London and provincial newspapers alike came to rely on the *Morning Chronicle* for the debates as well as accurate political news, and, though its position was in decline by 1807, these old links died hard. Papers throughout the country continued to revere the *Chronicle*, and almost all carried one or more of the six letters. Signed "A. B.," the letters highlighted the importance of the United States to Britain and railed against the government for being so shortsighted. According to A. B., the crisis with America was "the most important of all others to our country at this critical posture in her affairs. The State of Europe, calamitous and disastrous as it is to the Governments and Nations of that Continent, could not in the end very materially affect the prosperity of Great Britain, if she preserves her relations with the United States of America." Doubling in population every sixteen years, America was essential to Britain's economic future as a market. "If peace and harmony are preserved," one of the letters concluded, "you will want no other customers." War, A. B. warned, would drive Americans away and encourage them to manufacture their own goods rather than import them from Britain. British maritime rights mattered, but the government needed to be pragmatic. Impressing an estimated two hundred seamen from American ships a year was simply not worth risking "tens of millions" in trade annually. Besides, A. B. reminded readers, on the eve of the American Revolution, "the British government would hear of no relaxation or compromise in her system," and look at what happened.[2]

Public opposition to the American war was substantial. It was not a mirror of the American case against Britain, but a movement that reflected British interests. As the *Liverpool Mercury*, a venue for some of the most outspoken critics of the war, remarked in October 1812, "That *all* the demands of America are just, even her warmest friends in this country can scarcely contend."[3] Instead, British opposition to the war stemmed from exclusively British concerns about the health of the nation and its economy. Most of the war opposition stemmed from economic anxieties. Arguments for granting America greater consideration and latitude because of its commercial importance were not new. As early as the eve of the Seven Years' War, British proponents rested their case for armed intervention in North America on the grounds of America's commercial importance. As the *Whitehall Evening Post* remarked in 1755 in its call to send an army to defend the colonies against France and its American Indian allies, "whatever Nation remains sole Master of North America, must, in Consequence of that Acquisition, give Law in Europe."[4] Throughout the decade preceding the American Revolution, British opponents of coercion continued to argue that conciliation was the answer for the sake of preserving vital transatlantic trade links.[5] Despite Britain's efforts following American independence to shift its commercial ties to the European continent, the outbreak of war with France in 1793 meant that by 1812 the United States remained Britain's primary overseas market and was particularly important for manufacturers.[6] The Americans also continued to supply considerable raw materials, especially grain, lumber, and (increasingly) raw cotton, for Britain's textile mills. Much of the opposition to the government's American policy was therefore connected to the larger campaigns against the Orders in Council. When the Liverpool ministry suspended the orders, the potential opposition to the American war lost the glue that bonded it, allowing the savvy ministry, which was sensitive to public opinion, to avert a terrible domestic crisis. As a result, British opposition to the American war lacked coherence and a single platform.

Nevertheless, opponents, even though fewer and more disparate than they might have otherwise been, remained vocally critical of the government's policies. Exhausted from twenty years of war with France, many Britons complained that expansion of Britain's war efforts to North America was simply too much. Opponents of the American war insisted that even with the suspension of the orders, the British government remained culpable for the war; they questioned Britain's ability to prosecute a successful war in North America; they challenged the morality and necessity of going to war against Britain's cultural kin and fellow lover of liberty; and they worried that a war would press the United States to become a great naval power in order to protect its maritime interests, and thus create a new rival to Britain's supremacy over the waves. Ultimately, British opposition to the American war reflects how the British, regardless of whether they were in power themselves or criticizing those who were, firmly believed they were in command of the Anglo-American relationship. They viewed Britain as the protagonist rather than as the respondent.

British opposition to the war with America existed within a much broader critique of Britain's war with France—just as the War of 1812 itself played out within the broader global context of the Napoleonic Wars. The British people generally accepted the case for prosecuting the war against France, submitting to some two decades of the hardships and unprecedented rates of taxation that went with it. There were, however, plenty of detractors, ranging from republican radicals seeking revolution in Britain to middling men and women who were tired of paying taxes for a war that seemed endless. By the eve of the War of 1812, radical opponents of the war had been largely forced into silence or moderation in their public views, but war fatigue hung over Britain and passive criticism of war against France grew considerably as the British faced what appeared to be a never-ending struggle.[7] Napoleon's viselike grip on Europe appeared stronger than ever (and no one entertained hopes that he would in fact abdicate in less than two years after the United States declared war).

By 1812 the "Friends of Peace," as the broader movement against continuing the war against France had come to be known, were part of the national discussion on the war, producing petitions, supporting parliamentary candidates, and relentless pressing their case in the national press. Like their American antiwar counterparts, these men and women dressed their critiques in the language of patriotism and loyal pledges, emphasizing that patriotism compelled them to advocate for its best interest, which was peace. They expressed no love for France or desire for a revolution at home, and many had supported the war in earlier stages. They extensively used terms such as "liberal principles" and "rational Christianity," reflecting their roots in opposition to coercive measures against the American colonies in the 1770s and the slave trade, as well as in longstanding calls for moderate parliamentary reform and the repeal of acts that limited enfranchisement to practicing members of the Church of England.[8] In short, opposition to continuing the war against France was the latest in a long list of causes for these moderate reformers.

As Britain limped into 1812, the peace movement had grown considerably, attracting Britons ranging from manufacturers suffering under the Orders in Council to the heavily taxed middle class. In 1813 these groups joined forces with dissenting Protestants, who had similarly used the crisis caused by the American Revolution to push for parliamentary reforms that would have ended laws that discriminated against them. Petitions circulated around dissenting chapels and Sunday schools and manufacturing districts in the North and the

Midlands to garner upward of sixty thousand signatures calling for an end to the war with France.[9]

The corresponding critique in the national press was wide-ranging, reflecting broad dissatisfaction with the state of the nation. Calling the outspoken supporters "war croakers," newspapers across the country complained about the fruitlessness of continuing the war with France. As the *Morning Chronicle* remarked, removing Napoleon from power was an unrealistic and unnecessary goal: "we say, if the people of France like him we have no right to interfere." Containment of France was enough.[10] Other critics railed against the Russian government for pursuing scorched-earth tactics, in which Russians destroyed everything of use in the path of the French army, including Moscow. For the sake of the Russian people who suffered greatly from the policy, critics argued, it would have been better to surrender. "Humanity must shudder at the perusal of the twentieth Bulletin of the French Army, which describes the conflagration of Moscow," the *Liverpool Mercury* declared. "This war, hatched in the cabinets of the mistaken monarchs, who expected to aggrandize themselves, about twenty years ago . . . has," the paper continued, "in its progress displayed new and unknown features, strange and unusual forms of human desolation; but it remained for Russia to exhibit the cold and deadly policy of immolating provinces, and capitals, to any pretended military advantage."[11] Every setback on the Iberian Peninsula prompted fresh cries for an explanation of why Britain was wasting her wealth and sons on an "ungrateful" people whose emancipation from French rule offered little benefit to Britain.

The British, war critics complained, were the real victims of the war. No other nation was more militarized, with as many as one in five male Britons in arms by 1805, and the loss of life among mobilized British men was proportionately greater than any modern war before or since.[12] Contemporary Britons knew it. In October 1813, the *Aberdeen Chronicle* offered readers one of a slew of widely reprinted tables with men in arms as a percentage of the national population. This table noted that Britain's rate of mobilization was a full 20 percent higher than its allies' average and 39 percent higher than Russia's. Meanwhile, in France the rate was a mere two-thirds that of Britain.[13] Anecdotes of the human carnage appeared in newspapers alongside the official accounts, highlighting the personal nature of the human toll of the war. Among the most poignant accounts was "The Soldier's Wife," a poem reportedly written by a "very young person." The poem is narrated by Anne, the wife of a young farmer, Henry, who leaves his home and family to serve in the army. She describes the farm's decay, her worry, and her elation at the arrival of Henry's letters, as testament that "My Henry forgot not his duty and love." Meanwhile their "dear little boy, to be tall would jump higher, Or climb up my chair to read news from his Sire." The poem goes on to describe their hardships and concludes with a plea to God for peace:

Of what comforts to a million your power might bestow:
The comforts of peace, from which all blessings flow.[14]

To pay for the war, the British suffered unprecedented taxation; combined with
loans, the British government raised an impressive £1.5 billion to pay for the war.
By 1812, the British were paying per capita more than 35 percent of their annual
earnings in taxes—more than 50 percent higher than during the American
Revolution and double what they paid at the beginning of the eighteenth century.
The most loathed was the property tax. Introduced in 1798, it was the world's
first direct income tax, and it ultimately accounted for about 9 percent of
government revenues. Even worse was that taxes could pay for less than half the
costs of the war; mounting debts covered the rest.[15] A widely reprinted humorous
article about the national debt highlighted how farcical the situation had become.
Entitled "wimsichal [sic] calculations respecting the national debt," it offered a
series of curious calculations. Rounding the debt off at £700 million, the article
estimated that if converted to one-pound Bank of England notes, it would weigh
in excess of 61 tons and cover more than 4,315 acres. If converted into guineas
and placed in a row it would reach 10,521 miles, 558 yards, 1 foot, 6 inches. If
converted into shillings, the line would extend 220,959 miles, 1,048 yards, 2 feet,
8 inches, or "nearly nine times the circumference of the globe." If converted into
pennies, the article continued, the line "would extend seventeen times the
distance between the earth and the moon, and go twice round the earth, and five
times round the moon besides!" In total, the article offered twenty such
calculations, the last ones becoming more serious, pointing out that each Briton's
share of the debt was £58 6s 8d, well in excess of the average family's annual
income. "*This is the effect of* Glorious War," it concluded, "*of Oceans of Human
Blood we'll say nothing*."[16]

Worse still, critics argued, a handful of profiteers benefited from this massive
sacrifice of blood and treasure. William Cobbett regularly argued in his *Weekly
Register* that the war continued because too many people were invested in its
prolongation. "All those who have any thing to say as to public affairs, thrive by
war, and dread nothing so much as its termination," he cried. "I verily believe,
that peace would cause a million more tears to be shed, than all the butcheries of
war have." Almost every family receives wages for the soldiering of its men,
farmers have come to enjoy the high grain prices caused by the war, he continued, and "every new tax gives to the Government fresh accession of power, in
the attachment which its application purchases."[17] As the *Liverpool Mercury*
moaned, "War is become a habit."[18] Now fearing an end to the European war,
critics claimed, Britain's governors had secured continuation by forcing the
United States into an unnecessary conflict. "From the North of Europe, the Peninsula, and America," the *Aberdeen Chronicle* concluded, "we may expect to hear

Figure 7.1 George Cruikshank, "Sick of the Property Tax or Ministerial Influenza" (London, 1816). Library of Congress, Prints and Photographs Division, LC-USZC4-6858. One of a host of satirical prints attacking British taxation, this print depicts ministers vomiting various expenses and taxes into a large bag labeled "budget." Meanwhile the prince regent, known for his extravagant lifestyle, stands to the side with crutches to protect his gouty leg and demands more money for his various expenses, which are listed on the scrolls under his arms.

of sanguinary conflicts, which, if a sincere disposition towards Peace prevailed, might well be avoided."[19]

The Orders in Council became the locus of the British opposition to the government's handling of American affairs. Some sectors of the empire's economy heralded the introduction of the orders in 1807; others opposed them vehemently from the start. The orders contracted British overseas and domestic markets, and they alienated the United States, which bought nearly 80 percent of its imported goods from Britain.[20] The American government's response of a series of embargoes and nonintercourse acts, though ultimately even more costly for the United States, contributed to severe unemployment in the British manufacturing districts in the English midlands, northern counties, and Scotland and devastated commercial port cities.

By the end of 1811, the official value of British exports to the United States had fallen from a height of £8.6 million to a mere £1.43 million.[21] The *Carlisle Journal* estimated that "Birmingham alone has lost, by the interruption of the

American trade, the receipt of £1,200,000 per annum, four-fifths of which were paid to the workmen for labour, the raw material costing only one-fifth of the whole sum."[22] Because the United States both supplied the bulk of the raw cotton and served as a major market for the finished textiles, the weaving industries in places such as Manchester ground to a halt, putting tens of thousands either out of work or on reduced hours.[23] Liverpool relied on American trade for more than a quarter of its commerce, and the combination of the Orders in Council and American retaliation turned the bustling port into a commercial graveyard. An open letter to the electors of Liverpool in February 1812 declared that these were difficult times. Announcing that "the town of Liverpool is on a sudden arrested in its progress," the author estimated that more than one in six Liverpudlians "receive weekly aid from a charitable fund" and lamented that the "enterprising mechanic seeks in vain for employments; and the steady shopkeeper, without purchasers for his goods, unable to pay his rent and support his family, resigns his affairs into the hands of his creditors."[24] Worse still, most of the financing for overseas exchanges was handled by British, rather than American, banks, causing the financial sector to suffer too and contributing to more than one of the twenty-six banks that failed in 1810 alone.[25] In fact, the journey from British manufacturer to American consumer involved such an array of financiers, insurers, transporters, brokers, and shopkeepers that hardly anyone involved in commerce in either Britain or America could have escaped the fallout unscathed.[26]

A series of poor harvests made matters even worse as bread prices rose. Riots broke out, particularly in areas that most felt the pinch of unemployment, and workers began breaking the industrial machinery that they partly blamed for their joblessness.[27] The most infamous machine breakers were the Luddites, who first appeared in 1811, but they were not the only angry workers. Far more common were legal protests, such as petitions in 1811 that sought economic relief for the distressed cotton industry and together boasted the signatures of more than seventy thousand Manchester and Scottish weavers.[28] In the end the British government deployed twelve thousand troops to the troubled districts, more than it would send to North America until 1814.

Yet the British government, first led by the Duke of Portland and then by Spencer Perceval, refused to budge for nearly five years. The reasons were numerous, but they centered on the enormous pressure from the West India and shipping interests, which were losing out to American merchants, concerns that America's merchant fleet was draining Britain of its seamen, and the desire to wage an economic war on France, which relied heavily on the American merchant fleet for overseas trade. The government knew the orders would harm the manufacturers, but this weighed unfavorably against the potential for the West India interest, the shipping interest, and the landed interest, of which many of

Figure 7.2 William Elmes, "A Rosey Picture of the Times" (London, 1812). Library of Congress, Prints and Photographs Division. Drawn during the parliamentary hearings on the Orders in Council, the print depicts the French decrees and the orders as a suicidal game in which France and Britain see who will drown first. Meanwhile a group of Birmingham manufacturers appears with a petition against the Orders in Council.

the most powerful members of Parliament were a part and which had a deep-seated prejudice toward the new-monied provincial manufacturers.[29] Manufacturers, after all, competed with the landed interest for cheap labor, forcing Britain to deal with the likes of the United States for grain and markets for manufactured goods. When the British government did remove the Orders in Council, it literally did so over the prime minister's dead body. Only after Spencer Perceval was assassinated was reconsideration of the orders possible.[30]

The new ministry, led by Lord Liverpool, hardly represented a new direction for the government. Composed almost exclusively of men from the old Perceval and Portland ministries, the Liverpool ministry did not repeal the Orders in Council as an admission of the merits of free trade or the illegality of the orders, or as a result of intimidation by the United States. In fact, immediately after the war, the Liverpool government expressed its deep suspicion of the merits of free trade by ushering in the controversial Corn Law of 1815, which used a series of tariffs to protect British grain producers from cheaper (particularly American) imports. Called "one of the most naked pieces of class legislation in English history," the law also further demonstrated the tory elite's general suspicion of the intrinsic value of overseas commerce over domestic agriculture.[31] More-over, the British government did not repeal the orders in June 1812, but reserved the right to reinstate them at any point. As the *Liverpool Mercury* later remarked, "yet with all this mildness of reasoning it only disguises that unaccommodating spirit. . . . It is true, that the Orders in Council were rescinded, conditionally, but there has been no mention of any relinquishment of that principle upon which the Orders in Council were issued."[32] For British critics and Americans alike, this smacked of the imperial conceit that had shaped relations with the Ameri-can colonies since the 1760s, when Parliament began directly taxing the colo-nists without their consent and thus began paving the road to the American Revolution.

All of this raises the question of why the Liverpool administration suspended the Orders in Council at all. The British government's original condition for the orders' removal was that France first repeal the Berlin and Milan decrees; despite American and French claims that this had happened, hardly anyone in Britain, least of all the Liverpool ministry, accepted that this had been done by June 1812.

The answer can be found in examining the immediate domestic political situ-ation and the enormous pressure opponents in Britain brought to bear at a time when the tories were struggling to remain in power. The Perceval ministry endured brutal and relentless criticism from the opposition in Parliament and in the press over the Orders in Council. Reflective of thousands of similar public declarations, a damning editorial in the *Leeds Mercury* argued in early 1812 that the ministers "must be driven from the realm by the united voice of the people, or they will hold their fatal course until the vessel of the state is completely a wreck." The Orders in Council, the paper maintained, were ruining the economy and with it Britain's ability to wage war: "the advocates of the present Ministers and their favourite measure, the Orders in Council, are in this Country the most efficient friends of Napoleon."[33] Others accused the ministers of corruption, arguing, as the *Glasgow Journal* did, that they kept the Orders in Council so that ministers could profit by selling thousands of special licenses exempting neutral ships and their cargoes.[34] In June the *Liverpool Mercury* went so far as to accuse the "war party" of manufacturing a conflict with the United States "at all haz-ards" in order to profit from lucrative licenses during a war. "The pretence of this party is the maritime rights of Britain," asserted the paper, "but their object is to monopolize, by means of licenses, false oaths, and forged papers, a small portion of that commerce, of which our naval force, in time of war, would entirely deprive America."[35]

The campaign to repeal the Orders in Council received enormous popular support, as evidenced by the tens of thousands of names on hundreds of peti-tions from all over the country. Critics argued that the solution to the unemploy-ment, machine breaking, and general unrest was repeal of the Orders in Council

Figure 7.3 Charles Williams, "Which Drowns First or Boney's Improved Bucket" (London, 1812). Library of Congress, Prints and Photographs Division. This print is a twist on the theme of the suicidal nature of the French decrees and the Orders in Council. While Britain plunges headfirst into its bucket, Napoleon calmly leans over his bucket, which is being drained by a spout labeled "British licenses"—a critical reference to the vast system of special licenses the British government doled out to merchants that undercut the effectiveness of the trade restrictions.

and election of a new government. "If our Rules could but be prevailed upon to settle the dispute with America, so that we could have an open trade with the United States," complained a reader's letter to the *Leeds Mercury*, "I apprehend that all the Machinery so much dreaded both in Yorkshire and Nottingham, would be insufficient to supply the increased demand for our manufactures."[36] A petition to the prince regent from the hard-hit manufacturing town of Bolton, near Manchester, underscored that the situation had reached a crisis level, pleading that the "distress of which we complain, are so urgent a nature, that we cannot contemplate their continuance without dismay, and the most alarming apprehension." Workers were laboring for less than one-quarter of their normal wages, the petition complained, "whilst the necessaries of life are, since that period, nearly doubled in price." Such a situation was untenable with "Their pale and ghastly countenances—their squalid and ragged clothing—their houses emptied of furniture—their half-starved and half-clad children crying for bread." "Victory abroad," the petition argued, could not "compensate for a mass of wretchedness at home."[37]

In the spring of 1812 the Perceval ministry was forced to allow a parliamentary committee to reinvestigate the effects of the Orders in Council. Led by the young whig reformer Henry Brougham, the opponents of the orders paraded what seemed like an endless line of suffering merchants and manufacturers before Parliament. Witnesses included the likes of William Whitehouse, an ironmonger from West Bromwich, who detailed the suffering of the nail trade. The loss of the American market had meant that nail manufacturers laid off as many as ten thousand workers, or one-third of its workforce, and reduced wages for the remaining workers as much as 10 percent. Whitehouse himself had cut his own labor force by more than half in the previous six months.[38] Newspapers extracted portions of the testimony, which took place over six weeks and produced nearly seven hundred pages of evidence. A favorite of opposition newspapers was the attempt of James Stephen, the author of the anti-American *War in Disguise; or the Frauds of Neutral Flags* and architect of the Orders in Council, to intimidate a witness. Stephen, who sat on the parliamentary committee, arrogantly assumed his quarry to be a provincial bumpkin and so began with an attempt to intimidate the witness by asking him to describe precisely the Orders in Council. "Nay marry," the witness responded resolutely, "I never here of any body that knew, either what they were or what good they'd done, and I did not come hear to tell you that; but I can tell you one thing—before their time we'd a good trade with America, but now we've none, and that happen will *satisfy* you." "This answer," explained one account, "delivered in a strong Warwickshire accent, raised a general laugh against the learned Civilian."[39]

The pressure was intense as the largely provincial movement of merchants and manufacturers gained ground and became more politically ambitious. Brougham became a national hero in some circles, and reformers of all sorts sought to benefit from the clash that effectively pitted rising provincial interests against the more established London trading interests. Calls for abolition of slavery, repeal of the East India Company's monopoly, opposition to continuing the war with France, and electoral reform all started to mix at the edges with the demands for the repeal of the Orders in Council.

The key to understanding the suspension of the Orders in Council is the Liverpool ministry itself. Perceval had been an avid supporter of the orders from their inception; however, he was hardly alone. In fact, when he revisited the issue as chancellor of the exchequer in the spring of 1809, Perceval expressed some sensitivity to American complaints, remarking that "how far [any revisions] may be received by America as a fresh grievance" was "worth considering" and that American agitation might be offset with relaxation of regulation of its trade with the West Indies. Liverpool, who was secretary for war and the colonies at the time, responded in opposition to such concessions, "since a concession once made will never be retracted." Moreover, he argued that relaxing American trade with any part of the British Empire ran contrary to the purpose of the Orders in Council, thus betraying that for Liverpool at least the orders were as much about curbing the United States as about retaliating against France.[40] Lord Bathurst, who at the time was the president of the Board of Trade and would serve in the Liverpool ministry as secretary of state for war and the colonies during the War of 1812, also opposed any relaxation. No friend of the United States, Bathurst disliked the Americans and had a habit of sharing their confidential correspondence with other foreign powers.[41] In consequence, when Perceval was assassinated in May 1812, the Orders in Council hardly lost their sole benefactor in the government, making Madison's dismissal of the possible impact of Perceval's death on the Orders in Council seem reasonable.[42] However, Madison and his supporters failed once again to appreciate the context in which Britain's policies toward the United States were forged.

The Perceval ministry, founded on the ashes of the Portland ministry in 1809, was hardly rock-solid. Perceval had tried to form a broad coalition and even offered cabinet posts to opposition whigs, but they refused and he essentially formed his ministry as a slightly narrower version of Portland's cabinet. Perceval's unexpected death created a crisis, because no one commanded both enough support within Parliament and the confidence of the prince regent, who was filling in as head of state for his mentally ill father. The opposition press treated the remnants of the Perceval ministry brutally. Singling out Liverpool, Bathurst, and Castlereagh, the *Dublin Evening Post* asked, "What is the British Cabinet, in this day of peril, to have infused into it an increase of imbecility and rashness, in place of the great Statesman-like qualities, the integrity and the patriotism, which should adorn and direct the Councils of the Nation?"[43] The conservative press treated them little better, with the *Times* calling the remnants of the Perceval cabinet "a body of men so critically situated, and so doubtful of national support."[44] Conduct of the war against France, taxes, various personal scandals, the unpopularity of the prince regent, the Orders in Council, the economic crisis in the West Indies, and Catholic emancipation (which would have removed restrictions placed on Catholics in Britain and Ireland) were all divisive issues driving a wedge into the government. After nearly a month of attempts by others to form a government, the prince regent named Liverpool effectively by default.[45]

No one, including most members of the cabinet, expected the Liverpool ministry to survive long. Liverpool could hardly claim a mandate to govern, having not come to power following a general election; in fact, he was the third prime minister to serve since the last election.[46] Yet the Liverpool ministry lasted nearly fifteen years (and even then ended only owing to Liverpool's health) precisely because Liverpool and his leading ministers were savvy, experienced politicians who recognized when to set aside ideological differences for practical gain.

Unlike the Portland or Perceval ministries, Liverpool and his colleagues could not afford to entrench themselves on many major issues. Removing restrictions against Catholics had divided the British government for well over a decade, putting such potentially powerful tories as George Canning and Richard Wellesley, Marquess Wellesley, at odds first with Perceval and then Liverpool.[47] Though slightly more flexible than Perceval—Liverpool would later yield small concessions such as admitting English Catholics to the higher ranks of the armed forces—he firmly opposed admitting Catholics to Parliament.[48] Yet on becoming prime minister he quickly announced that his ministry would be neutral on the subject, thus stealing the thunder of Wellesley and Canning, who Liverpool believed were a far greater threat to his continuance in office than the opposition whigs. The simultaneous announcement that the ministry would review the Orders in Council with the expectation of suspending them was no coincidence, and the sudden reversal of policy can be explained in the same way as Catholic emancipation. Lord Castlereagh, the foreign secretary, remained indignant, commenting to William Wilberforce that "one does not like to own that we are forced to give way to our manufacturers."[49] Nevertheless, for the sake of continued power, giving way is exactly what he and the rest of the cabinet did.

The strategy was nothing short of masterful. The issue of Catholic emancipation never seriously threatened the Liverpool ministry. Suspension of the Orders in Council deflated the swelling provincial movement that threatened to embolden manufacturers into becoming far more serious reformers challenging the landed interest, London merchants' supremacy, and the government's ability to wage war against France—all central to the Liverpool ministry's continuation.

The public joy at the repeal of the Orders in Council was evident throughout the country, and many Britons assumed that Anglo-American discord was at an end. As the *Liverpool Mercury* happily observed, "The repeal of these noxious orders has every where revived the spirit of enterprise and industry: papers both from London and the provincial towns announce this pleasing truth almost unanimously." "In our town," it continued, "the merchant is again cheered with the prospect of honourable profits of a free and open trade, and the labouring porter again smiles amid the traffic on the loaded quay."[50] The *Glasgow Courier* informed readers that local merchants had been buying up goods to ship to America—"a proof that those who ought to be best acquainted with the state of America politics, have little doubt that that Government will embrace our proposals."[51] The *Exeter Flying-Post* concurred, remarking that the "opinion of the better informed American merchants" was that the suspension of the Orders in Council would result in "the termination of our disputes with that country very soon."[52] In fact, optimistic merchants wagered heavily that the suspension would result in a return to normal trade, shipping vast quantities of goods stockpiled in warehouses. According to one report, Liverpool merchants shipped two million

THE INSURRECTION OF THE PAPERS.

Figure 7.4 William Elmes, "The Insurrection Papers" (London, 1812). British Museum Catalogue, 11869. © Copyright the Trustees of the British Museum. The prince regent is inundated with papers marked as controversial bills and petitions. The largest is a "Catholic Petition" representing emancipation; a number of petitions from various provincial towns and cities representing complaints against the Orders in Council fly about the room. Clearly overwhelmed by all of the complaints, the prince regents tips his chair and knocks over a table. The print underlines the diversity and amount of complaints that beset and divided the nation when the Liverpool ministry formed.

yards of Manchester cotton calicos in six days that summer.[53] Even after news of a declaration of war arrived, the British remained optimistic; not until early autumn did the public accept that Britain and the United States were at war in earnest.

Criticism of Liverpool and other ministers continued from the most militant corners of the press, but to little effect. Such comments aside, the *Freeman's Journal* responded to the announcement that Castlereagh would continue as foreign secretary with the remark that "his Lordship has been always celebrated for having two strings to his bow, and we are firmly persuaded he would serve under Belzebub [sic]."[54] Yet, the immediate threats to the Liverpool ministry evaporated, and Liverpool and his colleagues felt sufficiently confident to call an early general election that autumn, which saw his support in the Commons increase by sixty seats, thereby giving him a comfortable working majority.[55] Without the galvanizing issue of the Orders in Council, even Henry Brougham lost his bid for a Liverpool seat in the general election to tories associated with the West India interest.[56]

The city of Liverpool and the surrounding region continued to suffer economically after the United States declared war, but the Liverpool ministry managed to avert a great deal of initial blame for the war. By suspending the Orders in Council that most Britons (and Americans for that matter) considered to be the source of the troubles, the Liverpool ministry shifted the blame to Madison and the Republicans in Congress. The opposition in Britain to the war would be pronounced, but it was nothing compared to the chaos that would have ensued had America declared war and Liverpool refused to remove the Orders in Council. When the Birmingham deputation returned with news of the repeal, the townspeople were elated. One observer described the scene in which townsmen released horses of the deputies' carriage "and the carriage was borne upon the shoulders, than drawn, by the tens of thousands of their townsmen rending the air with acclamations."[57] If "upon a modest calculation" some thirty thousand people turned out in Birmingham to cheer the end of the Orders in Council, it does not require a great stretch of the imagination to fathom the popular response to news of the refusal of a repeal of the orders followed by announcement of an American war. The Liverpool ministry, not the Madison administration, had cleverly altered the playing field. If there was to be war between the British Empire and the United States, the Americans would have to declare it, and they would need to construct their case without its primary stated grievance.

Without the locus of the Orders in Council, British opposition to the American war was scattered. Complaints about the economic suffering caused by the war were common in manufacturing regions throughout the conflict, although the suspension of the Orders in Council had taken away much of their edge, and entwining them with calls for political reform or removal of the ministry was rare after 1812. Unlike the protests over the Orders in Council, public opposition to impressment of American seamen never garnered substantial support in Britain. When Britain suspended the orders, leaving impressment as the major obstacle to peace, many one-time critics of the British government turned their frustrations on the implacable United States. Given the "awful state of the world," complained the *Aberdeen Journal*, surely this issue could be "mooted." "We do not mean to say (God forbid!) that the personal liberty of every citizen is not dear to the State of which he is a member," the paper explained, "but, surely, it is not to be set in the scale against the liberties and lives of the thousands who must suffer by war."[58]

Nevertheless, a few critics spoke out against Britain's practice of impressing sailors from American merchant ships. Some repeated the Americans' arguments that Britain had allowed naturalization for more than a century, referring to laws in the reigns of Anne, George I, and George II that extended the rights and privileges of Britons to foreign seamen who served a specified period of time on British ships.[59] As the 1814 Pamphlet *Why Are We still at War* complained, while British ships have "been half manned with foreigners—foreigners, with whose parent state we were actually at war, we have been issuing proclamations, threatening our own seamen with punishment for the very act which we have thus so strongly, and for so great a length of time, encouraged others."[60] Cobbett, a regular opponent of impressment in all forms, argued that British practices with regard to American ships were entirely unlawful. Even as late as December 1814, after most Americans had stopped talking about impressment, he refused to let the issue rest. In a public letter addressed to the prime minister, Cobbett insisted that the "Americans have denied us *no maritime right*; that is to say, nothing that any writer on public law; nothing that any usage of nations; nothing that any principle, any maxim; any practice even *our own*, at any former period, has held forth as a *right*."[61]

Despite the Liverpool ministry's attempts to avert blame, several critics still maintained that the war was ultimately the British government's fault. The *Liverpool Mercury* argued in August 1812, in response to news of the United States having declared war, that the ministry acted too late: "[O]ur ministers, by delaying to do what was just until domestic miseries forced the causes of commercial distress upon their notice, will probably have subjected the nation to the disgrace of seeing the justice, so tardily offered, rejected with indignation."[62] In Parliament, opponents of the war blamed the ministry for allowing such an unnecessary and fruitless war to erupt. In response to the prince regent's speech outlining Britain's case for war, Alexander Baring declared in the Commons that he did not accept the government's attempt to play the victim and therefore "could not consider America as being wholly to blame in the production of war." Correctly identifying the Perceval ministry's secret strategy, Baring pointed out that in April 1812 the prince regent told the world Britain would not revoke the Orders in Council unless France repealed its decrees to Britain's complete satisfaction. "From that moment that Declaration reached America," Baring argued, "she must have considered negotiation as hopeless, and have made up her mind to war." Britain shoved the United States into a corner, and the government could not pretend to be the injured party when the Americans pushed back.[63] Cobbett agreed, placing full blame on the Liverpool ministry. "It [the war] was *not* provoked by the American government but by us," he declared in September 1814. "It was *not* entered into their part for unjust purposes, but to vindicate the *personal* rights of its citizens."[64]

British critics were particularly skeptical from the start of the empire's ability to force the United States to yield. After measuring the size and capabilities of both sides' forces and factoring in the distance to the North American setting, the *Caledonian Mercury* doubted either side could compel the other to yield in a military contest, which made the whole affair pointless. "After four or five years of useless suffering," it impressively predicted three months before war erupted, "neither America nor Britain would be one whit nearer their respective objects."[65] Other commentators worried about the global impact of an American war, particularly how it would affect Britain's ability to prosecute its war in Europe. A letter in the *Carlisle Journal* reflected concerns that a war with America would expose the British Empire as a precariously balanced house of cards. In a by-then-familiar rehearsal of worst-case scenarios, the letter explained how an American war would force Britain to reallocate troops to protect Canada, enabling France to conquer Spain and Portugal. The Spanish Empire would be next. Meanwhile, American and French privateers would maraud the British West Indies. Combined with the unavoidable sugar glut that would accompany closure of American markets, the West Indian economy would decline and the islands would become an economic and defensive burden to Britain. This shift in commercial power, the letter continued, would mean the rise of France as a maritime power and the inevitable decline of Britain, leaving it to be either relegated to a second-rate power or conquered like so many other European countries. [66]

Such doomsday scenarios were not the domain of the radical fringe. Samuel Whitbread, member of Parliament for Bedford, called the possibility of a war with America "a great evil," in a speech before the House of Commons on the eve of war. "It was an easy thing to talk and write of putting down America, of inflicting chastisement . . . as if it was in the power of England to annihilate her," he remarked. "We might talk this well," he scolded, "but we could not put America down. She was there where we had placed her; it was not in the power of England to annihilate her, and it was therefore the interest of England to be her friend." Alexander Baring agreed, rhetorically asking, "If we were formerly unsuccessful, how could it be supposed that we could be now successful against a people whose population and resources had been tripled?"[67] Even after Britain began chalking up victories, opponents remained skeptical. As the *Leeds Mercury* reminded readers,

> Whoever will be at the pains to look back into the records of the last American war, will find a striking similarity in the accounts of that day and this . . . we had the address to chain victory to our chariot wheels, and our course was marked by a splendid career of glory; but with all these triumphs, the United States of America were severed from the British dominions.[68]

A related concern was that a war would make the United States economically and militarily stronger. British newspapers had printed American calls made in Congress and the press to develop American manufacturing for years, and the

Perceval ministry felt enough pressure to instruct its agents to investigate the matter. Yet the government displayed its insensitivity to the manufacturing interest by entirely dismissing the reports. In fact, when Augustus Foster, Britain's minister to the United States, reported that American manufacturing was in its early stages and would likely increase, the Board of Trade and the Perceval ministry dismissed it as an American bluff. Wellesley, as foreign secretary, even admonished Foster for being so gullible to American "insinuations of this kind" made "for political purposes."[69] The British in the manufacturing districts took such news more seriously. Glasgow's *Caledonian Mercury* produced a widely reprinted exhaustive report on the eve of the war detailing the growth and potential capacity of American cotton manufacturing, a trade that directly threatened tens of thousands of Britons engaged in weaving in Scotland, the North of England, and the Midlands.[70] Britain's manufacturing complained that cutting American markets off from British manufactured goods would force the Americans to invest in domestic production. The *Carlisle Journal*, whose readership included a substantial manufacturing interest, explained that the real danger of trade disputes and conflict with the United States was not immediate loss of trade, but that the "Americans have been compelled to establish manufactories of those articles with which they were not to be supplied by us; and these infant establishments (considering every part of the case) are represented to be in a flourishing condition."[71] Britain was on the brink of war with the United States, railed the *Leeds Mercury* in June 1812, and even though "This, by some of our hot politicians may not be considered as a subject of much regret, but to the manufacturers and the great mass of people, it will be an event pregnant with the direst evils."[72]

Critics also argued throughout the American war that the conflict itself would hurt Britain regardless of whether it won or not, because the war would spur the Americans into creating stronger and larger armed forces. Early American successes against the Royal Navy helped to foster such worries, as did the American versions of battle accounts that exaggerated their successes, which regularly circulated in the British press. As William Cobbett remarked in his public letter to the prince regent near the end of the war, "I always said, that this war, if continued for any length of time, would create a *Navy, a formidable Navy*, in America."[73] On this point war proponents concurred, regularly urging the government to prosecute the war in order to destroy America's naval capacity. "For we must not forget," warned a letter in the *Edinburgh Star*, "that she possesses all the requisites necessary for becoming a naval power of no mean eminence; the materials for ship-building are the native growth of her soil, the extensive line of coast affords an excellent nursery for seamen."[74] Even Britain's meticulously executed lightning strike on Washington resulted in warnings from such doomsayers as the *Aberdeen Chronicle*, which declared that "no more effectual means could be devised to stimulate the Americans in their exertion to create a Navy" than the humiliating destruction of their capital.[75]

Although most of the British press depicted the Americans as being in chaos following the burning of Washington, a number of commentators were wary of such claims. Cobbett questioned the completeness of the victory, emphasizing that for all their bravado the British bid a hasty retreat from Washington. "Why did our army not *remain* at Washington?" he stated, chiding that "[w]hen the French got to Berlin, Vienna, Naples, Hanover, Madrid, Amsterdam, they remained in them as long as they pleased." And as for the news that Britain left its dead and wounded behind, "Oh! Reader! how has Napoleon been abused for leaving behind *him* his sick and wounded when he retreated from Russia!"[76] Most critics, though, were similar to the *Liverpool Mercury*, which praised the capture of the capital but questioned the necessity of burning the government buildings that were of no military value. "Why burn the President's Palace?" it asked, noting "that was no Arsenal. Why burn the Houses of Congress? They were no fortifications." The paper then asked readers to consider the same for England: "Suppose a hostile army in London—suppose that army, not content with destroying the Docks and the Tower—Somerset House and the Admiralty . . . should set fire to Carlton House, to the Palace of St. James, and to the Courts of Westminster, under the pretence that these were Public Edifices?"[77]

At the heart of the matter, therefore, was critics' expectation that the United States had the status of a European foe. It was not a colony, where all sorts of depredations—slave revolts, slaughter of civilians, destruction of towns—were par for the course. Thus even though most accepted that warfare involving American Indians and colonial militia carried with it a degree of routine savage irregularity on both sides, conflicts between exclusively British and American forces carried the same expectations, at least for some, of limited warfare as might be practiced between Britain and Prussia and for which the British had a penchant for accusing the armies of Napoleon of violating. The *Leeds Mercury* asserted that such actions were "setting an evil precedent" for the European world, noting that "[i]n all modern wars, edifices exclusively appropriated to the purposes of civil government, have been respected, and we see no just reason why this usage should have been departed from in the present instance." Such brutality, worried the paper, might lower Britain's standing in Europe at a time when it was negotiating for the continent's future at the Congress of Vienna. After all, arguing for harsh sanctions against Napoleon was difficult when British troops were waging war "in the Bonapartian style" against a fellow civilized nation.[78] As described in more detail in Chapter 8 the British government felt considerable pressure from the European powers over the American war by the autumn, which events at Washington intensified. The Duke of Wellington informed Castlereagh in October that reports of the attack on Washington have "increased the ill temper and

Le baiser de Judas, ou la bonne foi Anglaise?

Figure 7.5 "Le baiser de Judas, ou la bonne foi Anglaise" (Paris?, 1814). British Museum Catalogue, 12312. © Copyright the Trustees of the British Museum. With the title "The kiss of Judas, or English good faith," the satirical print reflects both French criticism of the British attack on Washington and widespread agitation in France over British pressure on the defeated French to end the African slave trade. The hypocritical British soldiers cruelly set fire to the capital's buildings, including a hospital and church, showing blatant disregard for the rules of war—symbolized by the burning paper inscribed "Droit des Gens" [Law of Nations]. Meanwhile leering British officers duplicitously embrace African American slaves as false friends—suggesting plans to seize them as booty.

rudeness with which in too many instances His Majesty's subjects are treated in this town."[79] The French press universally condemned the British conduct at Washington, and a number of the articles appeared in translation in sympathetic British newspapers throughout the country. The *Aberdeen Chronicle* printed a lengthy one in October that compared the British to "pirates, who land upon a coast to ravage it, and then precipitately embark again, not feeling themselves sufficiently strong to occupy it and maintain their position." Tired of listening to the British harp about the evils of Napoleon, the author warned against the hypocrisy of the attack: "The English have often preached up excellent principles of morals and humanity: they have often and justly reproached their enemies with violating those principles; but let them beware—their edifying sermons and their severe reproaches will lose much of their force, if they themselves commit those excesses of which they accuse others."[80]

Although practical considerations received the most attention, what might be labeled moral concerns also shaped the antiwar discussion in Britain. Throughout the conflict with America, many Britons expressed their reluctance to wage a war against their former countrymen, against a liberty-loving people, and against a nation they believed held the moral high ground. Unlike during the American War of Independence, when most British critics shifted tactics during wartime to focus on the less inflammatory subjects of military strategy, critics of the War of 1812 boldly opposed the war itself throughout the conflict.[81]

The idea that Americans were the cultural kin of Britons was deep-rooted. It peaked during the Seven Years' War as part of a campaign to persuade the nation of the necessity of looking beyond Europe in its wars against France and sending an unprecedented number of troops and matériel to fight in a distant American wilderness about which most Britons knew precious little.[82] Depicting the colonists as loyal subjects and the colonies as an extension of Britain helped to create a moral imperative for Britain's overseas operations. During the crisis that preceded the American Revolution, British radicals and reformers borrowed heavily on this rhetoric to argue that if American colonists were British then they deserved the rights of Britons, which included the right not to be taxed without representation. As the London radical John Wilkes remarked, there was no difference between Boston in Massachusetts and Boston in Lincolnshire. For the large minority of Britons who opposed or reluctantly accepted the government's case for waging war on the colonists, these cultural similarities made the American Revolution a British civil war. The British government made similar arguments about the colonists being British, but the government interpreted this to mean that the colonists too were there subject to parliamentary rule and taxation. During the American War of Independence, most Britons came to perceive Americans as foreigners, but long-established habits died hard. Old whigs such as the Earl of Shelburne advocated lenient peace terms and preferential treatment of the United States in trade—measures that soon enraged the neomercantilists, particularly those concerned about America's steady takeover of the carrying trade.[83]

Lengthy laments for a second British Atlantic civil war were rare during the War of 1812 but the reluctance with which many Britons went to war against the people they perceived as fellow countrymen in 1775 echoed into 1812. As the *Morning Chronicle* remarked in an editorial condemning the war, "Every considerate man must deplore this calamity, not merely on the general abhorrence of war in itself; but of war with a people springing from our own loins, possessing the blessings of a Constitution as free as our own, and which makes them as enlightened as ourselves." Firmly laying the blame at the feet of the Liverpool ministry, the paper concluded that when two nations are so close, "a just policy would make us ardent and inseparable friends."[84] The Dublin *Free-man's Journal* fully concurred in its reaction to news that the first American vessels had been captured, declaring that "the war with the United States is an evil so much to be deprecated that we cannot enjoy the good that may be supposed to flow from it."[85]

For many critics of the war, the conflict highlighted Britain's being disconnected from its love of liberty, a loss for which the United States served as a painful reminder of what Britons could accomplish. Britons who had sympathized with American complaints in the 1760s and 1770s about parliamentary representation hoped for reforms. Catholic emancipation, the repeal of the Test and Corporation Acts that restricted the political rights of Protestant dissenters, relaxation of the property qualifications that excluded even lower middling Britons from voting, and redrawing of constituencies so as to eliminate the rotten boroughs and reflect demographic shifts northward and in favor of urban centers were just some of the changes for which Britons clamored. But the outbreak of the French Revolution halted reformers' momentum and postponed serious change for another generation. Francis Burdett argued in the House of Commons in January 1812 that Britain had betrayed its heritage in the American Revolution. The subsequent war against revolutionary France underlined this, he argued, noting that "a detestation of liberty had involved us in both." What happened, he wondered aloud, that made Britain the sort of country that fought republics in order to restore absolute monarchs to their thrones in France and Spain?[86]

A number of war critics argued that greed and jealousy had driven Britain to quarrel with the Americans. As a letter in the *Inverness Journal* explained, the United States flourished as an independent nation. During the past forty years its population doubled, "and their commercial prosperity has been so great, that they have excited the envy of Britain herself!" But therein lay the problem, the letter continued, as it created a jealousy between "two nations, who ought to have preserved a perpetual intercourse of reciprocal benefits with each other," leading to war.[87] "We had yet left, he would not say a single ally, but one remaining friend, and that friend was America," bemoaned Henry Brougham in the Commons. Yet the government decided to "violate this solitary friend ship, and for purposes the most sordid and the most atrocious, hasten a rupture, and sweep into this fund the spoils of American commerce."[88] Other members of Parliament were more direct. In rejecting the legality of the Orders in Council, Henry Arthur Herbert, of County Kerry, stated that "the policy of a war with America appeared to him to be as doubtful as the justice of it." John Hely Hutchinson went further, declaring "that if he were to judge between the two countries, he should be obliged to vote against his own; he should be forced to say, that England had acted most tyrannically and unjustly to America."[89]

Such open opposition to the war on moral grounds would have been anathema two generations earlier, but British attitudes toward imperialism had changed radically since the outbreak of the American Revolution. The trend toward a chauvinistic national imperialism grew from its roots in the Seven Years' War, but its progress did not go on unmolested. Imperial reformers such as Edmund Burke and William Wilberforce cut their teeth as critics of the government's handling of the American revolutionary crisis, and afterwards with their growing supporters they assaulted the most established imperial institutions: the East India Company (Burke) and the African slave trade (Wilberforce). The trial of Warren Hastings, the governor of Bengal, and the popular movement against the slave trade highlighted that British imperialism generated human consequences and that British overseas commercial wealth came at a moral price.[90] Together with the American Revolution, these experiences worked to create a lasting suspicion of imperial motives among politicians and public commentators alike.

Yet in other ways little had changed in terms of the governing ethos of the empire since the end of the Seven Years' War.[91] Authority was centralized more than ever, fostering a metropolitan arrogance that mired relations with colonists and natives alike; the American rebels had escaped British rule in 1783, but they continued to endure a deep-seated arrogance from those Britons, including George III, who had not fully recovered from what they perceived as the insult of the American Revolution.

Even Wilberforce laced his remarks about Americans in 1812 with a grating imperial arrogance. Weighing in on a lengthy Commons debate on American affairs in February 1812, he admitted that the government's primary fault was not sufficiently stroking the new nation's ego, patronizingly remarking that "It would be well if persons in high situations of government had been more abundant in their civilities to that nation, which, being a new one, was naturally more jealous of etiquette, possibly from feeling that it did not stand on as high ground as other and older states."[92] Cobbett criticized such attitudes, noting on one occasion in the spring of 1814, as British war supporters pressed their case for escalation of the war against America, "They see in it [the United States] an example of freedom, morality and happiness, the bare thought of which put them to torture. If they could consolidate all the people of America into one carcase, they would, having an army sufficiently strong, cut their throat at a single gash." "Such people," he continued, "delight in the news of destroyed American ships and towns and cannot wait to deploy Wellington and his army there." These Britons were bent on avenging the loss of the colonies, Cobbett concluded, and so he labeled it "re-colonization."[93]

War critics argued throughout the crisis and conflict that British animosity was nonsensical. Samuel Whitbread argued before the Commons in February

1812 that the economies of Britain and America were linked and complemen-
tary. Therefore, "he felt no jealousy of the prosperity of America, convinced as
he was, that with proper management here, the more she flourished, the more
would this country flourish."[94] A year later and seven months into the war, the
Aberdeen Chronicle concurred, declaring the "truth is, we are still unable to
bring ourselves to treat America as a great independent Power, we have not yet
forgiven the success of their Revolution, and the practical example of a state
thriving without a King, Court Influence, Peers, or Beggars."[95] The most vehement war proponents, such as Wellesley and Canning in Parliament and the
Edinburgh Star and the *Times* in the press, regularly attacked the Liverpool
ministry as being too soft on the Americans, often expressing their own lingering imperial attitude toward the Americans. The language and tone of the
Edinburgh Star's demand for escalation of the war in the spring of 1814 would
not have been out of place forty years earlier: "Vigorous war with America, till
America turns back in the spirit of peace to sue for reconciliation with her
outraged parent state."[96] In the *Times's* rejoicing at the burning of Washington,
it justified the attack on the grounds that Madison and his supporters were
traitors to *Britain* and that Washington was "the proud seat of that nest of traitors, whose accursed arts involved us in war with our brethren beyond the
Atlantic."[97]

Cobbett and other war critics bristled at such arrogance. "We *must* treat
America with respect," he railed. Without it there can be no peace, because
"Peace implies *treaty* and *confidence*; but, what confidence are we to have in a
nation such as our hirelings describe America to be? This arrogant, this insolent
tone must be dropped, or peace is impossible."[98] When news circulated that the
British delegation at the peace negotiations at Ghent were demanding major
trade and territorial concessions from the United States, opponents of the war
in Britain began to worry. The warmongers, argued "Pacificator" in a letter
reprinted throughout the country, had turned Madison into the new Napoleon
in order to justify their calls for stripping America of its lands, as Britain had
done to France: "the same sort of abusive terms that our newspapers applied to
Napoleon are now used as to Mr. Madison, and nothing will satisfy the haters
of the former but to see the latter, like him, deposed, and the American territory violated and dismembered, as has, in some measure, been the case with
France."[99]

Yet Madison was no tyrant, and the British were not liberators when it came
to the American war, Cobbett reminded his readers. "The President of America
rules according to well regulated laws, and a wise Constitution," he declared. "I
am led to suspect," he scolded, "that the love of freedom and independence on
the part of the Americans, is the grievance which excites our hatred."[100] Britain,
he argued, was the true aggrandizer, not the United States.

Ultimately, British domestic opposition to the war, not success on the battle-field or savvy American diplomacy, would dictate the pace and terms of the peace negotiations. When the Peace of Ghent was signed in late December, the British had not been defeated, and the United States was on the ropes. Britain had a regular army of veterans in North America roughly equal in size to the poorly equipped U.S. Army; and whereas the Britain's forces were increasing as more troops made their way across the Atlantic, the U.S. Army was hemor-rhaging troops to desertion owing to lack of pay and horrible conditions. Brit-ain won the naval war, and its warships could operate with impunity along the coasts of the United States. Britain was also capable of raising tens of millions of pounds a year in loans and taxes; the United States was effectively bankrupt. Moreover, the United States was showing signs of breaking up, with an in-creasing likelihood of a New England secession if the war continued into 1815. Yet, the British government in the late autumn of 1814 instructed its delegates in Ghent to make a deal of status quo ante bellum with the Americans by which neither side lost or gained anything, effectively declaring the contest a draw. This after just one short campaign season in which the British had the advan-tage, a season that saw only one setback, at Plattsburgh in which the invasion force was compelled to withdraw largely intact—a relatively minor issue in that the British force survived ready to fight the following spring. The British Empire clearly did not lack the tools to continue the war against the United States. Although a complete victory over the United States akin to what had been achieved over France was never truly in the cards, the British Empire would very likely have concluded substantially better peace terms if the war had con-tinued for another year.

The primary obstacle to continuing the war, and therefore the main reason for its conclusion, was the British public. Many Britons opposed the war from the start; others detested the Liverpool government; and even more were tired of being at war, regardless of who the enemy was in late 1814. The end of war in Europe meant the original causes of conflict with the United States—maritime rights and impressment—were for practical purposes obsolete. As the *Leeds Mercury* declared in April in response to news of peace in Europe, "We have only one wish, on this subject ungratified, that this peace may embrace America." After all, the editorial continued, "it will require great ingenuity to devise any reason for the prolongation of hostilities. The point which we are at issue with the United States, is not of the slightest importance in a time of peace."[101] The desire to chastise the United States, which war supporters had argued betrayed Britain by effectively siding with France, only went so far when the public began to realize how much the reprimand would cost. And the limit was a single failed offensive campaign. The Liverpool ministry was sensitive to public opinion from its inception. Realizing its vulnerability, the ministry backtracked on a number of major issues where the Perceval ministry had refused to budge, including the Orders in Council. Liverpool and his key colleagues, Bathurst and Castlereagh, worried that public support for the American war had never been strong, and they were unwilling to test that support by continuing the war for another year for fear it would threaten their own political power.

Ending the War and Constructing the Peace

When formal peace negotiations between Britain and the United States began in August 1814 in the ancient Flemish capital of Ghent, the American delegation was already close to exhaustion. Their diverse starting points, the different possibilities of peace negotiations, the difficulties of pre-telegraph communications, and intentional British delays created a slew of logistical nightmares. Albert Gallatin, Madison's former treasury secretary, had been in transit for a year with his son, and James A. Bayard, the sole Federalist in the American delegation, traveled first to Saint Petersburg, then to London, and finally to Ghent. John Quincy Adams, who was already in Saint Petersburg as the first minister of the United States to Russia, endured a harrowing trip to Ghent that included a three-week delay in Estonia thanks to unfavorable winds, followed by an unnecessary stop in Stockholm. Henry Clay, who had resigned the speakership of the House of Representatives to participate, had a smoother journey, arriving in a city only to find the negotiations had been moved only once. They then waited weeks for their British counterparts to arrive. Yet when the British delegation finally reached Ghent, the Americans dithered.

On arriving, the British delegation sent a note to the Americans inviting them to the British lodgings for a preliminary meeting to exchange credentials and discuss how to proceed. Having been appointed to negotiate a peace treaty more than a year earlier, having endured long and tedious ocean voyages to reach Europe, and having arrived weeks before the British delegates, the American plenipotentiaries had for some time been living with the anticipation of opening talks. Instead of getting to business, however, they preceded to scrutinize the brief note in an attempt to decipher a hidden meaning. Meeting at noon the following day, they deliberated for two hours, adjourned to eat, and then reconvened in the afternoon for more discussions. According to Adams, the Americans "were all of opinion that this first step of the British Commissioners was advancing, on their part, an offensive pretention to superiority." The insult, it seems, was that the British delegation had the audacity to invite the Americans to the British lodgings, rather than offering to convene at a supposedly neutral location (the fact that Ghent itself was garrisoned by the British army seems to have been beside the point). Citing an array of precedents that stretched back to the peace negotiations between England and Spain at Boulogne in the fifteenth century, Adams and Bayard meticulously constructed a case for construing the note as overt British high-handedness designed to push the Americans into a subordinate station. A frustrated Gallatin urged the easily offended Adams to overlook the issue, "not that he [Gallatin] felt differently," Adams noted in his diary, but because of his "aversion to clog the negotiation with any question of mere ceremony."[1]

After reconvening following a break for supper, they agreed to craft a note that offered to meet "at any place which may be mutually agreed upon" but told the messenger not to agree to the British lodgings and to suggest a neutral building. The British delegates did not put so much weight on small matters and replied almost immediately with a brief note readily agreeing to a preliminary meeting wherever the Americans wanted. When the two parties met the next day, the British cordially, and without deliberation, agreed to the American proposal of alternating meetings at each other's lodgings. Then the seemingly amenable British delegates presented the Americans with a substantial list of demands, including a sovereign state for the American Indians allied to Britain and territorial cessions to the British Empire. The encounter highlights the very different objectives—both in the war and at the negotiations—of the two camps. The Americans craved respect as a nation and as individuals to the point of distraction, while the British wanted tangible concessions that would limit American power in real terms. For the next five months, these competing objectives shaped the protracted negotiations at Ghent.

The historical significance of the War of 1812 is often overlooked on the grounds that the status quo ante bellum treaty concluding it did little more than return the United States and Britain to their prewar boundaries. Yet what is absent from the treaty is far more important and indicative of the war experience and the changing Anglo-American relationship than what is in it. The United States declared war on the grounds of neutral trading rights, resistance to impressment of its citizens, and British alliances with American Indians residing within the territory of the United States. The treaty resolved none of this. The Orders in Council had been removed, but the British reserved the right to invoke them at any time. Victory in Europe meant demobilization of the Royal Navy, thus eliminating the need to impress sailors from American ships, but the Treaty of Ghent was silent on this matter too. The subject of American Indians remained unsettled, but many of the American Indians living within the United States who had taken up arms entered into separate peace negotiations following the victory of the United States over the British–American Indian force at the Battle of the Thames (fought the previous October and resulting in the death of Tecumseh). Also, the Creek War, which neither the American nor the British government had necessarily perceived as part of the War of 1812, ended in the summer of 1814. In short, the grievances on which the American government based its case for war had been largely resolved, albeit only temporarily since Britain ceded no maritime rights and made no disavowal of its Indian allies.

On the surface it would seem that the war was an abysmal failure for the United States, because none of its grievances were addressed in any permanent fashion. Yet by the late summer of 1814, Madison's war aims had faded into the single goal of the union's survival. The Liverpool ministry's agenda, forged in the years preceding the outbreak of war and honed during the conflict, was easily as ambitious as anything conceived by Madison or the war hawks in Congress. The British demands included an independent Indian state carved entirely out of the American northwest, cessions of American territory around the Great Lakes and Maine, free navigation of the Mississippi River, and the right to keep anything conquered during the war—which many observers expected to include New Orleans and other parts of the Gulf Coast. In exchange, the British offered peace. In consequence, the negotiations at Ghent were not about Britain stifling American ambitions, but the reverse. The Americans, both in Ghent and the United States, were reactive, rather than proactive. The British government, not the Americans, dictated the subjects, tone, and speed of the negotiations, and whereas the United States had declared the war, Britain declared the peace.

Peace negotiations had been on the minds of the American and British governments since the war erupted. This was a war into which both sides, to some extent, bluffed their way, and once started both initially treated it as an escalation of the stakes in ongoing negotiations. Moreover, both nations pursued military strategies plainly aimed at forcing the other to negotiate on separate issues— such as the American strategy of invading Canada to compel the British to reconsider their stance on impressment. Both sides offered early armistices, albeit on unacceptable terms, and the British government did not even formally lay out its case for war until January 1813.

Peace appeared likely when, three months later, Alexander I, the Russian emperor, offered to mediate a peace. Madison leaped at the opportunity, believing that Russia, even if at that moment an ally of Britain, would be sympathetic to American arguments for neutrality and a quick end to the war. Russia and Britain were not close, having been thrown together more by a mutual desire to curb France than any sort of cultural closeness or shared understanding of good governance. In fact, Russia had regularly attempted to thwart the Royal Navy by leading European leagues of armed neutrality in the American Revolution and again in 1800. In April, James Monroe, as secretary of state, set about drafting instructions for the American plenipotentiaries, and in May Madison formally announced his acceptance of mediation. He publicly stated his expectation that Britain would follow suit, declaring, "[that] the sentiments of Great Britain towards that sovereign will have produced an acceptance of his offered mediation, must be presumed."[2] Two months later Gallatin and Bayard were on their way to Saint Petersburg to join John Quincy Adams and what they hoped would be a waiting British delegation. That summer, most commentators in the American press, like Madison, assumed the peace negotiations had begun and an end to the war was in sight. As Niles' Weekly Register confidently remarked, "It is perfectly understood, that the instructions to our envoys are so liberal and just, that Great Britain must accede to them; if she has a thousandth part of that regard for 'liberty and law' her friends attribute to her."[3]

When Gallatin and Bayard arrived in Russia, they received a cold reception. The British government rejected the offer of mediation outright on the grounds that Russian intervention was unacceptable, and it tactfully informed the emperor that he would do well to keep to his own affairs. As Castlereagh explained privately, "Great Britain may be driven out of a [European] Congress, but not out of her maritime rights, and, if the Continental Powers know their own interests, they will not hazard this. . . . The [Russian] Emperor, if he knows anything of England, must be convinced that no Government dare surrender the right of search for enemy's property, or British subjects."[4] Russia yielded to its ally, did not push the subject, and through intermediaries informed Castlereagh that the "business is at an end."[5] In consequence, the American envoys in Saint Petersburg were snubbed by the British and generally ignored by everyone else, prompting Albert Gallatin's young son James to confess in his diary that "Our position is a very embarrassing one. We plainly see we are not wanted."[6] After more than three months of languishing in Saint Petersburg waiting for fresh instructions that did not come, Albert Gallatin was determined to leave for London in order "to take his own course" and press matters there, but not until January 1814 did he and Bayard finally manage to depart.[7] Unbeknownst to Gallatin, the Madison administration had just accepted Britain's offer of direct talks. Although severely disappointed by Britain's rejection of Russia's offer—a point Monroe made perfectly clearly in his letter to Castlereagh formally accepting direct talks—the United States had little choice.[8]

The following spring in London, Gallatin father and son had an audience with Alexander I, during which the Russian emperor explained what had happened: Britain rejected the emperor's offer because of Britain's "former Colonial relations [with the United States], which are not forgotten." Not wanting to interfere with what Britain essentially defined as a domestic issue, Russia yielded.[9] Gallatin informed Monroe that the United States stood alone and could not look to Russia or any foreign power for assistance, explaining that "Whatever may be the object and duration of the war, America must rely on her own resources alone." Russia remained sympathetic, but Europe was too tired of war to risk another for the sake of America. "In a word," he concluded, "Europe wants peace, and neither will nor can at this time make war against Great Britain."[10]

A full nine months passed between Britain's offer of direct talks and the envoys' first meeting at Ghent. The slowness of transatlantic communications was partly to blame, but the Liverpool ministry in early 1814 was more concerned with publicly appearing to be pursuing peace than actually negotiating. It had not yet achieved its war aims, and successful conclusion of the war against France substantially increased Britain's prospects against the United States. The British government, which like the rest of the nation enjoyed full access to American newspapers, was perfectly aware of the domestic opposition Madison faced and the precarious state of America's finances. In other words, Britain had good reasons not to rush into peace in spring 1814.

Meanwhile the Americans were racing around Europe in an attempt to hurry matters. Gallatin, now in London, sent letters to Castlereagh's office urging acceleration of the talks; they sat there unanswered for weeks. Gallatin informed Monroe in May that "'England would in every point of view be at present preferable for the seat of negotiation to any other place" if it would hurry matters, but Clay and Adams seethed with indignation.[11] When considering a location for the talks, both outright refused to consider London, because such a venue would, according to Clay, represent further "condescension" from that "haughty people." Adams was apoplectic when he arrived in Sweden only to discover no one waiting for him and the talks again having been moved. "I cannot entertain a doubt that our conferences, wherever held," he sneered, "will be arrested at the threshold by an utter impossibility of agreement upon the basis of negotiations."[12] The pragmatic Gallatin had ignored such impulses when he met with Bathurst in May to determine a location. The brief meeting merely consisted of Gallatin and Bayard suggesting Amsterdam or the Hague, Bathurst countering with Ghent, and the Americans agreeing.

The advantages of conducting the negotiations at Ghent were entirely British. Ghent hosted a British garrison, its government was favorable to Britain, it was easily reached from London with a transit time of two to three days; perhaps most important, it was not a part of any major European power that might want to interfere in the disagreements between Britain and its former colonies. In fact, conquered and exchanged multiple times over the past century, Ghent's own future was uncertain in 1814.[13] The primary advantage to the Americans was that it meant discussions might formally begin. Even then, not until June did Gallatin learn that British envoys would not leave for Ghent until July at the earliest. Meanwhile Madison hoped that peace in Europe would pressure Britain to pursue a universal peace and fretted to Jefferson that the United States would have difficulty bearing the costs if the war continued.[14] Gallatin, recognizing America's vulnerable position and that Britain was in the lead, kept his frustrations private and proceeded to Ghent.

Modern historical accounts greatly underestimate British interest in the negotiations at Ghent, treating them as an unimportant sideshow to the Congress at Vienna, where Britain and the other European powers were simultaneously negotiating the fate of post-Napoleonic Europe. In contrast, American interest is taken for granted. The *Boston Spectator* remarked during the negotiations that "as it is the common custom, when acquaintances meet, to inquire of each other, what is the prospect of Peace, we feel persuaded that we need offer no apology for frequently introducing this subject in our speculations." "There is indeed nothing of a publick nature, at present, so interesting," the paper continued, "nothing on which there was ever such unanimity in the publick sentiment . . . we know not party, and scarcely an individual, who does not desire the return of Peace."[15]

The central tenet of the case against a lack of British interest in Ghent is the British plenipotentiaries themselves. Whereas the United States sent a delegation that included the former speaker of the House, the son of a president, and the former treasury secretary, the British mustered a second-rate band consisting of the undersecretary for war and the colonies, a retired admiral, and an expert in maritime law. James Gallatin was not initially impressed, complaining in his diary after the first encounter that the British had sent "men who have not made any mark and have no influence or weight."[16] This crew of "lesser talents," so the historical argument goes, was no match for the American diplomatic dream team that "was perhaps the ablest ever put together by the nation" and so "consistently outmaneuvered the enemy."[17]

Bruised American egos notwithstanding, the peace negotiations at Ghent mattered a great deal to the British public and the government. As the *Aberdeen Chronicle* remarked in September 1814, while like the rest of the nation's newspapers it closely followed the proceedings, "the public . . . expect, with much anxiety, the conclusion of the negotiations at Ghent."[18] As for claims of distractions from European affairs, the *Liverpool Mercury* argued that British affairs with North America "deserve, at present much more of our attention than any of the expected transactions at the Continental Congress [in Vienna]."[19] In consequence of such widely held concerns, the latest news and rumors from Ghent affected British markets throughout the autumn and early winter, particularly tobacco and cotton prices.[20] The peace negotiations also drew the attention of the nation's gamblers, as men and women wagered on the timing and terms of the peace. The betting became so popular and fierce that large wagers of fifty or more pounds became investments floated in the markets. Even as far away as Bermuda, the press followed the betting for the benefit of its invested readers, reporting the closing odds were two-to-one against peace by January 1 and four-to-three against peace before mid-January. It estimated that in excess of £200,000 was won (and that American agents profited by cheating).[21]

The Liverpool ministry in fact sent men appropriate for the task, not second-raters chosen as an afterthought. Although enjoying a comfortable majority in Parliament, the ministry had not managed to bring a number of the leading conservatives into the fold, such as George Canning and Lord Wellesley, who regularly berated the ministry for not being more aggressive with the Americans. Liverpool along with the all-important ministers Castlereagh and Bathurst were largely in agreement with what they wanted from the United States and the timetable they would follow. Moreover, these three men were political survivors who had weathered the storms of changing ministries by closely managing their own departments and by being adaptable when necessary. Powerful men such as Canning and Wellesley might have given more prestige to the delegation at Ghent, but they could not have been trusted to follow the ministry's directions; once at Ghent, there would be little the ministry could do about it, save remove the offender from negotiations—precipitating a political scandal that the still-fragile ministry could ill afford. Better to send proxies who would do the ministry's bidding, and considering that the round trip from London to Ghent was less than a week, such a tactic was entirely feasible. Thus the significance of the Ghent negotiations, not their lack of importance, led the Liverpool ministry to send plenipotentiaries of lesser prestige. The ministry pursued the same tactic at Vienna, again passing over prominent tory figures to accompany Castlereagh, who as foreign secretary led the British delegation, in favor of younger and more loyal men who could be tightly controlled, such as Bathurst's son and Castlereagh's undersecretary.

Though not prestigious, the front men for the Liverpool ministry at Ghent were solid choices. The ministry expected the Americans to push hard on maritime rights, which Britain would not yield in the slightest. To stonewall the Americans, the ministry sent two of the best navy men available: Lord Gambier, a retired admiral with a record of service in America; and William Adams, a prominent admiralty lawyer and leading authority on maritime rights.[22] Accompanying them was Henry Goulburn, who as undersecretary for war and the colonies had effectively run the British war effort against the Americans, and indeed much of the empire, for Bathurst. Although the youngest of either country's plenipotentiaries, at twenty-eight years old, Goulburn was a rising political star in Britain who would later become chancellor of the exchequer and home secretary. He was part of a new generation of politicians who began their careers in the later stages of the Napoleonic era. He was also a product of imperialism, descending from Englishmen who had made their fortunes in Jamaica, but now firmly part of the establishment, having attended Eton and Cambridge and married the eldest daughter of an English peer. A protégé of Spencer Perceval, Goulburn honeymooned at the prime minister's home. Goulburn was by far the most invested and politically astute of the three, and he quickly emerged as the leader—the intention of the ministry, and an impossibility had the delegation been officially led by someone more ambitious than the amiable Gambier.[23]

Although Goulburn emerged as the leader of the British delegation, he answered directly to Liverpool, Bathurst, and Castlereagh, who carefully choreographed the delegation's every significant move. The instructions the British envoys received were lengthy, meticulous, and unambiguous: they were to act precisely as stated and take no liberties, and, should something unforeseen arise, they were to seek further instructions immediately. Liverpool made his level of micromanagement clear in a letter to Bathurst in which he allowed the envoys only "to alter a word or a phrase, provided they adhered to the substance of what we sent them."[24] Thus, even though some of the American envoys might complain about the lacking prominence of the British delegation and historians might dismiss the seriousness with which Britain took the negotiations, the American envoys were, in fact, essentially dealing directly with the highest levels of the British government.

This created some tension, especially for Goulburn, who learned to detest the United States and the American envoys during the course of the war and his time at Ghent. His reports to Bathurst and Castlereagh are peppered with disdain and frustration at being bound by the ministry's directives, and within a month of arriving he regretted coming to Ghent at all, writing to Bathurst he wanted to return to his more useful post of running the war.[25] For Goulburn, the United States represented a direct threat to British maritime and North American interests. It was an aggressive and territorially ambitious state governed by "insolent" and unprincipled men who refused to recognize British supremacy. He thought the American envoys arrogant and vulgar, with the exception of Gallatin, and took issue with what he perceived as their childish disrespect, such as refusing to stand courteously with the rest of the audience when the British anthem of "God Save the King" was played at a public concert attended by both delegations.[26] At best, Goulburn thinly veiled his animosity. As Adams remarked after a private conversation with him in early September, "I found the more I conversed with him the more the violence and bitterness of his passion against the United States disclosed itself." Without a doubt, Adams concluded, "Goulburn is personally the most inveterate of the three Plenipotentiaries, and the most in the confidence of his Government."[27] It did not help that Adams and Clay teased the British envoys over their inability to act independently. Yet Goulburn had little choice in the matter. He was not politically significant or independent enough to challenge his masters—which is precisely why he was chosen for the task.

Two overriding British concerns shaped the context of the Ghent negotiations: the fragile peace in Europe and a desire to let the war in North America play out a little longer so as to secure a more favorable peace settlement. The autumn of 1814 became a balancing act as Liverpool, Castlereagh, Bathurst, and Goulburn furiously shared information from across Europe and the British Empire, constantly reassessing the situation and fretting over how change might affect public opinion—and with it the stability of the government.

Peace in Europe both aided and hindered British objectives in North America. Following the allies' occupation of Paris and Napoleon's abdication the previous spring, the leading powers of Europe—Britain, Russia, Austria, Prussia, and France—agreed to convene in Vienna that September to discuss the shape of Europe and its empires. The Congress of Vienna was full of decadence, splendor, and intrigue. The negotiations were never smooth; the allies had been each other's enemies over the past century just as much as France had. Vienna consumed most of Castlereagh's attention, and although he consulted on American matters he took a backseat to Liverpool and Bathurst, who remained in Britain and assumed Castlereagh's duties at the foreign office. An end to the war with France enabled massive redeployments of men and material to America, allowing Britain to go on the offensive. However, continuation of the war complicated Britain's standing in Vienna, because Britain's former allies, as well as France, were now neutral powers with regard to the American war. This made them sympathetic to complaints made by the United States about neutrals' trading rights, because they wanted to develop commercial links with the United States, which the Royal Navy's blockade complicated.[28] After all, if Britain blocked Russia's territorial ambitions in Germany, Russia could legitimately respond by pressing its neutral rights with regard to American trade. The French especially were sympathetic to the cause of the United States, often allowing American privateers to refit and sell their booty in French ports. The French press regularly abused the British over the American war, and the burning of Washington caused a great enough sensation in Paris that the Duke of Wellington felt compelled to smooth matters over with the French government and assure it that Britain had no interest in dismantling the United States.[29]

At various points during the Ghent negotiations each of the leading ministers in the Liverpool ministry expressed concern at how the American war was handicapping Britain's maneuvers, such as Liverpool's remark to Castlereagh at

Figure 8.1 George Cruikshank, "Preparing John Bull for a General Congress" (London, 1814). Library of Congress, Prints and Photographs Division, LC-USZ62-1556. In this satirical print, the artist describes the perilous balancing act the Liverpool ministry faced at the Congress of Vienna. John Bull as the personification of the British people is being set upon by little people representing all the conflicting interests and concerns the nation faced at Vienna. An Irishman holds an axe labeled "Catholic Bill," John Bull's left leg (marked "East Indies) is fought over by merchants arguing over free trade and the East India Company, and an American ship fires on his right leg, marked West Indies.

the end of October that "I cannot but feel apprehensive that some of our European Allies will not be indisposed to favour the Americans." Quite simply, he complained, continued war with the United States opened up opportunities for Britain's rivals to undermine it, particularly an increasingly assertive Russia.[30] The American envoys considered playing this to their advantage, but limited enquiries made it consistently clear to them that, though sympathetic to the Americans and willing to play the diplomatic game, no European power would risk a war with Britain.[31] The United States had plenty of friends, but none so great as thirty years earlier. As Clay explained in an August letter to Monroe, Europe "is too much exhausted' to come to the aid of the United States this time.[32] Gallatin's earlier

GENERAL CONGRESS.

audience with the Russian emperor in London had made this clear, as did a private letter from the Marquis de Lafayette, the American Revolutionary war hero and the most celebrated French friend of the United States. Lafayette bluntly urged the United States to withdraw from the war and sign a quick peace on the grounds that peace in Europe had removed the causes of the American war. He argued that continuing only made the United States look unreasonable and under the spell of the deposed Napoleon—charges against which Lafayette insisted he regularly defended the Madison administration—and increased the British desire for vengeance.[33]

Countering European pressure to make peace was the British government's desire to give the surge of British forces in North America a chance. Of course, plenty of vocal Americans also wanted to give the 1814 summer campaign season a run before finalizing a peace. Their number did not include the American delegates, who hoped to negotiate the treaty quickly, but other Americans argued that the U.S. Army was at its zenith finally, having veteran troops and able officers in its ranks who could successfully engage large bodies of British regulars for the first time. Thomas Barclay, the former British consul to New York who remained in America to handle prisoner-of-war exchanges, cast serious doubts on the Madison administration's sincerity about a quick peace in a report to Castlereagh. A regular source of information throughout the war, Barclay had his own private cipher and a direct line to the foreign office. Operating under the codename 76309 (or "Budha" when deciphered), Barclay erroneously depicted the Madison administration as staunchly hawkish, explaining in January 1814 that the United States expected to field an army of sixty thousand that year, which would enable another invasion of Canada—justifying "the general opinion" in America "that a treaty will not be concluded" any time soon. In February he sent further information of American troop movements, concluding that "this government is taking measures which indicate every thing but Peace." Madison, he argued, had little choice, as "the possession of Canada is necessary to the Existence of the present Administration." Barclay followed these comments in March and April with extracts from a supposed private letter he intercepted in which Monroe doubted the chances for the peace negotiations and a further declaration that "this Government does not intend to make peace under the proposed Negotiation."[34]

Armed with this information from Barclay, the Liverpool ministry did not hurry to Ghent. The ministry did not want a peace that would leave matters unresolved in North America or a strong United States that might renew war at the next opportunity, and ministers believed reinforcement of regular troops and ships would decide the war favorably for Britain. Once at Ghent, the envoys regularly played a waiting game at the behest of their masters in the ministry.[35] As Liverpool made clear in early September, the British envoys' job was to delay the Americans at Ghent long enough for the results of the present campaign to arrive. When he discovered the negotiations had nearly broke off, he was furious, writing to Castlereagh that "Our Commissioners had certainly taken a very erroneous view of our policy." If the present campaign, he explained, "should be as successful as our military preparations would lead us to expect," then Britain could dictate terms. In short, he concluded, "If our commander does his duty, I am persuaded we shall have acquired by our arms every point on the Canadian frontier which we ou[gh]t to insist on keeping."[36] Liverpool insisted on this stalling approach, informing Bathurst that his negotiators needed more finesse in handling the Americans, since the combined pressure of bankruptcy and British victories would ultimately mean the Americans could "be brought by degrees to our ultimatum."[37] Facing such criticism from his superiors, Goulburn quickly responded by assuring them he knew his mission and had a plan in motion. "As long as we answer their notes, I believe they will be ready to give us replies," Goulburn explained, and in just a few more weeks the weather conditions would be unfavorable for an Atlantic crossing, thus stranding the Americans in Ghent through the winter and preventing them from truly breaking off negotiations.[38]

Moreover, the foreign office's agents had tracked the movements of the American delegates throughout Europe, and Goulburn and the others knew that the Americans' finances were limited and that they would feel the pinch to make a deal when their credit ran out in December—by which time the success of British operations in America would be known.[39] The Americans suspected the British tactic, but there was little they could do. As Gallatin discovered in London, the British government would not be pushed, leaving the American envoys only the option of withdrawing from negotiations altogether. Gallatin, more than anyone, knew the precarious state of America's finances and how unlikely it was the Madison administration could continue the war through the following year, so he regularly placated his easily insulted colleagues and insisted they continue.

When negotiations opened at Ghent, the Madison administration had abandoned any serious expectation of compelling Britain to yield on issues of maritime rights. A year earlier, when Gallatin set off for Saint Petersburg, the Madison administration still harbored some hope of redress, as revealed in Monroe's long-winded instructions to the delegation in which he attempted to anticipate British arguments. The main issue, Monroe explained, was that Britain respect the sovereignty of the United States. So long as the British agreed to stay off American ships, Monroe and the administration would be more than satisfied. "I have to repeat," he instructed, "that the great object which you have to secure, in regard to impressment, is, that our flag shall protect the crew." In exchange, the United States was ready to make concessions to Britain, including banning all native-born Britons, even those who had become naturalized citizens of the United States, from American vessels. Yet even on the point of impressment, the American government's hardened position was cracking, and Monroe authorized the delegates to consider a treaty even if it did not resolve the issue.[40] As for Canada, Monroe expressed confidence in America's chances in the ensuing campaigns and boldly suggested that Britain yield its North American colonies in order to save both sides further trouble over what the United States would surely conquer eventually.

A year later the situation was fundamentally changed. Napoleon was defeated, British troops were in Paris, and the United States, having failed yet again to make significant inroads into Canada, was on the defensive. Leading London papers such as the *Times* and the *Courier* clamored for revenge against the United States—a nation that took advantage of Britain in its vulnerable state and now must suffer the empire's fury. While in London in the spring, Gallatin and Bayard read the papers with worry and watched as Britain prepared its invasion forces. Writing to Monroe in May, they informed him that British public opinion had swung decidedly against the United States. "The popular feeling is evidently strongly in favor of the prosecution of the war against us," they explained. "This sentiment is universal, and so powerful that it will be difficult for ministers to control it should they be disposed to peace." Peace might still be possible, but any expectation of British concessions on such major issues as impressment were out of the question, because "on this subject the opposition and the whole nation support the Ministry."[41] A month later Gallatin wrote to Monroe that the best the United States could achieve at this point was status quo ante bellum, and even this could not be ensured.[42] Meanwhile, Madison's cabinet met and agreed it no longer would require a peace treaty to include an end to impressment.[43] For its part, the Liverpool ministry instructed Britain's envoys to avoid any detailed discussion on such matters, because Britain would never yield on them; nor would Britain pay any reparations whatsoever for its enforcement of the Orders in Council. "The Right of Search and of withdrawing our Seamen from on board American merchant ships," Castlereagh instructed the envoys, "can never be given up."[44] In consequence, the maritime rights that were the declared basis of the war two years earlier did not even figure into the peace negotiations.

With America's once-lofty objectives reduced to preserving the prewar status quo, control of the negotiations fell entirely to Britain. The British initiated virtually all of the major discussions, and the terms over which the delegates argued came almost exclusively from the British side. The American delegation did not take this well. After all, their country had declared war in large part to compel Britain in particular and Europe generally to take the United States more seriously, and meeting with a second-tier British delegation in a provincial town of a second-rank power is hardly what the American government expected at the start of the war. Ghent was a harsh introduction to reality for the American delegation, which included two of America's greatest egos in Adams and Clay, both particularly feeling the indignity of their situation. They were important men in the United States and used to being treated as such; at Ghent they were merely important men from a relatively unimportant country that was being hammered by its former imperial masters. And as the Dutch, Spanish, Portuguese, Danish, and a host of other lesser powers of Europe that did not receive their own invitation to the Congress of Vienna already knew, there was a pecking order. As the newest, furthest, and militarily one of the weakest nations, the United States was nowhere in the vicinity of the first tier. Nevertheless, Adams fumed at the "overbearing and insulting . . . tone" of the British diplomatic notes and at being treated as social inferiors; and Clay railed at "the well known arrogance of the British character" in his reports to Monroe.[45]

Though accomplished as individuals, the American delegates hardly formed a well-oiled diplomatic machine. Only the Swiss-born Gallatin was widely respected in Europe. He merited an audience with the Russian Emperor, Lafayette had written to him, and on the one occasion Castlereagh passed through Ghent, he met only with Gallatin. Even the commander of the British forces in Europe, the Duke of Wellington, wrote privately to Gallatin, expressing his confidence in him, urging him to accept peace, and complimenting him on his reputation for reasonableness and civility.[46] Although such compliments flattered Gallatin, they likely chaffed at the sensitive egos of Adams and Clay, who developed an intense dislike of each other in Ghent. The brooding Adams rose early, read his Bible, and preferred simple pleasures. Clay enjoyed alcohol and gambling, showed no affinity for religion, and often went to bed just as Adams rose, forcing the envoys to delay starting their business day until the afternoon.[47] The pair overtly pursued sectional interests, with Clay suggesting concessions that would harm New England and dismissing Massachusetts's valor. He "rails at commerce and the people of Massachusetts, and tells what wonders the people of Kentucky would do if they should be attacked," complained Adams.[48] They argued incessantly in what Gallatin's son, James, diplomatically described as "strong language," and they often chose to write separate responses to British notes and then haggle over the interpretations, typically with Russell siding with Clay, Adams pouting over having his ideas largely ignored, and Gallatin attempting to smooth things over.[49] They also wrote separate reports to Monroe, in which they made digs at each other. Although Adams tended to respect Gallatin and follow his lead, it is clear Gallatin thought little of Adams. Influenced by his father, James noted in his diary after a day of sightseeing in Saint Petersburg that "Mr. Adams [is] very civil but has a disagreeable manner. He is from New England, a 'Yankee.'" When they met at Ghent a year later, Albert described his fear that Adams was not up for the task and that in the end he "will do harm" to the negotiations.[50] By late September, Adams was considering leaving and had gone so far as to review the terms of the delegates' lease with the landlord to enable an early departure.[51]

When the British delegates outlined Britain's conditions for peace, they treated the United States like a defeated nation. The British government had encouraged the United States into a war partly in order to curtail its power, and Britain's initial terms represented that intention. Even France, despite having a former emperor effectively imprisoned and Paris occupied by foreign troops in 1814, was not asked to make anywhere near the sorts of territorial concessions Britain demanded from the United States. In fact, in more than a century of wars with Britain, France had never been required to make comparable concessions of its home territory. But then France was a great power, and minor powers such as Poland and Saxony were carved up quite readily. Unfortunately for the United States, it was a minor power, which meant the Liverpool ministry's objectives and its chances of achieving them were entirely plausible for the period.

The British first demanded security for Canada, requiring the United States to relinquish control of the Great Lakes and parts of Maine. Under the pretense that Britain was the victim of American aggression, the delegates argued Britain had every right to secure its North American possessions from their neighbors to the south. That Britain had used Canada as a launching pad for its invasions of the United States both in the American Revolution and the War of 1812 was, of course, not mentioned. The Great Lakes were a natural border that hampered both sides from invading each other effectively. By assuming strategic control of the lakes—either by occupying both shores or allowing the British to militarize the lakes while prohibiting an American military presence—Britain would accomplish at Ghent what it had failed to achieve in the war. This would have laid bare the northern border of the United States and made it indefensible against a British attack from Canada. When the Americans were so bold as to contest Britain's claim to some of the coastal islands of Maine, the envoys revealed their intransigence by stating indignantly that the Americans "might as well contest their right to Northamptonshire."[52]

The theme of the British Empire standing up to the bullying American "aggrandizers" was the central pillar of the British position for the first three months of the negotiations. As Castlereagh explained in his initial instructions to the British envoys, "This [invasion of Canada] becomes the more alarming as part only of a general system of aggrandizement in the execution of which they [Americans] have possessed themselves of Louisiana and a part of Both the Floridas . . . whilst Spain was bravely contending for her Existence."[53] No note or conversation failed to portray the United States as an aggressor toward its neighbors. Of course, Britain knew all about aggrandizement, having added a further seventeen colonies to its empire along with tens of millions of people since going to war with France in 1793.[54]

Regardless, the envoys continually asserted that the British Empire was the injured party in the War of 1812, and as such Britain had every right to seek security against such a volatile, greedy neighbor. In an early September formal written exchange, the British accused the Jefferson and Madison administrations of being driven "by a spirit of aggrandizements, not necessary to their own security, but increasing with the extent of their Empire," noting "their progressive occupation of the Indian territories, by the acquisition of Louisiana, by the more recent attempts to wrest by force of arms from a nation in amity the two Floridas, and lastly by the avowed intentions of permanently annexing the Canadas to the United States." Had the United States kept to a naval war (the declared purpose of the war dealt primarily with maritime matters), or if the attack on Canada had been a mere diversion, British demands would be different, the delegates insisted. However, the United States invaded Canada with the express intent of annexing it, declaring "it is notorious to the whole world that the conquest of Canada and its permanent annexation to the United States was the declared object of the American Government." Had the United States succeeded, the British delegates asked incredulously, "is there any person who doubts that they would have availed themselves of their situation to obtain on the side of Canada important cessions of Territory, if not the entire abandonment of that Country by Great Britain?"[55]

Attempts to deny such claims were pointless. When Adams offered the weak protest at their second meeting that "the American Government never had declared the intention of conquering Canada," Goulburn replied by quoting the proclamation William Hull issued on his invasion of Upper Canada in July 1812, reprinted throughout the British Atlantic and unambiguously stating Canada was to be "emancipated." Adams answered that the American government had never endorsed Hull's proclamation (in fact it was partly crafted by Madison's cabinet). Goulburn sneered that it had not disowned the proclamation either.[56]

Even more worrying for the Americans was the British demand for the creation of an independent American Indian state for those Indians living within the United States who had allied with Britain during the war. Unfurling a massive, specially prepared, detailed map of North America, the British envoys outlined their plans. Amounting to over 250,000 square miles carved out of the northwest United States and including all or part of the modern states of Michigan, Illinois, Indiana, Ohio, Missouri, Iowa, Wisconsin, and Minnesota, the British demand required the United States to cede more than 15 percent of its territory.

According to Britain's initial terms, the new Indian state would be independent, but both Britain and the United States would secure its territorial integrity by agreeing not to acquire any of its land. As Goulburn explained to the American envoys, the new state would provide "a sort of barrier" between British North America and the United States and thus help "to prevent their future collision."[57] The British government had also promised that it would protect Indian territory in any peace negotiations with the United States in order to secure its alliance with Tecumseh and entice other Indians living on the U.S. side of the Great Lakes region and in the Ohio River Valley to ally with Britain. In fact, Bathurst explicitly stated the British government's promise to its Indian allies in a letter to Prevost in late 1812, declaring that Britain would secure a territory for them and "that whenever negotiations for Peace may be entered into, the Security of the Indian Possessions may not be either compromised or forgotten" and that Prevost and his officers were to make this clear to the Indians.[58] In 1814 the Liverpool ministry restated its pledge that it would not abandon its Indian allies, as the British government had done following the American Revolution. "Great Britain deems it inconsistent with honour and justice," declared a cabinet note sent to the American delegation in late August, "to leave those who have been her allies in the war dependent on any policy which the United States may see fit to adopt towards them."[59]

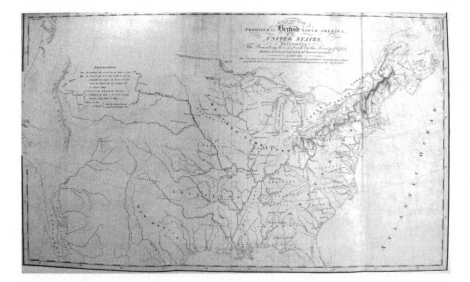

Figure 8.2 "Map of Frontier of British North America and the United States, describing the Boundary Line as fixed by the Treaty of 1783, and the New Line as proposed to secure the Independence of the Indians." The National Archives, Kew, FO 925/1410. With a scale of 100 miles to an inch, the map was created for the British delegation at Ghent. Shown to the American delegates, the map visually describes through use of colored boundary lines specifically the territory Britain demanded the Americans cede for creation of an American Indian state. Marked in bold green, its boundaries are roughly the Missouri River in the west, the Mississippi and Ohio Rivers to the south and east, and the Great Lakes and Canadian border to the North. In total the cession would have accounted for in excess of 15 percent of U.S. territory. The map reveals the seriousness of the demand and the extent of the British planning that had gone into it.

Britain's claim to represent the Indians was not entirely unorthodox. That a greater power would negotiate on behalf of a lesser power was standard practice in European diplomacy. In fact, as the British and Americans haggled at Ghent, the five major powers were negotiating at the Congress of Vienna on behalf of a host of nations. In theory, the practice simplified and hastened negotiations by limiting the number of players, and smaller nations benefited from having their grievances combined with the terms of a powerful nation. As Castlereagh explained to the British commissioners at Ghent, Britain claimed the right to represent and seek reparations for the Indians on the grounds they were formal allies, and as lesser powers they "are entitled to claim [protection] at our Hands."[60] In a conversation with Adams, Goulburn likened the relationship as akin to Britain's alliance with Portugal, which Britain was presently representing at Vienna.[61]

Britain's demands immediately put the Americans on the defensive. Clay wrote to Monroe at the start of the negotiations that they were prepared for extensive British demands, having carefully followed the discussion in the British press that summer, but the shock at the first formal meeting of learning the extent of those demands must have been shattering.[62] The delegates pleaded they could not negotiate on any territorial matters or on the Indians, on the grounds they had not received official instructions on the matter. In fact, neither official nor unofficial previous correspondence between the delegates and Monroe even hinted at these subjects, indicating the extent to which the British demands took the American delegates by surprise. Castlereagh was indignant and suspected the Americans of stalling, instructing that they be pressed, and sending a several-page explanation of why addressing the issue of the Indians *was* within the American plenipotentiaries' mandate.[63]

After several weeks of hard negotiating, the American delegation laid out its position in a formal note addressed to their British counterparts. Calling Britain's territorial demands "extraordinary," the note rejected accusations of a pattern of aggrandizement. They dismissed references to the Spanish Empire, insisting it had no relation to Anglo-American disagreements or the War of 1812, and they maintained that acquisition of Louisiana and Indian land was entirely legitimate. In consequence, they refused to discuss such topics. With regard to the U.S.-Canada border, the American delegates asserted, demanding that the United States leave its northern border defenseless for the sake of Canadian security was ridiculous considering that Britain's military establishment was by far the greater of the two nations. Alluding to Britain's impingement on the maritime rights of the United States, the note concluded that the best foundation for peace was not the ability of one side to threaten the other but instead "a mutual respect for the rights of each other, and in the cultivation of a friendly understanding between them."[64]

The longest portion of the note was reserved for the subject of the Indians. Adams and Clay argued vehemently, during the Americans' private deliberations, against including the Indians in *any* way in the treaty, while Bayard and Gallatin proved more flexible on both the Canadian border and the Indians. In a private meeting one evening with Goulburn a few days earlier, Adams revealed the prejudices he shared with many Americans. Describing the Indians in question as uncivilized peoples who did not have any sense of private property because they did not cultivate land, Adams declared that to create this Indian state was "to condemn vast regions of territory to perpetual barrenness and solitude that a few hundred savages might find wild beasts to hunt upon it, was a species of game law that a nation descended from Britons would never endure."[65]

At first the Americans dangerously underestimated the British, with Clay informing Monroe that he found the idea of "Britain attempting, without powers, to treat for savage tribes, scattered over our acknowleged [sic] territory, the very names of which she probably does not know," nothing short of "absurd." The British proposal, he sneered, "betrayed much ignorance of the political nature of that relation which has subsisted between Indians and the U. States." But on further reflection, Clay recognized his adversaries' guile and confessed that British pretense of ignorance was likely a mere tactic. He was right. Goulburn, the Liverpool ministry, and its agents in America were likely as well informed as the American delegates on Indian affairs thanks to a steady stream of reports from British agents in Canada and the United States and a capable Indian affairs department. More important, Clay ultimately discerned the true nature of the Liverpool ministry's intention: to hobble the United States and irrevocably impede its growth in favor of the British Empire in America. The proposal, "as we clearly understood it, in all its enormity," Clay explained, was "a proposition to sever our Country—made under the guise of a generous and disinterested attention to the welfare of their allies,—but urged in fact for the purpose of security to the British provinces."[66]

Adams and Clay initially prevailed among the American delegation, arguing in their note that including Indians in treaties between European states was unprecedented, which meant that asking the United States to do so now undermined its position as a state on a par with other European nations. The Americans recognized Britain's desire to include its allies in a peace as consistent with the laws of civilized nations, but they denied that the Indians were either civilized or independent nations, asserting that Britain had no right "to interfere in any manner with Indian tribes residing within the territories of the Untied States."[67] Playing their colonial past to their advantage for a change, the Americans asked, "What was the meaning of all the colonial charters granted by the British Monarchs, from that of Virginia by Elizabeth to that of Georgia by the immediate predecessors of the present King, if the Indians were the sovereigns and proprietors of the lands bestowed by those charters?" "It is this example," they continued, "which the United States, since they became by their independence the Sovereigns of the territory, have adopted and organised into a political system." In observance of this standing practice, they contended, the United States claimed not to interfere with those Indians residing in Canada.

The British stonewalled the Americans. In response to American complaints about the hundred thousand or more citizens living within the territory Britain wanted ceded to the Indians, the British envoys replied simply that "They must look after themselves."[68] In reply to American claims of sovereignty over the Indians, the British pretended that such a claim was mere hubris since many of the Indians in question had been in a state of rebellion since the United States attacked Tecumseh and his brother's headquarters at Prophetstown in the Indiana Territory in late 1811—a thinly veiled implication that if Britain's subjects could legally rebel in 1775 and be recognized as sovereign by European states, the Indians could do the same in 1811. In light of America's reputation, the delegates argued, Britain had no choice but to act out of humanitarianism. "The American government has now for the first time declared all Indian tribes to be its subjects," the British declared, "living upon sufferance within its territories, from whence it claims a right at any time to dispossess them, menacing thereby their final extinction. Against such a system the British government must formally protest." Although Britain's recent record toward Indians was better only in comparison to the United States, such sentiments were not entirely disingenuous. Liverpool, Bathurst, and Castlereagh all felt honor-bound to do their best for the Indians, but these were savvy, morally flexible men who had readily abandoned principle for the sake of power in the past. After all, this trait played no small part in making them one of the longest-lasting ministries in British history.

When the United States embarked on what it thought would be negotiations in Russia in 1813, the Madison administration and the war's supporters entertained high hopes. The press closely followed the Russian offer of mediation, and Madison publicly stated his expectation that Britain would accept. Well wishes appeared in print throughout the country on the departure of Gallatin and Bayard, with *Niles' Weekly Register* remarking that "They carry with them the best wishes and highest confidence of their fellow-citizens."[69] The Madison administration and the nation's press kept Americans well informed, regularly printing selected correspondence, including the lengthy official instructions Monroe gave to the plenipotentiaries. That summer, while the country believed its delegates were negotiating in Russia, bravado pervaded the pro-war press. The New York *Military Monitor* demanded expulsion of Britain from North America as "the only complete security which can be received against a recurrence of the injuries, which led to the present war." In consequence, it and others condemned the idea of a treaty that resulted in status quo ante bellum. "A treaty with such an enemy on the principle of the *status quo ante bellum*," the *Monitor* raged, "would be a mockery"; "drive [them] from America, else you will never have peace."[70]

When negotiations began at Ghent, the press prioritized peace news above all else, with papers such as Kentucky's *Union* making earnest pledges to readers to do anything and everything to keep them fully informed.[71] In consequence, even readers of the Williamsburg, Ohio, *Western American* had the same access to Monroe's diplomatic correspondence as did any reader in Washington or New York. By this time the American public was well aware of the escalating pressure in Britain on its government to make aggressive demands. Some commentators dismissed the cries in the British press for vengeance as mere bravado, but many Americans took the changing climate in Britain seriously, including the Madison administration, which effectively authorized the American envoys to agree to a status quo ante bellum treaty that June. By autumn the prospect of a quick peace at Ghent seemed shattered. Following the destruction of the nation's capital, Madison publicly informed Congress in September that the British government might not be considering peace seriously, pointing to its rejection of Russian mediation and "above all the principles and manner in which the war is now avowedly carried on."[72] The administration braced itself for another year of war and did what it could to prepare the country.

When news of Britain's initial demands reached the United States in October, it firmed American resolve. As the American envoys knew, no treaty along the lines of what the British originally proposed would be approved by the American government, because it would have meant the collapse of the Madison administration, likely disintegration of the Republicans, and quite possibly dissolution of the Union—or so many believed. Monroe declared in response to Britain's original terms, "the United States must relinquish no right, or perish in the struggle. There is not intermediate ground to rest on."[73] Madison confided in Jefferson that he expected the envoys to walk out of the negotiation in response to Britain's proposal.[74] News of Britain's territorial demands at Ghent confirmed public fears that Britain had shifted to an offensive strategy intent on destroying the United States, inflaming many former opponents of the war to take up arms. Even William Ellery Channing, the Massachusetts minister who repeatedly condemned the war in print and in person at prominent public occasions, shifted his stance. The situation was dire, he warned in a sermon that autumn: "the thought of invasion and slaughter mingles with the labours of the day." But at least now Americans were fighting a just, defensive war, enabling God to favor them. "The question now is—not whether we will carry invasion, slaughter, and desolation into an unoffending province," Channing declared, "but whether we will defend our firesides and altars—whether we will repel from our shores a hostile army." And on this question, he assured his audience, "our duty is clear": "whilst God gives us power we will not receive law as a conquered people."[75]

Among the most widely reprinted declarations of newfound support for the American war effort came from William Polk. A Revolutionary War hero who had survived alongside George Washington at Valley Forge, Polk was one of the most prominent Federalists in North Carolina. In 1812 he was offered a commission as a general in the United States Army, but at odds with Madison's causes for war, Polk declined. Yet in October 1814 he publicly switched his position in a detailed letter that appeared in most newspapers throughout the country. Singling out Britain's peace terms as the cause of his change of heart, Polk declared publicly that he would have remained a private citizen "had I not seen the degrading conditions demanded by the British Commissioners from the American government as the price of peace—conditions as new as they are humiliating: inadmissible under circumstances far more perilous than the present, and such as no American ought to succumb to." In consequence, he continued, "I hesitate not to declare my intention to unite with and support the government in such a system, as shall compel the enemy to respect our rights and bring the war to an honorable termination." Not to have his position mistaken as newfound support for Madison or the original case for war, Polk noted, "it is not, however, to be understood, that the avowed cause for the war or the manner in which it has been conducted have ever met my approbation."[76]

By winter, virtually no one in the United States believed that war would end soon or the United States would achieve its initial aims, and defeatism began to envelope the public discussion. Like most newspapers, the *Greensburgh & Indiana Register* endorsed and printed a lengthy defense of a status quo ante bellum treaty that stretched over two issues, asserting that such a treaty represented the best terms possible and that they were honorable.[77] The *National Intelligencer*, the Madison administration's unofficial newspaper, printed a slew of editorials and letters defending abandonment of neutral rights and impressment as war goals as a way to lower public expectations. The sophistry was admirable. In an early November editorial, the paper attempted to refute critics who had highlighted the administration's desertion of its stated reasons for declaring war by explaining that peace in Europe negated the need for the United States to press its maritime rights. Abandoning nearly two years of arguments about principal over practice, the editorial claimed that "It was the practice of impressment, not the claim of a right not in practice, that required the United States to go to war." After all, the *Intelligencer* continued, "The British King may insert this claim among his prerogatives, as he used to do among the titles his claim to the Kingdom of France." Though admitting that an article in the treaty prohibiting the practice would have been "agreeable," the real security derived from America's demonstration of its willingness to go to war over it. "If the British government had fully believed some years ago that her impressments and blockades, as practiced by her," the paper challenged, "would have produced war, and compared her gains by the former with her loss by the latter, is it not probable that peace with her would have remained to this day?" Thus, through a clever twist, the editorial asserted that the act itself of going to war, not waging it effectively or defeating Britain, achieved America's original war aims.[78] By these new criteria, the United States had already won. Now its envoys needed to see that the nation would escape the war intact.

Meanwhile, the Liverpool ministry wavered. The state of affairs in Europe and the British domestic political scene ultimately drove the actions of British government. As important as the war with America was, it was still essentially a colonial war in which even the most resounding success could not make amends for a disaster in Europe or at home. The prime minister and his colleagues had misjudged the

Americans' willingness to make a treaty on Britain's terms. As Liverpool remarked to Bathurst in September, following a series of exchanges with the Americans that made it clear they would not soon budge, "I confess I cannot believe that with the prospect of bankruptcy before them, the American government would not wish to make peace, if they can make it upon terms which would not give a triumph to their enemies."[79] Of course, the Americans' intransigence stemmed partly from the fact that neither they nor their government had anticipated Britain's territorial demands, and fresh instructions would take months in the slow world of transatlantic communications. Faced with such delays and mounting pressure at home and abroad, the Liverpool ministry yielded. The prime minister would ultimately call and lead the incremental retreat from Britain's initial demands, persuading Castlereagh and Bathurst and ordering Goulburn to follow.

Liverpool's centrality to the demise of Britain's hard-line position at Ghent stemmed largely from his responsibility for seeing the larger picture—carefully weighing the threats to the nation and the ministry's stability against potential gains. Liverpool, more than any other minister in Britain or prominent American leader, recognized the global context of the War of 1812. He understood the negotiations transpiring at Ghent and Vienna as connected, regularly remarking how events at one would play out in the other.

The autumn of 1814 was a precarious time in Europe, as the Congress of Vienna faced collapse and with it renewed war. Without Napoleon to bind the allies, they quickly fell into their old bickering habits as each nation pursued its own interest. Neither had much love for the other, they had all gone to war against each other at least once in the last century, and so intrigue, secret treaties, and backroom diplomacy prevailed. Britain's primary concern was a balance of power on the Continent, believing imbalance only encouraged aggression, and to achieve this it was willing to make major concessions to former enemies and work against former allies. Russia was perhaps the most powerful, and therefore a British target. To counter Russian power, Britain was willing to aid France's recovery by restoring many of its colonies and pursuing secret agreements.[80]

The American war hurt Britain's standing in Europe in two key ways. First, it made Britain look aggrandizing at a time of tit-for-tat diplomacy. The British government looked disingenuous arguing against the partition of lesser powers in Europe by Russia and Prussia while waging a war against the United States. After all, any pretense that Britain was a victim of American aggression and fighting solely to defend Canada and its maritime rights went out the window the moment Britain's terms at Ghent became known—which was immediate, thanks to the American delegation. France, which the Liverpool ministry wanted to court as an ally, was particularly sensitive to this, because the War of 1812 was unpopular with the French—many of whom had an affinity for the republican system of government and France's former ally. Second, continuing the war with the United States allowed the other powers to encroach on Britain's commercial hegemony over the Atlantic. They were, after all, neutrals, and Russia, which was militarily strong but economically weak, in particular saw an opportunity to enter the American trade the following year. Liverpool remarked with relief to Bathurst after concluding the Treaty of Ghent that peace with the United States would facilitate an alliance with France and "foil [Emperor] Alexander" by undercutting Russia's finances through keeping it out of lucrative American trade.[81]

More important to the short-term survival of the Liverpool ministry was the intense domestic pressure to alleviate the burdens of war. Although newspapers such as the *Times* and *London Courier* still clamored for chastisement of the United States, the national fury against the Americans in the wake of Napoleon's defeat subsided during the autumn. The British people grew increasingly weary of mobilization and taxation. Britain had lost a generation to its wars with Revolutionary and Napoleonic France, and repayment of the war debt would cost in excess of 30 percent of national government expenditure for nearly a century.[82] Many Britons were too tired of war to want revenge. As a letter in the *Edinburgh Star* remarked on the eve of the Ghent negotiations, "moderation is perhaps the best guarantee for the continuance of the peace. When degrading terms are imposed on a nation, it is evident from the history of the last few years . . . that they will be submitted to only so long as they cannot be successfully opposed."[83] As talks began, the *Aberdeen Chronicle* confidently remarked in a lengthy editorial on the negotiations at Ghent, with peace in Europe, "the public will, therefore, naturally expect, with much anxiety, the conclusion of the negotiations at Ghent." Besides, the *Chronicle* continued, Britain had no right to make harsh demands: "We daily hear much flippant talking of drubbing the Yankee—of bringing Jonathan to his senses—with other expressions of the like nature; but as yet, we have gained no decisive advantage over the Americans, and our losses during the war are more than equal to theirs."[84] After learning of Britain's initial terms for peace, the *Liverpool Mercury* lamented, "the expectation of any immediate peace with the United States of America, seems to be totally extinguished." The *Mercury* called the terms "impossible" and proclaimed they were designed to prolong the war for the benefit of the war contractors, suppliers, creditors and officials—people for whom "war expenditure may not only be useful, but even absolutely necessary."[85] The problem, declared the radical critic William Cobbett, was that Britain had become too arrogant in the wake of the defeat of Napoleon: "the truth is, we have been so stunned with vain boasts of our achievements; we have been so battened with the notion of our being *conquerors of France* that we are become stupid."[86]

Liverpool realized the British public's patience was limited. This compelled Castlereagh to pursue a policy of peace at almost any cost at Vienna, which in turn led to a push for a balance of power even when it meant thwarting its Russian

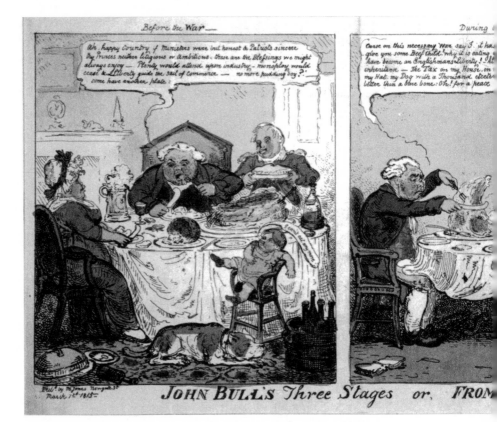

Figure 8.3 George Cruikshank, "John Bull's Three Stages or, From Good to Bad to Worse" (London, 1815). Library of Congress, Prints and Photographs Division, LC-USZC4-6863. The print satirizes the national frustration with the perceived economic decline of the British family even after peace. In the first scene, marked "Before the War," the plump family tucks into frothing beer and roast beef. In the second scene, "During the War," the family, including the dog, is noticeably thinner, the tablecloth is looking a little ragged, the food portions are smaller, and the beer has less froth. In the final scene, "Peace with the World," the family have declined noticeably. Now emaciated, they have moved from their original home, their clothes are in tatters, the mug is empty, and only bones are on offer for food. In the second and third scenes the father complains of the heavy taxes.

ally and bolstering the former enemy, France.[87] The War of 1812 figured indirectly into this equation because continuing it risked damage to the extremely delicate and complicated balance in Europe. More directly, the War of 1812 would cost no less than £10 million per annum on top of a large peacetime military establishment, according to the estimate Liverpool made in October.[88] This meant keeping many unpopular taxes, including the dreaded property tax, which was set to expire in 1816. And as Parliament would later confirm in 1815 as it axed wartime taxes, it was in no mood to do anything except provide relief—despite Liverpool's pleas.[89]

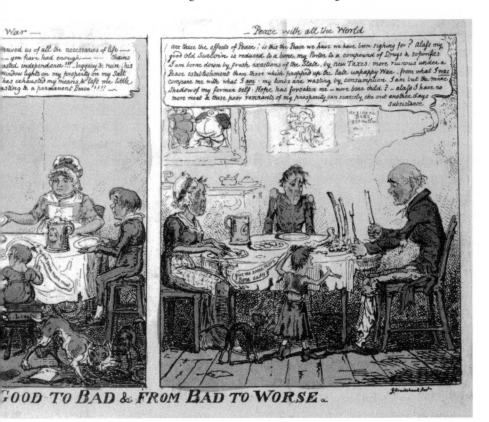

Liverpool would not yield without one last push, but when he informally polled his colleagues about keeping taxes in place on multiple occasions, he found limited enthusiasm. Castlereagh framed the issue in a letter to Liverpool in late August after American intransigence became apparent: "are we prepared to continue the war for territorial arrangement?" If not, he asked if it was better to make peace now and be done with it.[90] Liverpool's answer was to continue the war a while longer. The news in October of the burning of Washington boosted his confidence, and Bathurst sent fresh instructions to the British envoys to inform the Americans that in Britain's "generous" magnanimity it would not take advantage of the situation to make additional conditions for peace.[91] Although Clay confessed "I tremble indeed whenever I take up a late News paper," he and the other delegates did not panic, and soon afterwards they learned of Britain's failure at Plattsburgh and with it postponement of any British invasion plans until the next year.[92]

From that point forward, British softening on the major issues became a matter of policy at Ghent. The Liverpool ministry jettisoned plans for major territorial concessions on the Canadian border and abandoned any hope of a

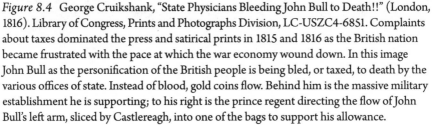

Figure 8.4 George Cruikshank, "State Physicians Bleeding John Bull to Death!!" (London, 1816). Library of Congress, Prints and Photographs Division, LC-USZC4-6851. Complaints about taxes dominated the press and satirical prints in 1815 and 1816 as the British nation became frustrated with the pace at which the war economy wound down. In this image John Bull as the personification of the British people is being bled, or taxed, to death by the various offices of state. Instead of blood, gold coins flow. Behind him is the massive military establishment he is supporting; to his right is the prince regent directing the flow of John Bull's left arm, sliced by Castlereagh, into one of the bags to support his allowance.

separate Indian state. American acknowledgment of the Indians in the treaty and a return to their 1811 borders would suffice. Liverpool had already retreated considerably from the idea of securing a separate state for the Indians, tangling with the less flexible stance of Bathurst and Goulburn. Writing to Bathurst in mid-September, Liverpool conceded that "I quite agree with you on the *absolute necessity* of including the Indians in the treaty of peace." Moreover, he continued with all the sincerity of a successful career politician with uncanny survival skills, "I would do more, if more has been promised; but I would not make a *sine qua non* of more, if more has not been promised." Liverpool knew perfectly well that more had been promised than a return to the Indians' prewar status, but he worried that harsh ultimatums would invigorate the American war spirit. "[W]e must recollect," he cautioned, "that if the ground upon which the negotiation terminated were popular . . . the war would then be rendered a war of despair, in which all private rights and interests would be sacrificed to the public cause."[93]

Softening was not a total collapse, however. Throughout October and November Liverpool struggled with how much Britain could yield before having to commit to continuing the war. For most of this period, Britain fell back to the position of *uti possidetis*—Latin for "as you possess," by which both sides keep whatever they held at the time of the treaty—on the assumption that Britain would finish the war with at least some gains, including parts of Maine and perhaps New Orleans. With this in mind, Goulburn advised urging Britain's Indian allies in the Ohio and Great Lakes to "occupy as advanced a position as they can with a view of procuring better terms for them, and through them for ourselves." Of course, Gallatin had taken a similar tactic in late August by advising Monroe to sign separate peace treaties with the hostile Indians as soon as possible, thereby eliminating the need for Britain to represent them at Ghent.[94] Writing in late October to Castlereagh at Vienna, Liverpool lamented the British failure at Plattsburgh but nonetheless saw a silver lining: the American victory enabled Madison to "cling to office," which would allow continuation of peace negotiations, which Liverpool described as concluding.[95] Just a week later he warned Castlereagh not to make or inflame enemies at Vienna, fearing that the war with America might continue to handicap Britain for some time. On the same day, he also wrote to the Duke of Wellington that "there can be, however, very little doubt" that peace would *not* come from the Ghent negotiations, because the Americans refused to yield any territory. "[T]hey never will cede any part of their dominions, even though they shall have been conquered by their enemies," he moaned. "This principle they bring forward during a war in which one of their chief efforts has been to conquer and annex Canada to the United States." Liverpool's new plan was simple: stall by tying them down with notes and requests for explanation, and hope that continued British attacks would bring the Americans to their senses.[96]

A week later, however, Liverpool reconsidered again, after concluding that his ministry was running out of time. Writing to Castlereagh, Liverpool explained his primary concern. Parliament would be called back into session soon, and its members expected to make massive, long-awaited cuts to government spending—cuts that continuing the war with America made extremely difficult. "The continuance of the American war," Liverpool worried, "will entail upon us a prodigious expense, much more than we had any idea of." The opposition's first action would be to request the government's papers on the American war to go before Parliament—papers that would enable opponents to discern the real cost of the war. The vote could be called as early as December, and the Liverpool ministry, still not the strongest of governments, could very well lose the vote and with it possibly their hold on power. As Liverpool had remarked earlier, he could hear the opposition's cries already: "We must expect, therefore, to hear it said that the property-tax is continued for the purpose of securing a better frontier for Canada." Others would question whether or not Britain could meet its promises made at Vienna, in particular the ability to take over a portion of Russia's massive debts and thus use this as leverage to thwart Russian territorial ambitions. And Liverpool expected that for all of the bluster of the *Times*, neither Parliament nor the greater public would make the sorts of sacrifice necessary for a colonial war.[97]

To shore up domestic support in case of a protracted war with the United States, Liverpool sought to send the Duke of Wellington to command Britain's war effort in America. There were perhaps other cards to play in this suit, but none carried as much conviction as linking the war effort to the nation's greatest war hero. As Liverpool explained to Castlereagh in early November, "His appointment will in itself be sufficient to obviate many difficulties and much embarrassment at home."[98] For his part, Wellington had mixed thoughts. Although kept as well apprised of British operations in North America and negotiations at Ghent as any cabinet member, Wellington had commented little officially until Liverpool pressed him to take command of the forces there. Writing to Liverpool in early November, Wellington explained that he did not want to leave Europe at present for fear of renewed war, but he would be willing to go if the American war continued. In terms of the war itself, he had little regard for the American army but doubted that he could be more effective than Prevost without naval superiority on the Great Lakes, commenting that there was no point in his going "only to prove the truth of Prevost's defense." In terms of the negotiations at Ghent, Wellington dealt a severe blow to the ministry's position. Britain, he asserted, had not fought successfully enough to merit any major American concessions of territory, and pursuing this would only prolong the war unnecessarily. "You can get no territory; indeed the state of your military operations, however creditable, does not entitle you to demand any," Wellington bluntly wrote Liverpool.[99]

Meanwhile Goulburn informed Bathurst that he did not think a quick peace was possible unless Britain would accept status quo ante bellum, "to which I presume we are not ready to accede." Goulburn advised an aggressive posture, but Liverpool gave the order to yield less than a week after he received Wellington's letter. In a letter to Castlereagh, Liverpool summarily declared that "we have determined, if all other points can be satisfactorily settled, not to continue the war for the purpose of obtaining or securing any acquisition of territory." His reasons were clear: the state of Britain's finances were poor, the opposition in Parliament "would be violently opposed" to continuing the war for territorial gain at the edge of the empire, the state of the negotiations at Vienna pointed to a strong possibility of renewed war, and Wellington advised peace.[100]

Liverpool reiterated this explanation shortly after the treaty was signed in a private letter to Canning, one of the most vocal critics in Parliament of a soft stance against the United States. Arguing that fighting for a "better frontier for

Canada" was not worth prolonging the war at the cost of continuing wartime taxation rates, Liverpool asserted that "from all I have heard, I do not believe it would have been possible to have continued it for the purpose of carrying on an American war" and that he wanted to end the conflict before the "impatience of the country on the subject had been manifested at public meetings or by motions in Parliament." The length of the Canadian border and the enormous disparity between the populations of British North America and the United States would make the war difficult, Liverpool added. Only New Orleans could be taken in the near future, and the war was not worth continuing on that account. Liverpool pleaded he had wanted to fulfill promises to "the Indians who were abandoned in the Treaty of 1783," and he deflected much of the blame for the status quo ante bellum nature of the treaty on Wellington in a likely effort to thwart Canning's public criticism of the terms. Whereas Canning would readily abuse Liverpool in public, he would tread more lightly with the enormously popular duke.[101]

Goulburn was livid. Learning of Liverpool's revised position in late November, Goulburn wrote immediately to Bathurst, expressing his "sincere regret at the alternative which the government feels itself compelled by the present state of affairs in Europe to adopt with respect to America." "You know that I was never much inclined to give way to the Americans," he concluded, knowing full well that Britain was abandoning its Indian allies to a dreadful fate and deeply regretting it. "I had till I came here no idea of the fixed determination which prevails in the breast of every American to extirpate the Indians and appropriate their territory," Goulburn lamented, "but I am now sure that there is nothing which the people of America would so reluctantly abandon as what they are pleased to call their natural right to do so." Nevertheless, Goulburn assured his superiors that he would proceed as ordered.[102] In the end, Goulburn endorsed a treaty he personally loathed and then became its apologist in the House of Commons, fielding questions from outraged members such as Canning and Wellesley who, like himself, could not believe the Liverpool ministry had been so lenient.[103] All he could do was grumble to John Quincy Adams, who along with Clay ungraciously mocked Goulburn for his lack of independence in the proceedings, that, had he had his way, the matter between Britain and the United States would not be finished.[104]

Once the Liverpool ministry determined to end the war, what followed was a mad rush to conclude it. Within two days of Goulburn's defeatist letter, an excited Adams wrote in his diary that "All the difficulties to the conclusion of a peace appear to be now so nearly removed, that my colleagues all considered it as certain."[105] Goulburn spent days "closeted with the American plenipotentiaries" wrapping up the terms in a process that primarily consisted of neither side yielding anything, ignoring the most controversial issues, and agreeing to set aside anything complicated, particularly commercial issues such as fishing and navigation rights, for later negotiations. To hurry matters further, Goulburn reined in any attempts by the Americans to stall for further concession by telling them that if they decided to consult with their government, all terms that were agreed would be open for reconsideration.[106] Liverpool also insisted on making the end of hostilities conditional on formal ratification by the government of the United States. The move was not an effort to prolong the war to allow the British to take New Orleans; instead, it was a move to further pressure the United States to accept the treaty as written. If the American government demurred, the war would continue, he explained to Castlereagh, and Britain had plenty of troops and ships in place to intimidate the Americans.[107] Besides, if the Americans rejected the treaty, once again he could plausibly lay the blame at the feet of the American government and then proceed as originally planned in 1812.

When the envoys signed the treaty on Christmas Eve, Goulburn could hardly hide his disgust. He believed Britain had let the Americans off too lightly and betrayed the promises the British government made to its American Indian allies—promises that as undersecretary of state for war and the colonies he had helped craft and relay. He would have left Ghent immediately, he explained to Bathurst, but the townspeople annoyingly insisted on holding a fete to celebrate the treaty.[108] In contrast, the Americans enjoyed the celebrations. On Christmas day, both delegations joined together with the town's leaders for a Christmas feast in which they enjoyed roast beef and plum pudding from England and listened to a Ghent band's rendition of "God Save the King" and "Yankee Doodle" as they toasted one another's heads of state. The young James Gallatin was quite moved, calling it "a scene to be remembered." "God grant there may be always peace between the two nations," he concluded. "I never saw father so cheerful; he was in high spirits."[109] Two weeks later, the town hosted a banquet, where the Americans remained amiable and Goulburn continued in his sour mood. The leading American delegates' more private views were mixed but more reflective of their personalities than any belief that the treaty was less than a success. Adams appealed to God, writing in his diary after signing the treaty that "I cannot close the record of this day without a humble offering of gratitude to God for the conclusion to which it has pleased him to bring the negotiations of peace at this place." Gallatin stated simply to Monroe that the terms were the best the delegates could do, and he hoped that America's naval success would prompt greater respect from European nations. Clay was less grateful to the Divine but nevertheless thankful that although the terms were "undoubtedly not such as our Country expected at the commencement of the War," he had no doubt that in the present situation "they cannot be pronounced very unfavorable," concluding "I think [we lose] no honor."[110] Perhaps most reflective of how humbling the experience at Ghent had been for the Americans, as well as how grateful they were to have escaped with their nation intact, is that none of them complained when the British delegates held the signing at their residence and listed their names before those of the Americans.

Conclusion: Who Won the War of 1812?

After signing the Treaty of Ghent, the British government included a caveat: the war would not end until the U.S. government formally ratified the treaty. An American refusal was a plausible possibility. After all, Thomas Jefferson had declined even to send the last one (the 1806 Monroe-Pinkney Treaty) to Congress for its consideration, and the American peace delegates had failed to win any concessions from Britain with regard to their country's originally stated reasons for declaring war. To transport the treaty to Washington, the British sent Anthony St. John Baker, a midlevel but experienced diplomat, who had served in the United States and been at Ghent. Running the foreign office during Lord Castlereagh's absence at the Congress of Vienna, Lord Bathurst provided explicit instructions. Baker had the power only to exchange treaties, not enter negotiations, which meant the United States could either accept or reject the treaty, not revise it. If the Americans refused to ratify, Baker was to leave for Halifax, but not before leaking the entire contents of the treaty to the American press in hopes of using public opinion to pressure the American government into reconsidering. Bathurst and his fellow ministers knew full well how public opinion could alter the course of governments, having been held hostage themselves for two and a half years. If Madison and Congress still refused to budge, Baker was then to return to London.[1]

As it turned out, the British had no reason to worry. Baker reported to Castlereagh from the American capital in February that the Madison administration and Congress had practically trampled each other in their rush to ratify the treaty. In fact, according to Baker, "it bore such evident marks of haste, that Mr. Monroe entreated me to delay the departure [of the British conveying ship] until Monday morning in order that an opportunity might be afforded of putting it into some better condition."[2] What was one of the most ambiguous wars in American and British history was finally over, but the most confusing part remained: determining the victor.

Throughout the Anglo-American Atlantic world, politicians, government officials, and public commentators debated this topic without reaching a consensus.

A few observers, such as Glasgow's *Caledonian Mercury*, found the subject vulgar: "As to the question so eagerly contested in some of the London newspapers, which of the two nations have done most mischief to the other in the war, we have really too much respect for the good sense of our readers to enter into such a controversy." Peace, the *Mercury* declared, "is the great object of war. This object we have attained, and it is surely not very humane to boast at what an expense of human misery it has been purchased."[3] Of course, the *Mercury* was critical of the war from the start, laying blame at various points on both the American and British governments for bringing the two nations to a war that was detrimental to the manufacturing and commercial interests of cities like Glasgow. From the vantage point of the *Mercury* and dozens of newspapers like it, there could be no winner. As the *Aberdeen Chronicle* remarked the same day, "the shortest follies are the best" and for that the "restoration of Peace with America forms a just subject of joy and congratulation." But while many suffered as a result of the war, others plainly benefited.

Yet the status quo ante bellum terms of the peace treaty should not lull anyone into thinking the war was a draw. After all, few European-style wars in this period ended conclusively. The decisiveness of the victory over France in 1815 was the exception, not the rule, and it had taken more than two decades and the lives of a generation of young men to achieve it. Even then, the victors were not able to dictate terms to France, and Britain returned many of its imperial conquests. Ambiguous conclusions to European wars both allowed multiple sides to declare victory and drove many nations to declare war shortly after making peace in order to pursue unresolved issues. But this was not the case with Britain and the United States, because the War of 1812 proved sufficiently conclusive to curtail future conflicts. Although tensions ran high on multiple occasions, the United States did not go to war with a European nation again until the Spanish American War in 1898. Europe managed to keep its conflicts from erupting into global wars, and the Europeans effectively stayed out of North American conflicts, such as the Mexican American War, the American Civil War, and the many conflicts between the United States and the American Indians—a sharp contrast to the preceding centuries. This was in no small part because the true primary issue of the War of 1812—whether or not the United States would be respected as a sovereign nation rather than humbled as a quasi-part of the British Empire—was resolved, and Britain had lost.

News of the Treaty of Ghent reached London within two days of its signing, and within a week it fully circulated throughout the British Isles. Most newspapers devoted an entire issue to the subject, and some, such as the *Caledonian Mercury*, even printed a second edition in order to inform readers. Most Britons were surprised by the sudden turn of events. Because the British government had kept a fairly tight lid on news emanating from Ghent, British newspapers relied on American sources in Europe (which overplayed American reluctance to accept peace) and American newspapers (whose most recent editions to reach Britain carried the resolute rejection of Britain's harsh initial terms). As the *Exeter Flying-Post* remarked, "The Peace comes probably very unexpected upon our readers; for the last American documents had assumed such a tone . . . that no one supposed that the same breath that blew the blast of war could have been playing to the American commissioners the dulcet notes of peace."[4]

Most were elated at the news. As joyful as peace in Europe was, it was not complete for many Britons so long as the war with the United States continued. After all, Britain had more troops in Canada than would fight at Waterloo. Alluding to the Biblical account of the angelic chorus's announcement of the birth of Jesus, with which its readers would have been familiar, the *Leeds Mercury* declared its joy: "This Country, thanks to the good Providence of God, is now at Peace with Europe, with America, and with the World. . . . There is at length 'Peace on Earth,' and we trust the revival of 'Good-will among men' will quickly follow the close of national hostilities."[5] In manufacturing towns such as Beith in Scotland, which relied heavily on producing textiles for American markets, the joy was overwhelming. As one participant observed: "When the news of the American peace reached Beith, the inhabitants ordered the bells to be rung for an hour; and on Monday evening last the town was finely illuminated."[6] Others were less magnanimous. Having suffered for the better part of the past decade from Anglo-American disagreements, commentators from Liverpool were especially bitter. As the *Liverpool Mercury*, which harshly criticized the British government over the Orders in Council and the war, remarked, "The sincere gratification which this even affords us, may be measured by the tone of execration in which we have ever commented upon a contest as abhorrent as it was impolitic." The war, the *Mercury* complained, should never have transpired, and at the very least it should have ended with the conclusion of Britain's war with France the previous spring. "Now, do we indeed rejoice," it continued, "that in spite of the wishes and prayers of a greedy and sanguinary war party, our Government has seen the necessity of not suffering hostilities" to continue.[7] The *Morning Chronicle*, which at times castigated ministers over their handling of the war, placed the peace with the United States in a larger context. The war, the *Chronicle* asserted, was a "lesson" to the sovereigns haggling at the Congress of Vienna "that peace can alone have a chance for durability, that is founded on justice and moderation!" There is no point in governments pursuing "demands, which they cannot accomplish without perpetuating the horrors of war." Such policies, the *Chronicle* concluded, only lead to bitterness and renewed war—a concern that haunted postwar Europe.[8]

British critics of the war expressed disappointment that it had taken so long to conclude, but many of the war's proponents asserted their fury over the terms on which it had ended. The debate that transpired over the next two months was fierce and widespread; as Dublin's *Freeman's Journal* noted, the "Treaty with America continues to occupy the most prominent place among public subjects."[9] The *Times*, long critical of what it considered the Liverpool ministry's lack of resolve in prosecuting the American war, was the most vocal critic of the treaty. After printing a summary of the terms, the *Times* consoled its readers by stating "that there is yet a hope that this disgraceful Treaty may fail of obtaining a ratification" and so publicly appealed directly to the prince regent to reject it and "liberate us from the trammels of a deceptive and treacherous negotiation." The Americans were down, the *Times* declared, and now was the time to kick them hard. Yes, it admitted, wartime taxation in Britain was oppressive and thus "the great argument for peace." "But all such questions are relative," it continued, insisting that the United States was suffering far more, facing a doubling of taxes and military conscription—"a measure till now unheard of in the history of the Republic." Meanwhile, news was arriving that New England "is openly with drawing itself from the Union." "And, at such a moment," raged the *Times*, "we tender to our hopeless antagonist the unlooked-for boon of peace!"[10] On further reflection a few days later, the *Times* published a lengthy editorial expressing irritation at the peace celebrations, claiming that thoughtful Britons were troubled by the terms and complaining that the timing of the treaty made it seem as if Britain had partly capitulated to the United States. The *Times* lamented that "The painful anticipation of vulgar and insolent triumph from adversaries on whom we had looked down with contempt" awaited the British, along with "the certainty that we should be considered both in America and Europe as partly beaten and partly intimidated into pacification."[11]

For the next month the *Times* was relentless, arguing in almost daily editorials that the peace was a fiasco for Britain, damaging its military reputation and showing weakness before its rivals in Europe. Peace on these terms, the *Times* and its like-minded supporters in the press argued, only invited future conflict with the United States. As the equally irate *Edinburgh Star* argued, any peace with the United States was just a truce until the Americans were beaten and severely humbled. Reflecting the new attitude in Britain that victory was not complete without removal of the opponent's government and conquest of its territory, the *Star* declared that "Our opinion has been from the first . . . that nothing but convincing them of our decided superiority will ever make them cordially our friends; they are spoiled children, who should be whipped, not flattered into friendship." The Americans will strike again, the paper warned, unless Britain deals them such a blow that "they perceive [Canada] to be unattainable."[12]

Although the *Times* represented those who perceived the American war as a loss, few in Britain pretended the war was a national victory, including those who welcomed the peace. When officials of the City of London gathered to construct its traditional address to the prince regent on an end to the war, they outright refused to endorse a conflict that many of them had opposed. In the resulting address they ambiguously referred to the war as "that series of political calamities which, whatever may have been their causes, or in whatever degree they were unavoidable, have at various periods of their disastrous court filled His Majesty's loyal subjects with anxiety for the welfare of these kingdoms." Neither in the debate nor in the address did they highlight British successes: the blockade of America's shores, destruction of a sizable portion of the American merchant fleet, victories in Canada over the invaders from the United States, or destruction of the American capital. Instead, the congratulations to the prince regent stemmed from the joy of peace itself. The petitioners depicted the conflict as an extension of the European wars—"but an effect of the mutual hostilities of the pre-existing Beligerents"—and so they tactfully linked the happiness of the conclusion of the American war with the great euphoria of a general peace befalling the British Empire, a peace that meant a return to commerce and elimination of taxes "such as we hope never again have the occasion to name."[13] Thus, for many Britons peace, and with it tax relief, overshadowed the importance of a clear victory in North America.

When news of the treaty reached the United States in mid-February, the nation was already celebrating. A month earlier Andrew Jackson and his motley force soundly defeated an army of British regulars nearly three times its size at New Orleans in the bloodiest and most decisive battle of the war—a defeat in which the British suffered more casualties than in all the other battles of the war combined. Although a misconception that the war had ended before the battle—the peace treaty did not take effect until the United States ratified it on February 16—New Orleans nevertheless did not have an impact on the war's outcome. It did, however, shape how the Americans received the end of the war by creating the illusion of military victory. In contrast, the British paid scant attention to it; news arrived at the same time as both the national debate on the Corn Law (an intensely controversial bill that introduced substantial protections for British grain producers and permanently inflated the price of the national dietary staple of bread) and the announcement of Napoleon's escape from Elba and the beginning of his Hundred Days that would end at the Battle of Waterloo.[14] Thus even though Americans would remember the wars of the period for the final victory at New Orleans (ignoring their later defeat at Mobile Point), Britain would commemorate Waterloo for generations, conveniently forgetting the defeat at New Orleans.[15]

The news met with universal jubilation across the United States as editors, clergymen, and politicians fell over each other in a race to offer the grandest praise. As the British would with Waterloo, the Americans in 1815 seized the image of the victory at New Orleans as evidence of American greatness and allowed it to color the entire conflict. In a celebratory sermon, Stephen Bovell typified many Americans' elation by boasting to his Virginian congregation that the Battle of New Orleans "will cause more tears to flow in England than any action fought by the British troops since Lord Wellington took the field in Spain in 1810." Not content with such a claim, he challenged any doubter to "search the annals of the most celebrated heroes and conquerors from the earliest ages down to the present . . . no instance has ever occurred in which a victory so decisive was obtained at the expense of so small a number of lives."[16] Speaking before the House of Representatives, George Troup, a Georgia Republican, also typified the unrestrained joy and exaggerated claims that swept the nation. "The God of Battles and of Righteousness took part with the defenders of their country," he declared, "and the foe was scattered before us as chaff before the wind. It is, indeed, a fit subject for the genius of Homer, of Ossian, or Milton." Not content with confining his boasts to New Orleans, he, like so many others, proceeded to reinterpret the war itself. "Europe has seen that, to be formidable on the ocean, we need but will it," Troup proclaimed. "Europe will see that, to be invincible on land, it is only necessary that we judiciously employ the means which God and Nature have bountifully placed at our disposal. The men of Europe . . . are not a match for the men of America."[17] In consequence, the terms of the treaty mattered relatively little to the celebrating Americans. As Charles Ingersoll, a congressman from Pennsylvania, observed as the House of Representatives awaited details of the terms of the Treaty of Ghent, "The terms of the treaty are yet unknown to us. But the victory at Orleans has rendered them glorious and honorable, be that what they may."[18] At a time of such triumphalism, there was little room for disappointment.

Combined with the news of New Orleans, the conclusion of the war sent a rapid wave of jubilation across the country. Within two days of arriving at New York, the news reached Washington, Boston, and Philadelphia. Within three days it reached Maine, and within a week almost all Americans heard it.[19] By the end of February, towns and cities across the country were advertising their celebration plans in newspapers and broadsides. In Hallowell, Maine, the inhabitants began a day of festivities with an eighteen-gun salute, followed by an afternoon gathering at the town meetinghouse, where "appropriate passages from scripture were read," followed by prayer and "selections of sacred music adapted to the occasion." The rest of the day "was devoted to mutual congratulations; and mirth and hilarity beamed on every countenance." As with most other celebrations across the county, this included an illumination

Figure 9.1 Title page of "Battle of the Memorable 8th of 1815. Composed for the Piano Forte by P. Laroque of New Orleans, and Most Respectfully Dedicated by him to the Fair Sex of America" (Philadelphia, 1815). The United States was awash with triumphal ballads, poetic tributes, paintings, engravings, and narrative accounts of the Battle of New Orleans, which, like this one, proclaimed Andrew Jackson "The Hero of New Orleans."

of the town that evening along with fireworks. Unique to Hallowell was the parading of a decorated sailboat through the streets—"to the gratification of the juvenile part of the town."[20] At Charleston, the evening illumination was on a grander scale and included a range of transparencies and banners hanging from windows emblazoned with the names of the American plenipotentiaries and that of Andrew Jackson.[21] In Boston, the Federal Street Theatre constructed a special exhibit on its stage including "Transparencies, Emblems,

Mottos, etc." that celebrated peace, America's naval prowess, and the fallen generals and naval captains. Audiences were invited to view the exhibit as the theater's chorus sang a variety of patriotic hymns.[22] Emphasizing that these were national celebrations, most newspapers provided accounts of local celebrations along with those from across the country, so that the people of Hallowell knew about the banners in Charleston, and readers of the *Western Monitor* in Kentucky had full details of the parade in Hartford, Connecticut. As the *Monitor* remarked in a March issue, "This day's mail brought us little else than universal expressions of gladness at the return of peace. Every city town and village from New-York to Lexington . . . vied with each other in manifestations of joy at the return of this inestimable blessing."[23]

Madison and his supporters were quick to claim the peace as a victory. The president himself wasted no time in declaring a carefully worded victory in his first public statement following the arrival of the treaty: "Peace, at all times a blessing, is peculiarly welcome, therefore, at a period when the causes for war have ceased to operate; when the government has demonstrated the efficiency of its powers of defence; and when the nation can review its conduct without regret, and without reproach."[24]

The supporting press was far bolder. The *National Intelligencer* produced a widely reprinted poetic "Tribute to American Valor" that began by mockingly asking "Where are Britannia's glories now?" and claimed that its laurels now adorn America's "Naval Band, and the Heroes of the Land."[25] As news of British disgruntlement with the peace terms, as exemplified by the *Times*, made its way to the United States, many American editors embraced the stories, gleefully depicting them as representative of national British sentiments and as further evidence of America's victory.

The sermon of John Latta to his parish in the town of Newcastle, Delaware, on the national day of thanksgiving for peace on April 13 encapsulates how many Americans narrated the war as a victory and as a second war of independence. Britain, he argued, "entertained towards us a grudge" for "they had never forgiven us for what they called our rebellion." The prosperity of the United States merely filled the British with "jealousy and envy," and so they embraced the war as an opportunity to "chastise [us] for our insolence, haughtiness, and presumption." As in the first war of independence, the Americans faced and overcame internal divisions and escaped the indignity of being a "vassal" of Britain. Equally important, he concluded, the United States had undeniably demonstrated its martial prowess. "No nation can, without a miracle, expect to enjoy its independence and its rights, unless it be respected and feared on account of its military strength," he declared. Pointing to "the success of our arms at New Orleans," Latta asserted that the United States had proven itself and thereby secured its independence.[26] Latta's sentiments were echoed in sermons,

orations, and newspaper columns throughout the country. As a mass-distrib-
uted broadside poster in Boston declared, the United States had won independence again, and its people had a new George Washington:

> Great Washington of peerless name,
> Our country gain'd immortal fame;
> Where veteran Jacksons presence cheers,
> A second Washington appears.

"This" day of celebration, the broadside declared, "is freedom's holiday."[27]

Even though virtually all Americans embraced the conclusion of the war, a
vocal minority remained reluctant to declare it a victory or credit Madison. As
John Smith, a Salem minister, explained to his congregation on the day of national thanksgiving, "rejoicing at the return of peace" does not "imply approbation of the late war."[28] The *Boston Spectator* criticized the public for being so
blinded by the joy of peace as to examine properly the terms of the treaty.
According to the *Spectator*, in failing to achieve its stated goals the American
government, "has shown Great Britain her strength and our weakness." After all,
the paper continued, "Mr. Madison's flag 'FREE TRADE AND SAILORS'
RIGHTS'" was nowhere to be seen in the public celebrations of peace.[29] Kentucky's *Western Monitor* was less critical of the terms, but like a number of commentators across the country it blasted Madison for trying to claim a victory,
declaring that "We have but little patience in hearing Mr. Madison indulge in a
language so inconsistent, in the face of this nation & in the view of such a vast
number of opposing facts as exist." Madison would be far more respected, the
disappointed *Monitor* continued, if "he had told congress and the nation that he
had been mistaken, and that he was compelled to make peace on the terms proposed, although falling entirely short of those for which the war was waged."[30]
What critics of the war did appreciate, however, was the printing presses that
enabled discussion and critique of the war. Humphrey Moore, a clergyman in
the New Hampshire village of Milford, spoke for former war critics across the
nation when he declared in a peace sermon that "The freedom of the press is
necessary to the general diffusion of political knowledge, and to the preservation
of civil rights."[31]

Despite the terms and the suffering of the past, most critics agreed that
Americans should embrace the peace. As Moore declared in his sermon, "Wives,
who lately were trembling alive for the fate of their husbands in their country's
service, are freed from their fearful apprehensions. Children are no longer
disturbed in their slumbers with visions of their fathers fallen on the field of
battle."[32] Moreover, critics had little doubt that continuing the war would have
been disastrous. As Benjamin Tappin remarked in an address to the Washington

Benevolent Society of Kennebec, Maine, "Had hostilities been protracted through another season, we must have suffered far more, than had yet befallen us."[33] But, critics of the war argued, Americans' gratitude for the peace was not owed to Madison and his cohort. "Fourteen years of misrule have cruelly" reversed America's happiness, complained one. God, not Madison, put an end to the war, declared John Smith from his Massachusetts pulpit. "God denied them [Madison and Congress] the means of continuing the war," and "the goodness of God appeared, in his *refusing to prosper* invading armies, on either side, during the late war. This ought to be noticed, with sincere gratitude, as one event, which led to peace."[34] But according to Susan Mansfield, a Boston minister's wife, such entreaties fell on deaf ears. "Few, alas! appear to recognize God as the author of the blessing, and their consequent obligations to Him," she remarked with disappointment. Instead, she complained, they see it entirely in terms of personal benefit and opportunity: "Few appear to regard [peace] in any other light, than as it affects the prices of goods, or the advantages of trade, or the indulgence of luxury."[35] Americans had returned to their true prowess: commerce.

While the war's supporters and critics disagreed on a great deal, most commentators came to a consensus on a number of key points in the wake of the war's conclusion. First, they agreed that the United States prospered in peace, not war, and that the conclusion of the war was good, despite disagreement on whether the terms merited claims of an American victory.

Second, there was an overwhelming consensus the United States had suffered from partisanship and disunity during the war. Marked with the stain of secessionist intrigue, New Englanders went out of their way to insist on their loyalty to the United States. Once again echoing the words of commentators throughout New England that winter and spring, Humphrey Moore declared, to "preserve domestic peace it is necessary to moderate the rage of party spirit," and the first step was "submission to the laws" of the land. "It is very supposable that a single law or a code of laws will not equally affect all parts of the community"; however, he warned in thinly-veiled allusion to the secessionist spirit that had lately swept through New England, "If the laws are unconstitutional, constitutional means should be used to produce their repeal."[36] But the lesson went both ways. As the war-supporting *Missouri Gazette* reflected through a reader's letter, wars waged by republics such as the United States required greater support to be successful, and for this the government needed better reasons to go to war. "Succeeding administrations will learn, that in adopting measures involving the consequences of war, the concurrence of a bare majority is not sufficient."[37]

Third, Americans from across the political spectrum agreed on the need for stronger defenses. Regardless of what national leaders might claim in public, the war had been a military embarrassment for the United States, and the victory at New Orleans, no matter how decisive, could not entirely erase the embarrassment of the United States suffering the destruction of its capital, nor the inability to conquer a weaker neighbor, Canada. Madison raised the subject immediately, calling construction of a larger regular peacetime army the "best security for the continuance of peace" in the message he sent to Congress with the Treaty of Ghent.[38] For their part, the war's opponents tried to claim a share of any military success by highlighting the valor of the state militias and the American forces in defending the United States in late 1814. They also credited the Federalists with the success of the navy; as one critic remarked, "In rendering a just tribute to the heroism exhibited on the land, we ought not to forget the child and boast of federalism,—*Our Navy*."[39] In consequence, Congress had little difficulty passing a peacetime military establishment of more than twelve thousand men, nearly four times what it was in 1807. The following year it passed an $8 million program to build the navy that Congress had rejected three years earlier on the eve of the war.[40]

Finally, Americans were optimistic about the future. As with most New England wartime sermons, Daniel Clark Sanders admonished the government from his Sherburne, Massachusetts, pulpit for going to war against Britain, but he concluded on a sanguine, rather than dour, note. "We witness this day a rare sight," he declared, "all Christendom in a state of profound and universal peace. The whole world was never, perhaps, more tranquil since the Augustan age."[41] War hovered over Europe's future prospects like "the thick smoke of a volcano," declared a Philadelphian, but "ours are lighted by a cloudless sun."[42]

The case for a British victory in the War of 1812 relies primarily on a narrow interpretation of the war's causes and of the conflict itself. The standard argument asserts that the United States declared war over three stated issues: the commercial maritime rights of neutrals, the impressment of sailors from American merchant ships, and Britain's involvement with the American Indians living within the borders of the United States. Britain yielded none of these points in the Treaty of Ghent, and so according to the specific terms as defined by the American declaration of war, the United States lost. Most historical analyses of the war have embraced the idea of a British victory on these grounds, and, if limited to these criteria, the British clearly won.[43]

Even though Britain ultimately repealed the Orders in Council, the government never admitted any wrongdoing. It refused to offer compensation to Americans who had lost their ships or cargoes, and it made no pledges against introducing similar measures in the future. Impressment died as an issue only because America's declaration of war gave the Royal Navy every right to board American ships and seize its sailors with impunity. Thousands languished in British prisons in Canada, Africa, the West Indies, and Britain by the war's end; many were also put on board British ships. By the time the War of 1812 ended, the Royal Navy was demobilizing rather than recruiting—releasing 50,000 from service at the end of 1814 and a further 60,000 by the end of 1816, from a starting point of 130,000—thus eliminating the need for impressment.[44] In fact, Britain's victory on the point of impressment was so clear that the Madison administration agreed to support a treaty that did not include it before formal peace negotiations began, and at Ghent neither side even bothered to raise it with any conviction.

The situation regarding those Indians living in the United States who allied themselves to Britain was more complicated. As in most colonial wars, the Indians were the worst losers by virtually every criterion, and those who allied themselves to Britain during the War of 1812 were no exception. They lost their primary war leader in Tecumseh and a larger number of warriors, and were compelled to accept the prewar borders of 1812—borders that played a key role in fueling a powerful resistance movement in the first place. Further south, the Creek Indians suffered far worse. Although the Red Sticks were the ideological comrades of Tecumseh and Tenskwatawa's followers, they did not forge a close alliance with the British, whose campaigns along the Gulf Coast came too late to affect the Creek War. Without hope of British advocacy at Ghent, the Creek Indians lost some 22 million acres at the Treaty of Fort Jackson in August 1814—land that came not just from the breakaway Creek Red Sticks but also from the Creek and Cherokee allies of the United States.[45] Worse still, as Henry Goulburn woefully predicted at Ghent, the Indians in the western United States were largely eradicated over the next generation—many during the presidency of John Quincy Adams, who at Ghent had completely disregarded the notion that Indians could improve the lands they occupied, or even truly own them for that matter.[46]

Yet from the British perspective the subject of Indians could still be tallied in the victory column. The United States had objected to Britain's interference, and the Treaty of Ghent did not admonish the British for doing so; nor did the British pledge not to act similarly in the future. In fact, Britain compelled the United States to change its policies toward Indians living within its territory by including them in the Treaty of Ghent and returning them to their prewar status. In consequence, Britain set the precedent of treating the Indians living within the territorial boundaries of the United States as separate, if not entirely sovereign, peoples from the Americans—a major concession that caused a great deal of resistance and consternation for the American delegates at Ghent. Unfortunately for the Indians involved, the precedent came too late in the struggle for North America, because by 1815 Indian power was largely broken and European powers were not willing to help rehabilitate it.

In terms of military objectives, the British did exceedingly well. The primary strategy of the United States was to conquer Canada, and it failed miserably. Even when the United States had every apparent advantage at the start of the war, it failed. In fact, when the two delegations met at Ghent, the Americans were the ones pleading for a return of territory. To a large extent this unexpected outcome was enabled by the defeat of France in April 1814, which no one could have predicted when the United States declared war in June 1812. Nevertheless, even before the British began redeploying troops from Europe in the summer of 1814 the army acquitted itself admirably, successfully defending a vast territory inhabited by what was at best a largely apathetic population. Moreover, the domestic and maritime security of the West Indies allowed Britain to redeploy enough troops to triple the force of regulars in Canada in 1813 and mount limited offensive operations.[47] Thus, even if Napoleon had hung on for a few more years, there is nothing to suggest that Canada would have fallen to American arms.

In this sense, British North America (or at least those who wanted to keep Canada British) were winners. The loyalists, who served disproportionately in the colonial militia, organized an empirewide charity drive, vocally pronounced Canadians' fidelity with the empire and detestation of American republicanism, and succeeded in persuading the British of Canada's importance. Britain ultimately demonstrated its willingness to defend Canada against its neighbor and, more important, the ability to do so effectively. Although suffering a series of postwar economic setbacks and growth issues, partly caused by policies that aimed to exclude citizens of the United States from settling in British North America, Canada strengthened ties to the empire through an increase in British immigration and through prospering—albeit to some extent at the hands of Britain's former Indian allies, whose lands the British raided almost with as much impunity as the United States did. By 1824, the population of Upper Canada had increased 250 percent over its prewar level.[48]

This is not to suggest that Canadians were happy with the peace terms. Many complained violently in the press about the government's actions—a critical tone that was largely absent from the Canadian press during the war. Aligning themselves with the likes of the London *Times*, whose editorials damning the Treaty of Ghent found a wide audience in Canada, critics in British North America were furious. From the perspective of British North America, Britain was winning the war in 1814, and the peace treaty whose terms seemingly declared the war a draw did not reflect that success. Magnanimity was easier for members of Parliament who had the luxury "to speak with cold blooded indifference about the infliction of ruin upon friends at the distance of 3,000 miles," sneered a letter in the *Montreal Herald*.[49] Echoing similar sentiments from across British North America, as well as the British Empire, a letter in the *New Brunswick Courier* declared that the Treaty of Ghent was repeating the mistakes of the treaty that concluded the American Revolution: "the greatest Nation in the world will again be made the dupe of the most contemptible people ever recorded in history." Returning the prewar borders, the letter explained, left Canada and the Indians as vulnerable as before, and so "Upper Canada will have been sold, and

Lower Canada in the bargain."[50] Another letter in the *Montreal Herald* scolded the British government for abandoning its Indian allies so abruptly. Such actions, the letter lamented, sent a clear message of Britain's policy toward those Indians who had proven instrumental in Britain's prosecution of the war:

> Get all the aid you can from the Indians for our purposes, but take special care, and I strictly enjoin one and all of you, that if they shall be retaliated upon by the enemy for affording us this aid, and in consequence get their villages and fields of corn destroyed, (as actually happened) and their wives and children thereby threatened with starvation, as also themselves with extermination, you are upon no accounts to send a man to assist in their defence, because it would offend His Excellency James Madison Esq. and be liable to misinterpretation.

Although no fan of the Indians themselves, the author worried about what might happen when the United States next attacked Canada and Britain called on the Indians for aid: either the Indians would refuse or there would be no Indians left to assist.[51]

Much of this anxiety stemmed from the widespread belief that peace would not last. From the hindsight of two centuries, one can see how events played out in the nineteenth century to create a period for Europe and North American that was positively tranquil in comparison to the century that proceeded 1815. Yet from the vantage point of those living in 1815, an alternative history is easy to imagine. As the *Edinburgh Star* declared, "the present peace is but a truce. Canada is an object they [the Americans] will never lose sight of . . . and the moment Britain again become entangled in continental warfare (for which our Statesmen seem to have a natural predilection), the United States will find some pretext for invading these provinces."[52] And renewed war in Europe seemed likely following a century in which Britain spent more years at war with France than not. In fact, as the British and Americans celebrated peace with each other, Napoleon was again marching across France and amassing an army. Had he succeeded, or the Congress of Vienna failed, or any number of regional European conflicts erupted into a greater war (as one ultimately would in 1914 and plunge Europe into a world war), the United States could have again found itself at the mercy of the Royal Navy, whose global dominance only increased in the early decades of the nineteenth century.[53] The unresolved issues involving impressment and neutral trade might have all reappeared, and the military strategies available to the United States would not have been significantly different— namely, invasion of Canada and limited naval warfare. Henry Clay, who on concluding negotiations at Ghent went to London to secure a commercial treaty, certainly thought Europe had fallen back into a state of war when he learned of

Napoleon's march across France. Declaring "Wonderful age! wonderful man! wonderful nation!" in reference to Napoleon and France, Clay wondered if this would mean a return to Britain's former policies of trade restrictions and impressment from American ships. After all, he of all people realized that the recent peace treaty between Britain and the United States resolved none of these issues.[54] Had Britain reintroduced these measures, the United States was in an even worse position to offer resistance in 1815 than in 1812, because Britain held complete naval supremacy in North America, a large army of regulars in Canada poised to invade, and all the financial tools necessary to wage a global war. But, just as it did in 1783, when the British occupied Charleston and New York and could field a regular army superior to Washington's, Britain elected not to pursue its case despite having an enormous strategic advantage. Once again, what Britain elected not to do, rather than what it might have done, is what truly mattered in the end. And Britain, not the United States, ultimately chose to give up the fight when domestic resolve waned.

Interpreting Britain as the overall victor in the War of 1812 overlooks a central argument of this book: just as the United States attempted to compel Britain to respect American sovereignty, Britain pursued a prewar and wartime agenda that aimed to humble the United States and demonstrate that Britain could ignore American national sovereignty as it saw fit. Britain did not go to war simply to protect its maritime rights. It went to war to crush an emerging rival. Using descriptors such as "chastise," "insolent," and "children," a succession of British ministries sought to put the former colonies in their so-called place. The British government was prepared to go to war, if need be, to accomplish this; in fact, at times it encouraged the American government to declare war. Once the Liverpool ministry was able to go on the offensive in 1814, it did so with glee, employing policies and plans that had been circulating for years: pillaging the Atlantic coastline and mounting invasions of the United States via Canada and through the Gulf coast.

The British government's objectives were plainly revealed in the original peace terms the plenipotentiaries laid out at Ghent in August 1814. They demanded the United States relinquish more than a fifth of its territory in order to give British North America a massive strategic advantage in any future war, and to provide a sovereign state for those Indian allies of Britain who lived in the northwestern United States. Moreover, the British government was in direct negotiation with New England secessionists, whose number included the governor of Massachusetts, and Britain was prepared to offer material military support if they seceded. Had Britain's plans prevailed, the United States would have been either dismantled into two or more lesser states or, if the Madison administration acquiesced to the secessionists' demands in order to maintain the Union, reduced to a nation stripped of much of its territory and ruled by a federal government too weak to mount effective campaigns against its hostile neighbors of American Indians, the British Empire, and the Spanish Empire. American manifest destiny would have been dead, and the federal government would have lacked the power or tools to build and fund a navy capable of protecting the nation's maritime interests. The United States would have been truly humbled, perhaps permanently.

Britain failed to meet its objectives. Campaigning in North America proved difficult, particularly when Britain went on the offensive. Whereas Britain successfully raided the Atlantic coast and seized parts of what is now the state of Maine, its forces proved unable to follow up those successes with major invasions. A far more important factor than American defensive efforts, however, was the British public. As at the end of the American War of Independence, the British public and Parliament proved unwilling to endure continued heavy taxation for the sake of the British Empire in North America. In fact, Lord Liverpool and his fellow ministers were so certain of this in late 1814 that they were unwilling even to put it before a parliamentary vote. Although Britain had every advantage in the war notwithstanding its setback at Plattsburgh, Liverpool instructed his negotiators at Ghent to offer generous terms to the Americans, because he knew the nation would not willingly continue the war into the next year. Ironically, this reluctance to continue the war highlights the limits of British imperial will at the beginning of what has so often been labeled "Britain's imperial century." Apparently the assertion of British supremacy overseas had a price limit, and in the case of the United States in 1814 that limit was less than the £10 million Liverpool had estimated it would cost to continue the war.

The British government's plans in the War of 1812 backfired. Rather than humbling the United States, the war helped to create a nation that was far more powerful and resolute in its expansionist plans. The experience forged capable soldiers and proved the quality of America's seamen. As John Le Couteur, a young British lieutenant who served in Canada for the duration of the war, remarked of the American army at the war's end, "They had turned out very good soldiers. There officers were gallant and enterprizing. . . . They would have a fine army ten years hence and [for] that, we should keep twenty thousand men in Canada."[55] Americans' confidence in their navy, which had received scant attention let alone widespread admiration before 1812, was at an all-time high. As Stephen Bovell proudly rejoiced in his thanksgiving sermon delivered in Virginia at the end of the war, "To every true American it must be a subject of boastful and gratifying reflection, that we have in this manner taught the Tyrant of the Ocean to feel our maritime consequence."[56] Following the War of 1812, the United States committed to creating a substantial navy, a larger and better organized professional army, and a national bank that would better enable the federal government to fund these ventures as well as wage wars. These were all plans Congress rejected as it prepared for war in 1812. As *Niles' Weekly Register*, a bulwark of prewar opposition to these measures, remarked in May 1815, "the best way to avoid war is probably to be prepared to meet it with firmness and effect" and therefore create a military deterrent more powerful than what the United States previously had, which earlier only invited European aggression and disdain.[57]

More specifically, the War of 1812 was a victory for those Americans who supported territorial expansion and the goal of subjugating the continent. At the time most closely affiliated with the Republican supporters of Madison, their views and future were embodied most by men such as Andrew Jackson. Equally hostile to Europeans and American Indians, Jackson had called Florida an "asylum" from which the British and Spanish could incite Indians to "rapine and bloodshed."[58] His answer was invasion, annexation, and expansion, and he and his kind would readily bend the U.S. Constitution and use the federal government to assert the supremacy of the United States over the North American continent. Ironically, this meant that although the war with Britain had been fought primarily at sea and in the north, it was the whites of the landlocked and southern states who most benefited—the representatives of whom in Congress had been the core supporters of a declaration of war in 1812. The settlement of the War of 1812 for them translated into fresh lands for expansion and the entrenchment of slavery as plantations mushroomed across the lands the United States seized from American Indians and the Spanish during the war years and the immediate aftermath.

The War of 1812, or at least Americans' interpretation of it, became a source of the national confidence from which men like Jackson would later draw. As Albert Gallatin reflected in returning from the peace negotiations at Ghent, "The war has renewed the national feelings and character which the Revolution had given, and which were daily lessening. The people are now more American. They feel and act more as a nation."[59] The victories at Plattsburgh and New Orleans allowed Americans to reassert the revolutionary myth that ordinary Americans in arms were invincible on their home soil, and local celebrations of the American Revolution began to incorporate selected elements of the War of 1812 into the national memory.[60] Moreover, the New England secessionists had been quieted, and the Federalist party was finished, with the Republicans' national leadership embracing some of the federalists' ideology regarding a stronger centralized government and armed forces. The postcolonial chip on many Americans' shoulders endured, but after 1815 it was rooted more in their interpretations of the past than in pressing concerns about the present.[61] And while the United States enjoyed a détente with British North America, the Americans aggressively pursued expansionist designs against their other neighbors. It proceeded almost at once to move against the Indians living within its territorial boundaries, simultaneously promoting additional white settlement, limiting Indians' movement across the border, and severely restricting British traders.[62] In the decade following the war, Indiana, Illinois, and Missouri all achieved statehood with lands Britain had tried to wrench from the United States at Ghent for the purpose of creating an independent Indian state.

Meanwhile, the United States continued to assert itself in the Southwest under the leadership of Jackson. The Treaty of Fort Jackson remained in place, even though local British officers argued that it violated Article IX of the Treaty of Ghent, which stipulated "all tribes or nations of Indians" who took up arms against the United States would be returned to their 1811 borders. The United States insisted that the article pertained only to those Indians still at war at the time of treaty ratification, but more important, the British government refused even to listen to the Creek delegation that traveled to London, let alone lodge a formal complaint.[63] Completely disregarding Spanish sovereignty once again, the United States vigorously pursued hostile Indian and African American communities in Spanish East Florida, culminating in the July 1816 bombardment and capture of "Negro Fort" on the Apalachicola River, which killed more than 270 people in it—many of whom were families seeking refuge. The leaders were captured and tortured, and those who were not killed were brought to Alabama and Georgia and sold into slavery—a flagrant violation of the 1807 federal law prohibiting transportation of slaves across the national boundaries of the United States.[64] Four years after the War of 1812, the United States formally acquired the Spanish Floridas through the Adams-Onís Treaty, which also settled the western boundary disputes of the Louisiana Purchase, as well as any lingering doubts about its legitimacy.

The empire of the United States was larger and more secure than ever from external threats; and as James Austin declared at the 1815 Fourth of July celebration on Lexington's green, the site of the first battle of the American Revolution, Madison and his supporters in the field had fulfilled the dream of independence. "Speaking [England's] language, reading her history and her journals, deriving our laws, our taste, our fashions from her example, we believed in that magnanimity and greatness which she claimed as her national attributes," he remarked. "The storm of war has cleared the intellectual atmosphere of these clouds of prejudice, and opened to our view the dark realities of truth."[65] While war resulted in the triumph of the Republicans and the western and southern expansionists and slaveholders who led them, it also highlighted the deep fractures that ran throughout the United States and the tentativeness of many Americans' loyalty to a united national future. The War of 1812 ensured that Britain was no longer America's master. But the question of who would be masters *within* the United States remained.

ABBREVIATIONS

Adams Memoirs	*Memoirs of John Quincy Adams, Comprising Portions of His Diary from 1795 to 1848*, ed. Charles Francis Adams (Philadelphia, 1874), vol. 3.
AC	*Annals of Congress: Debates and Proceedings in the Congress of the United States, 1789–1824*, 42 vols. (Washington, DC, 1834–1856).
ASP: FR	*American State Papers, I: Foreign Relations*, 6 vols. (Washington, D.C. 1832–1859).
ASP: MA	*American State Papers, 5: Military Affairs*, 7 vols. (Washington, D.C. 1832–1861).
Brock Correspondence	*The Life and Correspondence of Major-General Sir Isaac Brock*, ed. Ferdinand Brock Tupper (London, 1845).
CBJM	James Morton Smith, ed., *The Republic of Letters: The Correspondence Between Thomas Jefferson and James Madison*, 3 vols. (New York, 1995).
Clay Papers	James F. Hopkins and Robert Seager, eds., *The Papers of Henry Clay*, 11 vols. (Lexington, 1959–1992).
CO	Colonial Office records, National Archives, Kew, UK (formerly the Public Record Office).
DRICSD	Documents Relating to the Invasion of Canada and the Surrender of Detroit, 1812, ed. Ernest A. Cruikshank (Ottawa, 1912).
FO	Foreign Office records, National Archives, Kew, UK (formerly the Public Record Office).
Gallatin Papers	Henry Adams, ed., *The Writings of Albert Gallatin*, 3 vols. (New York, 1960).
HC Debates	T. C. Hansard, ed., *Parliamentary Debates*, 1st ser., 41 vols. (London, 1803–1820).

James Gallatin Diary	James Francis Gallatin, ed., *The Diary of James Gallatin: Secretary to Albert Gallatin A Great Peace Maker, 1813–1827* (New York, 1916).
Oxford DNB	*Oxford Dictionary of National Biography*, 60 vols., ed. H. C. G. Matthew and Brian Harrison (Oxford, 2004).
TNA	The National Archives, Kew, UK (formerly the Public Record Office).
WSD	*Supplementary Despatches, Correspondence, and Memoranda of Field Marshal Arthur, Duke of Wellington, K. G.*, ed. A. R. Wellesley, 15 vols. (London, 1858–1872).

NOTES

Introduction

1. Anthony St. John Baker to Lord Castlereagh, Mar. 23, 1815, FO 5/106.
2. The figure of seven hundred thousand is from the often-used estimate of William Wood, *The War with the United States: A Chronicle of 1812* (Toronto, 1915), 21.
3. William Dunlop, ed., *Tiger Dunlop's Upper Canada* (Toronto, 1967), 35.
4. For a concise discussion of the nomenclature of the period, see Daniel Walker Howe, *What Hath God Wrought: The Transformation of America, 1815–1848* (New York, 2007), 4–6. Howe aptly calls it the "communications revolution."
5. For an excellent summary of the historiography, see Donald R. Hickey, "The War of 1812: Still a Forgotten Conflict?" *Journal of Military History* 65 (2001): 741–42. Hickey's own *The War of 1812: A Forgotten Conflict* (Urbana, 1989) and Richard Buel, Jr., *American on the Brink: How the Political Struggle over the War of 1812 Almost Destroyed the Young Republic* (New York, 2005) are two exceptions in that their analyses of the conflict relay some public understandings of the war. Alan Taylor, *The Civil War of 1812: American Citizens, British Subjects, Irish Rebels, & Indian Allies* (New York, 2010) includes excellent accounts of the motivations, experiences, and roles of the war's ordinary participants along the U.S.-Canada border.
6. Jon Latimer, *1812: War with America* (Cambridge, MA, 2008), 59.
7. *AC*, 24: 1380–81. (See Abbreviations for full bibliographic information on this and other sources.)
8. For recent and especially scathing reviews of America's military performance, see especially Jon Latimer, *1812: War with America* (Cambridge, MA, 2008); and Taylor, *Civil War of 1812*. On America's strategy with regard to Canada, see especially J. C. A. Stagg, "James Madison and the Coercion of Great Britain: Canada, the West Indies, and the War of 1812," *William & Mary Quarterly*, 3d ser., 38 (1981); and 3–34; Peter J. Kastor, "Toward 'the Maritime War Only': The Question of Naval Mobilization, 1811–1812," *Journal of Military History* 61 (1997): 455–80.
9. *Star*, Jan. 31, 1812.
10. *Carthage Gazette*, July 18, 1812.
11. Delivered May 30, 1812, and reprinted in *Niles' Weekly Register*, June 13, 1812.
12. For a description of the Portugal comparison, see John Quincy Adams's diary entry for Sept. 1, 1814, *Adams Memoirs*, 24.
13. Two important exceptions are Bradford Perkins, *Prologue to War, 1805–1812* (Berkeley, 1974), which examines the origins of the war from the perspective of national politics in America and Britain but generally discounts the war's importance to Britain at the time and British history in general; and Jeremy Black, *The War of 1812 in the Age of Napoleon* (Norman, OK, 2009), which places the military narrative within the broader context of the Napoleonic Wars.

14. For just a few examples, see Gordon S. Wood, *Empire of Liberty: A History of the Early Republic, 1789–1815* (New York, 2009), 689–90; Hickey, "The War of 1812": 765; George C. Herring, *From Colony to Superpower: U.S. Foreign Relations Since 1776* (New York, 2008), 127; Mark Zuehlke, *The War of 1812 and the Brokering of an Uneasy Peace* (Toronto, 2006), 4; Roy Muir, *Britain and the Defeat of Napoleon 1807–1815* (New Haven, CT, 1996), 232; Boyd Hilton, *A Mad, Bad, and Dangerous People? England 1783–1846* (Oxford, 2006), 230–31; Arthur Herman, *To Rule the Waves: How the British Navy Shaped the Modern World* (New York, 2004), 411; and Latimer, *War with America*, 35.

15. Linda Colley, *Britons: Forging of the Nation 1707–1837* (New Haven, CT, 1992); C. A. Bayly, *Imperial Meridian: The British Empire and the World 1780–1830* (London, 1989). For counterweight that deemphasizes British exceptionalism but still recognized aspects of British uniqueness, see Stephen Conway, *Britain, Ireland, and Continental Europe in the Eighteenth Century* (Oxford, 2011).

16. Hickey, "War of 1812": 765; Christopher D. Hall, *British Strategy in the Napoleonic War 1803–1815* (Manchester, UK, 1992), 200.

17. See especially Frank L. Owsley, Jr., and Gene A. Smith, *Filibusters and Expansionists* (Tuscaloosa, 1997); and J. C. A. Stagg, *Borderlines in Borderlands: James Madison and the Spanish-American Frontier, 1776–1821* (New Haven, 2009).

18. R. C. Nash, "The Organization of Trade and Finance in the British Atlantic Economy, 1600–1830," in *The Atlantic Economy During the Seventeenth and Eighteenth Centuries: Organization, Operation, Practice, and Personnel*, ed. Peter A. Coclanis (Columbia, SC, 2005); Peter Marshall, "The First and Second British Empire: A Question of Demarcation," *History* 49 (1964): 13–23; B. H. Tolley, "The Liverpool Campaign Against the Order in Council and the War of 1812," in *Liverpool and Merseyside: Essays in the Economic and Social History of the Port and Its Hinterland*, ed. J. R. Harris (London, 1969), 98–145; and G. E. Watson, "The United States and the Peninsular War, 1808–1812," *Historical Journal* 19 (1976), 859–76; Roger Knight and Martin Wilcox, *Sustaining the Fleet, 1793–1815: War, the British Navy and the Contractor State* (London, 2010), 11.

19. For examples, see Christopher Mulvey, *Transatlantic Manners: Social Patterns in Nineteenth-Century Anglo-American Travel Literature* (Cambridge, 1990); John E. Crowley, *The Invention of Comfort: Sensibilities and Design in Early Modern Britain and Early America* (Baltimore, 2000); Maxine Berg, *Luxury and Pleasure in Eighteenth-Century Britain* (Oxford, 2005), 136–38; James Raven, *The Business of Books: Booksellers and the English Book Trade* (London, 2011), 144–53; and Elizabeth Aldrich, *From the Ballroom to Hell: Grace and Folly in Nineteenth-Century Dance* (Evanston, IL, 1991).

20. See especially Kariann Akemi Yokota, *Unbecoming British: How Revolutionary America Became a Postcolonial Nation* (New York, 2011); and the essays in R. A. Burchell, ed., *The End of Anglo-America: Historical Essays in the Study of Cultural Divergence* (Manchester, 1991).

21. For examples, see Troy Bickham, *Savages Within the Empire: Representing American Indians in Eighteenth-Century Britain* (Oxford, 2005), chapter 1; Robin Reilly and George Savage, *Wedgwood the Portrait Medallion* (London, 1973), 331–32; Troy Bickham, "Eating the Empire: Intersections of Food, Cookery and Imperialism in Eighteenth-Century Britain," *Past & Present* 198 (2008): 71–110.

22. Jane Errington, *The Lion, the Eagle, and Upper Canada: A Developing Colonial Ideology* (Kingston, Ontario, 1987).

23. *Times*, Nov. 28, 1812.

24. Donald E. Graves, *Merry Hearts Make Light Days: The War of 1812 Journal of Lieutenant John Le Couteur, 104th Foot* (Ottawa, 1994), 133–34, 135. Buckmaster of Bond Street was an elite London tailor, and Joseph Manton was one of the best-known gunsmiths in London. For an especially illuminating look at how the conflict played out as a civil war on the U.S.-Canadian border region, see Taylor, *Civil War of 1812*.

25. *York Gazette*, Aug. 29, 1812.

26. *Tiger Dunlop*, 44–45.

27. Lord Bathurst to Baker, Dec. 31, 1814, FO 5/105.

28. Advertised in the *Carlisle Journal*, May 30, 1812.

29. For a sampling of the extensive literature on the British press, see especially Hannah Barker, *Newspapers, Politics and English Society, 1695–1855* (London, 2000); Troy Bickham, *Making Headlines: The American Revolution as Seen Through the British Press* (DeKalb, IL, 2009), chapters 1, and 2; Jeremy Black, *The English Press, 1621–1861* (Stroud, UK, 2001); C. Y. Ferdinand, *Benjamin Collins and the Provincial Newspaper Trade in the Eighteenth Century* (Oxford, 1997); and Bob Harris, *Politics and the Rise of the Press: Britain and France, 1620–1800* (London, 1996). On the American press during this period, see especially Richard D. Brown, *The Strength of the People: The Idea of an Informed Citizenry in America, 1650–1870* (Chapel Hill, NC, 1996), chapter 4; Richard Buel, Jr., "Freedom of the Press in Revolutionary America: The Evolution of Libertarianism, 1760–1820," in Bernard Bailyn and John B. Hench, eds., *The Press and the American Revolution* (Boston, 1981); John C. Nerone, *Violence Against the Press: Policing the Public Sphere in U.S. History* (New York, 1994); Jeffrey L. Pasley, *"The Tyranny of Printers": Newspaper Politics in the Early American Republic* (Charlottesville, VA, 2001); Paul Starr, *The Creation of the Media: Political Origins of Modern Communications* (New York, 2004); and Marcus Daniel, *Scandal and Civility: Journalism and the Birth of American Democracy* (New York, 2009), who argues persuasively for the weakness of political parties' control of journalism, despite the partisan nature of politics at the time.
30. See for example, *Niles' Weekly Register*, June 20 and Aug. 1, 1812.
31. *Oracle*, July 6, 1799, quoted in Timothy Jenks, *Naval Engagements: Patriotism, Cultural Politics, and the Royal Navy 1793–1815* (Oxford, 2006), 16–17.
32. *HC Debates*, Feb. 13, 1812, 21: 762–63; Madison to Jefferson, Feb. 7, 1812, *CBJM*, 3: 1687; Madison to Jefferson, May 10, 1814, *CBJM*, 3: 1742; Clay to Monroe, *Clay Papers*, 1: 963; and Clay to Monroe, Oct. 26, 1814, *Clay Papers*, 1: 996.
33. *York Gazette*, Jan. 22, 1812.
34. Benedict Anderson, *Imagined Communities: Reflections on the Origin and Spread of Nationalism*, rev. ed. (London, 1991).
35. Margaret Bayard Smith to Maria Kirkpatrick, Sept. 11, 1814, in *The First Forty Years of Washington Society in the Family Letters of Margaret Bayard Smith*, ed. Gaillard Hunt (New York, 1906), 117.
36. On the significance of the Fourth of July and the American Revolution in the culture of American politics, see especially David Waldstreicher, *In the Midst of Perpetual Fetes: The Making of American Nationalism, 1776–1820* (Chapel Hill, NC, 1997), especially chapter 1. See also Joanne Freeman, *Affairs of Honor: National Politics in the New Republic* (New Haven, CT, 2001); and Len Travers, *Celebrating the Fourth: Independence Day and the Rites of Nationalism in the Early Republic* (Amherst, MA, 1997).
37. Jabez Chickering, *An Oration Pronounced at Dedham . . . July 4, 1812* (Boston, 1812), 10.
38. Daniel Webster, *An Address Delivered Before the Washington Benevolent Society, at Portsmouth, July 4, 1812*, 2nd ed. (Portsmouth, NH, 1812), 7.
39. *Times*, Nov. 28, 1812.
40. Jefferson to Madison, June 29, 1812, *CBJM*, 3: 1699.
41. Nancy F. Koehn, *The Power of Commerce: Economy and Governance in the First British Empire* (Ithaca, 1994), 3–18.
42. See especially Fred Anderson, *Crucible of War: The Seven Years War and the Fate of Empire in British North America* (New York, 2000); H. V. Bowen, "British Conception of Global Empire, 1756–83," *Journal of Imperial and Commonwealth History* 26 (1998), 1–27; Colley, *Britons*; Eliga Gould, *The Persistence of Empire: British Political Cultures in the Age of the American Revolution* (London, 2000); Bob Harris, "'American Idols': Empire, War and the Middling Ranks in Mid-Eighteenth-Century Britain," *Past and Present* 150 (1996): 111–41; P. J. Marshall, "A Nation Defined by Empire, 1755–1776," in *Uniting the Kingdom? The Making of British History*, ed. Alexander Grant and Keith Stringer (London, 1995), 208–22; and Kathleen Wilson, *Sense of the People: Culture and Imperialism in England, 1715–1785* (London, 1995).
43. P. J. Marshall, "Empire and Authority in the Later Eighteenth Century," *Journal of Imperial and Commonwealth History* 15 (1987): 105–22. This thesis is elaborated and refined in his *Making and Unmaking of Empires: Britain, India, and America c. 1750–1783* (Oxford, 2005).

44. Gordon S. Wood, *The Radicalism of the American Revolution* (New York, 1991).
45. For the most influential proponent of this view, see Jack P. Greene's *The Quest for Power: The Lower Houses of Assembly in the Southern Royal Colonies, 1689–1776* (Chapel Hill, NC, 1963) among his other works.
46. The quotation is from a petition sent to James Madison, cited in Adam Rothman, *Slave Country: American Expansion and the Origins of the Deep South* (Cambridge, MA, 2005), 120.
47. Marshall, *Making and Unmaking of Empires*; Christopher Leslie Brown, *Moral Capital: Foundations of British Abolitionism* (Chapel Hill, NC, 2006); and J. R. Osborn, "India, Parliament and the Press Under George III" (D.Phil. thesis, University of Oxford, 1999).
48. *Jamaica Magazine*, Sept. 1813, p. 744.

Chapter 1

1. Joseph Otis Osgood, *An Oration, Commemorative of American Independence. Pronounced at Salisbury, July Fourth, 1810* (Newburyport, 1810). 16.
2. See especially David Waldstreicher, *In the Midst of Perpetual Fetes: The Making of American Nationalism, 1776–1820* (Chapel Hill, 1997); Steven Watts, *The Republic Reborn: War and the Making of Liberal America, 1790–1820* (Baltimore, 1987), 9–14; Richard D. Brown, *The Strength of the People: The Idea of an Informed Citizenry in America, 1650–1870* (Chapel Hill, NC, 1996), chapter 4; and J. M. Opal, *Beyond the Farm: National Ambitions in Rural New England* (Philadelphia, 2008).
3. See especially Kariann Akemi Yokota, *Unbecoming British: How Revolutionary America Became a Postcolonial Nation* (New York, 2011); and R. A. Burchell, "The Role of the Upper Class in the Formation of American Culture, 1780–1840," in *The End of Anglo-America: Historical Essays in the Study of Cultural Divergence*, ed. R. A. Burchell (Manchester, 1991), 184–212. For examples, see Christopher Mulvey, *Transatlantic Manners: Social Patterns in Nineteenth-Century Anglo-American Travel Literature* (Cambridge, 1990); John E. Crowley, *The Invention of Comfort: Sensibilities and Design in Early Modern Britain and Early America* (Baltimore, 2000); James Raven, *The Business of Books: Booksellers and the English Book Trade* (London, 2011), 144–53; and Elizabeth Aldrich, *From the Ballroom to Hell: Grace and Folly in Nineteenth-Century Dance* (Evanston, IL, 1991). On the English assumption of social superiority toward Americans, see Christopher Mulvey, *Transatlantic Manners: Social Patterns in Nineteenth-Century Anglo-American Travel Literatures* (Cambridge, 1990).
4. Gordon S. Wood, *Empire of Liberty: A History of the Early Republic, 1789–1815* (New York, 2009), 622.
5. See especially Paul Semonin, *American Monster: How the Nation's First Prehistoric Creature Became a Symbol of National Identity* (New York, 2000); Lee Alan Dugatkin, *Mr. Jefferson and the Giant Moose: Natural History in Early America* (Chicago, 2009); and Stanley Hedeen, *Big Bone Lick: The Cradle of American Paleontology* (Lexington, 2008).
6. See especially Peter J. Kastor, *The Nation's Crucible: The Louisiana Purchase and the Creation of America* (New Haven, 2004); Jon Kukla, *A Wilderness So Immense: The Louisiana Purchase and the Destiny of America* (New York, 2003); James E. Lewis, Jr., *The Louisiana Purchase: Jefferson's Noble Bargain?* (Charlottesville, VA, 2003).
7. Francis Blake, *An Oration, Pronounced at Worcester, (Mass.) on the Thirty-Sixth Anniversary of American Independence, July 4, 1812* (Worcester, 1812), 17.
8. Peter Nicolaisen, "John Adams, Thomas Jefferson, and the Dutch Patriots," in *Old World, New World: America and Europe in the Age of Jefferson*, ed. Leonard J. Sadosky, Peter Nicolaisen, Peter S. Onuf, and Andrew J. O'Shaughnessy (Charlottesville, VA, 2010), 105–30.
9. Jeremy Black, *The War of 1812 in the Age of Napoleon* (Norman, OK, 2009), 5.
10. Leonard J. Sadosky, *Revolutionary Negotiations: Indians, Empires, and Diplomats in the Founding of America* (Charlottesville, VA, 2009), 4.
11. On the British side, see especially Maxine Berg, *Luxury and Pleasure in Eighteenth-Century Britain* (Oxford, 2005); C. A. Bayly, *The Birth of the Modern World 1780–1914: Global Connections and Comparisons* (Oxford, 2004); Troy Bickham, "Eating the Empire: Intersections of Food, Cookery and Imperialism in Eighteenth-Century Britain," *Past & Present* 198

(2008): 71–110. On the American side, see especially Wood, *Empire of Liberty*, 322–24 and 354–56; David Jaffee, *A New Nation of Goods: The Material Culture of Early America* (Philadelphia, 2010); Richard Bushman, *The Refinement of America* (New York, 1992); John Crowley, *The Invention of Comfort* (Baltimore, 2001); and Winifred Barr Rothenberg, *From Market-Places to a Market Economy: The Transformation of Rural Massachusetts, 1750–1850* (Chicago, 1992).

12. Adam Smith, *An Inquiry into the Nature and Causes of the Wealth of Nations* (Dublin, 1801), 1: 359.

13. See especially T. H. Breen, *The Marketplace of Revolution: How Consumer Politics Shaped American Independence* (New York, 2004), chapter 6; Timothy Morton, "Blood Sugar," in *Romanticism and Colonialism*, ed. Timothy Fulford and Peter Kitson (Cambridge, 1998); Clare Midgley, "Slave Sugar Boycotts, Female Activism and the Domestic Base of British Anti-Slavery Culture," *Slavery and Abolition* 17 (1996): 137–62; Bickham, "Eating the Empire."

14. Jan de Vries, *The Industrious Revolution: Consumer Behavior and the Household Economy, 1650 to the Present* (Cambridge, 2009). On the "motivational revolution" in the early American republic, see J. M. Opal, *Beyond the Farm: National Ambitions in Rural New England* (Philadelphia, 2008).

15. Bayly, *Birth of the Modern World*, 99.

16. Ted Widmer, *Ark of Liberties: America and the World* (New York, 2008), 66; R. C. Nash, "The Organization of Trade and Finance in the British Atlantic Economy, 1600–1830," in *The Atlantic Economy During the Seventeenth and Eighteenth Centuries: Organization, Operation, Practice, and Personnel*, ed. Peter A. Coclanis (Columbia, SC, 2005), 120; James R. Fichter, *So Great a Proffit: How the East Indies Trade Transformed Anglo-American Capitalism* (Cambridge, MA, 2010).

17. Donald Hickey, *The War of 1812: A Forgotten Conflict* (Urbana, 1989), 9; Stanley Elkins and Eric McKitrick, *The Age of Federalism* (New York, 1993), 826n; Curtis P. Nettles, *The Emergence of a National Economy, 1775–1915* (New York, 1962), 235 and 396; Mark Zuehlke, *The War of 1812 and the Brokering of an Uneasy Peace* (Toronto, 2006), 65.

18. On the importance of the American market to Britain, see for example, J. C. A. Stagg, *Mr. Madison's War: Politics, Diplomacy, and Warfare in the Early American Republic, 1783–1830* (Princeton, 1983), 14; Curtis P. Nettles, *The Emergence of a National Economy, 1775–1915* (New York, 1962), 232–36; and B. H. Tolley, "The Liverpool Campaign Against the Order in Council and the War of 1812," in *Liverpool and Merseyside: Essays in the Economic and Social History of the Port and Its Hinterland*, ed. J. R. Harris (London, 1969), 98–145.

19. Tolley, "The Liverpool Campaign," 101–6.

20. Trafalgar did not so much reconfigure naval power in favor of Britain as it emphasized on an epic scale the impotence that had plagued the French navy for much of the Napoleonic Wars. For a concise description of the state of the French navy during the Napoleonic Wars, see Jonathan R. Dull, *The Age of the Ship of the Line: The British & French Navies, 1650–1815* (Lincoln, NE, 2009), chapter 7.

21. Russell to Castlereagh, April 25, 1812, FO 5/90.

22. Wood, *Empire of Liberty*, 655–57.

23. Silvia Marzagalli, "The Failure of a Transatlantic Alliance? Franco-American Trade, 1783–1815," *History of European Ideas* 34 (2008): 456–64.

24. Stephen Conway, *The War of American Independence 1775–1783* (London, 1995), 133–34 and 157–58; Andrew Jackson O'Shaughnessy, *An Empire Divided: The American Revolution and the British Caribbean* (Philadelphia, 2000), 208–10; Troy Bickham, *Making Headlines: The American Revolution as Seen Through the British Press* (DeKalb, IL, 2009), chapter 5.

25. Jeremy Black, *Britain as a Military Power, 1688–1815* (London, 2006), 268–69; Douglas Hay and Nicholas Rodgers, *Eighteenth-Century English Society* (Oxford, 1997), 153; J. E. Cookson, *The British Armed Nation, 1793–1815* (Oxford, 1997), 95; Linda Colley, *Britons: Forging of the Nation 1707–1837* (New Haven, 1992), chapter 7. As a rough comparison, this average rate of taxation is 25 percent higher than it was in the United States in 2007 and slightly lower than in Britain for the same year.

26. *"Free Trade and Sailor's Rights!" An Address to the Independent Electors of the State of New York*, 2nd ed. (Albany, 1813), 6.

27. *AC*, 23: 492. (See Abbreviations for full bibliographic information on this and other sources.)

28. *AC*, 23: 601.

29. Augustus Foster to Richard Wellesley, Marquess Wellesley, April 3, 1812, FO 5/85.

30. Jabez Chickering, *An Oration Pronounced at Dedham . . . July 4th, 1812* (Boston, 1812), 15.

31. Roger H. Brown, *The Republic in Peril: 1812* (New York, 1964), 18.

32. John Burnham, *An Oration Pronounced at Hillborough, New-Hampshire; July 4, 1810* (Concord, New Hampshire, 1810), 20.

33. Reprinted in *Niles' Weekly Register*, Jan. 11, 1812.

34. Madison to Jefferson, May 25, 1812, *CBJM*, 3: 1696.

35. Madison to Jefferson, May 30, 1812, *CBJM*, 3: 1697.

36. Clay to unknown, June 18, 1812, *Clay Papers*, 1: 674.

37. James Madison, *Message from the President of the United States . . . on the Subject of Our Affairs with Great Britain* (Washington, 1812), 4.

38. Hickey, *Forgotten Conflict*, 11.

39. Some 6,500 Americans signed on for service in the Royal Navy during this period, particularly as American embargoes created high unemployment among American sailors. Jon Latimer, *1812: War with America* (Cambridge, MA, 2008), 31; Robert E. Cray, Jr., "Remembering the USS *Chesapeake*: The Politics of Maritime Death and Impressment," *Journal of the Early Republic* 25 (2005): 462; Scott Thomas Jackson, "Impressment and Anglo-American Discord, 1787–1818" (Ph.D. diss., University of Michigan, 1976), 156–57; and Paul Gilje, *Liberty on the Waterfront: American Maritime Culture in the Age of Revolution* (Philadelphia, 2003), 157–61.

40. See for example, *An Address to Masters of Vessels on the Objects of the Boston Society for the Religious and Moral Improvement of Seamen* (Boston, 1812); *The Adventures of a Bible* (Boston, 1813); and the series *Prayers, Social and Private, to Be Used at Sea*, published in Boston throughout the period.

41. Cray, "Remembering the *Chesapeake*," 445–71.

42. Latimer, *War with America*, 7.

43. For an excellent comprehensive examination of the practice of impressment, see Denver Alexander Brunsman, "The Evil Necessity: British Naval Impressment in the Eighteenth-Century Atlantic" (Ph.D. diss., Princeton University, 2004), who concludes that, as unsavory as the system was, it worked. On the Royal Navy's strength, see Stephen Conway, *The British Isles and the War of American Independence* (Oxford, 2000), 17–18; Arthur Herman, *To Rule the Waves: How the British Navy Shaped the Modern World* (New York, 2004), 413; Nicholas Rogers, *The Press Gang: Naval Impressment and Its Opponents in Georgian Britain* (London, 2007), 122.

44. See especially Rogers, *Press Gang*; and Jesse Lemisch, "Jack Tar in the Streets: Merchant Seamen in the Politics of the American Revolution," *William and Mary Quarterly*, 3d ser. 25 (1969): 371–407.

45. Douglas Hay and Nicholas Rogers, *Eighteenth-Century English Society* (Oxford, 1997), 157–58.

46. Christopher Lloyd, *The British Seaman, 1200–1860: A Social Survey* (London, 1968), 195 and appendix A for the number of navy seamen during each year of the war; Paul M. Kennedy, *The Rise and Fall of British Naval Mastery* (1976), 123–47; Jackson, "Impressment and Anglo-American Discord," 33–4, 436.

47. Latimer, *War with America*, 31.

48. Jackson, "Impressment and Anglo-American Discord," 52–53.

49. Douglass Bradburn, *The Citizenship Revolution: Politics and the Creation of the American Union 1774–1804* (Charlottesville, VA, 2009), 105.

50. Monroe to Foster, June 8, 1812, FO 5/104.

51. *Niles' Weekly Register*, July 25, 1812.

52. For a complete compilation of the British aliens who registered under the acts, see Kenneth Scott, *British Aliens in the United States During the War of 1812* (Baltimore, 1979).

53. Bradburn, *Citizenship Revolution*, 106.

54. Ibid., 140.

55. Gilbert Youmans and Greg Stratman, "American English: the Transition from Colonialism to Independence," in *The End of Anglo-America: Historical Essays in the Study of Cultural Divergence*, ed. R. A. Burchell (Manchester, UK, 1991), 137–59.

56. Gilje, *Liberty on the Waterfront*, 163–69.

57. "Minute: Impressment of American Seamen," dated Feb. 21, 1812, FO 5/104.

58. James Madison, *Message from the President of the United States to both Houses of Congress . . . November 4, 1812* (Washington, 1812), 15.

59. Madison, *Message from the President of the United States . . . on the Subject of Our Affairs with Great Britain*, 10.

60. Monroe to Foster, June 10, 1812, printed in *Message from the President . . . Transmitting Copies of a Correspondence between Mr. Monroe and Mr. Foster, Relating to the Alleged Encouragement by the British Government of the Indians to Commit Depradations on the Inhabitants . . . June 11, 1812* (Washington, 1812), 10–11; Jefferson to Madison, June 29, 1812, *CBJM*, 3: 1699.

61. *Niles' Weekly Register*, March 7, 1812.

62. Alan Taylor, *The Civil War of 1812: American Citizens, British Subjects, Irish Rebels, & Indian Allies* (New York, 2010), 101.

63. The *Times* referred to the Indians this way in its Feb. 14, 1812, issue.

64. Gregory Evans Dowd, *A Spirited Resistance: The North American Indian Struggle for Unity, 1745–1812* (Baltimore, 1992).

65. Dowd heavily emphasizes the role of "sacred power" in his *A Spirited Resistance*. For more on the internal divisions, see especially Richard White, *The Middle Ground: Indians, Empires, and Republics in the Great Lakes Region, 1650–1815* (Cambridge, UK, 1991), chapter 15; and Frank Lawrence Owsley, Jr., *Struggle for the Gulf Borderlands: The Creek War and the Battle of New Orleans 1812–1815* (Gainesville, FL, 1981).

66. Armstrong Starkey, *European and Native American Warfare, 1675–1815* (Norman, OK, 1998), 156.

67. Andrew R. L. Cayton, *Frontier Indiana* (Bloomington, IN, 1996), 252.

68. Benjamin Drake, *Life of Tecumseh and His Brother the Prophet* (Gloucester, UK, 2009), 138–39.

69. J. C. A. Stagg, *Mr. Madison's War: Politics, Diplomacy, and Warfare in the Early American Republic, 1783–1830* (Princeton, NJ, 1983), 177–88.

70. Adam Jortner, *The Gods of Prophetstown: The Battle of Tippecanoe and the Holy War for the American Frontier* (New York, 2011).

71. Quoted in Angela Pulley Hudson, *Creek Paths and Federal Roads: Indians, Settlers, and Slaves and the Making of the American South* (Chapel Hill, NC, 2010), 92.

72. See especially Owsely, *Struggle for the Gulf Borderlands*; Hudson, *Creek Paths*, especially chapter 3; Kathryn E. Holland Braund, *Deerskins and Duffels: The Creek Indian trade with Anglo-America, 1685–1815* (Lincoln, NE, 1993).

73. Owsley, *Struggle for the Gulf Borderlands*, 8–9 and chapter 2.

74. *Alexandria Daily Herald*, June 10, 1812.

75. William Ellery Channing, *A Sermon Preached in Boston, July 23, 1812, The Day of Publick Fast* (Boston, 1812), 9.

76. Asa Aikens, *An Oration, Pronounced before the Republican Citizens of Windsor, on Their Celebration . . . of American Independence* (Windsor, VT, 1812), 1.

77. Quoted in Black, *War of 1812*, 42.

78. *Edinburgh Magazine*, Nov. 1758, p. 402.

79. *Carthage Gazette*, July 18, 1812.

80. Allen, *His Majesty's Indian Allies*, 116.

81. Colin G. Calloway, *Crown and Calumet: British-Indian Relations, 1783–1815* (Norman, OK, 1987), 17.

82. *Quebec Gazette*, Dec. 19, 1811.

83. See especially, Troy Bickham, *Savages Within the Empire: Representing American Indians in Eighteenth-Century Britain* (Oxford, 2005); Robert S. Allen, *His Majesty's Indian Allies: British Indian Policy in the Defence of Canada, 1774–1815* (Toronto, 1992); Calloway, *Crown and Calumet*; and Kate Flint, *The Transatlantic Indian, 1776–1930* (Princeton, 2009), 13–15.

84. *Ipswich Journal*, Feb. 21, 1812.
85. Allen, *His Majesty's Indian Allies*, 88.
86. Allen, *His Majesty's Indian Allies*, 106–15; and Carl Benn, *The Iroquois in the War of 1812* (Toronto, 1998), especially chapter 3.
87. Allen, *His Majesty's Indian Allies*, 122.
88. See especially Frank L. Owsley, Jr. and Gene A. Smith, *Filibusters and Expansionists* (Tuscaloosa, 1997); and J. C. A. Stagg, *Borderlines in Borderlands: James Madison and the Spanish-American Frontier, 1776–1821* (New Haven, 2009).
89. Jefferson to Madison, June 6, 1812, *CBJM*, 3: 1697.
90. Charles J. Cox, *Oration Delivered before the Washington Association of Philadelphia* (Philadelphia, 1813), 19.
91. Wood, *Empire of Liberty*, 661.
92. First articulated by Louis M. Hacker, the land-hunger thesis was quickly challenged by Julius W. Pratt (*Expansionists of 1812*, New York, 1925) and has been largely rejected by historians since. Yet it occasionally receives credit in general histories, such as Widmer, *Ark of Liberties*, 83–85. For the best discussion of the early historiography of the origins of the war, see Bradford Perkins, ed., *The Causes of the War of 1812: National Honor or National Interest?* (New York, 1962).
93. For an excellent review of U.S. relations with the Spanish Empire in the Americas, see James E. Lewis Jr., *The American Union and the Problem of Neighborhood: The United States and the Collapse of the Spanish Empire, 1783–1829* (Chapel Hill, 1998). On the "Patriot War" in East Florida, see James G. Cusick, *The Other War of 1812: The Patriot War and the American Invasion of Spanish East Florida* (University Press of Florida, 2003). On American involvement in the 1812–13 rebellion in Texas, see Donald E. Chapman, *Spanish Texas, 1519–1821* (Austin, 1992), 233–40; and Richard W. Gronet, "The United States and the Invasion of Texas," *The Americas* 25 (1969): 281–306. J. C. A. Stagg downplays direct involvement of the Madison administration in the Texas rebellion in "The Madison Administration and Mexico: Reinterpreting the Gutiérrez-Magee Raid of 1812–1813," *William and Mary Quarterly*, 3rd ser., 59 (2002): 449–80.
94. *Military Monitor*, May 10, 1813; *Carthage Gazette*, July 8, 1812.
95. *City Gazette*, April 12, 1812. Although Cusick rightly argues for greater inclusion of the conflict in East Florida in studies of the War of 1812, he makes clear that the Patriot War is best understood as a regional affair (*The Other War of 1812*, especially 11–12 and 300–301 in terms of the experience, organization, and objectives).
96. Madison to Jefferson, Feb. 7, 1812, *CBMJ*, 1687.
97. J. C. A. Stagg, "James Madison and the Coercion of Great Britain: Canada, the West Indies, and the War of 1812," *William & Mary Quarterly*, 3rd ser., 38 (1981): 3–34; Peter J. Kastor, "Toward 'the Maritime War Only': The Question of Naval Mobilization, 1811–1812," *Journal of Military History* 61 (1997): 460.
98. *AC*, 23: 476.
99. Jonathan B. Smith, *Oration Delivered on the Fourth of March, 1813, Before the Association of Democratic Young Men of the City and Liberties of Philadelphia* (Philadelphia, 1813), 20.
100. *Free Trade and Sailor's Rights*, 14.
101. Reprinted in *Niles' Weekly Register*, Dec. 28, 1811.
102. Reprinted in *Niles' Weekly Register*, Oct. 24, 1812.
103. William Parkinson, *A Sermon, Delivered in the Meeting House of the First Baptist Church of the City of New-York* (New York, 1812), 24–25.
104. *Free Trade and Sailor's Rights*, 11.

Chapter 2

1. William Kingsford, *The History of Canada* (Toronto, 1887–98), 8: 579.
2. *Leeds Mercury*, Aug. 8, 1812.
3. See especially Troy Bickham, *Savages Within the Empire: Representing American Indians in Eighteenth-Century Britain* (Oxford, 2005); H. V. Bowen, "British Conception of Global Empire, 1756–83," *Journal of Imperial and Commonwealth History*, 26 (1998), 1–27; Bob

Harris, "'American Idols': Empire, War and the Middling Ranks in Mid-Eighteenth-Century Britain," *Past and Present* 150 (1996): 111–41; P. J. Marshall, "A Nation Defined by Empire, 1755–1776," *Uniting the Kingdom? The Making of British History*, ed. Alexander Grant and Keith Stringer (London, 1995), 208–22; and Eliga Gould, *The Persistence of Empire: British Political Cultures in the Age of the American Revolution* (London, 2000).

4. See especially Troy Bickham, *Making Headlines: The American Revolution as Seen Through the British Press* (DeKalb, IL, 2009); Bickham, "Eating the Empire: Intersections of Food, Cookery and Imperialism in Eighteenth-Century Britain," *Past & Present* 198 (2008): 71–110; Kathleen Wilson, *Sense of the People: Culture and Imperialism in England, 1715–1785* (London, 1995); Bickham, "'A Conviction of the Reality of Things': Material Culture, North American Indians and Empire in Eighteenth-Century Britain," *Eighteenth-Century Studies* 39 (2005): 29–47; and Marius Kwint, "Astley's Amphitheatre and the Early Circus in England, 1768–1830" (D.Phil. diss., University of Oxford, 1994), chapter 6.

5. See especially Bickham, *Making Headlines*; Christopher Leslie Brown, *Moral Capital: Foundations of British Abolitionism* (Chapel Hill, NC, 2006); J. R. Osborn, "India, Parliament and the Press Under George III" (D.Phil. thesis, University of Oxford, 1999); Nicholas B. Dirks, *The Scandal of Empire: India and the Creation of Imperial Britain* (Cambridge, MA, 2008).

6. See especially J. M. Bumsted, "'Things in the Womb of Time': Ideas of American Independence, 1633 to 1763," *William and Mary Quarterly*, 3d ser. 31 (1974): 534–64; and Paul W. Mapp, *The Elusive West and the Contest for Empire, 1713–1763* (Chapel Hill, NC, 2011), especially part IV.

7. Quoted in Reginald Horsman, *The Causes of the War of 1812* (Philadelphia, 1962), 49.

8. See especially Peter J. Kastor, *The Nation's Crucible: The Louisiana Purchase and the Creation of America* (New Haven, CT, 2004); Jon Kukla, *A Wilderness So Immense: The Louisiana Purchase and the Destiny of America* (New York, 2003); James E. Lewis, Jr., *The Louisiana Purchase: Jefferson's Noble Bargain?*(Charlottesville, VA, 2003).

9. *Bermuda Gazette and Weekly Advertiser*, Aug. 1, 1812.

10. *Royal Gazette*, Mar. 15, 1812.

11. Bickham, *Making Headlines*, chapter 7.

12. *Edinburgh Star*, Sept. 11, 1812.

13. Boyd Hilton, *A Mad, Bad, and Dangerous People? England 1783–1846* (Oxford, 2006), 57–64 and 110–13.

14. Quoted in Alan Taylor, *The Civil War of 1812: American Citizens, British Subjects, Irish Rebels, & Indian Allies* (New York, 2010), 111.

15. *Democracy Unveiled; In a Letter to Sir Francis Burdett, Bart. M.P. by T. Adams, Lately Resident in the United States* (London, 1811), ii.

16. For a more detailed discussion of the Baltimore riots in this book, see Chapter 6. For more comprehensive examinations of the riots, see Donald Hickey, *The War of 1812: A Forgotten Conflict* (Urbana, IL, 1989), chapter 3; and Paul A. Gilje, "The Baltimore Riots of 1812 and the Breakdown of the Anglo-American Mob Tradition," *Journal of Southern History* 13 (1980): 547–64.

17. *Caledonian Mercury*, Sept. 10, 1812; *London Examiner*, Sept. 13, 1812; *Cobbett's Weekly Political Register*, Sept. 19, 1812.

18. *A View of the State of Parties in the United States of America; Being an Attempt to Account for the Present Ascendancy of the French, or Democratic Party, in that Country* (Edinburgh, 1812), 63.

19. *On the Past Relations Between Great Britain and the United States* (London, 1813), 37 and 38.

20. *Freeman's Journal*, Mar. 10, 1812.

21. This is most elegantly argued in John Brewer, *The Sinews of Power: War, Money and the English State, 1688–1783* (Cambridge, MA, 1990).

22. The average annual duty on sugar between 1767 and 1771 was about £500,000: T [Treasury: Miscellaneous Record] 64/276B/388, TNA. The duty on coffee in 1774 was £115,126 8s 8d: T 64/276B/316, TNA. For the costs of naval ships and their maintenance, see Brewer, *Sinews of Power*, 34–35.

23. See especially Brewer, *Sinews of Power*, chapter 8; Don Herzog, *Poisoning the Minds of the Lower Orders* (Princeton, 1998); and Bickham, *Making Headlines*, chapter 1.

24. Frederick Morton Eden, *Address on the Maritime Rights of Great Britain*, 2nd ed. (London, 1808), 14.

25. Margarette Lincoln, *Representing the Royal Navy: British Sea Power, 1750–1815* (Aldershot, UK), especially 6–7.

26. *London Gazette*, May 16, 1812.

27. Eden, *Maritime Rights of Great Britain*, 22.

28. Francois Crouzet, "America and the Crisis of the British Imperial Economy, 1803–1807," in *The Early Modern Atlantic Economy*, ed. John J. McCusker and Kenneth Morgan (Cambridge, 2000), 299–301, 303–5; Ted Widmer, *Ark of Liberties: America and the World* (New York, 2008), 66; R. C. Nash, "The Organization of Trade and Finance in the British Atlantic Economy, 1600–1830," in *The Atlantic Economy During the Seventeenth and Eighteenth Centuries: Organization, Operation, Practice, and Personnel*, ed. Peter A. Coclanis (Columbia, SC, 2005), 120.

29. John Brown, *The Mysteries of Neutralization; or, the British Navy Vindicated From the Charges of Injustice and Oppression towards Neutral Flags* (London, 1806), 2 and 61.

30. Leonard J. Sadosky, "Reimagining the British Empire and America in an Age of Revolution," in *Old World, New World: America and Europe in the Age of Jefferson*, ed. Leonard J. Sadosky, Peter Nicolaisen, Peter S. Onuf, and Andrew J. O'Shaughnessy (Charlottesville, VA, 2010), 83–104.

31. Stephen Conway, *The British Isles and the War of American Independence* (Oxford, 2000), 17–18; and Arthur Herman, *To Rule the Waves: How the British Navy Shaped the Modern World* (New York, 2004), 413.

32. See for example, Charles Bosanquet, *Thoughts on the Value, to Great Britain, of Commerce in General; and on the Value and Importance of the Colonial Trade in Particular* (London, 1807).

33. John Baker Holroyd, Earl of Sheffield, *Strictures on the Necessity of Inviolably Maintaining the Navigation and Colonial System of Great Britain* (London, 1804), 21. On arguments during and shortly after the American Revolution, see Sadosky, "Reimagining the British Empire and America in an Age of Revolution."

34. Sheffield, *Strictures*, 2–3.

35. On West Indian planters' presence and power in Britain during this era, see Andrew Jackson O'Shaughnessy, *An Empire Divided: The American Revolution and the British Caribbean* (Philadelphia, 2000), especially chapter 1 and 107, 206–8; Lillian M. Penson, "The London West India Interest in the Eighteenth Century," *English Historical Review* 30 (1921): 373–92; and James Raven, *Judging New Wealth: Popular Publishing and Responses to Commerce in England, 1750–1800* (Oxford, 1992), chapter 11. The number of MPs in the group depends on how one defines it, but contemporaries and historians place the figure between thirteen and forty: Sir Lewis Namier, *England in the Age of the American Revolution*, 2nd ed. (London, 1961), 234–36.

36. See especially James Raven, *Judging New Wealth: Popular Publishing and Responses to Commerce in England, 1750–1800* (Oxford, 1992), particularly chapters 10, and 11.

37. See especially Timothy Morton, "Blood Sugar," in *Romanticism and Colonialism*, ed. Timothy Fulford and Peter Kitson (Cambridge, 1998); Clare Midgley, "Slave Sugar Boycotts, Female Activism and the Domestic Base of British Anti-Slavery Culture," *Slavery and Abolition* 17 (1996): 137–62; Brown, *Moral Capital*; and Seymour Drescher, *Abolition: A History of Slavery and Antislavery* (Cambridge, 2009), chapter 8.

38. *A Permanent and Effectual Remedy Suggested for the Evils under which the British West Indies Now Labour. In a Letter from a West India Merchant to a West India Planter* (London, 1807), 6–14; Crouzet, "America and the Crisis of the British Imperial Economy," 279; Rebecca Hartkopf Schloss, *Sweet Liberty: The Final Days of Slavery in Martinique* (Philadelphia, 2009), 46–71.

39. For examples from 1807, see *Permanent and Effectual Remedy*, 5–6; *Outline of a Plan for the Better Cultivation, Security, & Defense of the British West Indies: Being the Original Suggestion for Providing an Effectual Substitute for the African Slave Trade, and Preventing the Dependence of Those Colonies on America for Supplies* (London, 1807); Joseph Lowe, *An Inquiry into the State of the British West Indies* (London, 1807).

40. *Report from the Committee on the Commercial State of the West India Colonies* (London, 1807). On the general importance of this sort of public investigation and the attempt to relate numerical values to the well-being of Parliament's constituents, see Joanna Innes, *Inferior Politics: Social Problems and Social Politics in Eighteenth-Century Britain* (Oxford, 2009), chapter 4.

41. Macall Medford, *Oil Without Vinegar and Dignity Without Pride: Or, British, American, and West Indian Interests Considered*, 2nd ed. (London, 1807), 40. Medford, an American who was long resident in Britain, opposed tighter trade restrictions.

42. Joseph Lowe, *An Inquiry into the State of the British West Indies* (London, 1807), x.

43. *Permanent and Effectual Remedy*, 5–6.

44. The pamphlet enjoyed at least four editions between its first publication in 1805 and 1807, and it was widely extracted in the newspaper and periodical press.

45. James Stephen, *War in Disguise; or, The Frauds of Neutral Flags*, 3rd ed. (London, 1806), 121, 219.

46. Jon Latimer, *1812: War with America* (Cambridge, MA, 2008), 19; and J. E. Cookson, *The Friends of Peace: Anti-War Liberalism in England, 1793–1815* (Cambridge, 1982), 220. Among the more humorous attacks is a poem panning Stephen and his pamphlet in the Dec. 17, 1814, issue entitled "War in Disguise; or, an Apology for his Majesty's Navy."

47. Denis Gray, *Spencer Perceval: The Evangelical Prime Minister 1762–1812* (Manchester, 1963), 169.

48. Douglass Bradburn, *The Citizenship Revolution: Politics and the Creation of the American Union 1774–1804* (Charlottesville, 2009), 140.

49. Scott Thomas Jackson, "Impressment and Anglo-American Discord, 1787–1818" (Ph.D. diss., University of Michigan, 1976), 51. The vast majority of sailors were lost to disease. On the breakdown of causes of loss, see Dudley Pope, *Life in Nelson's Navy* (London, 1987), 131.

50. Taylor, *Civil War of 1812*, 104.

51. Latimer, *War with America*, 32.

52. Britain agreed to the treaty, but Jefferson rejected and refused to send it to the Senate for ratification on the pretence that the treaty did not satisfactorily resolve the issue of impressment.

53. "Question submitted to Sir John Nicholl His Majesty's Advocate General by Lord Holland and Lord Auckland—November 1st, 1806," FO 5/104; "Principles and Positions applying to the American Question," FO 5/104, f. 92–94.

54. Michael Lewis, *The Navy in Transition: A Social History* (London, 1965), 312–13.

55. Christopher Lloyd, *The British Seaman, 1200–1860: A Social Survey* (London, 1968), 159.

56. "Minute: Impressment of American Seamen," dated Feb. 21, 1812, FO 5/104.

57. Asa Aikens, *An Oration, Pronounced before the Republican Citizens of Windsor, on Their Celebration . . . of American Independence* (Windsor, VT, 1812), 1.

58. William Crafts, *An Oration Delivered in St. Michael's Church before the Inhabitants of Charleston, South Carolina . . . in Commemoration of the Independence of the United States* (Charleston, 1812), 19.

59. Joseph Richardson, *An Oration . . . Before the Citizens of the County of Plymouth, on the Anniversary of American Independence* (1812), 23.

60. Jackson, "Impressment and the Anglo-American Discord," 73–76, estimates that although foreigners made up roughly 25 percent of ships' crews operating out of New England ports, foreigners constituted up to 90 percent of ships' crews in Southern ports.

61. Berkeley to Bathurst, Aug. 13, 1807, in F. Bickley, ed., *Historical Manuscripts Commission: Report on the Manuscripts of Earl Bathurst, preserved at Cirencester Park* (London, 1923), 63–65. On Berkeley's career, see Brian Mark De Toy, "Wellington's Admiral: The Life and Career of George Berkeley, 1753–1818," (Ph.D. diss., Florida State University, 1997); and "Sir George Cranfield Berkeley," *Oxford DNB.*

62. Such attitudes led Berkeley to order the HMS *Leopard's* lethal attack on the USS *Chesapeake* earlier that summer. Although ultimately denounced by Britain, the attack hardly ruined Berkeley, who enjoyed continued support in Britain and assumed the more illustrious post of commander-in-chief of the coast of Portugal, where he won acclaim before retiring in July 1812.

63. Joseph Marryat, *Concessions to America the Bane of Britain; or the Cause of the Present Distressed Situation of the British Colonial and Shipping Interests Explained, and the Proper Remedy Suggested* (London, 1807), 23 and 36–37. On the Marryat's associations, see François Crouzet, "America and the Crisis of the British Imperial Economy, 1803–1807," 313.

64. *Animating Hints; for British Statesmen; British Merchants; and Britons in General: On Going to War with America* (London, 1811), 14.

65. *Bahama Gazette,* July 9, 1812.

66. *Glasgow Courier,* Jan. 7, 1812.

67. Bradford Perkins, *Prologue to War, 1805–1812* (Berkeley, 1974), 61–64. On France's minimal direct impact on the War of 1812, see Lawrence S. Kaplan, "France and the War of 1812," *Journal of Southern History* 57 (1970): 36–47.

68. *Bahama Gazette,* July 5, 1812.

69. *Edinburgh Star,* Sept. 25, 1812.

70. Festus Foster, *An Oration . . . in Commemoration of the Thirty-Seventh Anniversary of American Independence* (Brattleboro, VT, 1813), 15.

71. John Lowell, *Mr. Madison's War* (New York, 1812), preface.

72. *An Inquiry into the Past and Present Relations of France and the United States of America* (London, 1811), 86.

73. Troy Bickham, "Sympathizing with Sedition? George Washington, the British Press, and British Attitudes During the American War of Independence," *William and Mary Quarterly,* 3d ser. 59 (2002): 102–22.

74. *Edinburgh Star,* Feb. 18, 1812; *Freeman's Journal,* Mar. 12, 1812; *Times,* Oct. 14, 1812.

75. See especially Bickham, *Making Headlines;* James E. Bradley, "The British Public and the American Revolution: Ideology, Interest and Opinion," in *Britain and the American Revolution,* ed. H. T. Dickinson (London, 1998), 124–54; Wilson, *Sense of the People,* chapter 5; Paul Langford, "London and the American Revolution," in John Stevenson, ed., *London in the Age of Reform* (Oxford, 1977), 55–78; John Sainsbury, *Disaffected Patriots: London Supporters of Revolutionary America, 1769–1782* (Montreal, 1987); Brown, *Moral Capital,* especially chapter 3; Edmund Burke, *Reflections on the Revolution* (London, 1790); Hilton, *A Mad, Bad, and Dangerous People,* 59–60; and Linda Colley, *Britons: Forging of the Nation 1707–1837* (New Haven, 1992), 254–57.

76. *Morning Herald,* Feb. 2, 1797.

77. *A View of the State of Parties in the United States of America; Being an Attempt to Account for the Present Ascendancy of the French, or Democratic Party, in that Country* (Edinburgh, 1812), 30–31.

78. *View of the State of Parties in the United States of America,* 79.

79. *Jamaica Magazine,* May 1813, pp. 355–56.

80. Castlereagh to Foster, Apr. 10, 1812, FO 5/83.

81. For a concise discussion of Madison's handling of French duplicity over the repeal of the decrees, see Stagg, "Malcontents," 566–72.

82. Castlereagh to Foster, Apr. 10, 1812, FO 5/83.

83. *Remarks on . . . the Encouragement of the British Shipping Interest, and the Cultivation of Naval Stores, in Upper and Lower Canada* (London, 1805); D'arcy Boulton, *Sketch of His Majesty's Province of Upper Canada* (London, 1805).

84. Hugh Gray, *Letters from Canada, Written during a Residence there in the years 1806, 1807, and 1809* (London, 1809), 74.

85. *Times,* Feb. 14, 1812.

86. Isaac Brock to brother Irving Brock, Jan. 10, 1811, *Brock Correspondence,* 70–71; and Dec. 31, 1809, *Brock Correspondence,* 54.

87. "Richard Cartwright," *Dictionary of Canadian Biography* (Toronto, 1966–1994); and Jane Errington, *The Lion, the Eagle, and Upper Canada: A Developing Colonial Ideology* (Kingston: McGill-Queen's University Press, 1987), 1–3.

88. *York Gazette,* Feb. 26, 1812.

89. *Quebec Gazette,* Aug. 19, 1812.

90. *Montreal Herald,* Feb. 29, 1812 and Mar. 7, 1812.

91. Reprinted in the *York Gazette,* Feb. 4, 1812.

92. *York Gazette*, Feb. 26, 1812.
93. *Montreal Gazette*, Jan. 27, 1812.
94. *Quebec Mercury*, Feb. 12, 1812.
95. *York Gazette*, Aug. 29, 1812.
96. John Strachan, *A Sermon Preached at York before the Legislative Council and House of Assembly* (York, 1812), 4; J. L. H. Henderson, *John Strachan 1778–1867* (Toronto, 1969).
97. *Kingston Gazette*, July 14, 1812.
98. *Kingston Gazette*, Mar. 3, 1812.
99. *Quebec Gazette*, May 28, 1812.
100. Strachan, *Sermon Preached at York*, 3.
101. Jefferson to William Duane, Aug. 4, 1812, in *The Writings of Thomas Jefferson*, ed. Albert Ellery Bergh (Washington, D. C., 1907), 13: 180–81.
102. *York Gazette*, Mar. 4, 1812.

Chapter 3

1. For a fuller narrative, see Richard Buel, Jr., *America on the Brink: How the Political Struggle Over the War of 1812 Almost Destroyed the Young Republic* (New York, 2005), 141–43; Donald Hickey, *The War of 1812: A Forgotten Conflict* (Urbana, 1989), 37–39; and Bradford Perkins, *Prologue to War, 1805–1812* (Berkeley, 1974), 369–72. For the letters, see James Madison, *Message from the President of the United States Transmitting Copies of Certain Documents Obtained from a Secret Agent of the British Government, Employed in Fomenting Disaffection to the Constituted Authorities, and in Bringing about Resistance to the Laws; and Eventually, in Concert with a British Force, to Destroy the Union of the United States* (Washington, 1812).
2. *New England Palladium*, Mar. 17 and 27, 1812.
3. *Edinburgh Star*, May 5, 1812. The Henry letters were the primary topic of debate in the House of Commons on April 23.
4. *Aberdeen Journal*, May 6, 1812.
5. *Carlisle Journal*, May 9, 1812.
6. Craig to Castlereagh, Apr. 10, 1808, FO 5/92; Castlereagh to Craig, July 7, 1808, FO 5/92; Foster to Wellesley (encrypted), Mar. 24, 1812, FO 5/85; and Castlereagh to Foster, May 7, 1812, FO 5/83.
7. The bumbling, mismanagement, and distractions of a succession of British ministries in the era of the American Revolution are vividly detailed in Peter D. G. Thomas's three-volume history, *British Politics and the Stamp Act Crisis: The First Phase of the American Revolution 1763–1767* (Oxford, 1975); *The Townshend Duties Crisis: The Second Phase of the American Revolution, 1767–1773* (Oxford, 1987); and *Tea Party to Independence: The Third Phase of the American Revolution, 1773–1776* (Oxford, 1991).
8. For an elaboration of the thesis that factionalism and sectionalism prevented, rather than caused, conflict in the early republic, see Scott A. Silverstone, *Divided Union: The Politics of War in the Early American Republic* (Ithaca, 2004), especially chapter 3.
9. Gordon S. Wood, *Empire of Liberty: A History of the Early Republic, 1789–1815* (New York, 2009), 661.
10. Mark Zuehlke, *The War of 1812 and the Brokering of an Uneasy Peace* (Toronto, 2006), 67; Perkins, *Prologue to War*, 344–45.
11. Zuehlke, *War of 1812*, 65.
12. Ronald L. Hatzenbuehler and Robert L. Ivie, "Justifying the War of 1812: Toward a Model of Congressional Behavior in Early War Crises," *Social Science History* 4 (1980): 453–77.
13. *AC*, 23: 481.
14. Lorri Glover, *Southern Sons: Becoming a Man in the New Nation* (Baltimore, 2007); and Margaret Kincaid Latimer, "South Carolina—A Protagonist of the War of 1812," *American Historical Review* 61 (1956): 914–29.
15. *AC*, 23: 481.
16. Printed in *Niles' Weekly Register*, Dec. 28, 1811.
17. *American Mercury*, Mar. 18, 1812.

18. [Maine] *American Advocate*, June 2, 1812.
19. Jon Latimer, *1812: War with America* (Cambridge, MA, 2008), 7. Foster wrote to Castlereagh on May 3, 1812, that Madison's reelection plans were being held hostage by Clay and the war hawks, FO 5/85; Foster reiterated this to Castlereagh on June 21, 1812, FO 5/86.
20. Clay to William W. Worsley, Apr. 4, 1812, *Clay Papers*, 1: 643.
21. Clay to Jesse Bledsoe, *Clay Papers*, 1: 675.
22. On the limitations of Clay and the war hawks, see especially J. C. A. Stagg, "James Madison and the 'Malcontents': The Political Origins of the War of 1812," *William and Mary Quarterly*, 3d ser. 33 (1976): 557–85.
23. Jefferson to Madison, Feb. 19, 1812, *CBJM*, 3: 1688.
24. For examples, see *Aberdeen Journal* Oct. 21, 1812; *Edinburgh Star*, Dec. 18, 1812; *Times*, Jan. 1, 1813; William Hamilton (British agent in Boston) to Castlereagh, July 21, 1812, FO 5/89.
25. Cited in Alan Taylor, *The Civil War of 1812: American Citizens, British Subjects, Irish Rebels, & Indian Allies* (New York, 2010), 140.
26. Stagg, "Malcontents," 570.
27. Donald H. Kagin, "Monetary Aspects of the Treasury Notes of the War of 1812," *Journal of Economic History* 44 (1984): 69–88.
28. The U.S. Army's authorized size at this point was nearly sixty-three thousand officers and men. On the state of the American army and navy, see Latimer, *War with America*, 54–59; Hickey, *A Forgotten Conflict*, 90–91; William B. Skelton, "High Army Leadership in the Era of the War of 1812: The Making and Remaking of the Officer Corps," *William and Mary Quarterly*, 3d ser. 51 (1994): 253–74.
29. Peter J. Kastor, "Toward 'the Maritime War Only': The Question of Naval Mobilization, 1811–1812," *Journal of Military History* 61 (1997): 455–80.
30. *National Intelligencer*, Aug. 29, 1811.
31. On the size of the American station, see Taylor, 128 n. 14.
32. *National Intelligencer*, Dec. 5, 1811.
33. Reginald C. Stuart, *War and American Thought: From the Revolution to the Monroe Doctrine* (Kent, OH, 1982), 99; Wood, *Empire of Liberty*, 9–10; Perkins, *Prologue to War*, 410–25; and Walter R. Borneman, *1812: The War That Forged a Nation* (New York, 2004).
34. Roger H. Brown, *The Republic in Peril: 1812* (New York, 1964), 45.
35. Foster to Richard Wellesley, Marquess Wellesley, Apr. 2, 1812, FO 5/85.
36. Stagg, "Malcontents."
37. James Madison, *Message from the President of the United States, to Both Houses of Congress at the Commencement of the First Session of the Twelfth Congress* (Washington, 1811), 8–9.
38. Party was the single most determinative factor in predicting congressional votes. Ronald L. Hatzenbuehler, "Party Unity and the Decision for War in the House of Representatives, 1812," *William and Mary Quarterly*, 3d ser. 29 (1972): 367–90; Perkins, *Prologue to War*, 410.
39. See especially, Jeremy Black, *Britain as a Military Power, 1688–1815* (London, 2006), 268–69; Douglas Hay and Nicholas Rodgers, *Eighteenth-Century English Society* (Oxford, 1997), 153; J. E. Cookson, *The British Armed Nation, 1793–1815* (Oxford, 1997), 95; Linda Colley, *Britons: Forging of the Nation 1707–1837* (New Haven, 1992), chapter 7; John Brewer, *The Sinews of Power: War, Money and the English State, 1688–1783* (Cambridge, MA, 1990); and Roger Knight and Martin Wilcox, *Sustaining the Fleet, 1793–1815: War, the British Navy and the Contractor State* (London, 2010).
40. Patricia Y. C. E. Lin, "Caring for the Nation's Families: British Soldiers' and Sailors' Families and the State, 1793–1815," in *Soldiers, Citizens and Civilians: Experiences and Perceptions of the Revolutionary and Napoleonic War, 1790–1820*, ed. Alan Forrest, Karen Hagemann, and Jane Rendall (London, 2009), 103–6.
41. Wood, *Empire of Liberty*, 292–93.
42. Jeremy Black, *The War of 1812 in the Age of Napoleon* (Norman, Oklahoma, 2009), 9, argues that this was America's most severe handicap in prosecuting the war.
43. Reginald C. Stuart, *War and American Thought: From the Revolution to the Monroe Doctrine* (Kent, OH, 1982), 101.
44. Latimer, *War with America*, 59.

45. *Niles' Weekly Register*, Dec. 14, 1811.
46. *Niles' Weekly Register*, June 27, 1812.
47. *"Free Trade and Sailor's Rights!" An Address to the Independent Electors of the State of New York*, 2nd ed. (Albany, 1813), 4.
48. Clay speaking in the House of Representatives, Jan. 9, 1813, *Clay Papers*, 1: 762.
49. Castlereagh to Foster, Apr. 10, 1812, FO 5/83.
50. *London Gazette*, Apr. 21, 1812.
51. Madison to Jefferson, Apr. 3, 1812, *CBJM*, 3: 1691.
52. Foster to Castlereagh, May 3, 1812, FO 5/85.
53. *Niles' Weekly Register*, June 27, 1812.
54. *Niles' Weekly Register*, July 25, 1812.
55. Cited in J. C. A. Stagg, *Mr. Madison's War: Politics, Diplomacy, and Warfare in the Early American Republic, 1783–1830* (Princeton, 1983), 4.
56. *AC*, 23: 426.
57. Clay to Thomas Bradley, Dec. 18, 1813, *Clay Papers*, 1: 842.
58. Taylor, *The Civil War of 1812*, 138.
59. Ibid., 106–8.
60. C. P. Lucas, *The Canadian War of 1812* (Oxford, 1906), 9.
61. Alan Taylor, "The Late Loyalists: Northern Reflections of the Early American Republic," *Journal of the Early Republic* 27 (2007): 1–34. See also Stuart Ivison and Fred Rosser, *The Baptists in Upper and Lower Canada Before 1820* (Toronto, 1956), chapters 3–4.
62. Cited in Taylor, *The Civil War of 1812*, 141.
63. *National Intelligencer*, Apr. 14, 1812.
64. *AC*, 23: 143–44.
65. Jefferson to William Duane, Aug. 4, 1812, in *The Writings of Thomas Jefferson*, ed. Albert Ellery Bergh (Washington, DC, 1907), 13: 180–81.
66. *Bahama Gazette*, Feb. 16, 1812.
67. *Times*, Feb. 24, 1812.
68. *Montreal Herald*, Feb. 29, 1812.
69. Madison to Jefferson, June 22, 1812, *CBJM*, 3: 1698; Madison to Jefferson, Aug. 17, 1812, *CBJM*, 3: 1702.
70. Captain Layman, *Outline of a Plan for the Better Cultivation, Security, & Defense of the British West Indies: Being the Original Suggestion for Providing an Effectual Substitute for the African Slave Trade, and Preventing the Dependance of Thos Colonies on America for Supplies* (London, 1807), 36; *A Permanent and Effectual Remedy Suggested for the Evils under which the British West Indies Now Labour. In a Letter from a West India Merchant to a West India Planter* (London, 1807), 5–6; Joseph Lowe, *An Inquiry into the State of the British West Indies* (London, 1807).
71. On snobbery toward manufacturing wealth, see James Raven, *Judging New Wealth: Popular Publishing and Responses to Commerce in England, 1750–1800* (Oxford, 1992), especially chapter 11. On the Orders in Council highlighting a London-provincial divide, see Cookson, *Friends of Peace*, chapter 9.
72. *Cobbett's Weekly Political Register*, Feb. 15, 1812.
73. Charles Cameron to Liverpool, July 16, 1812, CO 23/59.
74. Foreign Office to Foster, Jan. 28, 1812 (marked "secret"), FO 5/83.
75. *Royal Gazette and Bahama Advertiser*, Jan. 12, 1812.
76. *Bahama Gazette*, Feb. 18, 1813.
77. Anthony St. John Baker to Castlereagh, Oct. 31, 1812, FO 5/88. On American involvement in the 1812–13 rebellion in Texas, see Donald E. Chapman, *Spanish Texas, 1519–1821* (Austin, 1992), 233–40; and Richard W. Gronet, "The United States and the Invasion of Texas," *Americas* 25 (1969): 281–306. J. C. A. Stagg downplays the direct involvement of the Madison administration in the Texas rebellion in "The Madison Administration and Mexico: Reinterpreting the Gutiérrez-Magee Raid of 1812–1813," *William and Mary Quarterly* 3d ser., 59 (2002): 449–80.
78. *Jamaica Magazine*, Feb. 1812.

79. Roy Muir, *Britain and the Defeat of Napoleon 1807–1815* (New Haven, CT, 1996), chapter 12.
80. *Times*, May 16, 1812.
81. On British mobilization, see especially J. E. Cookson, *The British Armed Nation, 1793–1815* (Oxford, 1997); and Austin Gee, *The British Volunteer Movement, 1794–1814* (Oxford, 2003).
82. Douglas Hay and Nicholas Rogers, *Eighteenth-Century English Society* (Oxford, 1997), 153.
83. Jeremy Black, *Britain as a Military Power*, 269; Kagin, "Monetary Aspects," 71.
84. For this reason, any estimation of the actual financial cost of the War of 1812 for Britain is suspect.
85. For an overview of expansion during the Napoleonic Wars, see especially C. A. Bayly, *Imperial Meridian: The British Empire and the World 1780–1830* (London, 1989).
86. On British dependency on American grain, see G. E. Watson, "The United States and the Peninsular War, 1808–1812," *Historical Journal* 19 (1976), 859–76; Knight and Wilcox, *Sustaining the Fleet*, 54.
87. Jefferson to Madison, Apr. 17, 1812, *CBJM*, 3: 1692–93; quoted in Muir, *Britain and the Defeat of Napoleon*, 237.
88. Muir, *Britain and the Defeat of Napoleon*, 237.
89. Foster to Castlereagh, Apr. 21, 1812, FO 5/85.
90. The quoted phrase is from Frederick Morton Eden, *Address on the Maritime Rights of Great Britain*, 2nd ed. (London, 1808), 12.
91. Margaret Law Callcott, ed., *Mistress of Riversdale: The Plantation Letters of Rosalie Stier Calvert, 1795–1821* (Baltimore, 1991), 194, 203, 239, and 246.
92. Foster to Wellesley, Jan. 11, 1812, FO 5/84.
93. Foster to Wellesley, Mar. 22, 1812, FO 5/85.
94. Foster to Wellesley, Apr. 2, 1812, FO 5/85.
95. Foster to Castlereagh, Apr. 23, 1812, FO 5/85.
96. Foster to Castlereagh, June 21, 1812, FO 5/86.
97. Buel, *America on the Brink*, 153–54.
98. Russell to Castlereagh, June 26, 1812, FO 5/90.
99. Brown, *Republic in Peril*, 96; Perkins, *Prologue to War*, 352–53.
100. Letter in cipher from Foster to Wellesley, Feb. 4, 1812, FO 5/84.
101. Foster to Wellesley (marked "secret"), Mar. 12, 1812, FO 5/84.
102. Baker to Castlereagh, Oct. 31, 1812, FO 5/88.
103. Foster to Wellesley, Jan. 16, 1812, FO 5/84.
104. Foster to Wellesley (marked "secret"), Mar. 12, 1812, FO 5/84.
105. For a more detailed discussion, see Chapter 7.
106. Castlereagh to Foster (marked "private"), Apr. 10, 1812, FO 5/83.
107. Liverpool to Prevost, May 15, 1812, CO 43/23.
108. *Edinburgh Star*, Feb. 18, 1812.
109. Russell to Castlereagh, Aug. 24, 1812, FO 5/91.
110. Castlereagh to Russell, Aug. 29, 1812, FO 5/91.
111. Russell to Castlereagh, Sept 12, 1812, FO 5/91.
112. Russell to Castlereagh, n.d., FO/91; Russell to William Hamilton, Sept. 16, 1812, FO 5/91.
113. Castlereagh to Russell, Sept. 18, 1812, FO 5/91.

Chapter 4

1. Jeremy Black, *The War of 1812 in the Age of Napoleon* (Norman, OK, 2009), 44.
2. On British commanders' concern about their ability to defend British North America, see especially Prevost to Liverpool, May 18, 1812, CO 42/146; and Bathurst to Prevost, Aug. 10, 1812, CO 43/23.
3. On Madison's thoughts on rejecting a ceasefire, see Madison to Jefferson, Aug. 17, 1812, *CBJM*, 3: 1703.
4. *Missouri Gazette*, Sept. 12, 1812.
5. Monroe to Clay, Aug. 28, 1812, *Clay Papers*, 1: 722.
6. Jefferson to Madison, Nov. 6, 1812, *CBJM*, 3: 1707.

7. The governor's message was printed in full in *Niles' Weekly Register*, Jan. 9, 1813.

8. Clay to Caesar A. Rodney, Dec. 29, 1812, *Clay Papers*, 750.

9. James Madison, *Message from the President . . . November 5th, 1811* (Washington, 1811), 6.

10. *National Intelligencer*, Mar. 6, 1813.

11. Steven Watts, *The Republic Reborn: War and the Making of Liberal America, 1790–1820* (Baltimore, 1987).

12. Ibid., 62.

13. Joseph Richardson, *An Oration Pronounced July 4, 1812, Before the Citizens of the County of Plymouth, On the Anniversary of American Independence* (Boston, 1812), 16.

14. *City Gazette*, July 7, 1812.

15. *National Intelligencer*, Aug. 11, 1812.

16. Reprinted in the *National Intelligencer*, Jan. 6, 1813.

17. Harry S. Laver, "Refuge of Manhood: Masculinity and the Militia Experience in Kentucky," *Southern Manhood: Perspectives on Masculinity in the Old South*, ed. Craig Thompson Friend and Lorri Glover (Athens, GA, 2004); Lorri Glover, *Southern Sons: Becoming Men in the New Nation* (Baltimore, 2007), 155.

18. *Carthage Gazette*, Mar. 14, 1812.

19. Monroe to Clay, Aug. 28, 1812, and Sept. 17, 1812, *Clay Papers*, 1: 723 and 1727.

20. Dianne Graves, *In the Midst of Alarms: The Untold Story of Women and the War of 1812* (Cap-Saint-Ignace, Quebec, 2007), 157–58.

21. Margaret Law Callcott, ed., *Mistress of Riversdale: The Plantation Letters of Rosalie Stier Calvert, 1795–1821* (Baltimore, 1991), 197, 239, 260, 265.

22. *Alexandria Daily Gazette*, May 28, 1814.

23. For an extensive discussion of the tensions between public politics and domestic prescriptions, see especially Rosemarie Zagarri, *Revolutionary Backlash: Women and Politics in the Early American Republic* (Philadelphia, 2007); Linda K. Kerber, *Women of the Republic: Intellect and Ideology in Revolutionary America* (Chapel Hill, NC, 1980); and Mary Beth Norton, *Liberty's Daughters: The Revolutionary Experience of American Women, 1750–1800* (Ithaca, NY, 1981).

24. *Military Monitor*, Sept. 14, 1812.

25. See especially Linda Colley, *Britons: Forging the Nation, 1707–1837* (New Haven, 1992), chapter 6; Joan Landes, *Women and the Public Sphere in the Age of the French Revolution* (London, 1988); and Elaine Chalus, *Elite Women in English Political Life, 1754–1790* (Oxford, 2005).

26. Colley, *Britons*, 260.

27. *General Evening Post*, Oct. 22, 1776.

28. Kerber, *Women of the Republic*, 111; Zagarri, *Revolutionary Backlash*, 99–100.

29. Zagarri, *Revolutionary Backlash*, 94–97.

30. *Federal Republican*, Oct. 30, 1812.

31. *Missouri Gazette*, Sept. 25, 1813.

32. William Crafts, *An Oration Delivered in St. Michael's Church, Before the Inhabitants of Charleston, South Carolina . . . in Commemoration of the Independence of the United States* (Charleston, 1812), 25.

33. *Military Monitor*, Sept. 14, 1812.

34. Zagarri, *Revolutionary Backlash*, 98–102.

35. J. C. A. Stagg, *Mr. Madison's War: Politics, Diplomacy, and Warfare in the Early American Republic, 1783–1830* (Princeton, 1983), 170.

36. Gordon S. Wood, *Empire of Liberty: A History of the Early Republic, 1789–1815* (New York, 2009), 674.

37. Phinehas Cooke, *An Oration Delivered at Keene, N. H. . . . Being the Anniversary of American Independence* (Keene, NH, 1813). Historians have discredited the idea that the Continental Army's rank and file was made up of land-owning American citizens by the end of the revolution. See especially Charles Royster, *A Revolutionary People at War: The Continental Army and the American Character, 1775–1783* (Chapel Hill, NC, 1979).

38. Jon Latimer, *1812: War with America* (Cambridge, MA, 2008), 108; James H. Broussard, *The Southern Federalists, 1800–1816* (Baton Rouge, 1978), chapter 11.

39. James Madison, *Message from the President . . . at the Commencement of the First Session of the Thirteenth Congress* (Washington, 1813), 10.

40. For an excellent detailed strategic analysis of these campaigns, see Latimer, *War with America*. Many of the comments here regarding the quality of the troops and their officers and the overall military strategies are derived from Latimer's analysis.

41. Madison, *Message from the President . . . at the Commencement of the Second Session of the Thirteenth Congress*, 16.

42. Graves, *In the Midst of Alarms*, 361.

43. Wood, *Empire of Liberty*, 684–85.

44. *Pendleton Messenger*, May 29, 1813.

45. Madison, *Message from the President . . . at the Commencement of the Second Session of the Thirteenth Congress*, 8.

46. *Boston Spectator*, Sept. 17, 1814.

47. *Niles' Weekly Register*, Feb. 15, 1815.

48. Colin G. Calloway, *Crown and Calumet: British-Indian Relations, 1783–1815* (Norman, OK, 1987), 221; Latimer, *War with America*, 64–66.

49. Latimer, *War with America*, 69.

50. Wood, *Empire of Liberty*, 679.

51. James Madison, *Message from the President . . . at the Commencement of the Second Session of the Twelfth Congress* (Washington, 1812), 4–5.

52. *Niles' Weekly Register*, June 12, 1813.

53. *National Intelligencer*, Apr. 13, 1813.

54. Brock to Hull, Aug. 15, 1812, in *DRICSD*, 144.

55. Calloway, *Crown and Calumet*, 202.

56. Graves, *In the Midst of Alarms*, 262.

57. Richard Bache, *Oration Delivered at Spring Garden . . . of the City and County of Philadelphia* (Philadelphia, 1813), 6.

58. Jonathan B. Smith, *Oration Delivered on the Fourth of March, 1813, Before the Association of Democratic Young Men of the City and Liberties of Philadelphia* (Philadelphia, 1813), 20–21.

59. *National Intelligencer*, Nov. 25, 1813.

60. *Baltimore Whig*, May 27, 1813, cited in Alan Taylor, *The Civil War of 1812: American Citizens, British Subjects, Irish Rebels, & Indian Allies* (New York, 2010), 206.

61. Wood, *Empire of Liberty*, 686–87; Daniel Walker Howe, *What Hath God Wrought: The Transformation of America, 1815–1848* (New York, 2007), 5; Armstrong Starkey, *European and Native American Warfare, 1675–1815* (Norman, OK, 1998), 158–59.

62. Madison, *Message from the President . . . at the Commencement of the Second Session of the Thirteenth Congress*, 7.

63. Bathurst to Prevost, Aug. 10, 1812, CO 42/147.

64. *Carlisle Journal*, Oct. 10, 1812.

65. *Aberdeen Journal*, June 2, 1813.

66. Troy Bickham, *Savages Within the Empire: Representing American Indians in Eighteenth-Century Britain* (Oxford, 2005). On this subject, see also Tim Fulford, *Romantic Indians: Native Americans, British Literature, and Transatlantic Culture 1756–1830* (Oxford, 2006); and the essays in Tim Fulford and Kevin Hutchings, eds., *Native Americans and Anglo-American Culture, 1750–1850: The Indian Atlantic* (Cambridge, 2009).

67. Hugh Gray, *Letters from Canada, Written During a Residence there in the years 1806, 1807, and 1809* (London, 1809), 157–62.

68. *Times*, Feb. 14, 1812; *Ipswich Journal*, Feb. 21, 1812.

69. *York Gazette*, Dec. 26, 1812.

70. Brock to Liverpool, Aug. 29, 1812, in *DRICSD*, 192.

71. Brock to Colonel Edward Baynes, York, Aug. 4, 1812, in *DRICSD*, 119–20.

72. For a compelling account of the Iroquois in the War of 1812, see Carl Benn, *The Iroquois in the War of 1812* (Toronto, 1998).

73. Brock to Liverpool, York, Aug. 29, 1812, in *DRICSD*, 191.

74. Captain Roberts to Major Glegg, July 29, 1812, in *DRICSD*, 101.

75. Donald E. Graves, *Merry Hearts Make Light Days: The War of 1812 Journal of Lieutenant John Le Couteur, 104th Foot* (Ottawa, 1994), 126–29, 174.

76. Calloway, *Crown and Calumet*.

77. Liverpool to Brock, Nov. 16, 1812, CO 42/352.

78. Black, *War of 1812*, 130–32.

79. Wood, *Empire of Liberty*, 682.

80. Bache, *Oration Delivered at Spring Garden*, 5.

81. Arthur Herman, *To Rule the Waves: How the British Navy Shaped the Modern World* (New York, 2004), 413; Latimer, *War with America*, 84.

82. *Ipswich Journal*, Feb. 7, 1812.

83. Peter J. Kastor, "Toward 'the Maritime War Only': The Question of Naval Mobilization, 1811–1812," *Journal of Military History* 61 (1997): 455–80.

84. Brown Emerson, *The Causes and Effects of War. A Sermon, Delivered in Salem, August 20, 1812, the Day of National Humiliation and Prayer* (Salem, 1812), 11.

85. *Niles' Weekly Register*, Sept. 12, 1812 and Dec. 26, 1812.

86. Charles J. Cox, *Oration Delivered Before the Washington Association of Philadelphia* (Philadelphia, 1813), 20.

87. *Missouri Gazette*, Sept. 25, 1813.

88. Jefferson to Madison, May 21, 1813, *CBJM*, 3: 1720.

89. *Niles' Weekly Register*, Dec. 26, 1812.

90. *National Intelligencer*, Feb. 14, 1814; Lucile Gafford, "The Boston Stage and the War of 1812," *New England Quarterly* 7 (1934): 327–35.

91. For an example, see the *American Advocate*, May 15, 1813.

92. Reprinted in the *Alexandria Gazette*, Dec. 23, 1812.

93. *National Intelligencer*, July 8, 1813.

94. *American Advocate*, July 16, 1814.

95. Daniel Webster, *An Address Delivered Before the Washington Benevolent Society, at Portsmouth, July 4, 1812* (Portsmouth, 1812), 19.

96. *Federal Republican*, Nov. 27, 1812.

97. *Military Monitor*, Dec. 14, 1812.

98. Condy Raguet, *Oration Delivered Before the Washington Benevolent Society* (Philadelphia, 1814), 14.

99. See especially Margarette Lincoln, *Representing the Royal Navy: British Seapower, 1750–1815* (London, 2002). Though agreeing with other historians on the importance of the navy to national public culture, Timothy Jenks's *Naval Engagements: Patriotism, Cultural Politics, and the Royal Navy 1793–1815* (Oxford, 2006) offers a more complicated view, arguing that the relationship was often strained and the public was often critical.

100. For Goulburn's reflections, see Wilbur Devereaux Jones, "A British View of the War of 1812 and the Peace Negotiations," *Mississippi Valley Historical Review* 45 (1958): 481–87, which is a complete transcription of Goulburn's memoirs related to the War of 1812.

101. *Times*, Oct. 7, 1812.

102. *London Gazette*, Dec. 4, 1812.

103. *Times*, Mar. 20, 1813.

104. For examples, see the *Oxford Journal*, Oct. 10, 1812, and Nov. 28, 1812.

105. *Caledonian Mercury*, Jan. 2, 1813.

106. Budiansky, *Perilous Fight*, 234.

107. *Morning Chronicle*, Dec. 28, 1812.

108. *Times*, Dec. 30, 1812.

109. All the letters appeared in a single pamphlet, *The Letters on the Subject of the Naval War with America, which Appeared in the Courier, Under the Signature of Nereus* (London, 1813). For a closer analysis of Croker and the letters, see Budiansky, *Perilous Fight*, 194–96.

110. *Naval Chronicle*, Nov. 1812, pp. 386–87. On the *Naval Chronicle*, see Jenks, *Naval Engagements*, 159–68.

111. *London Gazette*, Feb. 5, 1814.

112. *Liverpool Mercury*, July 16, 1813.

113. *Edinburgh Star*, Aug. 17, 1813.

114. *Times*, July 8, 1813.

115. Budiansky, *Perilous Fight*, 288–89; Jerome R. Garitee, *The Republic's Private Navy: The American Privateering Business as Practiced in Baltimore in the War of 1812* (Middletown, CT, 1977), 191–94. The figures assume an exchange rate of £1 for $4.40 and the standard wage of eleven pence a day for an ordinary seaman in the Royal Navy.

116. *Western American*, Sept. 24, 1814.

117. Donald Hickey, *The War of 1812: A Forgotten Conflict* (Urbana, IL, 1989), 97. The British government estimated capturing a total of 8,974 men on American privateers, *Papers Relating to the War with America. Ordered, by the House of Commons, to be Printed* (London, 1815), which can be found in CO 42/160. On prisoners, see also Robin F. A. Fabel, "Self-Help in Dartmoor: Black and White Prisoners in the War of 1812," *Journal of the Early Republic* 9 (1989): 165–66.

118. Gerard T. Altoff, *Amongst My Best Men: African-Americans and the War of 1812* (Put-in-Bay, Ohio, 1996), 28–30.

119. The number of privateers is difficult to estimate accurately. Five hundred letters of marquee were issued by Congress during the war to more than 250 ships, but other ships operated without official authorization. For British official estimates of the number of American privateers captures, see CO 42/160. On the relative success of privateers during the war, see especially Budiansky, *Perilous Fight*, 289; Reuben Elmore Stivers, *Privateers and Volunteers: The Men and Women of Our Reserve Naval Forces: 1766 to 1866* (Annapolis, 1975), 56–57, 60; Wade G. Dudley, *Splintering the Wooden Wall: The British Blockade of the United States, 1812–1815* (Annapolis, MD, 2003), 138–39; Paul Gilje, *Liberty on the Waterfront: American Maritime Culture in the Age of Revolution* (Philadelphia, 2003), 173–74.

120. Latimer, *War with America*, 90; Dudley, *Splintering the Wooden Wall*, 141–42; and Gilje, *Liberty on the Waterfront*, 173.

121. *Morning Chronicle*, Oct. 22, 1812.

122. John Boileau, *Half-Hearted Enemies: Nova Scotia, New England and the War of 1812* (Halifax, 2005), 29–30; Faye M. Kert, *Prize and Prejudice: Privateering and Naval Prize in Atlantic Canada in the War of 1812* (St. Johns, Newfoundland, 1997).

123. *Glasgow Chronicle*, Nov. 3, 1812.

124. *Bermuda Gazette and Weekly Advertiser*, May 15, 1813.

125. "Further Papers Relating to the War with America," CO 42/160. However, some historians' estimates put the Americans slightly ahead of this figure. See George F. Emmons, *Navy of the United States from the Commencement, in 1775, through 1853* (Washington, D.C, 1853); Dudley, *Splintering the Wooden Wall*, 138.

126. *Morning Chronicle*, Dec. 21, 1813.

127. Dudley, *Splintering the Wooden Wall*, 82–83.

128. *Liverpool Mercury*, Aug. 26, 1814.

129. For a collection of the petitions, see "Further Papers Relating to the War with America," CO 42/160.

130. Reprinted in the *Aberdeen Chronicle*, Sept. 7, 1814.

131. *Freeman's Journal*, Sept. 25, 1814.

132. Wood, *Empire of Liberty*, 689.

133. For a detailed discussion of the blockade, see Dudley, *Splintering the Wooden Wall*.

134. *American Advocate*, July 16, 1814; and *Western American*, Oct. 1, 1814.

135. These claims are based on the prices posted in the *Baltimore Price-Current*, which published the availability and prices of an enormous range of commodities weekly.

136. Taylor, *Civil War of 1812*, 407.

137. Wood, *Empire of Liberty*, 684, 692. For an overview of American finances, see Hickey, *The War of 1812*, chapter 5; Black, *War of 1812*, 213. For an acute analysis of the treasury's measures and failures, see Donald H. Kagin, "Monetary Aspects of the Treasury Notes of the War of 1812," *Journal of Economic History* 44 (1984): 69–88. Gallatin issued paper currency with some success, but the federal government's third issue failed miserably.

138. Madison to Jefferson, May 10, 1814, *CBJM*, 3: 1742.

139. Wood, *Empire of Liberty*, 689; Hickey, *Forgotten War*, 241–45.

140. *Boston Spectator*, Nov. 5, 1814; *Western Monitor*, Dec. 20, 1814.

141. James Madison, *Message of the President… to Both Houses of Congress, at the Commencement of the First Session of the Thirteenth Congress* (Washington, 1813), 4.

142. Black, *War of 1812*, 149; Christopher D. Hall, *British Strategy in the Napoleonic War 1803–1815* (Manchester, UK, 1992), 197–98; Rory Muir, *Britain and the Defeat of Napoleon 1807–1815* (New Haven, CT, 1996), 332.

Chapter 5

1. Prevost to Bathurst, Jan. 6, 1814, CO 42/156.

2. Margaret Bayard Smith to Maria Kirkpatrick, July 20, 1813, in *The First Forty Years of Washington Society in the Family Letters of Margaret Bayard Smith*, ed. Gaillard Hunt (New York, 1906), 89.

3. *Cobbett's Weekly Political Register*, Feb. 15, 1812.

4. Prevost to Liverpool, May 18, 1812, CO 42/146; and Bathurst to Prevost, Aug. 10, 1812, CO 43/23.

5. Liverpool to Prevost, Apr. 20, 1812, CO 42/147.

6. Bathurst to Prevost, Aug. 10, 1812, CO 42/147.

7. Bathurst to Prevost, Nov. 16, 1812, CO 42/147.

8. *Oxford Journal*, Oct. 10, 1812.

9. *Jamaica Magazine*, Nov. 1812, 284.

10. *Times*, Nov. 28, 1812.

11. *Leeds Mercury*, July 31, 1813.

12. Alan Taylor, *The Civil War of 1812: American Citizens, British Subjects, Irish Rebels, & Indian Allies* (New York, 2010), 56; David Mills, *The Idea of Loyalty in Upper Canada, 1784–1850* (Kingston, Ontario, 1988), 6–7; Colin M. Coates, "French Canadians' Ambivalence to the British Empire," in *Canada and the British Empire*, ed. Phillip Buckner (Oxford, 2008), 186–88.

13. Luca Codignola, "'France's Cromwell' to 'Consummate Brigand': North Atlantic Catholics and Napoleon, 1789–1815," in *Napoleon's Atlantic: The Impact of Napoleonic Empire in the Atlantic World*, ed. Christophe Belaubre, Jordana Dym, and John Savage (Leiden, 2010), 25–44.

14. Arthur Bowler, *The War of 1812* (Toronto, 1973), 14; "George Prevost," *Oxford DNB*.

15. Prevost to Liverpool, July 6, 1812, CO 42/147; Robert Christie, *The Military and Naval Operations in the Canadas, During the Late War with the United States* (Quebec, 1818), 61; Sean Mills, "French Canadians and the Beginning of the War of 1812: Revisiting the Lachine Riot," *Histoire sociale/Social History*, 76 (2005).

16. Mills, "Revisiting the Lachine Riot," 48.

17. Jane Errington, *The Lion, the Eagle, and Upper Canada: A Developing Colonial Ideology* (Kingston, Ontario, 1987), especially Chapter 3.

18. Brock to Prevost, York, Feb. ?, 1812, *Brock Correspondence*, 130; Brock to Liverpool, 23 March 1812, CO 42/352.

19. Docs, Brock to Prevost, York, July 28, 1812, 99.

20. Brock to Colonel Baynes, July 29, 1812, in *DRICSD*, 106–7.

21. Brock to Col. Baynes, York, Aug. 4, 1812, in *DRICSD*, 120.

22. William Dunlop, ed., *Tiger Dunlop's Upper Canada* (Toronto, 1967), 4. On desertion from the British regiments in Canada, see Taylor, *The Civil War of 1812*, 106–8.

23. George Sheppard, *Plunder, Profit, and Paroles: A Social History of the War of 1812 in Upper Canada* (Montreal, 1994), 55–57.

24. Ibid., 59–64.

25. Ibid., especially 70–73, 79–87.

26. For examples, see Prevost to Bathurst, Aug. 17, 1812, *DRICSD*, 160–64, Sheaffe to Bathurst, Dec. 31, 1812, CO 42/352; Prevost to Bathurst, Apr. 21, 1813, CO 42/150; and Sheppard, *Plunder, Profit, and Paroles*, 6.

27. Sheppard, *Plunder, Profit, and Paroles*, 85–86.

28. James J. Talman, ed., *Loyalist Narratives from Upper Canada* (Toronto, 1946), lxi.

29. Sheppard, *Plunder, Profit, and Paroles*, 61.

30. Ibid., 91.
31. Prevost to Bathurst, Dec. 11, 1813, CO 42/152.
32. The examples are taken from *The Report of the Loyal and Patriotic Society of Upper Canada with an appendix and a list of subscribers and benefactors* (Montreal, 1817). For the total estimate, see Sheppard, *Plunder, Profit, and Paroles*, 101.
33. Arthur Bowler, *The War of 1812* (Toronto, 1973), 82–83.
34. Stuart Sutherland, ed., *"A Desire of Serving and Defending My Country": The War of 1812 Journals of William Hamilton Merritt* (Toronto, 2001), 42.
35. *Kingston Gazette*, Nov. 7, 1812.
36. Sheppard, *Plunder, Profit, and Paroles*, 101.
37. *Report of the Loyal and Patriotic Society of Upper Canada*, 101. Frey received $50 compensation.
38. The advertisement offering a hundred-dollar reward for information ran in the *Kingston Gazette* for most of the spring.
39. Donald E. Graves, *Merry Hearts Make Light Days: The War of 1812 Journal of Lieutenant John Le Couteur, 104th Foot* (Ottawa, 1994), 78, 126–27.
40. Sheppard, *Plunder, Profit, and Paroles*, 21–22, 120–22.
41. Ibid., 109–13; Alan Taylor, "The Late Loyalists: Northern Reflections of the Early American Republic," *Journal of the Early Republic* 27 (2007): 24.
42. Graves, *Merry Hearts*, 134.
43. Drummond to Bathurst, Apr. 12 1814, CO 42/355.
44. Sheppard, *Plunder, Profit, and Paroles*, 160–62.
45. Ibid., 153.
46. Ibid., 148–52.
47. John Boileau, *Half-Hearted Enemies: Nova Scotia, New England and the War of 1812* (Halifax, 2005), especially 18–30.
48. Boileau, *Half-Hearted Enemies*, 23 and 60–61; and Faye M. Kert, *Prize and Prejudice: Privateering and Naval Prize in Atlantic Canada in the War of 1812* (St. Johns, Newfoundland, 1997).
49. Graves, *Merry Hearts*, 78.
50. *New Brunswick Courier*, Aug. 3, 1814, and Sept. 3, 1814.
51. *Canadian Courant*, Nov. 26, 1814.
52. Dianne Graves, *In the Midst of Alarms: The Untold Story of Women and the War of 1812* (Cap-Saint-Ignace, Quebec, 2007), 247.
53. *New Brunswick Courier*, Sept. 3, 1814.
54. *Montreal Herald*, July 18, 1812.
55. *New Brunswick Courier*, Aug. 3, 1814.
56. *Quebec Gazette*, Aug. 19, 1812.
57. The Quebec Act of 1774 consolidated Britain's gains from the 1763 Treaty of Paris by attaching the British North American interior roughly east of the Mississippi River and north of the Ohio River to Quebec.
58. The petition is reprinted in the *Kingston Gazette*, Oct. 16, 1813. Prevost duly forwarded to Bathurst.
59. Drummond to Bathurst, Jan. 2, 1815, CO 42/356. McSwiney received the requested pardon.
60. *Kingston Gazette*, Nov. 17, 1812.
61. Drummond to Bathurst, Jan. 10, 1814, CO 42/355. The report included the assembly's records.
62. *New Brunswick Courier*, Aug. 13, 1814.
63. *York Gazette*, Nov. 19, 1812.
64. *Kingston Gazette*, Feb. 22, 1814.
65. *Kingston Gazette*, Apr. 20, 1813.
66. John Strachan, *A Sermon Preached at York, Upper Canada, On the Third of June, Being the Day Appointed for a General Thanksgiving* (Montreal, 1814), 17, 29.
67. *New Brunswick Courier*, Sept. 3, 1814.
68. *York Gazette*, Feb. 4, 1812.

69. *Montreal Gazette*, Nov. 17, 1812.
70. Bathurst to Prevost, Oct. 31, 1813, CO 43/23.
71. *Liverpool Mercury*, Dec. 4, 1812.
72. *HC Debates*, Nov. 30, 1812, 24: 73.
73. *An Account of the Official and Real Value of Exports from Great Britain, to the British Colonies in North America; in the Years ending the 5th of January 1810, 1811, 1812, 1813, 1814;—distinguishing British Manufactures from Foreign Merchandize* (London, 1814).
74. *On the Past Relations Between Great Britain and the United States* (London, 1813), 4.
75. David Anderson, *Canada: Or, A view of the Importance of the British American Colonies* (London, 1814).
76. *The Report of the Loyal and Patriotic Society of Upper Canada with an appendix and a list of subscribers and benefactors* (Montreal, 1817); *Kingston Gazette*, Dec. 4, 1813. On British charities and North America, see P. J. Marshall, "Who Cared About the Thirteen Colonies? Some Evidence from Philanthropy," *Journal of Imperial and Commonwealth History* 27 (1999): 53–67; Troy Bickham, *Savages Within the Empire: Representing American Indians in Eighteenth-Century Britain* (Oxford, 2005), chapter 6.
77. *Times*, July 5, 1813.
78. *The Report of the Loyal and Patriotic Society of Upper Canada with an appendix and a list of subscribers and benefactors* (Montreal, 1817).
79. Drummond to Council and Assembly of Upper Canada at close of session in March, n.d., CO 42/356.
80. Castlereagh to Bathurst, Oct. 4, 1814, *Historical Manuscripts Commission. Report on the Manuscripts of Earl Bathurst, Preserved at Cirencester Park*, ed. F. Bickley (London, 1923), 295–96.
81. *York Gazette*, Apr. 8, 1815.
82. *Royal Gazette and Bahama Advertiser*, Dec. 18, 1813.
83. *Journals of the Assembly of Jamaica* (Kingston, Jamaica, 1816), 12: 486. A Bahamas select committee complained in December 1813 that its colony paid two to three times the insurance rates of other West Indian colonies; for the report, see Dec. 9, 1813, CO 23/61.
84. *Jamaica Magazine*, Oct. 1812.
85. Beckwith to Goulburn, Dec. 1, 1813, CO 28/82.
86. *Jamaica Magazine*, Feb. 1813.
87. *Royal Gazette and Bahama Advertiser*, Nov. 26, 1814.
88. "Committee Formed to Enquire into Effects of American War on Commerce and Agriculture," *Journals of the Assembly of Jamaica* 12: 486–88. The report was submitted on December 8.
89. On the trials and tribulations of the British West Indies during the American War of Independence, see Andrew Jackson O'Shaughnessy, *An Empire Divided: The American Revolution and the British Caribbean* (Philadelphia, 2000), 238–48.
90. *Journals of the Assembly of Jamaica*, 12: 486.
91. CO 28/81.
92. The Orders in Council, Oct. 26, 1813 effectively affirmed what Barbados and other colonial governments were already doing.
93. *Bahama Gazette*, Aug. 1, 1813; Cameron to Bathurst, Aug. 4, 1813, CO 23/60.
94. George Horsford, acting governor of Bermuda, to Bathurst, Oct. 14, 1812, CO 37/69.
95. Horsford to Bathurst, Nov. 1, 1812, CO 37/69.
96. From the "Committee Formed to Enquire into Effects of American War on Commerce and Agriculture," 12: 487.
97. This is based on the governor's official monthly reports to the Secretary of State. CO 137/34.
98. Ibid., CO 23/59–60.
99. Ibid., CO 137/34–41.
100. CO 28/82.
101. CO 23/59 includes a copy of the counter memorial, signed by seventy-three men.
102. Governor Charles Cameron to Liverpool, July 16, 1812, CO 23/59.
103. Morrison to Bathurst, Sept. 4, 1812, CO 137/134.
104. *Royal Gazette and Bahama Advertiser*, Jan. 12, 1814.

105. Reprinted in the *Bahama Gazette*, July 5, 1812.
106. *Bermuda Gazette*, Aug. 1, 1812.
107. Christopher D. Hall, *British Strategy in the Napoleonic War 1803–1815* (Manchester, 1992), 197–98.
108. f. 132–33 Bathurst to Prevost, Nov. 5, 1813, CO 43/23; f. 133–37 Bathurst to Prevost, Dec. 15, 1813, CO 43/23; f. 157–59 Bathurst to Prevost, July 11, 1814, CO 43/23.
109. Hall, *British Strategy*, 197–98.
110. Bathurst to Prevost, July 11, 1814, CO 43/23.
111. Bathurst to Colonel Sir George Beckwith, Mar. 18, 1813, CO 43/23.
112. Jon Latimer, *1812: War with America* (Cambridge, MA, 2008), 171, C. J. Barlett and Gene A. Smith, "A 'Species of Milito-Nautico-Guerilla-Plundering Warfare': Admiral Alexander Cochrane's Naval Campaign Against the United States, 1814–1815," in *Britain and America Go to War: The Impact of War and Warfare in Anglo-America, 1754–1815*, ed. Julie Flavell and Stephen Conway (Gainesville, FL, 2004), 184–86. Although formed from the royalist French army, the Chasseurs Britanniques had by 1812 become a motley crew of Frenchmen drawn from all walks of life and political principles; they were, in effect, mercenaries.
113. *American Mercury*, July 16, 1813.
114. Ruddock F. Mackay, ed., *From Trafalgar to the Chesapeake: Adventures of an Officer in Nelson's Navy. Vice Adm. William Stanhope Lovell* (Annapolis, MD, 2003), 152.
115. Latimer, *War with America*, 320.
116. *Kingston Gazette*, Jan. 1, 1814.
117. Graves, *In the Midst of Alarms*, 348.
118. *New Brunswick Courier*, Aug. 3, 1814.
119. Bathurst to Prevost, Mar. 5, 1814, CO 43/23.
120. *Aberdeen Journal*, June 22, 1814.
121. *Times*, Oct. 3, 1814.
122. *Royal Gazette and Bahama Advertiser*, Mar. 25, 1814.
123. *London Gazette*, Jan. 9, 1813.
124. *Exeter Flying-Post*, Feb. 25, 1813.
125. *Edinburgh Star*, Jan. 15, 1813.
126. *Carlisle Journal*, Aug. 8, 1812.
127. Liverpool to Castlereagh, Oct. 21, 1814, in *WSD*, 9: 367.
128. *Times*, Sept. 28, 1814, and Oct. 20, 1814.
129. *Times*, Oct. 19, 1814.
130. *A Compressed View of the Points to be Discussed, in Treating with the United States of America; A.D. 1814* (London, 1814), 1.
131. *Exeter Flying-Post*, Mar. 10, 1814.
132. *Edinburgh Star*, May 24, 1814.
133. *Times*, June 2, 1814.
134. *New Monthly Magazine and Universal Register*, Oct. 1814, 267.
135. Donald Hickey, *The War of 1812: A Forgotten Conflict* (Urbana, IL, 1989), 196–201; Anthony S. Pitch, *The Burning of Washington: The British Invasion of 1814* (Annapolis, MD, 1998).
136. *Western Monitor*, Sept. 9, 1814.
137. *Niles' Weekly Register*, Sept. 24, 1814.
138. The French Revolutionary and Napoleonic Wars are littered with atrocities on all sides against civilians that led to the death of more than a million noncombatants across the world. The Royal Navy bombardment of neutral Denmark's capital of Copenhagen in 1807 resulted in destruction of much of the city and the death of thousands of inhabitants; in following the successful siege of Badajoz in April 1812, the victorious British army pillaged and brutalized the inhabitants for three days before order was restored, resulting in the death of thousands of Spanish civilians.
139. *Niles' Weekly Register*, Sept. 24, 1814.
140. *Niles' Weekly Register*, Sept. 10, 1814.
141. *Niles' Weekly Register*, Oct. 27, 1814.

142. Albrecht Koschnik, "Young Federalists, Masculinity, and Partisanship During the War of 1812," in *Beyond the Founders: New Approaches to the Political History of the Early American Republic*, eds. Jeffrey L. Pasley, Andrew W. Robertson, and David Waldstreicher (Chapel Hill, NC, 2004), 159–79.

143. *Edinburgh Star*, Sept. 30, 1814.

144. *Glasgow Courier*, Oct. 1, 1814.

145. *New Monthly Magazine*, Oct. 1814, 365–66.

146. *Bermuda Gazette and Weekly Advertiser*, Oct. 8, 1814.

147. *Morning Chronicle*, Sep. 28, 1814.

148. *London Gazette*, Nov. 8, 1814.

149. *Royal Gazette and Bahama Advertiser*, Sept. 24, 1814.

150. Bathurst to Prevost, Aug. 22, 1814, CO 43/23.

151. *Times*, Oct. 19, 1814.

152. For assessments of Prevost, see especially Wesley B. Turner, *British Generals in the War of 1812: High Command in the Canadas* (Montreal, 1999), chapter 2; C. P. Lucas, *The Canadian War of 1812* (Oxford, 1906), 209–13; and Jeremy Black, *The War of 1812 in the Age of Napoleon* (Norman, OK, 2009), 162–63.

153. *Tiger Dunlop's Upper Canada*, 31.

154. *Royal Gazette and New Brunswick Advertiser*, Oct. 17, 1814.

155. The collection of letters was published that summer as *The Letters of Veritas, Re-Published from the Montreal Herald; Containing a Succinct Narrative of the Military Administration of Sir George Prevost, During his Command in the Canadas; Whereby it will Appear Manifest that the Merit of Preserving Them from the Conquest, Belongs Not to Him* (Montreal, 1815).

156. Prevost to Bathurst, Nov. 6, 1814, CO 42/157.

157. Liverpool to Castlereagh, Oct. 21, 1814, in *WSD*, 9: 367.

Chapter 6

1. William Ellery Channing, *A Sermon Preached in Boston, July 23, 1812, The Day of the Publick Fast* (Boston, 1812), here citing pages 5, 6, 7, 13, 9.

2. For comprehensive, but sometimes differing, views on this broader subject, see especially Nathan O. Hatch, *The Democratization of American Christianity* (New Haven, 1989); and John Butler, *Awash in a Sea of Faith: Christianizing the American People* (Cambridge, MA, 1990).

3. Quoted in Rosemarie Zagarri, *Revolutionary Backlash: Women and Politics in the Early American Republic* (Philadelphia, 2007), 100.

4. William Gribben, *The Churches Militant: The War of 1812 and American Religion* (New Haven, 1973), 19–23. *Boston Gazette* cited on p. 21.

5. David Osgood, *A Solemn Protest Against the Late Declaration of War* (Cambridge, MA, 1812), 5.

6. James H. Broussard, *The Southern Federalists, 1800–1816* (Baton Rouge, 1978), especially chapters 19, and 20. Reflective of his time, Broussard uses a strict nomenclature of Federalist and Republican to describe the newspapers, but 'opposition' and 'pro-administration' might better describe their politics. See also John E. Talmadge, "Georgia's Federalist Press and the War of 1812," *Journal of Southern History* 19 (1953): 488–500.

7. Albrecht Koschnik, "Young Federalists, Masculinity, and Partisanship During the War of 1812," in *Beyond the Founders: New Approaches to the Political History of the Early American Republic*, ed. Jeffrey L. Pasley, Andrew W. Robertson, and David Waldstreicher (Chapel Hill, NC, 2004), 159–79.

8. *Alexandria Daily Gazette*, May 26, 1813.

9. Jeremy Black, *The War of 1812 in the Age of Napoleon* (Norman, OK, 2009), 43.

10. *Western Monitor*, Mar. 10, 1815.

11. Broussard, *Southern Federalists*, especially chapters 19, and 20.

12. *Alexandria Daily Gazette*, June 29, 1813.

13. *Niles' Weekly Register*, Sept. 12, 1812.

14. James Boswell, *The Life of Samuel Johnson* (Dublin, 1792), 2: 211–12.

15. This extract even made the front page of *Niles' Weekly Register*, June 12, 1813.

16. Condy Raguet, *Oration Delivered before the Washington Benevolent Society at the Second Anniversary Meeting* (Philadelphia, 1814), 16. Raguet soon emerged as a leading banker and later became America's first ambassador to Brazil, an appointment made by President James Monroe.

17. William Ellery Channing, *A Sermon Preached in Boston, August 20, 1812, The Day of Humiliation and Prayer, Appointed by the President of the United States, in Consequence of the Declaration of the War Against Britain* (Boston, 1812), 5.

18. Daniel Webster, *An Address Delivered Before the Washington Benevolent Society, at Portsmouth [New Hampshire], July 4, 1812* (Portsmouth, 1812), 21.

19. *Salem Gazette*, July 21, 1812.

20. *Salem Gazette*, July 7, 1812.

21. *AC*, 23: 259–61.

22. *Niles' Weekly Register*, Sept. 12, 1812.

23. DeWitt Clinton, *Jefferson Against Madison's War . . . For a Peace President. By a True Republican* (Boston, 1812), 16.

24. Charles J. Cox, *Oration Delivered before the Washington Association of Philadelphia* (Philadelphia, 1813), 20.

25. *Investigator*, Mar. 15, 1813.

26. *Carolina Federal-Republican*, July 3, 1813.

27. Cox, *Oration*, 19.

28. *Boston Patriot*, June 30, 1813.

29. Clinton, *Jefferson Against Madison's War*, 15.

30. Reprinted in the *Salem Gazette*, July 21, 1812.

31. *Trenton Federalist*, Jan. 29, 1812.

32. Osgood, *A Solemn Protest Against the Late Declaration of War*, 3.

33. Channing, *Sermon Preached in Boston, July 23, 1812*, 16.

34. Francis Brown, *The Evils of War. A Fast Sermon, Delivered At North-Yarmouth* (Portland, 1814), 17.

35. Elizabeth Ann Seton to Juliana Scott, Mar. 14, 1814, in *Letters of Mother Seton to Mrs. Julianna Scott*, ed. Joseph B. Code (New York, 1960), 234.

36. Rebecca Gratz to Benjamin Gratz, 1814?, in *Letters of Rebecca Gratz*, ed. David Philipson (Philadelphia, 1929), 5.

37. Nathan S. S. Beman, *A Sermon, Delivered at the Meeting House of the Second Parish in Portland, August 20, 1812: On the Occasion of the National Fast* (Portland, 1812), 7.

38. Paul Gilje, *Liberty on the Waterfront: American Maritime Culture in the Age of Revolution* (Philadelphia, 2003), 173–74.

39. *Salem Gazette*, July 7, 1812.

40. Brown, *Evils of War*, 6 and 12.

41. Mark Zuehlke, *The War of 1812 and the Brokering of an Uneasy Peace* (Toronto, 2006), 67.

42. Delivered May 30, 1812, and printed in *Niles' Weekly Register*, June 13, 1812.

43. Brown, *Evils of War*, 6

44. Gribben, *Churches Militant*, 20.

45. Brown Emerson, *The Causes and Effects of War. A Sermon Delivered in Salem, August 20, 1812, the Day of National Humiliation and Prayer* (Salem, 1812), 4.

46. Printed in the *Ohio Weekly Recorder*, Feb. 16, 1815.

47. James Abercrombie, *Two Sermons . . . Being Days of Fasting, Humiliation and Prayer* (Philadelphia, 1812), 33.

48. Osgood, *Solemn Protest*, 9.

49. *AC*, 23: 259–61. It was passed by the Massachusetts House of Representatives on June 2, 1812, and presented to Congress on June 11, 1812.

50. *Address, to the Republican Citizens of the State of New-York* (Albany, 1813), 6.

51. Delivered May 30, 1812, and reprinted in *Niles' Weekly Register*, June 13, 1812.

52. On the Federalist focus on internal threats, see Linda K. Kerber, *Federalists in Dissent: Imagery and Ideology in Jeffersonian America* (Ithaca, 1970), 199–200.

53. James Sloan, *Address to the Citizens of the United States, but More Particularly those of the Middle and Eastern States*, 3rd edition (Philadelphia, 1812), 6.

54. The pamphlet was published anonymously. DeWitt Clinton, *The Republican Crisis: Or, an Exposition on the Political Jesuitism of James Madison, President of the United States of America* (Alexandria, 1812).
55. *Western Monitor*, Jan. 13, 1815. On the lack of genuine interest in sailors' suffering, see especially Robert E. Cray, Jr., "Remembering the USS Chesapeake: The Politics of Maritime Death and Impressment," *Journal of the Early Republic* 25 (2005): 445–71.
56. John Lowell, *Perpetual War, the Policy of Mr. Madison* (Boston, 1812), 6, 19, 28.
57. Reprinted in *Niles' Weekly Register*, June 12, 1812.
58. *Festus Foster, An Oration Pronounced before the Washington Benevolent Society, of the County of Franklin in the Town of Northfield. In Commemoration of the Thirty-Seventh Anniversary of American Independence* (Brattleboro, VT, 1813), 15.
59. Lucius Horatio Stockton, *An Address Delivered Before the Convention of the Friends of Peace of the State of New Jersey, July 4, 1814* (Trenton, 1814), 4.
60. *Federal-Republican*, Sept. 18, 1813.
61. On the use of slavery as a rhetorical tool in public debates during the War of 1812, see Matthew Mason, *Slavery and Politics in the Early American Republic* (Chapel Hill, NC, 2006), chapter 2.
62. Sloan, *Address to the Citizens of the United States*, 12.
63. Charles J. Cox, *An Oration Delivered before the Washington Association* (Philadelphia, 1813), 4–6.
64. For example, the *New Brunswick Courier* devoted large portions of two issues to the speech, Mar. 4 and 11, 1813.
65. *Address, to the Republican Citizens of the State of New-York* (Albany, 1813), 5.
66. Samuel Clesson Allen, *An Oration Delivered at Greenfield, July 6, 1812* (Greenfield, Massachusetts, 1812), 16.
67. *Salem Gazette*, July 7, 1812.
68. *Alexandria Gazette*, June 29, 1812.
69. Osgood, *Solemn Protest*, 14.
70. On the tradition of restraint in eighteenth-century riots, see E. P. Thompson, "The Moral Economy of the English Crowd," *Past & Present* 50 (1971): 76–136. Paul A. Gilje, "The Baltimore Riots of 1812 and the Breakdown of the Anglo-American Mob Tradition," *Journal of Southern History* 13 (1980), 547–64.
71. For a comprehensive narrative of the Baltimore riots, see Hickey, *War of 1812*, ch. 3.
72. An account of the assault in Savannah can be found in the North Carolina *Star*, July 3, 1812. Broussard, *Southern Federalists*, 156–57; Talmadge, "Georgia's Federalist Press," May 4, 1813, and Oct. 29, 1813.
73. *Greensburgh & Indiana Register*, July 9, 1812.
74. *Mercury*, Aug. 8, 1812.
75. *Salem Gazette*, July 17 and 21, 1812.
76. George Washington Parke Custis, *Oration of Mr. Custis, of Arlington; with an Account of the Funeral Solemnities in Honor of the Lamented Gen. James M. Lingan* (Washington City, 1812), 12–13.
77. Richard Buel, Jr., *America on the Brink: How the Political Struggle over the War of 1812 Almost Destroyed the Young Republic* (New York, 2005), 163–64.
78. Foster, *An Oration Pronounced before the Washington Benevolent Society*, 12.
79. Hickey, *War of 1812*, 70.
80. Hext McCall, *An Oration, Delivered in St. Michael's Church, Before the Inhabitants of Charleston, South Carolina, on the Fourth of July 1810* (Charleston, 1810), 4; Thomas McAdory Owen and Marie Bankhead Owen, *History of Alabama and Dictionary of Alabama Biography* (Chicago, 1921), 3: 831.
81. Jabez Chickering, *An Oration Pronounced at Dedham . . . July 4th, 1812* (Boston, 1812), 5.
82. *Missouri Gazette*, Oct. 23, 1813. The editorial was largely reprinted from the *Boston Patriot*.
83. Sloan, *Address to the Citizens of the United States*, 10.
84. *Boston Spectator*, Mar. 26, 1814.
85. Buel, *America on the Brink*, 205–6.
86. *American Mercury*, Aug. 3, 1813.

87. George W. Stanley, *An Oration, Delivered at Wallingford, April 4, 1814; in Celebration of the Late Glorious Events in Europe; which have resulted in the Overthrow of the Tyrant of France, and the Restoration of Civil Liberty to the Enslaved Nations of the Continents* (New Haven, 1814), 3, 10.

88. For descriptions, see the *Daily Advertiser and Repository*, June 16, 1814; *New England Palladium*, June 17, 1814.

89. William Ellery Channing, *A Discourse, Delivered in Boston at the Solemn Festival in Commemoration of the Goodness of God in Delivering the Christian World from Military Despotism* (Boston, 1814).

90. *Salem Gazette*, July 12, 1814.

91. Daniel Webster, *Papers of Daniel Webster: Speeches and Formal Writings* (Hanover, NH, 1986), 1: 19–30.

92. *American Mercury*, Aug. 26, 1812.

93. *National Intelligencer*, Aug. 14, 1812.

94. *"Free Trade and Sailor's Rights!" An Address to the Independent Electors of the State of New York* (Albany, 1813), 12.

95. Richard Bache, *Oration Delivered at Spring Garden ... to a Very Numerous and Respectable Company of Democratic Republicans, of the City and County of Philadelphia* (Philadelphia, 1813), 7.

96. *Niles' Weekly Register*, June 27, 1812.

97. Asa Aikens, *An Oration, Pronounced before the Republican Citizens of Windsor, on Their Celebration ... of American Independence* (Windsor, VT, 1812), 5.

98. *Military Monitor*, Sept. 14, 1812.

99. *Niles' Weekly Register*, June 27, 1812.

100. *American Advocate*, July 2, 1812.

101. *Boston Patriot*, Sept. 11, 1813.

102. See for example, George Hough, *A Defence of the Clergy of New-England ... and Condemning the Policy of the Present War* (Concord, 1814), the bulk of which first appeared as a series of letters in the *Concord Gazette*; and James Abercrombie, *Two Sermons ... Being Days of Fasting, Humiliation and Prayer* (Philadelphia, 1812), who published his sermons specifically in retaliation for what the pro-war press had said about him.

103. Gribben, *Churches Militant*, 91.

104. Ibid., 105–6. This sort of attitude of cautious support for the national government and disdain for the French Revolution and Napoleon as destroyers of the church is evident among the senior Catholic clergy in the British Empire as well as the United States. See Luca Codignola, "'France's Cromwell' to 'Consummate Brigand': North Atlantic Catholics and Napoleon, 1789–1815," in Christophe Belaubre, Jordana Dym, and John Savage, eds., *Napoleon's Atlantic: The Impact of Napoleonic Empire in the Atlantic World* (Leiden, 2010), 25–44.

105. Gribben, *Churches Militant*, 70.

106. William Parkinson, *A Sermon, Delivered in the Meeting House of the First Baptist Church, in the City of New-York* (New York, 1812).

107. Joseph Richardson, *An Oration, Pronounced July 4, 1812, Before the Citizens of the County of Plymouth on the Anniversary of Independence* (Boston, 1812), 16, 21.

108. *National Intelligencer*, Mar. 22, 1813.

109. *Boston Spectator*, Apr. 30, 1813.

110. *American Advocate* (Maine), July 2, 1812.

111. Parkinson, *Sermon*, 23.

112. *National Intelligencer*, July 8, 1813.

113. John Burnham, *An Oration Pronounced at Hillsborough, New-Hampshire; July 4, 1810, the Anniversary of American independence* (Concord, New Hampshire, 1810), 20.

114. *AC*, 23: 1410.

115. *Niles' Weekly Register*, June 27, 1812.

116. Gerry to Madison, May 19, 1812, cited in Hickey, *War of 1812*, 28.

117. Steven Watts, *The Republic Reborn: War and the Making of Liberal America, 1790–1820* (Baltimore, 1987), 61.

118. Berkeley to Bathurst, Aug. 13, 1807, in *Historical Manuscripts Commission. Report on the Manuscripts of Earl Bathurst, preserved at Cirencester Park*, ed. F. Bickley (London, 1923), 63–65.

119. Latimer, *War with America*, 348.
120. Beckwith to Bathurst, Nov. 26, 1813, CO 28/82; Beckwith to Bathurst, Jan. 18, 1814, CO 28/83; and Bathurst to Beckwith, Feb. 10, 1814, CO 29/83.
121. *Northern Grievances, Set Forth in a Letter to James Madison* (New York, 1814).
122. *Boston Spectator*, Nov. 5, 1814.
123. Mason, *Slavery and Politics in the Early American Republic*, 52–63.
124. For the best discussion of the Hartford convention and its limited outcome, see James M. Banner, Jr., *To the Hartford Convention: The Federalists and the Origins of Party Politics in Massachusetts, 1789–1815* (New York, 1970).
125. Clinton, *Jefferson Against Madison's War*, 11; *Western Monitor*, Aug. 3, 1814.
126. *Western Monitor*, Jan. 27, 1815.
127. *National Intelligencer*, Jan. 15, 1813.
128. *Niles' Weekly Register*, Nov. 20 and 26, 1814.
129. Printed in *Niles' Weekly Register*, Nov. 26, 1814.
130. Ibid., Feb. 11, 1815.
131. *Western American*, Feb. 11, 1815.
132. *Union*, Feb. 17, 1815.
133. Buel, *America on the Brink*, 219–22; and J. C. A. Stagg, *Mr. Madison's War: Politics, Diplomacy, and Warfare in the Early American Republic, 1783–1830* (Princeton, 1983), 477–78.
134. *Northern Grievances, Set Forth in a Letter to James Madison* (New York, 1814), 13.
135. Enclosed with Sherbrooke's letter to Bathurst, Nov. 20, 1814, CO 217/93.
136. Bathurst to Sherbrooke, Dec. 13, 1814, CO 218/29.

Chapter 7

1. Troy Bickham, *Making Headlines: The American Revolution as Seen Through the British Press* (DeKalb, IL, 2009), chapter 1; and P. D. G. Thomas, "The Beginning of Parliamentary Reporting in Newspapers, 1768–1774," *English Historical Review* 74 (1959): 623–36.
2. *The Six Letters of A.B. on The Differences Between Great Britain and the United States of America, with a preface by the Editor of the Morning Chronicle* (London, 1807), 4, 6, 12, 19.
3. *Liverpool Mercury*, Oct. 30, 1812.
4. *Whitehall Evening Post*, Sept. 4, 1755.
5. See especially, Bickham, *Making Headlines*, chapter 3; J. H. Plumb, "British Attitudes to the American Revolution," in his *In the Light of History* (Boston, 1972); Sheldon S. Cohen, *British Supporters of the American Revolution 1775–1783* (Rochester, NY, 2004); Jerome R. Reich, *British Friends of the American Revolution* (London, 1998); and John Sainsbury, *Disaffected Patriots: London Supporters of Revolutionary America, 1769–1782* (Montreal, 1987).
6. Stephen Conway, *Britain, Ireland, and Continental Europe in the Eighteenth Century: Similarities, Connection, Identities* (Oxford, 2011), 94–97.
7. For examples, see especially Mark Philip, *The French Revolution and British Popular Politics* (Cambridge, 1991); Ceri Crossley and Ian Small, *The French Revolution and British Culture* (Oxford, 1989); Albert Goodwin, *The Friends of Liberty: The English Democratic Movement in the Age of the French Revolution* (Cambridge, MA, 1979); H. T. Dickinson, *British Radicalism and the French Revolution, 1789–1815* (Oxford, 1989); and Dickinson, *The Politics of the People in Eighteenth-Century Britain* (London, 1995), chapters 7, and 8. For a close study of how loyalism and radicalism both became more centrist in practice in the first decade of the nineteenth century, see Katrina Navickas, *Loyalism and Radicalism in Lancashire, 1798–1815* (Oxford, 2009).
8. James E. Bradley, "The British Public and the American Revolution: Ideology, Interest and Opinion" in *Britain and the American Revolution*, ed. H. T. Dickinson (London, 1998), 124–54.
9. For an analysis of the petitions, see J. E. Cookson, *The Friends of Peace: Anti-War Liberalism in England, 1793–1815* (Cambridge, 1982), chapter 10.
10. *Morning Chronicle*, Feb. 9, 1814.
11. *Liverpool Mercury*, Oct. 16, 1812.

12. This figure includes militia and volunteers. J. E. Cookson, *The British Armed Nation, 1793–1815* (Oxford, 1997), 95; Clive Emsley, *British Society and the French Wars, 1793–1815* (London, 1979), 169.

13. *Aberdeen Chronicle*, Oct. 16, 1813.

14. *Liverpool Mercury*, June 19, 1812.

15. As a rough contemporary comparison, this average rate of taxation is 25 percent higher than it was in the United States in 2007 and slightly lower than in Britain for the same year. See Jeremy Black, *Britain as a Military Power, 1688–1815* (London, 2006), 268–69; Douglas Hay and Nicholas Rodgers, *Eighteenth-Century English Society* (Oxford, 1997), 153; Cookson, *British Armed Nation*, 95; Linda Colley, *Britons: Forging of the Nation 1707–1837* (New Haven, CT, 1992), chapter 7. Emsley, *British Society and the French Wars*, 169–70; and Martin Daunton, *Trusting the Leviathan: The Politics of Taxation in Britain, 1799–1914* (Cambridge, 2001), especially chapter 2.

16. *Liverpool Mercury*, Jan. 17, 1812. The emphasis is in the original passage.

17. *Cobbett's Weekly Register*, Nov. 20, 1813.

18. *Liverpool Mercury*, July 16, 1813.

19. *Aberdeen Chronicle*, Apr. 10, 1813.

20. J. C. A. Stagg, *Mr. Madison's War: Politics, Diplomacy, and Warfare in the Early American Republic, 1783–1830* (Princeton, 1983), 14.

21. B. H. Tolley, "The Liverpool Campaign Against the Orders in Council and the War of 1812," in *Liverpool and Merseyside: Essays in the Economic and Social History of the Port and Its Hinterland*, ed. J. R. Harris (London, 1969), 106.

22. *Carlisle Journal*, June 20, 1812.

23. Tolley, "Liverpool Campaign," 107–18.

24. *Liverpool Mercury*, Feb. 28, 1812.

25. Emsley, *British Society and the French Wars*, 153.

26. For excellent diagrams illustrating the anatomy of the Liverpool-Philadelphia trade, see Sheryllynne Haggerty, *The British-Atlantic Trading Community, 1760–1810: Men, Women, and the Distribution of Goods* (Boston, 2006), 192 and 201.

27. See especially Brian Bailey, *The Luddite Rebellion* (New York, 1998); John Stevenson, *Popular Disturbances in England, 1700–1870* (London, 1998), chapter 7; and Adrian Randall, *Riotous Assemblies: Popular Protest in Hanoverian England* (Oxford, 2006), chapter 11.

28. Emsley, *British Society and the French Wars*, 155.

29. James Raven, *Judging New Wealth: Popular Publishing and Responses to Commerce in England, 1750–1800* (Oxford, 1992), especially chapters 10, and 11.

30. Perceval was assassinated in the lobby of the House of Commons by John Bellingham, a merchant who had lost his fortune in the Russian trade and been imprisoned there. On his release, he sought compensation from the British government, which he was denied. He took out his frustrations on Perceval, and he did not resist capture.

31. On tory resistance to free trade imperialism, see especially Bernard Semmel, *The Rise of Free Trade Imperialism: Classical Political Economy, the Empire of Free Trade and Imperialism* (Cambridge: Cambridge University Press, 1970), chapters 1–3. On the Corn Law of 1815, see especially Boyd Hilton, *Corn, Cash, Commerce: The Economic Policies of the Tory Governments 1815–1830* (Oxford: Oxford University Press, 1977), 3–30.

32. *Liverpool Mercury*, Jan. 15, 1813.

33. *Leeds Mercury*, Jan. 11, 1812.

34. *Glasgow Journal*, Mar. 6, 1812.

35. *Liverpool Mercury*, June 26, 1812.

36. *Leeds Mercury*, Mar. 28, 1812.

37. Printed in the *Liverpool Mercury*, Apr. 24, 1812.

38. *Minutes of Evidence, Taken before the Committee of the Whole House, to whom it was Referred, to Consider of the several Petitions which have been Presented to the House, in this session of Parliament, relating to the Orders in Council* (London, 1812), 19–20.

39. *Leeds Mercury*, June 6, 1812.

40. Berkeley to Bathurst, Aug. 13, 1807, in *Historical Manuscripts Commission. Report on the Manuscripts of Earl Bathurst, preserved at Cirencester Park*, ed. F. Bickley (London, 1923), 87–89.

41. Denis Gray, *Spencer Perceval: The Evangelical Prime Minister 1762–1812* (Manchester, 1963), 170–77 and 451.

42. Madison to Jefferson, June 22, 1812, *CBJM*, 3: 1698.

43. *Dublin Evening Post*, May 23, 1812.

44. *Times*, May 20, 1812.

45. Norman Gash, *Lord Liverpool: The Life and Political Career of Robert Banks Jenkinson Second Earl of Liverpool 1770–1828* (Cambridge, MA, 1984), 90–96.

46. The narrative of events discussed here is largely taken from Gray, *Spencer Perceval*; and Gash, *Lord Liverpool*.

47. Boyd Hilton, *A Mad, Bad, and Dangerous People? England 1783–1846* (Oxford, 2006), 200.

48. Gash, *Lord Liverpool*, 93–96.

49. Emsley, *British Society and the French Wars*, 160.

50. *Liverpool Mercury*, July 10, 1812.

51. *Glasgow Courier*, June 27, 1812.

52. *Exeter Flying-Post*, July 25, 1812.

53. *Liverpool Mercury*, July 10, 1812.

54. *Freeman's Journal*, June 11, 1812.

55. Hilton, *Mad, Bad, and Dangerous People*, 198; John W. Derry, *Politics in the Age of Fox, Pitt and Liverpool* (London, 2001), 116.

56. Tolley, "Liverpool Campaign," 120–21.

57. Cookson, *Friends of Peace*, 235.

58. *Aberdeen Journal*, July 21, 1813.

59. The most referenced were 6 Anne, C. 37, S. 20; 1 Geo I. C. 4; 13 Geo. II. C. 3.

60. *Why Are We Still at War? Or the American Question Considered* (London, 1814), 569–70.

61. *Cobbett's Weekly Political Register*, Dec. 17, 1814.

62. *Liverpool Mercury*, Aug. 7, 1812.

63. *HC Debates*, Feb. 18, 1813, 24: 630.

64. *Cobbett's Weekly Political Register*, Sept. 24, 1814.

65. *Caledonian Mercury*, Mar. 9, 1812.

66. *Carlisle Journal*, Mar. 28, 1812.

67. *HC Debates*, Feb. 13, 1812, 21: 783.

68. *Leeds Mercury*, July 31, 1813.

69. Board of Trade to William Hamilton, Jan. 18, 1812, FO/92; Foreign Office to Foster, Feb. 1, 1812, FO 5/83.

70. *Caledonian Mercury*, June 6, 1812.

71. *Carlisle Journal*, July 4, 1812.

72. *Leeds Mercury*, June 13, 1812.

73. *Cobbett's Weekly Political Register*, Dec. 17, 1814.

74. *Edinburgh Star*, Jan. 15, 1813.

75. *Aberdeen Chronicle*, Oct. 8, 1813.

76. *Cobbett's Weekly Journal*, Oct. 8, 1814.

77. *Liverpool Mercury*, Oct. 17, 1814.

78. *Leeds Mercury*, Oct. 1, 1814.

79. Wellington to Castlereagh, Oct. 4, 1814, *WSD*, vol. ix, 314–16.

80. *Aberdeen Chronicle*, Oct. 15, 1814.

81. For the shift in the public discussion, see Bickham, *Making Headlines*; for the shift in the parliamentary discussion, Frank O'Gorman, "The Parliamentary Opposition to the Government's American Policy 1760–1782," in H. T. Dickinson, ed., *Britain and the American Revolution* (London, 1998), 97–123.

82. See especially Eliga Gould, *The Persistence of Empire: British Political Cultures in the Age of the American Revolution* (London, 2000); Bob Harris, "'American Idols': Empire, War and the Middling Ranks in Mid-Eighteenth-Century Britain," *Past and Present* 150 (1996): 111–41; and P. J. Marshall, "A Nation Defined by Empire, 1755–1776," *Uniting the Kingdom? The Making of British History*, ed. Alexander Grant and Keith Stringer (London, 1995), 208–22; H. V. Bowen, "British Conception of Global Empire, 1756–83," *Journal of Imperial and Commonwealth History* 26 (1998), 1–27.

83. Stephen Conway, "From Fellow-Nationals to Foreigners: British Perceptions of the Americans, circa 1739–1783," *William and Mary Quarterly* 3rd ser., 59 (2002). For an examination of the "neomercantilists," see Leonard J. Sadosky, "Reimagining the British Empire and America in an Age of Revolution," in Leonard J. Sadosky, Peter Nicolaisen, Peter S. Onuf, and Andrew O'Shaughnessy, eds., *Old World, New World: America and Europe in the Age of Jefferson* (Charlottesville, VA, 2010), 83–104.

84. *Morning Chronicle*, July 31, 1812.

85. *Freeman's Journal*, Oct. 5, 1812.

86. *HC Debates*, Jan. 7, 1812, 21: 18.

87. *Inverness Journal*, Oct. 7, 1814.

88. *HC Debates*, Jan. 21, 1812, 21: 258.

89. Ibid., Feb. 13, 1812, 21: 792.

90. Christopher Leslie Brown, *Moral Capital: Foundations of British Abolitionism* (Chapel Hill, NC, 2006); Nicholas B. Dirks, *The Scandal of Empire: India and the Creation of Imperial Britain* (Cambridge, MA, 2006); and J. R. Osborn, "India, Parliament and the Press Under George III" (D.Phil. thesis, University of Oxford, 1999).

91. P. J. Marshall, *Making and Unmaking of Empires: Britain, India, and America c. 1750–1783* (Oxford, 2005).

92. *HC Debates*, Feb. 13, 1812, 21: 789.

93. *Cobbett's Weekly Political Register*, May 7, 1814.

94. *HC Debates*, Feb. 13, 1812, 21: 771.

95. *Aberdeen Chronicle*, Feb. 27, 1813.

96. *Edinburgh Star*, May 24, 1814.

97. *Times*, Sept. 28, 1814.

98. *Cobbett's Weekly Political Register*, Jan. 2, 1813. The emphasis is in the original passage.

99. Ibid., Dec. 24, 1814.

100. Ibid., Oct. 8, 1814.

101. *Leeds Mercury*, Apr. 23, 1814.

Chapter 8

1. *Adams Memoirs*, 3–4.

2. James Madison, *Message from the President . . . to Both Houses of Congress, at the Commencement of the First Session of the Thirteenth Congress. May 25, 1813* (Washington, 1813), 4.

3. *Niles' Weekly Register*, Aug. 24, 1813.

4. Castlereagh to Sir George Cathcart, July 14, 1813, in *British Diplomacy, 1813–1815: Select Documents Dealing with the Reconstruction of Europe*, C. K. Webster (London, 1921), 14.

5. Cathcart to Castlereagh, Aug. 5, 1813, *Documents Dealing with the Reconstruction of Europe*, 16.

6. *James Gallatin Diary*, 5.

7. Ibid., 12.

8. Monroe to Castlereagh, Jan. 5, 1814, FO 5/100. See also James Madison, *Message of the President . . . to Both Houses of Congress, at the Commencement of the Second Session of the Thirteenth Congress* (Washington, 1813), 3.

9. *James Gallatin Diary*, 24–25.

10. Gallatin to Monroe, June 13, 1814, *Gallatin Papers*, 1: 628.

11. Gallatin and Bayard to Monroe, May 6, 1814, *Gallatin Papers*, 1: 612–13.

12. Quoted in Mark Zuehlke, *The War of 1812 and the Brokering of an Uneasy Peace* (Toronto, 2006), 274–75.

13. Following the final defeat of Napoleon in 1815, Ghent became part of the United Kingdom of Netherlands until the Belgian Revolution fifteen years later, when Ghent became part of the Kingdom of Belgium.

14. Madison to Jefferson, May 10, 1814, *CBJM*, 3: 1742.

15. *Boston Spectator*, Feb. 12, 1815.

16. *James Gallatin Diary*, 27–28.

17. "Lesser talents," Taylor, *Civil War of 1812*, 412; "was perhaps the ablest," George C. Herring, *From Colony to Superpower: U.S. Foreign Relations Since 1776* (Oxford, 2008), 129; "consistently outmaneuvered," Hickey, *Forgotten War*, 281. See also Latimer, *1812: War with America*, 360–61; Wood, *Empire of Liberty*, 695–96; Perkins, *Castlereagh and Adams*, 59–61; and Walter R. Borneman, *1812: The War That Forged a Nation* (New York, 2004), 263.

18. *Aberdeen Chronicle*, Sept. 17, 1814.

19. *Liverpool Mercury*, Oct. 17, 1814.

20. For detailed discussions, see for example ibid., Aug. 19, 1814, and *Times*, Nov. 26, 1814.

21. *Bermuda Gazette*, Jan. 14, 1815.

22. For details of their lives, see Zuehlke, *War of 1812*, 278–79.

23. On Goulburn, see Brian Jenkins, *Henry Goulburn, 1784–1856: A Political Biography* (London, 1996); Neville Thompson, *Earl of Bathurst and the British Empire, 1762–1834* (Barnsley, Yorkshire, 1999), 53; Wilbur Devereux Jones, "A British View of the War of 1812 and the Peace Negotiations," *Mississippi Valley Historical Review* 45 (1958): 481–87.

24. Liverpool to Bathurst, Oct. 1, 1814, *WSD*, 9: 298–99. Supplementary Despatches [WSD], Correspondence, and Memoranda of Field Marshal Arthur, Duke of Wellington, K. G., 15 vols. (London, 1858–1872).

25. Goulburn to Bathurst, Ghent, Sept. 5, 1814, *WSD*, 9: 221–22.

26. Jenkins, *Goulburn*, 84–85.

27. *Adams Memoirs*, 24–26.

28. Thompson, *Bathurst*, 83.

29. Wellington to Castlereagh, Oct. 4, 1814, *WSD*, 9: 314–15.

30. Liverpool to Castlereagh, Oct. 28, 1814, *WSD*, 9: 382–83.

31. Clay to Crawford, Oct. 17, 1814, *Clay Papers*, 1: 989.

32. Clay to Monroe, Aug. 18, 1814, *Clay Papers*, 967.

33. La Fayette to Gallatin, May 2, 1814, *Gallatin Papers*, 1: 620.

34. Barclay to Castlereagh, marked "Private Cypher," May 20, 1813, FO 5/95; Barclay to William Hamilton, Feb. 16, 1814, f. 20 in cipher, FO 5/100; Barclay to Castlereagh, Mar. 17, 1814, FO 5/100; Barclay to Castlereagh (in cipher) Apr. 9, 1814, FO 5/100.

35. Jenkins, *Goulburn*, 82.

36. Liverpool to Castlereagh, Sept. 2, 1814, *WSD*, 9: 214.

37. Liverpool to Bathurst, Sep. 11, 1814, *WSD*, 9: 240.

38. Goulburn to Bathurst, Sep. 16, 1814, *WSD*, 9: 265–67.

39. Gallatin to Monroe, Dec. 24, 1814, *Gallatin Papers*, 644. The British had access to almost all of the American correspondence sent from Europe, including the delegates' banking records. The primary exception was correspondence sent directly from Ghent, because the American delegation typically used its own couriers. The British had also broken the cipher Adams used in Russia. For some of the letters the British intercepted and copied, see FO 5/98. It is discussed in a foreign office letter dated June 22, 1813, FO 5/98.

40. Monroe's instruction to the plenipotentiaries, May 15, 1813, *ASP: FR*, 3: 695–700.

41. Gallatin and Bayard to Monroe, London, May 6, 1814, 1: 612.

42. Gallatin to Monroe, June 13, 1814, *Gallatin Papers*, 1: 629.

43. Borneman, 266; Taylor, *Civil War of 1812*, 413.

44. Castlereagh instructions to the commissioners, July 28, 1814, FO 5/101; Castlereagh to commissioners, Aug. 14, 1814, FO 5/101.

45. For the reaction to the British note of September 20, see *Adams Memoirs*, 37. Clay to Monroe, Aug. 18, 1814, *Clay Papers*, 1: 963.

46. Albert Gallatin burned the letter, but it is described by his son; *James Gallatin Diaries*, 34.

47. *Adams Memoirs*, 32 and 61.

48. Ibid., 53.

49. *James Gallatin Diaries*, 28; Zuehlke, *War of 1812*, 390.

50. Ibid., 30.

51. *Adams Memoirs*, 23–24.

52. On Maine, see *Adams Memoirs*, 20.

53. Castlereagh's instructions to the commissioners, July 28, 1814, FO 5/101.

54. Hilton, *A Mad, Bad, and Dangerous People*, 241.

55. For the British commissioners' response to the American complaint, see Sept. 4, 1814, FO 5/102.
56. Taylor, *Civil War of 1812*, 414.
57. Goulburn to Bathurst, Aug. 9, 1814, *WSD*, 9: 177–78.
58. Bathurst to Prevost, Dec. 9, 1812, CO 42/147.
59. British diplomatic note to the American envoys, Aug. 26, 1814, *WSD*, 9: 194–96.
60. Castlereagh's instructions to the commissioners, July 28, 1814, FO 5/101.
61. *Adams Memoirs*, 25.
62. Clay to Monroe, Aug. 18, 1814, *Clay Papers*, 967.
63. Castlereagh to commissioners, Aug. 14, 1814, FO 5/101.
64. For the September 9, 1814, diplomatic note from the American delegation to the British delegation, see *WSD*, 9: 249–55.
65. *Adams Memoirs*, 24–6.
66. Clay to Monroe, Aug. 18, 1814, *Clay Papers*, 964.
67. American response note to the British delegation, Sep. 9, 1814, *WSD*, 9: 251.
68. *James Gallatin Diaries*, 27–28.
69. *Niles' Weekly Register*, May 15, 1813.
70. *Military Monitor*, Aug. 2, 1813.
71. *Union*, Oct. 22, 1814.
72. This was reprinted throughout the country; see, for example, *Niles' Weekly Register*, Sept. 24, 1814.
73. Monroe to Will B. Giles, chairman of the Committee of the Senate on Military Affairs, Oct. 17, 1814, in *ASP: MA*, 1: 514–17.
74. Madison to Jefferson, Oct. 10, 1814, *CBJM*, 3: 1746.
75. William Ellery Channing, *A Sermon, Delivered in Boston . . . at the Request of the Hearers* (Boston, 1814), 6–7 and 14.
76. *National Intelligencer*, Oct. 25, 1814.
77. *Greensburgh & Indiana Register*, Jan. 21, 1815.
78. *National Intelligencer*, Nov. 5, 1814.
79. Liverpool to Bathurst, Sept. 11, 1814, *WSD*, 9: 240.
80. On the intrigue at Vienna, see especially Roy Muir, *Britain and the Defeat of Napoleon 1807–1815* (New Haven, CT, 1996), chapter 18; Harold George Nicholson, *The Congress of Vienna: A Study in Allied Unity, 1812–1822*, 2nd edition (London, 1948); and Adam Zamoyski, *Rites of Peace: The Fall of Napoleon & the Congress of Vienna* (New York, 2007).
81. Liverpool to Bathurst, Jan. 16, 1815, *Historical Manuscripts Commission. Report on the Manuscripts of Earl Bathurst, Preserved at Cirencester Park*, ed. F. Bickley (London, 1923), 324.
82. Latimer, *War with America*, 37.
83. *Edinburgh Star*, June 7, 1814.
84. *Aberdeen Chronicle*, Sept. 17, 1814.
85. *Liverpool Mercury*, Sept. 23, 1814.
86. *Cobbett's Weekly Register*, Nov. 5, 1814.
87. Norman Gash, *Lord Liverpool: The Life and Political Career of Robert Banks Jenkinson Second Earl of Liverpool 1770–1828* (Cambridge, MA, 1984), 113–14.
88. Liverpool to Castlereagh, Oct. 28, 1814, *WSD*, 9: 382.
89. Jeremy Black, *The War of 1812 in the Age of Napoleon* (Norman: OK, 2009), 207; and Gash, *Liverpool*, 126–27.
90. Castlereagh to Liverpool, Aug. 28, 1814, *WSD*, 9: 192–93.
91. Bathurst, who was running the foreign office in Castlereagh's absence, to the British commissioners, Sep. 27, 1814, FO 5/101; Liverpool to Bathurst, Sept. 30, 1814, *Historical Manuscripts Commission. Report on the Manuscripts of Earl Bathurst, Preserved at Cirencester Park*, ed. F. Bickley (London, 1923), 294–95; and Liverpool to Wellington and Castlereagh, Sep. 27, 1814, *WSD*, 9: 290.
92. Clay to Crawford, Oct. 17, 1814, *Clay Papers*, 1: 988.
93. Liverpool to Bathurst, Sept. 11, 1814, *WSD*, 9: 240.
94. Gallatin to Monroe, Aug. 20, 1814, *Gallatin Papers*, 1: 637–39.
95. Liverpool to Castlereagh, Oct. 21, 1814, *WSD*, 9: 367.

96. Ibid., Oct. 28, 1814, *WSD*, 9: 382–83; Liverpool to Wellington, Oct. 28, 1814, *WSD*, 9: 384.
97. Liverpool to Castlereagh, Nov. 2, 1814, *WSD*, 9: 402; Liverpool to Castlereagh, Oct. 28, 1814, *WSD*, 9: 382–83; Muir, *Britain and the Defeat of Napoleon*, 339–40.
98. Liverpool to Castlereagh, Nov. 4, 1814, *WSD*, 9: 404–5.
99. Wellington to Liverpool, Nov. 9, 1814, *WSD*, 9: 424–26.
100. Liverpool to Castlereagh, Nov. 18, 1814, *WSD*, 9: 438.
101. Liverpool to Canning, Dec. 28, 1814, *WSD*, 9: 513–15.
102. Goulburn to Bathurst, Ghent, Nov. 25, 1814, *WSD*, 9: 452–54.
103. Jenkins, *Goulburn*, 89.
104. Ibid., 88.
105. *Adams Memoirs*, 71.
106. Goulburn to Bathurst, Dec. 1, 1814, *WSD*, 9: 460–61.
107. Liverpool to Castlereagh, Dec. 23, 1814, *WSD*, 9: 495.
108. Goulburn to Bathurst, Dec. 30, 1812, *WSD*, 9: 516–17.
109. *James Gallatin Diaries*, 35–36.
110. *Adams Memoirs*, 126; Gallatin to Monroe, Dec. 25, 1812, *Gallatin Papers*, 1: 645; and Clay to Monroe, Dec. 25, 1814, *Clay Papers*, 1: 1007.

Conclusion

1. Bathurst to Baker, Dec. 31, 1814, FO 5/105.
2. Baker to Castlereagh, Feb. 19, 1815, FO 5/106.
3. *Caledonian Mercury*, Dec. 31, 1814.
4. *Exeter Flying-Post*, Dec. 29, 1812.
5. *Leeds Mercury*, Dec. 31, 1814. The reference is to Luke 2:14.
6. *Edinburgh Star*, Jan. 13, 1815.
7. *Liverpool Mercury*, Dec. 30, 1814.
8. *Morning Chronicle*, Dec. 27, 1814.
9. *Freeman's Journal*, Jan. 5, 1814.
10. *Times*, Dec. 26, 1814.
11. Ibid., Dec. 28, 1812.
12. *Edinburgh Star*, Feb. 3, 1815.
13. For reports on the debates in the London Common Council on the address, see the *Morning Chronicle*, Jan. 13, 1815; the address itself, which appeared in newspapers throughout the country, was first printed in the government's official newspaper, the *London Gazette*, on Feb. 25, 1815.
14. Public and government reactions were shock at the defeat, but it received little attention in Britain. For examples of comment, see *Morning Chronicle*, Mar. 9, 1815, and *Times* of the same day, which was grateful that the British public discussion had moved on to other topics.
15. British forces took Fort Bowyer at Mobile Point (modern Alabama) on February 12, just before they learned of the peace of Ghent.
16. Stephen Bovell, *A Thanksgiving Sermon, Delivered April 13th, 1815. On Occasion of the Treaty of Peace* (Abingdon, Virginia, 1815), 15, 16.
17. *AC*, 28: 1156.
18. Ibid., 1159.
19. For an interesting assessment that gives a breakdown of the travel of the news in the measurement of hours, see Maine's *American Advocate*, Feb. 18, 1815.
20. *American Advocate*, Feb. 25, 1815.
21. Ibid., Mar. 9, 1815.
22. Lucile Gafford, "The Boston Stage and the War of 1812," *New England Quarterly* 7 (1934): 332–33.
23. *Western Monitor*, Mar. 10, 1815.
24. James Madison, *Message from the President . . . Transmitting the Treaty of Peace and Amity between the United States and His Britannic Majesty* (Washington, 1815), preface.
25. Ohio *Western American*, Mar. 4, 1815.

26. John E. Latta, *A Sermon Preached at New-Castle . . . for the Restoration of Peace* (Wilmington, 1815).

27. *Peace on Honorable Terms to America Ratified . . .* (broadside), Feb. 17, 1815 (Boston, 1815).

28. John Smith, *A Sermon Preached . . . on Account of Peace with Great Britain* (Haverhill, MA, 1815), 5.

29. *Boston Spectator*, Feb. 18, 1815.

30. *Western Monitor*, Mar. 10, 1815.

31. Humphrey Moore, *An Oration Prepared to be Delivered at Nottinghamwest, N.H. . . . in Celebration of the Late Peace* (Amherst, 1815), 14.

32. Ibid., 4.

33. Benjamin Tappin, *An Address, Delivered at the Request of the Washington Benevolent Society of Kennebec, at Their Celebration of Peace, March 2d, 1815* (Hallowell, 1815), 6.

34. Smith, *Sermon Preached*, 7.

35. *Memoirs of the Late Mrs. Susan Huntington, of Boston, Mass., Consisting Principally of Extracts from her Journal and Letters: with the Sermon Occasioned by her Death*, 2nd edition, ed. Benjamin B. Wisner (Boston, 1826), 121.

36. Moore, *An Oration Prepared to be Delivered at Nottinghamwest, N.H.*, 11, 12.

37. *Missouri Gazette*, Mar. 24, 1815.

38. Madison, *Message from the President . . . Transmitting the Treaty of Peace and Amity between the United States and His Britannic Majesty*, preface.

39. *An Oration, Delivered at the Washington Association of Philadelphia, and the Washington Benevolent Society of Pennsylvania, on the Fourth of July, 1815* (Philadelphia, 1815), 12.

40. Jeremy Black, *The War of 1812 in the Age of Napoleon* (Norman, OK, 2009), 232–33.

41. Daniel Clark Sanders, *An Address, Delivered in Sherburne . . . Occasioned by the Celebration of the Peace of Ghent* (Dedham, MA, 1815), 13.

42. *An Oration, Delivered at the Washington Association of Philadelphia . . . Fourth of July, 1815*, 16.

43. For an example of this line of argument, see Donald R. Hickey, "The War of 1812: Still a Forgotten Conflict?" *Journal of Military History* 65 (2001): 743; John Latimer, *1812: War with America* (Cambridge, MA, 2008), 400–401; Black, *War of 1812*, 203; and J. C. A. Stagg, *Mr. Madison's War: Politics, Diplomacy, and Warfare in the Early American Republic, 1783–1830* (Princeton, 1983), 501.

44. Nicholas Rogers, *The Press Gang: Naval Impressment and Its Opponents in Georgian Britain* (London, 2007), 122.

45. Gordon S. Wood, *Empire of Liberty: A History of the Early Republic, 1789–1815* (New York, 2009), 686–87.

46. Daniel Walker Howe, *What Hath God Wrought: The Transformation of America, 1815–1848* (New York, 2007), 74–76; for John Quincy Adams's remark, see *Adams Memoirs*, 10 and 27–28.

47. Christopher D. Hall, *British Strategy in the Napoleonic War 1803–1815* (Manchester, 1992), 197–98.

48. See especially Latimer, *War with America*, 43; Sheppard, chapter 7; Alan Taylor, *The Civil War of 1812: American Citizens, British Subjects, Irish Rebels, & Indian Allies* (New York, 2010), 436–37; Black, *War of 1812*, 225.

49. *Montreal Herald*, June 7, 1815.

50. *New Brunswick Courier*, Mar. 18, 1815.

51. *The Letters of Veritas, Re-Published from the Montreal Herald; Containing a Succinct Narrative of the Military Administration of Sir George Prevost, During his Command in the Canadas; Whereby it will Appear Manifest that the Merit of Preserving Them from the Conquest, Belongs Not to Him* (Montreal, July 1815), 60.

52. *Edinburgh Star*, Feb. 3, 1815.

53. Arthur Herman, *To Rule the Waves: How the British Navy Shaped the Modern World* (New York, 2004).

54. *Clay Papers*, 2: 11.

55. Donald E. Graves, *Merry Hearts Make Light Days: The War of 1812 Journal of Lieutenant John Le Couteur, 104th Foot* (Ottawa, 1994), 223.

56. Bovell, *A Thanksgiving Sermon*, 11.

57. *Niles' Weekly Register*, May 13, 1815.
58. Adam Rothman, *Slave Country: American Expansion and the Origins of the Deep South* (Cambridge, MA, 2005), 121.
59. Quoted in William Wood, *The War with the United States: A Chronicle of 1812* (Toronto, 1915), 170–71.
60. See especially Wood, *Empire of Liberty*, 696–99; Howe, *What Hath God Wrought*, 17–18; Clifton Hood, "A Usable Past: Urban Elites, New York City's Evacuation Day, and the Transformations of Memory Culture," *Journal of Social History* 37 (2004): 883–913.
61. See especially Sam W. Haynes, *Unfinished Revolution: The Early American Republic in a British World* (Charlottesville, VA, 2010), especially chapter 5.
62. Taylor, *Civil War of 1812*, 437–38; and Colin G. Calloway, *Crown and Calumet: British-Indian Relations, 1783–1815* (Norman, OK, 1987), 240–48.
63. Black, *War of 1812*, 222.
64. Howe, *What Hath God Wrought*, 76–77.
65. James T. Austin, *An Oration, Pronounced at Lexington Mass. in Commemoration of the Independence of the United States of America, and the Restoration of Peace. 4th July, 1815* (Boston, 1815), 15.

INDEX

Page numbers in bold refer to illustrations.